From the author of DDD, the famous data display debugger, now comes the definitive book on debugging. It takes the reader on a systematic tour through the entire debugging process, starting with problem tracking, testing for debugging, and reproducing problems, all the way to state-of-the-art tools such as generating mock objects for replaying hard-to-reproduce events, automatically zeroing-in on fault inducing input, and isolating probable causes for faults.

If you are a seasoned programmer and think you know everything there is to know about debugging, think again. Zeller's book is chock-full with advice, insight, and tools to track down defects in programs, for all levels of experience and any programming language.

The book is lucidly written, explaining the principles of every technique without boring the reader with minutiae. And best of all, at the end of each chapter it tells you where to download all those fancy tools. A great book for the software professional as well as the student interested in the frontiers of automated debugging.

— Walter F. Tichy, Professor
University Karlsruhe, Germany

Although many programmers consider debugging as the most painful part of software development, few books are available for computer science students and practitioners to learn about scientific methods in debugging.

In this book, Andreas Zeller does an excellent job introducing useful debugging techniques and tools invented in both academia and industry. The book is easy to read and actually very fun as well — don't overlook all the bug stories included.

I strongly recommend this book to graduate and undergraduate students interested in software engineering research. It will not only help you discover a new perspective on debugging, but it will also teach you some fundamental static and dynamic program analysis techniques in plain language.

— Miryung Kim, Graduate Student
Computer Science & Engineering, University of Washington

Andreas Zeller's Why Programs Fail *lays an excellent foundation for practitioners, educators, and researchers alike. Using a disciplined approach based on the scientific method, Zeller provides deep insights, detailed approaches, and illustrative examples.*

— David Notkin, Professor
Computer Science & Engineering, University of Washington

WHY PROGRAMS FAIL

WHY PROGRAMS FAIL

A Guide to Systematic Debugging

ANDREAS ZELLER

ELSEVIER

MORGAN KAUFMANN PUBLISHERS

dpunkt.verlag

HEIDELBERG

AMSTERDAM • BOSTON • HEIDELBERG • LONDON • NEW YORK • OXFORD
PARIS • SAN DIEGO • SAN FRANCISCO • SINGAPORE • SYDNEY • TOKYO
MORGAN KAUFMANN PUBLISHERS IS AN IMPRINT OF ELSEVIER

Copublished by Morgan Kaufmann Publishers and dpunkt.verlag

Morgan Kaufmann Publishers

		dpunkt.verlag	
Senior Editor	Tim Cox	Senior Editor	Christa Preisendanz
Publishing Services Manager	Simon Crump		
Assistant Editor	Richard Camp		
Editorial Assistant	Jessica Evans		
Cover Design	Maria Ilardi Design		
Cover Image	© Stockdisk / Getty Images		
Composition	VTEX		
Technical Illustration	Dartmouth Publishing, Inc.		
Copyeditor	Daril Bently		
Proofreader	Jacqui Brownstein		
Indexer	Broccoli Information Management		
Interior printer	Maple-Vail Book Manufacturing Group		
Cover printer	Phoenix Color		

Morgan Kaufmann Publishers is an imprint of Elsevier.
500 Sansome Street, Suite 400, San Francisco, CA 94111

Available in Germany, Austria, and Switzerland from dpunkt.verlag
Rinstraße 19B, 69115 Heidelberg, Germany
http://www.dpunkt.de

This book is printed on acid-free paper.

Library of Congress Cataloging-in-Publication Data
Zeller, Andreas.
    Why programs fail: a guide to systematic debugging / Andreas Zeller.
        p. cm.
    Includes bibliographical references and index.
    ISBN -13: 978-1-55860-866-5
    ISBN -10: 1-55860-866-4
        1. Debugging in computer science. I. Title.

QA76.9.D43Z45 2005
005.1'4–dc22   2005049837

ISBN -13: 978-1-55860-866-5
ISBN -10: 1-55860-866-4
dpunkt ISBN: 3-89864-279-8

For information on all Morgan Kaufmann publications,
visit our Web site at *www.mkp.com* or *www.books.elsevier.com*

Printed in the United States of America
    06 07 08 09   5 4

For my family

ABOUT THE AUTHOR

Andreas Zeller is a computer science professor at Saarland University, Germany. His research centers on programmer productivity: What can be done to ease the life and work of programmers? Among Linux and Unix programmers Zeller is best known for GNU DDD, a debugger front-end with built-in data visualization. Among academics and advanced professionals, Zeller is best known for delta debugging, a technique that automatically isolates failure causes for computer programs.

His work is equally divided between teaching, reading, writing, programming, and flying back and forth across the Atlantic. He lives with his family in Saarbrücken, on the German border with France.

CONTENTS

How to...

FOREWORD

In *Federalist 51*, James Madison wrote: "If men were angels, no government would be necessary." If he lived today, Madison might have written: "If software developers were angels, debugging would be unnecessary." Most of us, however, make mistakes, and many of us even make errors while designing and writing software. Our mistakes need to be found and fixed, an activity called debugging that originated with the first computer programs. Today every computer program written is also debugged, but debugging is not a widely studied or taught skill. Few books, beyond this one, present a systematic approach to finding and fixing programming errors.

Be honest: does debugging seem as important, difficult, or worthy of study as writing a program in the first place? Or, is it just one of those things that you need to do to finish a project? Software developers though spend huge amounts of time debugging — estimates range up to half or more of their day. Finding and fixing bugs faster and more effectively directly increases productivity and can improve program quality by eliminating more defects with available resources. Preventing mistakes in the first place would be even better, but no one has yet found the technique to prevent errors, so effective debugging will remain essential.

Improved programming languages and tools can supplant, but not eliminate debugging, by statically identifying errors and by dynamically detecting invariant violations. For example, the type system in modern languages such as Java and C# prevents many simple mistakes that slip by C programmers. Moreover, these languages' run-time bounds checks stop a program when it strays out of bounds, which may be billions of instructions before the error manifests itself. Unfortunately there are countless ways in which a program can go wrong, almost all of which languages and tools cannot detect or prevent. For example, in recent years there has been considerable work in verifying sequences of operations in a program. Tools can ensure that a file is opened before a program reads it, but they cannot check that the correct file is accessed or that the program properly interprets its contents. If either mistake occurs, someone still must debug the program to understand the error and determine how to fix it.

In addition, debugging can be an enjoyable activity that shares the thrill of the hunt and chase found in a good detective novel or video game. On the other hand, a protracted, unsuccessful search for a bug in your code quickly loses its charm, particularly when your boss is asking repeatedly about your (lack of) progress. Learning to debug well is essential to enjoying software development.

This book can teach you how to debug more effectively. It is a complete and pragmatic overview of debugging, written by a talented researcher who has developed many clever ways to isolate bugs. It explains best practices for finding and fixing errors in programs, ranging from systematically tracking error reports, reproducing failures, observing symptoms, isolating the cause, and correcting defects. Along with basic techniques and commonly used tools, the book also explores the author's innovative techniques for isolating minimal input to reproduce an error and for tracking cause and effect through a program.

Studying this book will make you a better programmer. You will be able to find and fix errors in your code (and your colleague's code) faster and more effectively, a valuable skill that will enable you to finish projects earlier and produce programs with fewer defects. Also, if you read between the lines you will learn how to write code that is more easily tested and debugged, which further increases your ability to find and correct defects. And thinking hard about what can go wrong with your program can help you avoid mistakes in the first place, so you have less to debug.

James Larus
Microsoft Research
August, 2005

PREFACE

THIS IS A BOOK ABOUT BUGS in computer programs — how to reproduce them, how to find them, and how to fix them such that they do not occur. This book teaches a number of techniques that allow you to debug any program in a systematic, and sometimes even elegant, way. Moreover, the techniques can widely be automated, which allows you to let your computer do most of the debugging. Questions this book addresses include:

- How can I reproduce failures faithfully?

- How can I isolate what is relevant for the failure?

- How does the failure come to be?

- How can I fix the program in the best possible way?

Once you understand how debugging works, you will not think about debugging in the same way. Instead of seeing a wild mess of code, you will think about causes and effects, and you will systematically set up and refine hypotheses to track failure causes. Your insights may even make you set up your own automated debugging tool. All of this allows you to spend less time on debugging, which is why you are interested in automated debugging in the first place, right?

HOW THIS BOOK CAME TO BE WRITTEN

Although I work as a researcher, I have always considered myself a programmer, because this is how I spend most of my time. During programming, I make mistakes, and I have to debug my code. I would like to say that I am some type of *überprogrammer* — that I never make mistakes — but I am only human, just like anyone else.

During my studies, I have learned that an ounce of prevention is more than worth a pound of cure. I have learned many ways of preventing mistakes. Today, I teach them to my students. However, in striving for prevention we must not forget about the cure. If we were doctors, we could not simply refuse treatment just because our patient had not taken all possible preventions.

So, rather than designing yet another ultimate prevention I have sought good cures. This same pragmatic attitude has been adopted by other researchers around the globe. I am happy to report that we have succeeded. Today, a number of advanced debugging techniques are available that widely *automate the debugging process.*

These techniques not only automate debugging but turn debugging from a black art into a systematic and well-organized discipline that can be taught just like any software engineering topic. Thus, I created a course on automated debugging and reworked the lecture notes into a book. The result is what you see before you.

AUDIENCE

This book is intended for computer professionals, graduate students, and advanced undergraduates who want to learn how to debug programs systematically and with automated support. The reader is assumed to be familiar with programming and manual testing, either from introductory courses or work experience.

WHAT THIS BOOK IS AND WHAT IT IS NOT

This book focuses on the *cure* of bugs — that is, the act of isolating and fixing the defect in the program code once a failure has occurred. It only partially covers *preventing* defects. Many other books are available that provide an in-depth treatment of this topic. In fact, one might say that most of computer science is concerned with preventing bugs. However, when prevention fails there is need for a cure, and that is what this book is about.

OVERVIEW OF CONTENT

This book is divided into 15 chapters and an appendix. Chapters 1, 6, and 12 are prerequisites for later chapters.

At the end of each chapter, you will find a section called "Concepts," which summarizes the *key concepts* of the chapter. Some of these concepts are denoted "How To." These summarize *recipes* that can be easily followed. (The "How To"s are listed in the table of contents.) Furthermore, each chapter ends with practical *exercises*, for verifying your knowledge, and a "Further Reading" section. The content of this book is organized as follows.

Chapter 1: How Failures Come to Be

Your program fails. How can this be? The answer is that the programmer creates a defect in the code. When the code is executed, the defect causes an infection in the program state, which later becomes visible as a failure. To find the defect, one must reason backward, starting with the failure. This chapter defines the essential concepts when talking about debugging, and hints at the techniques discussed subsequently — hopefully whetting your appetite for the remainder of this book.

Chapter 2: Tracking Problems

This chapter deals with the issue of how to *manage* problems as reported by users — how to track and manage problem reports, how to organize the debugging process, and how to keep track of multiple versions. This information constitutes the basic framework in which debugging takes place.

Chapter 3: Making Programs Fail

Before a program can be debugged, we must set it up such that it can be *tested* — that is, executed with the intent to make it fail. In this chapter, we review basic testing techniques, with a special focus on automation and isolation.

Chapter 4: Reproducing Problems

The first step in debugging is to *reproduce* the problem in question — that is, to create a test case that causes the program to fail in the specified way. The first reason is to bring it under control, such that it can be observed. The second reason is to verify the success of the fix. This chapter discusses typical strategies for reproducing an operating environment, including its history and problem symptoms.

Chapter 5: Simplifying Problems

Once we have reproduced a problem, we must *simplify* it — that is, we must find out which circumstances are not relevant to the problem and can thus be omitted. This process results in a test case that contains only the relevant circumstances. In the best case, a simplified test case report immediately pinpoints the defect. We introduce *delta debugging*, an automated debugging method that simplifies test cases automatically.

Chapter 6: Scientific Debugging

Once we have reproduced and simplified a problem, we must understand how the failure came to be. The process of arriving at a theory that explains some aspect of the universe is known as *scientific method*. It is the appropriate process for obtaining problem diagnostics. We introduce basic techniques of creating and verifying hypotheses, creating experiments, conducting the process in a systematic fashion, and making the debugging process explicit.

Chapter 7: Deducing Errors

In this chapter, we begin exploring the techniques for creating hypotheses that were introduced in Chapter 6. We start with *deduction* techniques — reasoning from the *abstract* program code to the *concrete* program run. In particular, we present *program slicing*, an automated means of determining possible origins of a variable value. Using program slicing, one can effectively narrow down the number of possible infection sites.

Chapter 8: Observing Facts

Although deduction techniques do not take concrete runs into account, observation determines *facts* about what has happened in a concrete run. In this chapter, we look under the hood of the actual program execution and introduce widespread techniques for examining program executions and program states. These techniques include classical logging, interactive debuggers, and postmortem debugging — as well as eye-opening visualization and summarization techniques.

Chapter 9: Tracking Origins

Once we have observed an infection during debugging, we need to determine its origin. We discuss *omniscient debugging*, a technique that records an entire execution history such that the user can explore arbitrary moments in time without ever restarting the program. Furthermore, we explore *dynamic slicing*, a technique that tracks the origins of specific values.

Chapter 10: Asserting Expectations

Observation alone is not enough for debugging. One must *compare* the observed facts with the expected program behavior. In this chapter, we discuss how to automate such comparisons using well-known *assertion* techniques. We also show how to ensure the correct state of important system components such as memory.

Chapter 11: Detecting Anomalies

Although a single program run can tell you quite a bit, performing multiple runs for purpose of comparison offers several opportunities for locating *commonalities* and *anomalies* — anomalies that frequently help locate defects. In this chapter, we discuss how to detect anomalies in code coverage and anomalies in data accesses. We also show how to infer invariants from multiple test runs automatically, in order to flag later invariant violations. All of these anomalies are good candidates for identification as infection sites.

Chapter 12: Causes and Effects

Deduction, observation, and induction are all useful in finding *potential* defects. However, none of these techniques alone is sufficient in determining a *failure cause*. How does one identify a cause? How does one isolate not just *a* cause but *the* actual cause of a failure? This chapter lays the groundwork for techniques aimed at locating failure causes systematically and automatically.

Chapter 13: Isolating Failure Causes

This chapter is central to automating most of debugging. We show how delta debugging isolates failure causes automatically — in program input, in the program's thread schedule, and in program code. In the best case, the reported causes immediately pinpoint the defect.

Chapter 14: Isolating Cause-Effect Chains

This chapter presents a method of narrowing down failure causes even further. By extracting and comparing program states, delta debugging automatically isolates the *variables and values* that cause the failure, resulting in a cause-effect chain of the failure: for example, "variable x was 42; therefore p became null, and thus the program failed."

Chapter 15: Fixing the Defect

Once we have understood the failure's cause-effect chain, we know how the failure came to be. However, we must still locate the origin of the infection — that is, the actual location of the defect. In this chapter, we discuss how to narrow down the defect systematically — and, having found the defect, how to fix it.

Appendix: Formal Definitions

For the sake of readability, all formal definitions and proofs have been grouped in the Appendix.

Bibliography

The bibliography presents a wide range of sources of further reading in the topics covered by the text.

Index

The book ends with a major index.

SUPPLEMENTS, RESOURCES, AND WEB EXTENSIONS

Much of the material covered in this book has never been discussed in a textbook before. The later chapters have not been widely tested in practice, and like any book on an evolving field this one will benefit from more refinement and from further work. In other words, this book is full of bugs, and I welcome any comments on this book. You can write to the author care of Morgan Kaufmann, or e-mail me at zeller@whyprogramsfail.com. There is also a web page at

http://www.whyprogramsfail.com

for late-breaking information and updates (read: fixes).

ADVICE FOR INSTRUCTORS

I have used this book for three graduate courses on automated debugging. Each course consisted of approximately 15 lectures of 90 minutes each. Essentially, there was one lecture per chapter. The exercises stem from these courses (and their exams). For your convenience, my presentation slides for these courses are available in Keynote and Powerpoint format. Instructions on how to access them are available at

http://www.whyprogramsfail.com

If you prefer to make your own slides, all of the original illustrations for this book are also available at this site.

ADVICE FOR READERS

Typographics

To keep things simple, most examples in this book use the standard input/output mechanisms—that is, the *command line* and the *console*. In all of these examples, `typewriter font` stands for program output, and **`bold typewriter font`** for user input. The command line prompt is denoted by a dollar sign ($), and the cursor by an underscore (_). The following is a simple example. The user invokes the `hello` program, which prints the text `Hello, world!` on the console.

```
$ ./hello
Hello, world!
$ _
```

Programming Environment

The concepts and techniques discussed in this book do not depend on a particular programming environment or operating system. To illustrate the techniques, though, I frequently use *command-line tools*, typically from the Linux/UNIX community. In addition to saving space, this is a matter of simplicity: these command-line tools provide a functional core similar to that found in almost all sophisticated programming environments. Therefore, you should have no trouble transferring the examples to your personal programming workbench.

ACKNOWLEDGMENTS

Many people have had a part in the development of this book. The author would like to thank everybody who reviewed drafts of the manuscript or parts of it: Philipp Bouillon, Holger Cleve, David Cok, Michael Ernst, David Evans, Roland Illig, Clint Jeffery, Dieter Kranzlmüller, Jens Krinke, Andreas Leitner, Raimondas Lencevicius, Bil Lewis, Ben Liblit, Christian Lindig, Edu Metz, Robert Muth, Stephan Neuhaus, Jeff Offutt, Kerstin Reese, Zoltan Somogyi, Peter Weißgerber, Thomas Zimmermann, and the students of the *Automated Debugging* courses at Saarland University and the University of Washington. Philipp Bouillon, Silvia Breu, Holger Cleve, and Martin Mehlmann also helped with conception of the exercises. Christa Preisendanz of dpunkt Verlag and Tim Cox of Morgan Kaufmann Publishers were most helpful. And finally, my family has supported me enormously while writing this book—it's great to have you with me.

Have fun debugging!

Andreas Zeller
Saarbrücken, Germany
July 2005

For the Snark's a peculiar creature, that won't
Be caught in a commonplace way.
Do all that you know, and try all that you don't:
Not a chance must be wasted to-day!

— LEWIS CARROLL
The Hunting of the Snark (1876)

## CHAPTER 1

HOW FAILURES COME TO BE

Y OUR PROGRAM FAILS. HOW CAN THIS BE? The answer is that the programmer creates a defect in the code. When the code is executed, the defect causes an infection in the program state, which later becomes visible as a failure. To find the defect, one must reason backward, starting with the failure. This chapter defines the essential concepts when talking about debugging, and hints at the techniques discussed subsequently — hopefully whetting your appetite for the remainder of this book.

1.1 MY PROGRAM DOES NOT WORK!

Oops! Your program fails. Now what? This is a common situation that interrupts our routine and requires immediate attention. Because the program mostly worked until now, we assume that something external has crept into our machine — something that is natural and unavoidable; something we are not responsible for, namely, a bug.

If you are a user, you have probably already learned to live with bugs. You may even think that bugs are unavoidable when it comes to software. As a programmer, though, you know that bugs do not creep out of mother nature into our programs. (See Bug Story 1 for an exception.) Rather, bugs are inherent parts of the programs we produce. At the beginning of any bug story stands a human who produces the program in question.

The following is a small program I once produced. The `sample` program is a very simple sorting tool. Given a list of numbers as command-line arguments, `sample` prints them as a sorted list on the standard output ($ is the command-line prompt).

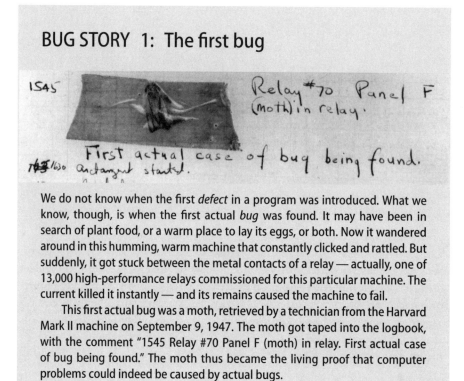

BUG STORY 1: The first bug

We do not know when the first *defect* in a program was introduced. What we know, though, is when the first actual *bug* was found. It may have been in search of plant food, or a warm place to lay its eggs, or both. Now it wandered around in this humming, warm machine that constantly clicked and rattled. But suddenly, it got stuck between the metal contacts of a relay — actually, one of 13,000 high-performance relays commissioned for this particular machine. The current killed it instantly — and its remains caused the machine to fail.

This first actual bug was a moth, retrieved by a technician from the Harvard Mark II machine on September 9, 1947. The moth got taped into the logbook, with the comment "1545 Relay #70 Panel F (moth) in relay. First actual case of bug being found." The moth thus became the living proof that computer problems could indeed be caused by actual bugs.

```
$ ./sample 9 7 8
Output: 7 8 9
$ _
```

Unfortunately, sample does not always work properly, as demonstrated by the following failure.

```
$ ./sample 11 14
Output: 0 11
$ _
```

Although the sample output is sorted and contains the right number of items, some original arguments are missing and replaced by bogus numbers. Here, 14 is missing and replaced by 0. (Actual bogus numbers and behavior on your system may vary.) From the sample failure, we can deduce that sample has a bug (or, more precisely, a *defect*). This brings us to the *key question* of this chapter:

> HOW DOES A DEFECT CAUSE A FAILURE, AND HOW CAN WE FIX IT?

1.2 FROM DEFECTS TO FAILURES

In general, a failure such as that in the `sample` program comes about in the four stages discussed in the following.

1. *The programmer creates a defect.* A defect is a piece of the code that can cause an infection. Because the defect is part of the code, and because every code is initially written by a programmer, the defect is technically created by the programmer. If the programmer creates a defect, does that mean the programmer was at fault? Not necessarily. Consider the following.

   - The original requirements did not foresee future changes. Think about the Y2K problem, for instance.

   - A program behavior may become classified as a "failure" only when the user sees it for the first time.

   - In a modular program, a failure may happen because of incompatible interfaces of two modules.

   - In a distributed program, a failure may be the result of some unpredictable interaction of several components.

   In such settings, deciding on who is to blame is a political, not a technical, question. Nobody made a mistake, and yet a failure occurred. (See Bug Story 2 for more on such failures.)

2. *The defect causes an infection.* The program is executed, and with it the defect. The defect now creates an *infection* — that is, after execution of the defect, the program state differs from what the programmer intended.

   A defect in the code does not necessarily cause an infection. The defective code must be executed, and it must be executed under such conditions that the infection actually occurs.

BUG STORY 2: F-16 Problems

A programmer who works for General Dynamics in Ft. Worth wrote some of the code for the F-16, and he has reported some neato-whiz-bang bug/feature they keep finding in the F-16.

- Because the F-16 is a fly-by-wire aircraft, the computer keeps the pilot from doing dumb things to himself. So if the pilot jerks hard over on the joystick, the computer will instruct the flight surfaces to make a nice and easy 4- or 5-G flip. But the plane can withstand a much higher flip than that. So when they were "flying" the F-16 in simulation over the equator, the computer got confused and instantly flipped the plane over, killing the pilot [in simulation]. And since it can fly forever upside down, it would do so until it ran out of fuel.

The remaining bugs were actually found while flying, rather than in simulation.

- One of the first things the Air Force test pilots tried on an early F-16 was to tell the computer to raise the landing gear while standing still on the runway. Guess what happened? Scratch one F-16. [...]

- The computer system onboard has a weapons management system that will attempt to keep the plane flying level by dispersing weapons and empty fuel tanks in a balanced fashion. So, if you ask to drop a bomb the computer will figure out whether to drop a port or starboard bomb in order to keep the load even. One of the early problems with that was the fact that you could flip the plane over and the computer would gladly let you drop a bomb or fuel tank. It would drop, dent the wing, and then roll off.

3. *The infection propagates.* Most functions result in errors when fed with erroneous input. As the remaining program execution accesses the state, it generates further infections that can spread into later program states. An infection need not, however, propagate continuously. It may be overwritten, masked, or corrected by some later program action.

4. *The infection causes a failure.* A failure is an externally observable error in the program behavior. It is caused by an infection in the program state.

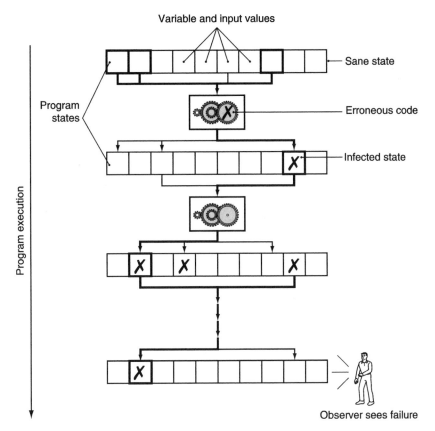

FIGURE 1.1 A program execution as a succession of states. Each state determines the following states — and where from defect to failure errors propagate to form an infection chain.

The program execution process is sketched in Figure 1.1. Each program state consists of the values of the program variables, as well as the current execution position (formally, the *program counter*). Each state determines subsequent states, up to the final state (at the bottom in the figure), in which we can observe the failure (indicated by ✗ in the figure).

Not every defect results in an infection, and not every infection results in a failure. Hence, having no failures does not imply having no defects. This is the curse of testing, as pointed out by Dijkstra. Testing can only show the presence of defects, but never their absence.

In the case of sample, though, we have actually experienced a failure. In hindsight, every failure is thus caused by some infection, and every infection is caused by some earlier infection, originating at the defect. This cause-effect chain from defect to failure is called an *infection chain*.

The issue of debugging is thus to identify the infection chain, to find its root cause (the defect), and to remove the defect such that the failure no longer occurs. This is what we shall do with the `sample` program.

1.3 LOST IN TIME AND SPACE

In general, debugging of a program such as `sample` can be decomposed into seven steps (List 1.1), whose initial letters form the word TRAFFIC.

1. Track the problem.

2. Reproduce the failure.

3. Automate and simplify.

4. Find infection origins.

5. Focus on likely origins.

6. Isolate the infection chain.

7. Correct the defect.

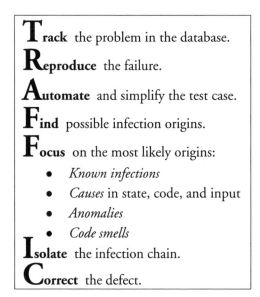

> **T**rack the problem in the database.
> **R**eproduce the failure.
> **A**utomate and simplify the test case.
> **F**ind possible infection origins.
> **F**ocus on the most likely origins:
> - *Known infections*
> - *Causes* in state, code, and input
> - *Anomalies*
> - *Code smells*
>
> **I**solate the infection chain.
> **C**orrect the defect.

LIST 1.1 The seven steps in debugging (TRAFFIC).

Of these steps, *tracking the problem* in a problem database is mere bookkeeping (see also Chapter 2 "Tracking Problems") and *reproducing the problem* is not that difficult for deterministic programs such as sample. It can be difficult for nondeterministic programs and long-running programs, though, which is why Chapter 4 discusses the issues involved in reproducing failures.

Automating the test case is also rather straightforward, and results in automatic simplification (see also Chapter 5 "Simplifying Problems"). The last step, *correcting the defect*, is usually simple once you have understood how the defect causes the failure (see Chapter 15 "Fixing the Defect").

The final three steps — from finding the infection origins to isolating the infection chain — are the steps concerned with *understanding how the failure came to be*. This task requires by far the most time and other resources. Understanding how the failure came to be is what the rest of this section and the other chapters of this book are about.

Why is understanding the failure so difficult? Considering Figure 1.1, all one need do to find the defect is to isolate the transition from a *sane* state (i.e., noninfected, as intended) to an *infected* state. This is a search in *space* (as we have to find out which part of the state is infected) as well as in *time* (as we have to find out when the infection takes place).

However, examination of space and time are enormous tasks for even the simplest programs. Each state consists of dozens, thousands, or even millions of variables. For example, Figure 1.2 shows a visualization of the program state of the GNU compiler (GCC) while compiling a program. The program state consists of about 44,000 individual variables, each with a distinct value, and about 42,000 references between variables. (Chapter 14 "Isolating Cause-Effect Chains" discusses how to obtain and use such program states in debugging.)

Not only is a single state quite large, a program execution consists of thousands, millions, or even billions of such states. Space and time thus form a wide area in which only two points are well known (Figure 1.3): initially, the entire state is sane (✔), and eventually some part of the state is infected (✘). Within the area spanned by space and time, the aim of debugging is to locate the defect — a single transition from sane (✔) to infected (✘) that eventually causes the failure (Figure 1.4).

Thinking about the dimensions of space and time, this may seem like searching for a needle in an endless row of haystacks — and indeed, debugging is largely a search problem. This search is driven by the following two major principles.

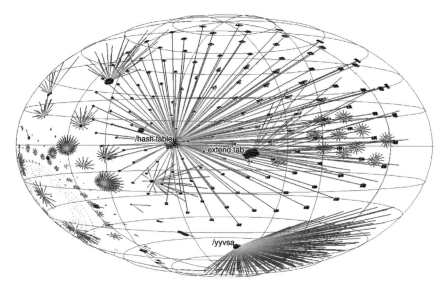

FIGURE 1.2 A program state of the GNU compiler. The state consists of 44,000 individual variables (shown as vertices) and about 42,000 references between variables (shown as edges).

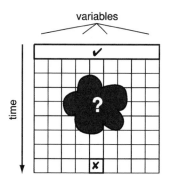

FIGURE 1.3 Debugging as search in space and time. Initially, the program state is sane (✔), eventually, it is infected (✘). The aim of debugging is to find out where this infection originated.

- *Separate sane from infected.* If a state is infected, it may be part of the infection propagating from defect to failure. If a state is sane, there is no infection to propagate.

- *Separate relevant from irrelevant.* A variable value is the result of a limited number of earlier variable values. Hence, only some part of the earlier state may be relevant to the failure.

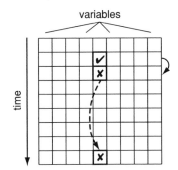

FIGURE 1.4 The defect that is searched. A defect manifests itself as a transition from sane state (✔) to infected state (✘), where an erroneous statement causes the initial infection.

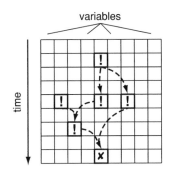

FIGURE 1.5 Deducing value origins. By analyzing the program code, we can find out that an infected variable value (✘) can have originated only from a small number of earlier variables (!).

Figure 1.5 illustrates this latter technique. The failure, to reiterate, can only have been caused by a small number of other variables in earlier states (denoted using the exclamation point, !), whose values in turn can only have come from other earlier variables. One says that subsequent, variable values *depend on* earlier values. This results in a series of *dependences* from the failure back to earlier variable values. To locate the defect, it suffices to examine these values only — as other values could not have possibly caused the failure — and separate these values into *sane* and *infected*. If we find an infected value, we must find and fix the defect that causes it. Typically, this is the same defect that causes the original failure.

Why is it that a variable value can be caused only by a small number of earlier variables? Good programming style dictates division of the state into *units* such that the information flow between these units is minimized. Typically, your programming language provides a means of structuring the state, just as it helps you to structure the program code. However, whether you divide the state into functions, modules, objects, packages, or components, the principle is the same: a divided state is much easier to conquer.

1.4 FROM FAILURES TO FIXES

Let's put our knowledge about states and dependences into practice, following the TRAFFIC steps (List 1.1).

- *Track the problem.* The first step in debugging is to *track the problem* — that is, to file a problem report such that the defect will not go by unnoticed. In our case, we have already observed the failure symptom: the output of sample, when invoked with arguments 11 and 14, contains a zero.

  ```
  $ ./sample 11 14
  Output: 0 11
  $ _
  ```

  An actual problem report would include this invocation as an instruction on how to reproduce the problem (see Chapter 2 "Tracking Problems" for details).

- *Reproduce the failure.* In case of the sample program, reproducing the failure is easy. All you need do is reinvoke sample, as shown previously. In other cases, though, reproducing may require control over all possible input sources (techniques are described in Chapter 4 "Reproducing Problems").

- *Automate and simplify the test case.* If sample were a more complex program, we would have to think about how to automate the failure (in that we want to reproduce the failure automatically) and how to simplify its input such that we obtain a minimal test case. In the case of sample, though, this is not necessary (for more complex programs, Chapter 5 "Simplifying Problems" covers the details).

- *Find possible infection origins.* Where does the zero in the output come from? This is the fourth step in the TRAFFIC steps: we must *find possible infection origins*. To find possible origins, we need the actual C source code of sample, shown in Example 1.1. We quickly see that the program consists of two functions: shell_sort() (which implements the shell sort algorithm) and main, which realizes a simple test driver around shell_sort(). The main function:

- Allocates an array a[] (line 32)

- Copies the command-line arguments into a[] (lines 33–34)

- Sorts a[] by invoking shell_sort() (line 36)

- Prints the content of a[] (lines 38–41)

By matching the output to the appropriate code, we find that the 0 printed by sample is the value of the variable a[0], the first element of the array a[]. This is the infection we observe: at line 39 in sample.c, variable a[0] is obviously zero.

Where does the zero in a[0] come from? Working our way backward from line 40, we find in line 36 the call shell_sort(a, argc), where the array a[] is passed by reference. This function might well be the point at which a[0] was assigned the infected value.

Unfortunately, shell_sort() in lines 6 through 25 is quite obscure. We cannot trace back the value of a[0] to a specific origin simply by *deduction* from the program code. Instead, we have to *observe* what actually happens in the failing run.

In principle, we can observe anything about the sample run, as sketched in Figure 1.6. We can even "execute" it on paper. However, this approach does not scale. We must focus on specific parts of the state or on specific moments in time. Relying on our earlier deduction on the origins of a[0], we focus on the execution of shell_sort().

We can easily find out that shell_sort() does not access any nonlocal variables. Whatever comes out of shell_sort() is determined by its input. If we observe the arguments at the invocation of shell_sort(), two things can happen.

- The arguments at the invocation of shell_sort are sane (i.e., are just as intended). In this case, the infection must take place *during* the execution of shell_sort, as sketched in Figure 1.7.

- The arguments are already infected. In this case, the infection must have taken place *before* the execution of shell_sort().

To find out how shell_sort() was actually invoked, we need a means of observing the state during execution. In this introduction chapter, we use the simplest of all observation techniques: we insert output statements in the code that *log* specific variables and their values when executed. For in-

```
 1   /* sample.c -- Sample C program to be debugged */
 2
 3   #include <stdio.h>
 4   #include <stdlib.h>
 5
 6   static void shell_sort(int a[], int size)
 7   {
 8       int i, j;
 9       int h = 1;
10
11       do {
12           h = h * 3 + 1;
13       } while (h <= size);
14       do {
15           h /= 3;
16           for (i = h; i < size; i++)
17           {
18               int v = a[i];
19               for (j = i; j >= h && a[j - h] > v; j -= h)
20                   a[j] = a[j - h];
21               if (i != j)
22                   a[j] = v;
23           }
24       } while (h != 1);
25   }
26
27   int main(int argc, char *argv[])
28   {
29       int *a;
30       int i;
31
32       a = (int *)malloc((argc - 1) * sizeof(int));
33       for (i = 0; i < argc - 1; i++)
34           a[i] = atoi(argv[i + 1]);
35
36       shell_sort(a, argc);
37
38       printf("Output: ");
39       for (i = 0; i < argc - 1; i++)
40           printf("%d ", a[i]);
41       printf("\n");
42
43       free(a);
44
45       return 0;
46   }
```

EXAMPLE I.I The sample program sorts given numbers — that is, mostly.

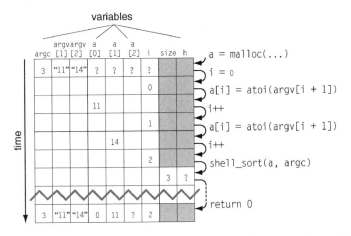

FIGURE 1.6 Observing the `sample` run. Using observation tools, we can observe the program state as it progresses through time.

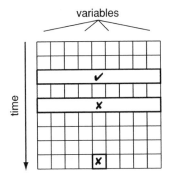

FIGURE 1.7 Observing a transition from sane to infected. If we know that an earlier state is sane (✔) and a later state is infected (✗), we can narrow down our search to isolate the transition between these two states.

stance, we could insert the following code in line 10 to have the values of the parameters `a[]` and `size` logged on the standard error channel whenever `shell_sort()` is invoked.

```
fprintf(stderr, "At shell_sort");
for (i = 0; i < size; i++)
    fprintf(stderr, "a[%d] = %d\n", i, a[i]);
fprintf(stderr, "size = %d\n", size);
```

• *Focus on the most likely origins.* After inserting the code and restarting `sample` with the arguments 11 and 14, you will find that at `shell_sort()` the values of the parameters are as follows.

```
a[0] = 11
a[1] = 14
a[2] = 0
size = 3
```

We see that `shell_sort` is invoked with *three* elements; that is, the array `a[]` to be sorted is [11, 14, 0]. This state is infected; that is, `a[]` should contain only two elements. As discussed previously, an infected state is likely to cause failures—and this particular state may well be the cause of our failure. Our hypothesis is that `shell_sort` properly sorts the three elements of `a[]` in place to [0, 11, 14]. Later on, though, only the first two elements of `a[]` will be printed, resulting in the failure output.

• *Isolate the origin of the infection.* According to our earlier reasoning, the infection must have occurred *before* the invocation of `shell_sort()`. Obviously, the parameter `size` is wrong. We can trace back its origin to the point at which `shell_sort()` is invoked: In line 36, we find the invocation

```
shell_sort(a, argc),
```

and find that the `size` parameter gets its value from the `argc` variable. However, `argc` is not the number of elements in `a[]`. It is the number of arguments to the `sample` program, including the name `sample` itself (`argc` is always *one more* than the number of elements in a). Thus, the following is our speculation about what is happening in our program.

1. The array `a[]` is allocated and initialized with the correct number of elements (2).

2. `shell_sort` is invoked such that the `size` parameter is 3 instead of 2 (the state is infected).

3. `size` being 3 causes `shell_sort()` to access `a[]` beyond the allocated space (namely, at `a[2]`).

4. The uninitialized memory at `a[2]` happens to be zero.

5. During the sort, `a[2]` is eventually swapped with `a[0]`, thus setting `a[0]` to zero (the infection has spread to `a[0]`).

6. Thus, the zero value of `a[0]` is printed, causing the failure.

You may wonder why `sample` actually worked when being invoked with the arguments 9 7 8. The defect was the same, and it caused the same infection. However, as `a[3]` in this case turned out to be larger than 9 it did not get swapped with another array element. At the return of `shell_sort()` the infection was gone, and thus the defect never showed up as a failure.

- *Correct the defect.* So far, we are still *speculating* about the failure cause. To deliver the final proof, we have to correct the defect. If the failure no longer occurs, we know that the defect caused the failure.

  In addition to prohibiting the failure in question we want to prohibit as many failures as possible. In our case, we achieve this by replacing line 36,

  ```
  shell_sort(a, argc);,
  ```

  with the correct invocation

  ```
  shell_sort(a, argc - 1);.
  ```

  Repeating the test with the fixed program, as follows, shows that the original failure no longer occurs.

  ```
  $ ./sample 11 14
  Output: 11 14
  $ _
  ```

  This resolves the `sample` problem.

1.5 AUTOMATED DEBUGGING TECHNIQUES

Essentially, we have solved the `sample` problem *manually* — that is, without using any specific tools. In principle, all debugging problems can be solved manually — by deduction from the source code and observation of what's going on in a program. (Purists might even argue that deduction alone suffices to prove a program correct, removing the need to fix defects.)

In practice, though, it is unwise to rely on manual debugging alone, as the computer can relieve you of most boring and tedious tasks. In particular, the `sample` program discussed earlier can be debugged almost automatically. Figure 1.8 depicts the automated debugging techniques discussed in the following.

- *Simplified input:* Chapter 5 "Simplifying Problems" introduces *delta debugging* — a technique that automatically narrows down the difference between

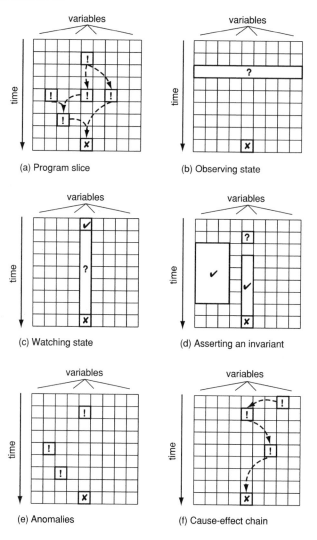

FIGURE 1.8 Some automated debugging techniques.

a passing and a failing run. Applied to program input, delta debugging returns a *simplified input* wherein each part contributes to the failure.

Applied to the failing sample run, delta debugging determines that each of the arguments 11 and 14 is relevant. The failure no longer occurs if sample is being called with one argument only.

• *Program slices:* Chapter 7 "Deducing Errors" explores basic deduction methods; that is, deducing from the (abstract) program code what can and cannot happen in the (concrete) program run. The most important technique is *slicing* — separating the part of a program or program run relevant to the failure. In Figure 1.8a, we can see that only a fraction of the state actually could have caused the failure. Applied to sample, a program slice could determine that a[0] got the zero value because of the values of a[2] and size, which is already a good hint.

- *Observing state:* Chapter 8 "Observing Facts" discusses *observation techniques*, especially using *debuggers*. A debugger is a tool that can make a program stop under specific conditions, which allows a programmer to observe the entire state (see Figure 1.8b). This allows us to tell the sane program state from the infected state. Using a debugger on sample, we would be able to observe the values of a[] and size at any moment in time without changing or recompiling the program.

- *Watching state:* Another important feature of debuggers, also discussed in Chapter 8, is that they allow us to *watch* small parts of the state to determine if they change during execution. As sketched in Figure 1.8c, this allows us to identify the precise moment at which a variable becomes infected. Using a debugger on sample, we would be able to watch the value of a[0] to catch the precise statement that assigns the zero from a[2].

- *Assertions:* When observing a program state, the programmer must still *compare* the observed values with the intended values — a process that takes time and is error prone. Chapter 10 "Asserting Expectations" introduces *assertions*, which are used to delegate this comparison process to the computer. The programmer specifies the expected values and has the computer check them at runtime — especially at the beginning and ending of functions (i.e., pre- and post-conditions). Such assertions typically include *invariants* over data structures that hold during the entire run.

  If all assertions pass, this means that the state is just as expected. When used to check invariants, as sketched in Figure 1.8d, assertions can mark large parts of the state as "sane," allowing the programmer to focus on the other parts.

  One specific instance of assertions are *memory assertions*, checking whether memory is accessed in a legal way. Applied to sample, tools exist that can easily identify that a[2] is accessed without being allocated or initialized. These tools are also discussed in Chapter 10.

- *Anomalies:* In general, we can assume that a program works well most of the time. If a program fails nonetheless, we can use our knowledge about the passing runs and focus on the *differences* between the passing runs and the failing run. Such differences point out *anomalies*, as sketched in Figure 1.8e.

Detecting anomalies requires techniques designed to *compare* program runs. It also requires techniques for creating *abstractions* over multiple runs. Chapter 11 "Detecting Anomalies" discusses these techniques.

Applied to sample, we can (for instance) compare the *coverage* of the two runs sample 11 (passing) and sample 11 14 (failing). It turns out that the statements where a[j] is assigned a value are executed only in the failing run, but not in the passing run. Hence, if we are looking for a zero value in a[0] these two lines might be a good starting point.

- *Cause-effect chains:* Chapter 14 "Isolating Cause-Effect Chains" applies delta debugging to *program states*, thus identifying in each state which particular variable(s) caused the failure. This results in a *cause-effect chain*, as sketched in Figure 1.8f. Although causes are not necessarily errors, they help to narrow down the relevant elements of a failure.

  Delta debugging on states is also the basis of the ASKIGOR automated debugging server. Its diagnosis, shown in Figure 1.9, summarizes how the failure came to be: variable argc was 3; hence, a[2] was zero; hence, sample failed.

All of these techniques can be combined to locate the defect systematically—and with a substantial degree of automation. Chapter 15 "Fixing the Defect" shows how the debugging techniques integrate and intertwine. In addition to these chapters focusing on concrete techniques, the following chapters focus on *prerequisites*.

- Tracking failures (Chapter 2 "Tracking Problems")

- Running tests automatically (Chapter 3 "Making Programs Fail")

- Reproducing failures (Chapter 4 "Reproducing Problems")

- Combining various reasoning techniques (Chapter 6 "Scientific Debugging")

- Finding failure causes systematically (Chapter 12 "Causes and Effects")

The first of these prerequisites is that a problem exist. Consequently, the next chapter starts with tracking and reproducing failures.

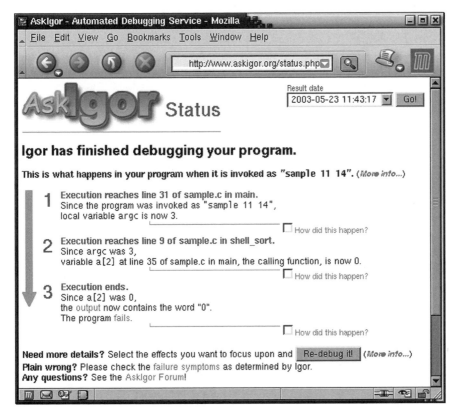

FIGURE 1.9 The ASKIGOR debugging server with a diagnosis for sample. Given an executable, a failing invocation, and a passing invocation, ASKIGOR automatically produces a diagnosis consisting of a cause-effect chain from invocation to failure.

1.6 BUGS, FAULTS, OR DEFECTS?

Before we close this chapter, let's examine our vocabulary. As illustrated at the beginning of this chapter, the word *bug* suggests something humans can touch and remove — and are probably not responsible for. This is already one reason to avoid the word *bug*. Another reason is its lack of precision. Applied to programs, a bug can mean:

- An incorrect *program code* ("This line is buggy")

- An incorrect *program state* ("This pointer, being null, is a bug")

- An incorrect *program execution* ("The program crashes; this is a bug")

This ambiguity of the term *bug* is unfortunate, as it confuses causes with symptoms: *The bug in the code caused a bug in the state, which caused a bug in the execution — and when we saw the bug we tracked the bug, and finally found and fixed the bug.* The remainder of this book uses the following more precise terms.

- *Defect:* An incorrect program code (a bug in the code).

- *Infection:* An incorrect program state (a bug in the state).

- *Failure:* An observable incorrect program behavior (a bug in the behavior).

The wording of the previous example thus becomes clearer: *The defect caused an infection, which caused a failure — and when we saw the failure we tracked the infection, and finally found and fixed the defect.*

The industry uses several synonyms of these terms. The IEEE standards define the term *fault* as here *defect* is defined. They also define *bug* as a fault, thus making it a synonym of *defect* — and *debugging* hence becomes the activity of removing defects in the software.

The terms *error* and *fault* are frequently used as a synonym of *infection*, but also for mistakes made by the programmer. Failures are also called *issues* or *problems*. In this book, we use *problem* as a general term for a questionable property of the program run. A problem becomes a *failure* as soon as it is considered incorrect.

Some defects cannot be attributed to a specific location in the software, but rather to its overall design or architecture. I call such defects *flaws.* In general, flaws are bad news, because they suggest major changes involved in fixing the problem.

So much for our family of bugs and related terms. Actually, your choice of one term over another shows two things. First, your wording shows how seriously you take the quality of your work. As Humphrey (1999) points out, the term *bug* "has an unfortunate connotation of merely being an annoyance; something you could swat away or ignore with minor discomfort." He suggests *defect* instead, and this book follows his advice. Likewise, the word *failure* is to be taken more seriously than *issue*. (If you find a *flaw*, you should be truly alarmed.)

Second, your choice shows whether you want to attribute failures to individuals. Whereas *bugs* seem to creep into the software as if they had a life of their own, *errors* and *faults* are clearly results of human action. These terms were coined by Edsger W. Dijkstra as pejorative alternatives to *bug* in order to increase the programmers' sense of responsibility. After all, who wants to create a fault? However, if a program does not behave as intended this may not be the effect of a human mistake (as discussed in Section 1.2). In fact, even a program that is *correct* with respect to its specification can still produce *surprises*. This is why I use the terms *defect* and *infection* instead of the guilt-ridden *faults* and *errors*. All of these definitions (and more) can be found in the Glossary.

1.7 CONCEPTS

✎ In general, a failure comes about in the following three stages. (See also List 1.2.)

1. The programmer creates a *defect* in the program code (also known as *bug* or *fault*).

2. The defect causes an *infection* in the program state.

3. The infection causes a *failure* — an externally observable error.

- Barron (2002) states that *roughly 22% of PCs and 25% of notebooks break down every year*, compared to 9% of VCRs, 7% of big-screen TVs, 7% of clothes dryers, and 8% of refrigerators.

- According to a U.S. federal study conducted by RTI (2002), software bugs are costing the U.S. economy an estimated *$59.5 billion each year.*

- Beizer (1990) reports that of the labor expended to develop a working program, *50% is typically spent on testing and debugging activities.*

- According to Hailpern and Santhanam (2002), validation activities (debugging, testing, and verification) can easily range from *50% to 75% of the total development cost.*

- Gould (1975) reports that out of a group of experienced programmers the three programmers best at debugging were able to find defects in about 30% the time and made only 40% as many errors as the three worst.

- In RTI (2002), developers estimate that improvements in testing and debugging could *reduce the cost of software bugs by a third*, or $22.5 billion.

LIST 1.2 Facts on debugging.

✎ *To debug a program*, proceed in seven steps (TRAFFIC):

- *Track:* Create an entry in the problem database (Chapter 2 "Tracking Problems").

- *Reproduce:* Reproduce the failure (Chapter 4 "Reproducing Problems").

- *Automate:* Automate and simplify the test case (Chapters 3 "Making Programs Fail" and 5 "Simplifying Problems").

- *Find origins:* Follow back the dependences from the failure to possible infection origins (Chapters 7 "Deducing Errors" and 9 "Tracking Origins").

- *Focus:* If there are multiple possible origins, first examine the following.

  1. *Known infections*, as determined by assertions (Chapter 10 "Asserting Expectations") and observation (Chapter 8 "Observing Facts")

  2. *Causes* in state, code, and input (Chapters 13 "Isolating Failure Causes" and 14 "Isolating Cause-Effect Chains")

  3. *Anomalies* (Chapter 11 "Detecting Anomalies")

  4. *Code smells* (Chapter 7 "Deducing Errors")

  Prefer automated techniques where possible.

- *Isolate:* Use scientific method (Chapter 6 "Scientific Debugging") to isolate the origin of the infection. Continue isolating origins transitively until you have an infection chain from defect to failure.

- *Correct:* Remove the defect, breaking the infection chain (Chapter 15 "Fixing the Defect"). Verify the success of your fix.

✎ Of all debugging activities, locating the defect (the find-focus-isolate loop in TRAFFIC) is by far the most time consuming.

✎ Correcting a defect is usually simple, unless it involves a major redesign (in which case we call the defect a *flaw*).

✎ Not every defect results in an infection, and not every infection results in a failure. Yet, every failure can be traced back to some infection, which again can be traced back to a defect.

1.8 TOOLS

Toward your own experimentation with techniques, the "Tools" section within chapters provides references where tools mentioned in the text are publicly available. Typically, the text provides a URL where the tool is available — often as an open-source download. If the tool is not publicly available, the reference describing it will be listed in the "Further Reading" section. You may want to ask the authors whether they make their tool available to you.

As this chapter is an introduction, references to tools will come in the later chapters. However, note that Clint Jeffery's *Algorithmic and Automatic Debugging Home Page* — a web page that collects links to debugging techniques and tools, and which will give you the latest and greatest in debugging — is available at:

```
http://www.cs.nmsu.edu/~jeffery/aadebug.html
```

1.9 FURTHER READING

To avoid breaking up the flow of the main text, references to related work are collected in a section at the end of each chapter. This first "Further Reading" section describes papers, books, and other resources relevant to the material covered in this chapter.

The story about the "first bug" was reported by Hopper (1981). Apparently, Hopper believed that this "first bug" coined the term *bug* for computer programs ("From then on, when anything went wrong with a computer, we said it had bugs in it."). However, as Shapiro (1994) points out, *bug* was already a common "shop" term in Edison's time (1878) for unexpected systems faults. The carryover to computers (certainly complex systems) is almost unavoidable.

Dijkstra's quote that testing can only show the absence of bugs stems from 1972. In 1982, Dijkstra was also among the first to criticize the word *bug* and suggest *error* instead. In 1989, he made clear that this wording would put "the blame where it belongs, viz., with the programmer who made the error."

The origin of the word *bug* is clarified by Beizer (1999). In 2000, he suggested dropping *fault* and *error* due to their pejorative aspect. The terms *bug* and *defect* are compared by Humphrey (1999). The term *infection* as well as the idea of an infection propagating from defect to failure were proposed by (Voas, 1992). Finally, in that this chapter serves as introduction to the book, we will now look into other material that serves as an introduction to debugging.

- *The Soul of a New Machine*, by Kidder (1981), tracks a team of engineers at Data General working on an innovative new computer. This is not a technical book but a well-orchestrated hymn to the man behind the machine. It describes the challenges and strains of debugging. It was winner of the Pulitzer prize for nonfiction.

- *Showstopper!*, by Zachary (1994), describes how Microsoft created Windows NT. Not too technical, it focuses on the people and their processes. Not too surprisingly, eventually finishing the product becomes a struggle with always resurfacing "showstopper" bugs.

- *Zen and the Art of Motorcycle Maintenance*, by Pirsig (1974), despite its title neither contains many facts on Zen nor many facts on motorcycle maintenance. It is an inquiry on what is good and what is not, in a clear engineer's language digging into the depths of philosophy — still a cult book today. The section on how a mechanic fixes a motorcycle is a must read.

- *Code Complete*, by McConnell (1993), is a practical handbook on how to construct software. "Practical" means "pragmatic" and "easily understandable." McConnell goes straight at the topic and tells you how to code and how not to code — and how to debug, of course.

- *The Practice of Programming*, by Kernighan and Pike (1999), describes best practices that help make individual programmers more effective and productive. Although just 250 pages long, barrels of wisdom and experience have been distilled in this book.

Bug Story 2, about the F-16 problems, was posted in *Risks* digest (vol. 3, issue 44), August 1986.

1.10 EXERCISES

EXERCISE 1.1. Relate the following statements to the terms *defect*, *infection*, *propagation*, and *failure*. Discuss how they (possibly) came to be, and how they (possibly) relate to the output.

- A program throws a null pointer exception.

- A print statement `printf("Helo World")` has a typo.

- A constant $\pi = 31.4$ is declared, but all but one test case pass.

- Variable z has the value 15.

- A bug is removed by fixing three files.

- A clock shows Greenwich mean time rather than the local time zone.

EXERCISE 1.2. Compile `sample` on your system. (You can download the source from http://www.whyprogramsfail.com/.) When compiling, enable all possible warning options you can find.

EXERCISE 1.3. Test `sample` on your system. Do the failures occur as described here? If not, can you find a test case that triggers a failure?

EXERCISE 1.4. Each of the following actions effectively fixes the `sample` program. Which are the advantages and disadvantages of these actions?

1. Insert a statement `argc = argc - 1` at the top of `main`, and replace all later occurrences of `argc - 1` by `argc`.

2. Change the loop in `shell_sort` such that it ends at `size - 1` instead of `size`.

3. Introduce a variable `size = argc - 1` at the top of `main`, and replace all later occurrences of `argc - 1` by `size`. Change the `shell_sort` invocation to `shell_sort(a, size)`.

4. Insert a statement `size = size - 1` at the top of `shell_sort`.

EXERCISE 1.5. "If we can prove a program is correct, we have no need for testing or debugging." Argue for and against this assertion. Use at least three arguments in either case.

EXERCISE 1.6. Perform a web search for as many occurrences of *bug*, *defect*, and *fault* you can find via the following.

1. On the entire Internet

2. On the web pages of your preferred software vendor

3. In computer-related newsgroups

You are in a little maze of twisty passages, all different.

—WILL CROWTHER,
Adventure game (1972)

## CHAPTER 2

TRACKING PROBLEMS

THIS CHAPTER DEALS WITH THE ISSUE OF HOW TO *manage* problems as reported by users: how to track and manage problem reports, how to organize the debugging process, and how to keep track of multiple versions. All of this constitutes the basic framework within which debugging takes place.

2.1 OH! ALL THESE PROBLEMS

Technically, a defect is created at the moment the programmer writes the appropriate code. However, its actual life cycle begins when some human spots the defect itself or one of its effects. Frequently, the human is a user, and the effect is a problem that needs to be solved.

Solving a user's problem is more than just debugging. At the start, we need to find out whether we can actually do something. Maybe the problem is a simple misunderstanding, or is caused by external components we cannot control. At the end, it does not suffice to fix the defect in our production code. To solve the user's problem, we also need to deploy the fix. All these steps involved in solving the problem need to be organized and managed. The life cycle of a software problem — from the first occurrence of a problem to its fix — can be summarized as the following five steps.

1. The user *informs* the vendor about the problem.

2. The vendor *reproduces* the problem.

3. The vendor *isolates* the problem circumstances.

4. The vendor *locates* and *fixes* the defect locally.

5. The vendor *delivers* the fix to the user.

As a programmer, you can be involved in each of these steps. First, you may always take the role of a user (for instance, when testing software or when working with third-party components). Later, you may be involved with reproducing, isolating, locating, and fixing the problem — the core of debugging. Finally, you may even be involved with delivering the fix.

Unless you are a one-person company with an elephant memory, this life cycle must be organized in some way. As a manager, you must be able to answer questions such as the following.

- *Which problems are currently open?* An open problem indicates that there is probably some defect in the software that must be fixed.

- *Which are the most severe problems?* Typically, the most severe problems are the first to get fixed.

- *Did similar problems occur in the past?* If there were similar problems, there may be a solution at hand that need only to be delivered.

Furthermore, the *user* may want to know the state of her problem — and be quickly informed about any progress made. Our challenge is thus:

> HOW CAN WE ORGANIZE THE LARGE-SCALE DEBUGGING PROCESS?

2.2 REPORTING PROBLEMS

To fix a problem, the developer must first be able to *reproduce it*. Otherwise, there would be no way of ascertaining further details about the problem. Worse, there would be no way of determining if the problem were fixed. The information required for this task is called a *problem report* (PR), also known as a *change request* (CR) or simply *bug report*. What goes into a problem report? The basic principle of problem reports is:

State all relevant facts.

Here, "relevant" means "relevant for reproducing the problem." However, determining the relevant facts can impose problems. How can the user know what is relevant or not?

Real-life problem reports frequently include *too much*, such as gigantic core dumps, entire hard disk content, and even entire drives. However, they may not include *enough*: "Your program crashed. Just wanted to let you know." (A 1999 problem report about the GNU DDD debugger.)

To get the right amount of information, it is usually a good idea to have a list of *specific items* that should be included in every problem report. If you write a problem report, be sure to include the following.

- *The product release:* This is the version number or some other unique identifier of the product. Using this information, the developer can recreate a local copy of the program in the version as installed in the user's environment.

  Example: `Perfect Publishing Program 1.1 for LemonyOS`

  If you can (for instance, if you are a tester), try to *generalize*. Does the problem occur under alternate releases, too? Does it occur in the most recent version?

- *The operating environment:* Typically, this is version information about the operating system. As problems may occur because of interactions between third-party components, information about such components may be useful as well.

  Example: `LemonyOS 2.3 with Primary Pretty Printer installed`

  Again, if you can, try to generalize. Does the problem occur under different operating environments, too? In our case, for instance, you might wish to check alternate operating systems or alternate printers.

- *The system resources:* Some problems occur only under limited resources. Therefore, it is advisable to include information about your system's memory, disk space, or CPU load:

  ```
  My system has one Googolbyte of RAM and
  2 Googolplexbytes of disk space.
  ```

- *The problem history:* This is a description of what has to be done to reproduce the problem, as a minimal set of steps necessary. Typically, this also includes any accessed resources, such as input or configuration files:

```
1) Create a document "bug.ppp" which includes
   the attached PNG graphic.
2) Print the document on the default printer.
```

This section is crucial: If the problem cannot be reproduced, it is unlikely to be fixed. If you can, have another user or tester repeat and review the steps described here.

If you can, *simplify* the problem as much as possible. If your database fails (say, on a 1,000-line SQL statement), the chances of getting the problem fixed are low — simply because such SQL statements do not occur this frequently in practice. But if you can simplify the SQL statement to three lines, such that the problem still persists, you're likely to get heard. Likewise, if certain circumstances are crucial for the problem to occur, be sure to include them. This gives developers a head start in debugging. (See Chapters 5 "Simplifying Problems" and 13 "Isolating Failure Causes" for more on this issue, especially on automating these steps.)

- *A description of the* expected *behavior:* This describes what should have happened according to the user.

  Example: `The program should have printed the document.`

- *A description of the* experienced *behavior:* These are the *symptoms* of the problem — what has happened in contrast to the expected behavior.

  Example:

  ```
  The program crashed with the following information

  *** STACK DUMP OF CRASH (LemonyOS)

    Back chain  ISA  Caller
    00000000    SPC  0BA8E574
    03EADF80    SPC  0B742428
    03EADF30    SPC  0B50FDDC  PrintThePage+072FC
  SnicketPC unmapped memory exception at
        0B512BD0 PrintThePage+05F50
  ```

As you are the bearer of bad news, it is important to remain *neutral.* Humor, sarcasm, or attacks will all divert developers from their goal — which is increasing the product quality. Just stay with the facts.

- *A one-line* summary: The one-line summary captures the essence of the problem. It is typically the basis for deciding the severity of the problem —

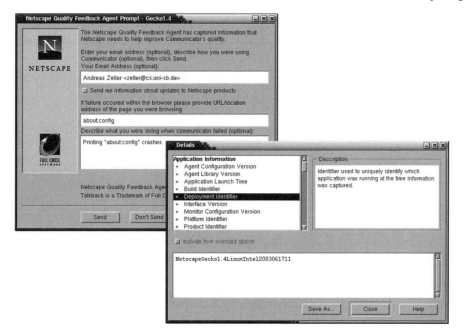

FIGURE 2.1 MOZILLA Talkback dialog. When MOZILLA fails, users can send relevant information to the MOZILLA developers.

that is, its impact on customers — and, consequently, the priority by which the problem will get fixed.

Example: PPP 1.1 crashes when printing documents with PNG graphics

Some products include specific functionality or stand-alone tools to produce standardized problem reports. Figure 2.1 shows the Talkback dialog, which appears when the MOZILLA web browser experiences a fatal failure. Clicking on Send forwards all relevant information (shown in the Details dialog) to the MOZILLA developers.

Talkback-like tools can also forward *internal* information to the vendor — for instance, a *core dump*, which records the state of the program at the moment it failed. Such core dumps can be read in and examined by developers (see Section 8.3.3 for details on how to perform such postmortem debugging).

If the error occurs after a long series of events, it is often difficult for the user to retrace all steps from the program invocation to the failure. Therefore, the program can also be set up to *record* important events in a *log file*, which can later be forwarded to and examined and reproduced by the vendor. (In Chapter 8 "Observing Facts," we will learn more about log files. Section 11.4 has more ideas on information that can be collected and sampled from users.)

In all of these cases, the *privacy* of the user is an important issue. It is very advisable that the user be aware of whatever information being sent to third parties (such as the vendor). This is not much of a risk with manually written problem reports, but it becomes an increasing risk with information collected automatically. Internal information (such as a core dump) cannot be interpreted by the user at all, and thus brings the greatest risk of an unwanted breach of privacy. In addition, log files about user interactions can be misused for all types of purposes, including third-party attacks. For these reasons, users should be made aware of any information your product may be collecting and forwarding. In addition, users should be able to turn off all recording features.

All of this applies to problems that occur in the field. If an in-house tester finds a problem, she should make every effort to fix the problem. This includes recording and providing as much information as possible.

2.3   MANAGING PROBLEMS

Most developer teams keep track of the current problems in their system using a single "problem list" document that lists all open or unresolved problems to date. Such a document is easy to set up and easy to maintain. However, associated problems include the folllowing.

- *Only one person at a time can work on the document.* Exception: The document is in a *version control system* that allows parallel editing and later merging.

- *History of earlier (and fixed) problems is lost.* Exception: The document is in a version control system and evolves together with the product.

- *Does not scale.* You cannot track hundreds of different issues in a simple text document.

The alternative to keeping a document is to use a *problem database*, which stores all problem reports. Problem databases scale up to a large number of developers, users, and problems.

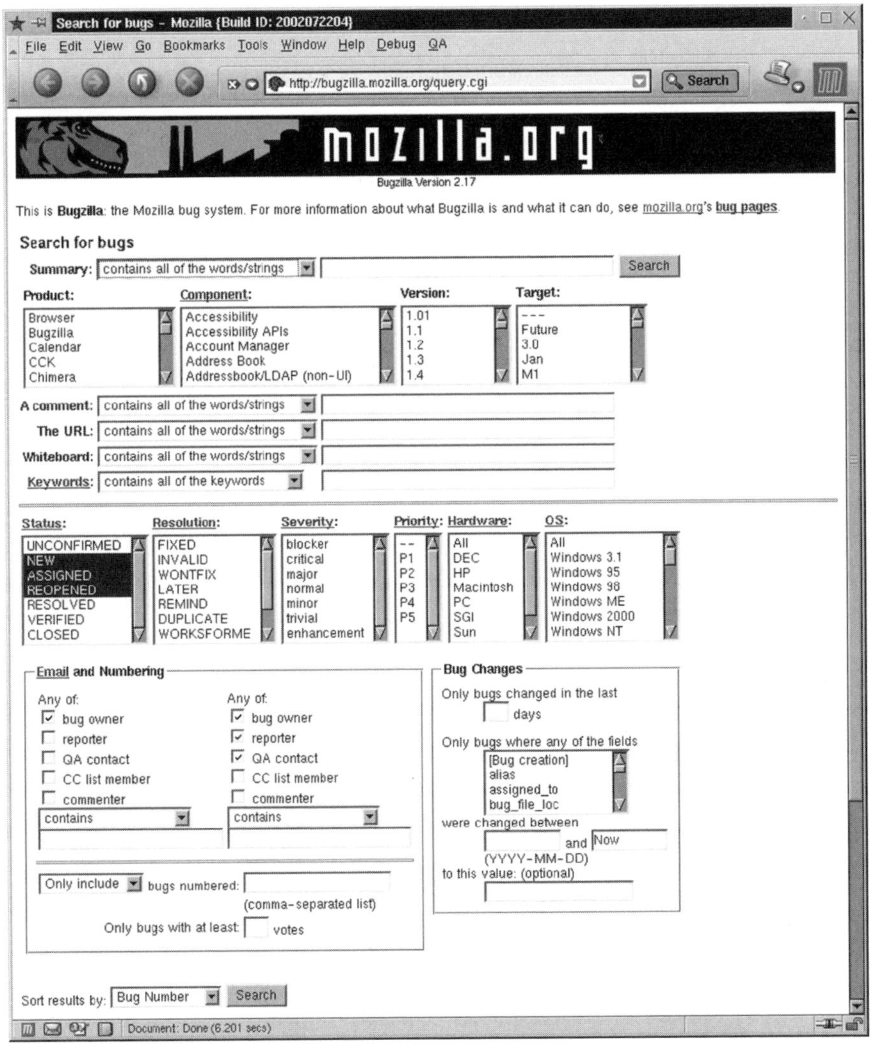

FIGURE 2.2 The BUGZILLA problem database. The database organizes all problem reports for MOZILLA.

Figure 2.2 shows an example of such a problem-tracking system. This is *BUGZILLA*, the problem-tracking system for the MOZILLA web browser. BUGZILLA employs a web browser as a user interface, which means that it can be accessed from anywhere (and by anyone, as MOZILLA is an open-source project). You can even install and adapt BUGZILLA for your own project. Note, though, that BUGZILLA (and other problem-tracking systems) are meant for developers, not for end users. Information provided from end users must be distilled and classified before it can be entered into the database.

2.4 CLASSIFYING PROBLEMS

Assume we want to report a problem in BUGZILLA (either because we are expert users and know how to enter a problem on a web site or because we are in charge of processing a user problem report). To report a problem, we must supply the required information (Section 2.2 has details on how to report problems) and *classify* the problem. The attributes BUGZILLA uses to classify problems, discussed in the following, are typical for problem-tracking systems.

2.4.1 Severity

Each problem is assigned a *severity* that describes the impact of the problem on the development or release process. BUGZILLA knows the following severity levels, from those with the greatest impact to those with the least.

- *Blocker:* Blocks development and/or testing work. This highest level of severity is also known as a *showstopper.*

- *Critical:* Crashes, loss of data, and severe memory leak.

- *Major:* Major loss of function.

- *Normal:* This is the "standard" problem.

- *Minor:* Minor loss of function, or other problem for which an easy workaround is present.

- *Trivial:* Cosmetic problem such as misspelled words or misaligned text.

- *Enhancement:* Request for enhancement. This means that the problem is not a failure at all, but rather a desired feature. Do not confuse this with missing functionality, though: if the product does not meet a requirement, this should be treated as a major problem.

Ideally, a product is not shipped unless all "severe" problems have been fixed; that is, major, critical, or blocker problems have been resolved, and all requirements are met. If a product is to be released at a fixed date, optional functions that still cause problems can be disabled.

The severity also determines our wording. In general, the word *problem* is just as a general term for a questionable property of the program run. A problem becomes a *failure* as soon as it is considered an incorrect behavior of the system. It is a *feature* if it is considered normal behavior ("It's not a bug, it's a feature!"). However, a *missing* or *incomplete* feature can also be a problem, as indicated by the *enhancement* category.

2.4.2 Priority

Each problem is assigned a specific *priority*. The higher the priority the sooner the problem is going to be addressed. The priority is typically defined by the management. In fact, it is the *main means* for management to express what should be done first and what later. The importance of the priority attribute when it comes to control the process of development and problem solving cannot be overemphasized.

2.4.3 Identifier

Each problem gets a unique *identifier* (a *PR number*; in BUGZILLA, *bug number*) such that developers can refer to it within the debugging process — in e-mails, change logs, status reports, and attachments.

2.4.4 Comments

Every user and developer can attach *comments* to a problem report — for instance, to add information about the circumstances of the problem, to speculate about possible problem causes, to add first findings, or to discuss how the problem should be fixed.

2.4.5 Notification

Developers and users can attach their e-mail address to a problem report. They will get notified automatically every time the problem report changes.

2.5 PROCESSING PROBLEMS

Assume that someone has entered a new problem report into the problem database. This problem report must now be *processed*. During this process, the prob-

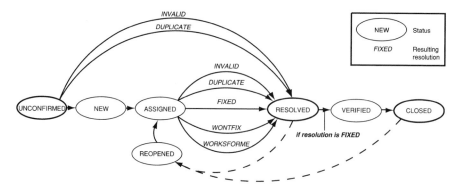

FIGURE 2.3 The life cycle of a problem in BUGZILLA. A problem starts UNCONFIRMED, is later ASSIGNED to a specific developer, and finally CLOSED with a specific resolution.

lem report runs through a *life cycle* (Figure 2.3) — from UNCONFIRMED to CLOSED. The position in the life cycle is determined by the *state* of the problem report. These states are described in the following.

- UNCONFIRMED: This is the state of any new problem report, as entered into the database. For example, Olaf is a happy user of the Perfect Publishing Program — until it suddenly crashes. Thus:

  1. Olaf reports the failure to Sunny at customer support.

  2. Sunny enters the failure details as a new problem report into the problem database. She reports how Olaf can reproduce the failure, ascertains the relevant facts about Olaf's configuration, and sets the severity to "normal." She also reports Olaf's contact address.

  3. The problem gets a PR number (say, PR 2074). Its initial state is UNCONFIRMED. Nobody has yet tried to reproduce it.

- NEW: The problem report is *valid*.

  – It contains the relevant facts. (Otherwise, its *resolution* becomes *INVALID*. See material following.)

  – It is not an obvious *duplicate* of a known problem. (Otherwise, its resolution becomes *DUPLICATE*. See material following.)

  A NEW problem need not necessarily be reproducible. This is being taken care of in the remainder of the life cycle. In our example, programmer Violet may be in charge of checking problem reports. Finding that PR 2074 was not known before, she sets its state to NEW.

- ASSIGNED: The problem is not yet resolved, but is already assigned to a developer (in BUGZILLA, to the *bug owner*). Mr. Poe, the manager, asks Violet to solve PR 2074. The state is now ASSIGNED.

- RESOLVED: The problem is resolved. The *resolution* tells what has become (for now) of the problem report.

  - *FIXED:* The problem is fixed.

  - *INVALID:* The problem is not a problem, or does not contain the relevant facts.

  - *DUPLICATE:* The problem is a duplicate of an existing problem.

  - *WONTFIX:* The problem described is a problem that will never be fixed. This may also be the case for problems that turn out to be features rather than failures. The following is a *WONTFIX* example. The MOZILLA browser does not display ALT texts for images as tooltips, which many consider a problem. However, the MOZILLA developers say this behavior is mandated by web standards and thus will not fix the "problem." (See bug #25537 at *bugzilla.mozilla.org.*)

  - *WORKSFORME:* All attempts at reproducing this problem were futile. If more information appears later, the problem may be reopened. If the resolution is *FIXED*, the fix must be verified (state VERIFIED) and finally delivered (state CLOSED). In our example, let's assume Violet is unable to reproduce PR 2074 in her environment. In this case, the following happens.

    1. Violet documents her attempts in additional comments to the problem report, and sets the resolution to WORKSFORME and the state to RESOLVED. However, could it be that Olaf has the product configured to use the metric system? She asks Sunny whether she could get further data.

    2. Sunny requests further information from Olaf and sets the state of PR 2074 to REOPENED.

    3. Violet is still responsible for PR 2074 (state ASSIGNED). With the new data, she can finally reproduce and fix the problem. The state becomes RESOLVED; the resolution is FIXED.

- VERIFIED: The problem is fixed. The fix has been verified as successful. The problem remains VERIFIED until the fix has been delivered to the user (for instance, by shipping a new release). Tester Klaus reviews Violet's fix. He gives his okay to integrate the fix in the current production release. The state of PR 2074 becomes VERIFIED.

- CLOSED: A new release (or patch) of the product was shipped. In this release, the problem no longer occurs. As soon as the fix is delivered to Olaf, the PR 2074 state is CLOSED.

- REOPENED: If a problem occurs again, it is assigned a state of REOPENED rather than NEW. It must be assigned again. In our example, if further users contact customer support about the problem Sunny can look up the problem in the problem-tracking system and point them to the new release.

All of these states and resolutions can (and should) be adapted to the process at hand. If there is no independent verification, for example, reports skip the VERIFIED state. If problems are fixed at the user's site (skipping shipment), the RESOLVED and CLOSED states become synonyms. On the other hand, if additional clearance is required before a fix gets accepted this can be expressed by additional states and resolutions.

2.6 MANAGING PROBLEM TRACKING

A good problem-tracking system is the basis for all daily work on problems and failures. If nobody files problem reports, it is useless. If nobody marks problems as resolved, it will quickly be filled with outdated information. Therefore, the following issues should be resolved.

- *Who files problem reports?* This could be support personnel only. In general, though, it is probably useful if any developer can add new entries. Advanced users and beta testers may also be enabled to file problem reports.

- *Who classifies problem reports?* The *severity* of a problem can be extracted from the initial report. Sometimes, the severity is determined only after the problem could be reproduced.

- *Who sets priorities?* To determine the priority of a problem, management must assess the *impact* of a problem — that is, not only its severity but the following.

    - Its likelihood

    - The number of users affected

    - The potential damage

Hence, the priority need not be correlated with the severity of a problem. A "blocker" problem in an alpha release may have lower priority than a "major" problem in a widely distributed product.

Many organizations use a *software change control board* (SCCB) to set priorities. This is a group of people who track problem reports and take care of their handling. Such a group typically consists of developers, testers, and configuration managers.

- *Who takes care of the problem?* All problem-tracking systems allow *assigning* problems to individual developers. This is also the task of an SCCB or like group.

- *Who closes issues?* This can be the SCCB or like group, the individual tester, or some quality assurance instance that verifies fixes (as in the scenario described previously).

- *What's the life cycle of a problem?* The BUGZILLA model, shown in Figure 2.3, is typical of problem databases but is by no means the only possible one. Depending on your individual needs, one can design alternate states and transitions. Problem-tracking systems may be configured to incorporate such processes.

2.7 REQUIREMENTS AS PROBLEMS

Problem-tracking systems need not be confined to maintenance. They can also be used during *development* of the product. In fact, they can be used from the very start, even when the product does not exist. In this setting, one enters *requirements* into the problem-tracking database, implying that each requirement not yet met is a problem. The severity of the problem indicates the importance of the requirement. Central requirements not yet met are marked as "major" problems. Minor or optional requirements could be marked as "requests for enhancement."

As requirements are typically broken down into subrequirements, the problem-tracking system should have a way of organizing problems *hierarchically.* That is, there should be a way of decomposing problems into subproblems, and of marking the problems as FIXED as soon as all subproblems are FIXED. In this fashion, requirement 1 is the product itself, and problem 1 thus becomes "the product is missing." As requirement 1 is broken down into a large number of individual features, so is the problem — with one subproblem for every feature. The product is ready for shipping when all problems are resolved —

indicated by problem 1 being FIXED, which implies that all features are now implemented.

A good problem-tracking system can *summarize* the problem database in the form of statistics (how many problems are still open, how many problems are being assigned to whom, and so on). A problem-tracking system may thus become the *primary tool* for organizing the debugging process, or the development process in general. The key is that managers check the problem-tracking system for outstanding issues, and assign appropriate priorities for developers. Eventually, your problem-tracking database will be a universal tool for resolving all types of problems — even those only remotely related to the product at hand (see Bug Story 3).

2.8 MANAGING DUPLICATES

If your problem-tracking system is well used, you may experience a meta-problem: *a lot of problem reports.* In September of 2003 the MOZILLA problem database listed roughly 8,300 UNCONFIRMED problems waiting to be assigned and resolved.

One reason for such a large number of problem reports is *duplicates.* If your program has several users and a defect, chances are that several users will experience similar failures. If all of these users send in problem reports, your problem-tracking system will quickly fill up with similar reports, all related to the same defect.

For instance, if your web browser crashes whenever it tries to render a drop-down list users will send in problem reports: "I opened web page X, and it crashed," "I opened web page Y, and it crashed," and so on. Processing all of these reports and finding out that each of the mentioned web pages includes a drop-down list takes a lot of time.

A partial solution to this problem is to *identify duplicates.* The idea is that within the problem-tracking system one can mark problems as a *duplicate* of another problem. Submitters of new problem reports can then be encouraged to search the problem database for similar problems first. If a similar problem is found, the new problem can be marked as a duplicate. When the initial problem is fixed, the developer can close the duplicates where the same failure cause occurs. Unfortunately, it is not always easy to spot duplicates. This is due to two conflicting goals.

- A problem report includes *as many facts* as possible, in that any of them may be relevant for reproducing the problem.

BUG STORY 3: Tracking Milk Issues at Microsoft

The following bug report is purported to originate from Microsoft's Excel group from 1994. Aliases have been removed. The T: indicates that the person was a tester, whereas D: stands for developer and P: for program manager.

```
------------------ ACTIVE - 05/12/94 - T:XXXXX ---------------------
: Go to the kitchen
: Grab a Darigold chocolate milk carton
: Read the ingredients list

--! Either Darigold has discovered a chocolate cow, or something's
  missing from the ingredients list. It only lists milk, vitamin A,
  and vitamin D.  So where does the chocolate/sugar flavor come from?
------------------ ACTIVE - 05/12/94 - T:XXXXX ---------------------
Moo info:
: Grab a Darigold 2% milk carton (NOT chocolate)
: Read the ingredients
--! Says it contains Cocoa, Sugar, Guar gum ...
Looks like the Chocolate
   and 2% ingredient lists have been swapped.
-------------- ASSIGNED to D:XXXXX - 05/12/94 - D:XXXXXXXX -----------
looks like an internals problem?
-------------- ASSIGNED to D:XXXXX - 05/12/94 - D:XXXXX ---------------
UI Problem. I'll take it.
-------------- ASSIGNED to D:XXXXX - 05/12/94 - D:XXXXX ---------------
They don't make milk at the Issaquah Darigold. Calling Ranier Ave.
-------------- ASSIGNED to D:XXXXX - 05/12/94 - D:XXXXX ---------------
I can't repro. Do you have the wrong MILKINTL.DLL?
-------------- ASSIGNED to D:XXXXX - 05/12/94 - T:XXXXXXXX -----------
By design? I think new US health labeling went into effect this month.
-------------- ASSIGNED to D:XXXXX - 05/12/94 - D:XXXXX ---------------
Wrong Department. Transferred from Distribution to Production.
Left voice mail for "Frank".
-------------- ASSIGNED to D:XXXXX - 05/12/94 - D:XXXXX ---------------
Reproduces in the Development Kitchen. Need a native
build of the Kitchen ...
-------------- ASSIGNED to D:XXXXX - 05/12/94 - D:XXXXX ---------------
This is a feature. IntelliSense labeling knew that you didn't want to feel
guilty about the chocolate in the milk, so it didn't list it on the box.
-------------- ASSIGNED to D:XXXXX - 05/12/94 - D:XXXX ---------------
Recommend postpone. Reading the ingredients is not a common user
scenario ...
-------------- RESOLVED - WON'T FIX - 05/12/94 - P:XXXXX --------------
Fixing the package is just a band-aid. We need to come up with a solution
that addresses the real problem in 96. My recommendation is
chocolate cows.

Please close and assign to DARIGOLD.
```

- Identifying duplicates requires *as few facts* as possible, because this makes it easier to spot the similarity.

The solution here is *simplification* — that is, to simplify a problem report such that only the relevant facts remain. We will come back to this issue in Section 5.1, on simplifying problems. Automated methods are presented in Chapter 5.

Even if all duplicates have been resolved, however, your database will eventually fill up with unresolved problem reports—problems that could not be reproduced, problems that may be fixed in a later version, and low-priority problems. This is less a problem of space or performance (modern databases can easily cope with millions of problem reports) than of *maintenance*, as your developers wade again and again through this swamp of unresolved bugs. Having thousands of unresolved problems is also bad for morale. The solution is to clean up the database by searching for *obsolete* problems. A problem report could be declared obsolete if, for instance:

- The problem will never be fixed—for instance, because the program is no longer supported

- The problem is old and has occurred only once

- The problem is old and has occurred only internally

Obsolete problem reports should show up only if explicitly searched for. If they ever show up again, you can recycle them by making them nonobsolete. In BUGZILLA, problems that will never be fixed are assigned a WONTFIX resolution.

2.9 RELATING PROBLEMS AND FIXES

Few products ever came out as a single version. Hence, whenever users report a problem they must state the version of the product in which the problem occurred. Without this, developers will not know which version to use when trying to reproduce the problem.

But even *with* a version identifier, are you prepared to access the specific version as released to your user? This means not only the binaries as shipped but every source that went into this specific release and all tools in their specific versions that were used to produce the binary. This is one of the key issues of *software configuration management*: to be able to recreate any given configuration any time.

To keep track of versions and configurations is something far too error prone to be done manually. Instead, use a *version control system* to support the task. Using version control has few costs and many benefits. *Not* using version control, though, makes your development process risky, chaotic, and generally unmanageable.

So, how do you manage your versions in order to track bugs? Simple: whenever a new version is shipped, mark its source base with an appropriate *tag*. Use this tag to recreate the source base — and together with the source base the product itself.

Another good thing about version control systems is the management of *branches* for storing *fixes*. The basic idea is to separate the evolution into two parts:

- A *main trunk* in which new features are tested and added

- *Branches* in which fixes (and only fixes) are added to stable versions

This separation allows vendors to ship out new fixed versions of stable products while developing new features for the next major release. The use of tags and branches is illustrated in Figure 2.4.

A product consists of two files, which have evolved independently into multiple revisions. Consider Figure 2.4. The initial release of the system, indicated by the dotted line, consisted of revision 1.1 of file A and revision 1.2 of file B. In the version control system, this is reflected by an appropriate tag of these revisions. Since then, file B has evolved into revision 1.3 with new features, but is as yet untested.

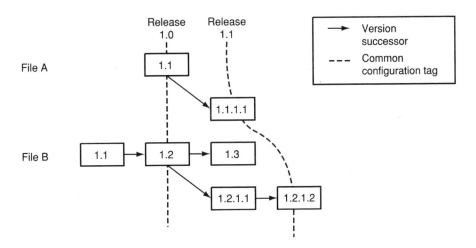

FIGURE 2.4 Tags and branches in version control. As a system progresses, individual releases are tagged such that they can be reconstructed on demand.

When a user now reports a problem that calls for a fix, what do we do? Do we ship the new, untested configuration with file B included? Usually not. Instead, based on the initial release, we create a *branch* for files A and B, containing the new versions 1.1.1.1 and 1.2.1.1, respectively. This branch holds only the indispensable *fixes* for the initial release, which can then be released as minor service updates (shown as release 1.1 in the figure). New, risky features still go to the main trunk. Eventually, all fixes from the branch can be *merged back* into the main trunk such that they will also be present in the next major releases. As maintainers routinely want to check whether a certain problem has been fixed in a specific release, be sure to relate problem reports to changes as follows.

- Within the problem-tracking system, identify the change in version control that fixed the problem. For instance, attach the branch identifier as a comment to the problem report:

  ```
  Problem fixed in RELEASE_1_1_BRANCH
  ```

- Within the version control system, identify the problem report number that is addressed by a specific change. This can be done in the log message given when the change is committed:

  ```
  Fix: null pointer could cause crash (PR 2074)
  ```

Such a relationship between problem tracking and version control works best when it is established *automatically.* Some version control systems integrate with problem-tracking systems such that the relationship between problems and fixes is maintained automatically. This allows for queries to determine which problem reports have occurred or fixed in which release.

As an example, consider the report of the TRAC system, shown in Figure 2.5. TRAC is a lightweight system that integrates version control and problem tracking. Its report shows which problems still persist in which version of the product.

2.10 RELATING PROBLEMS AND TESTS

Many developers use problem-tracking systems not only for problems as reported by end users but by problems encountered in-house. That is, as soon as a developer stumbles across a problem she reports it just as if an end user had told her about the problem.

In principle, this is a good thing, in that no problem remains unreported. However, the main way in which developers find problems is by *testing* the

Edgewall Trac | Trac Demo | Report: All active tickets by version - Mozilla Firebird

File   Edit   View   Go   Bookmarks   Tools   Help

http://trac-demo/trac/trac.cgi/report/5

trac
The link. No longer missing.

Login | Help/Guide | About Trac

| Wiki | Browser | Timeline | **Reports** | Search | New Ticket |

Report Index

All active tickets by version

ticket	version	status	severity	priority	component	owner	summary
#18		new	enhancement	high	ticket system	jonas	Unassigned tickets
#1		new	normal	high	general	jonas	Add a new project summary module. (My Page)
#68		new	major	normal	trac-admin	daniel	the command "component rename" should update existing tickets
#63	0.1	new	enhancement	highest	general	jonas	Session/user variables and storage
#69	0.1	new	blocker	normal	wiki	jonas	Default set of wiki pages
#11	0.1	new	normal	normal	general	jonas	(Web) configuration module is missing
#67	0.1	new	normal	normal	wiki	jonas	Inline HTML support
#73	1.0	assigned	enhancement	high	general	daniel	Trac should have a kitchen sink
#28	1.0	assigned	minor	normal	general	daniel	RSS Feed module
#38	2.0	new	enhancement	high	timeline	jonas	Wiki edit event collapsing
#41	2.0	new	enhancement	high	wiki	jonas	Alternate Interwiki-style links
#27	2.0	new	major	high	ticket system	jonas	Attaching files to tickets
#19	2.0	new	minor	high	report system	jonas	Changeable sort order
#12	2.0	new	normal	high	wiki	jonas	Write protected wiki pages
#14	2.0	new	normal	high	ticket system	jonas	Email/IM notification
#62	2.0	new	normal	high	wiki	jonas	Edit/change comments
#65	2.0	new	enhancement	low	trac-admin	daniel	Purge old versions of wiki pages.
#31	2.0	new	enhancement	lowest	ticket system	jonas	Bug dependencies/relations feature
#51	2.0	new	enhancement	lowest	general	jonas	HDF Dump
#53	2.0	new	enhancement	lowest	general	jonas	Viewing image changes/patches in a changeset
#17	2.0	new	trivial	lowest	general	jonas	Time zone support/preferences
#40	2.0	new	enhancement	normal	wiki	jonas	InterWiki links support
#13	2.0	new	normal	normal	ticket system	jonas	Add support for custom ticket fields

trac
The link. No longer missing.

Powered by Trac 0.1
By Edgewall Research & Development.

Visit the Trac open source project at
http://trac.edgewall.com/

FIGURE 2.5 Open issues as reported by the TRAC system. The report shows which problems persist for which version of the product.

program, and this induces a conflict between test outcomes and problem reports. Should a failing test be tracked in the problem database? And if so, how are we going to *synchronize* the problem database with the test outcomes?

Unless you have a problem-tracking system that neatly integrates with your test suite, I recommend keeping test outcomes separate from problem reports. There are several reasons for doing so.

- Test outcomes occur frequently — possibly (and hopefully) far more frequently than user's problem reports. Storing these test outcomes in the problem database would quickly flood the database — and divert from the actual problems in the field.

- If you use automated testing (Chapter 3 "Making Programs Fail"), you can at any time check test outcomes for any version, at the press of a button. Thus, there is no need for storing that information.

- Suppose a test fails. If you can find the defect and fix it right away, there is no need to enter a record in the problem-tracking system.

All of this boils down to one point: *Test cases make problem reports obsolete.* If a problem occurs during development, do not enter it into the problem-tracking system. Instead, write a *test case* that exposes the problem. This way, the test case will show that the problem is still present, and you can always check for the problem by running the test.

You *can* always use the problem-tracking system, though, for storing *ideas* and *feature requests* — that is, for anything that does not immediately translate into code or a test case. As soon as you start to implement the feature request, start writing a test case that exposes the lack of the feature, and close the entry in the problem-tracking system. Once the feature is implemented, the succeessive test case can be used to determine whether it meets expectations.

2.11 CONCEPTS

- ✎ Reports about problems encountered in the field are stored in a *problem database* and are classified with respect to status and severity.

- ✎ A problem report must contain all information that is *relevant to reproduce the problem.*

✎ *To obtain the relevant problem information*, set up a standard set of items that users must provide (see also Section 2.2, on reporting problems). This includes:

- Product release

- Operating environment

- Problem history

- Expected behavior

- Experienced behavior

✎ *To write an effective problem report*, make sure the report:

- Is *well structured*

- Is *reproducible*

- Has a descriptive *one-line summary*

- Is as *simple* as possible

- Is as *general* as possible

- Is *neutral* and stays with the facts

For details, see Section 2.2.

✎ Products can be set up to *collect and forward information* that may be relevant to reproduce the problem. Be aware of privacy issues, though.

✎ A typical life cycle of a problem starts with a status of UNCONFIRMED. It ends with CLOSED and a specific *resolution* such as FIXED or WORKSFORME (Figure 2.3).

✎ *To organize the debugging process*, have a *software change control board* that uses the problem database to: **HOW TO**

- Keep track of resolved and unresolved problems

- Assign a priority to individual problems

- Assign problems to individual developers

✎ *To track requirements*, one can also use a problem-tracking system. Each   **HOW TO**
requirement not yet met is a problem.

> ✎ *Keep problem tracking simple.* If it gets in the way, people won't use it.

HOW TO

> ✎ *To restore released versions,* use a version control system to *tag* all configurations as they are released to users.

> ✎ *To separate fixes and features,* use a *version control system* to keep fixes in branches and features in the main trunk.

HOW TO

> ✎ *To relate problems and fixes,* establish conventions to *relate problem reports to changes,* and vice versa (Section 2.9). Advanced version control systems integrate with problem-tracking systems to maintain this relationship automatically.

HOW TO

> ✎ *To relate problems and tests, make a problem report obsolete* as soon as a test case exists. When a problem occurs, prefer writing test cases to entering problem reports.

2.12 TOOLS

BUGZILLA

The BUGZILLA problem-tracking system can be found at:

```
http://www.bugzilla.org/
```

Its specific incarnation for MOZILLA is available for browsing at:

```
http://bugzilla.mozilla.org/
```

PHPBUGTRACKER

PHPBUGTRACKER is a lightweight problem-tracking system that is simpler to install and manage than BUGZILLA. It can be found at:

```
http://phpbt.sf.net/
```

ISSUETRACKER

Like PHPBUGTRACKER, ISSUETRACKER aims to be a lightweight problem tracker, with a special focus on being user friendly. If you want to toy with a problem-tracking system at your site, PHPBUGTRACKER or ISSUETRACKER might be your choice. ISSUETRACKER can be found at:

```
http://www.issue-tracker.com/
```

TRAC

TRAC is another lightweight problem-tracking system. Its special feature is that it integrates with version control. This makes it easier to track problems across multiple versions. Just as PHPBUGTRACKER and ISSUETRACKER, TRAC is open-source software, but with optional commercial support. TRAC can be found at:

```
http://trac.edgewall.com/
```

SOURCEFORGE

The SOURCEFORGE project provides automated project organization beyond simple problem tracking. It includes facilities such as discussion forums, public version archives, user management, and mailing lists. It is available to open-source projects. A simple registration suffices, and there is no installation hassle. SOURCEFORGE is also available as a commercial version to be installed at other sites and to manage commercial projects. SOURCEFORGE can be found at:

```
http://www.sf.net/
```

GFORGE

GFORGE is a fork of the original SOURCEFORGE code. Just as SOURCEFORGE, it provides problem tracking, discussion forums, public version archives, user management, mailing lists, and much more. In contrast to SOURCEFORGE, the GFORGE people do not host projects. Instead, you install the GFORGE software at your site. (Commercial support is available.) If you want a single open-source package that manages the entire development life cycle, GFORGE delivers. GFORGE can be found at:

```
http://www.gforge.org/
```

2.13 FURTHER READING

Regarding problem-tracking systems, there is not too much information available except from those provided by vendors. Mirrer (2000) addresses the issue of obsolete test cases. For him, organizing a problem-tracking system is like "organizing your socks": once in a while, an overflowing sock drawer has to be cleaned up.

Kolawa (2002) comments on the relationship between problem-tracking systems and testing. He states that problem-tracking systems "should be used exclusively as a place to store feedback when you cannot immediately modify the code." Otherwise, you should create a reproducible test case.

Advanced problem-tracking systems can do an even better job of integrating with version control systems. The *Software Configuration Management* FAQ posting of the `comp.software.config-mgmt` newsgroup contains a large list of problem-tracking systems and their integration within software configuration management. The newsgroup can be found at:

`http://www.daveeaton.com/scm/`

Finally, if you want to keep your customers happy, see Phil Verghis' help desk FAQ at:

`http://www.philverghis.com/helpdesk.html`

2.14 EXERCISES

EXERCISE 2.1. Write a bug report for the `sample` problem (Section 1.1). Justify the amount of information you gave.

EXERCISE 2.2. Visit the MOZILLA problem-tracking site at
`http://bugzilla.mozilla.org/`
and answer the following questions:

1. How many problems have been entered as NEW into BUGZILLA in the past three days?

2. How many of these are critical (or even blocking)?

3. How many of these are invalid? Why?

4. How many unresolved or unconfirmed problems are there in the currently released version?

5. Which is the worst currently unresolved problem?

6. According to problem priority, which problem should you address first as a programmer?

EXERCISE 2.3. What are the major differences between a dedicated problem-tracking system such as MOZILLA and a general organizing and messaging tool such as Microsoft Outlook?

EXERCISE 2.4. Which other problems (in addition to software) could be managed using a problem-tracking system?

Six Stages of Debugging:

1. That can't happen.
2. That doesn't happen on my machine.
3. That shouldn't happen.
4. Why does that happen?
5. Oh, I see.
6. How did that ever work?

—ANONYMOUS

3

MAKING PROGRAMS FAIL

B EFORE A PROGRAM CAN BE DEBUGGED, we must set it up such that it can be *tested* — that is, executed with the intent to make it fail. In this chapter, we review basic testing techniques, with a special focus on automation and isolation.

3.1 TESTING FOR DEBUGGING

User reports are not the only way of learning about problems. Typically, most problems (and in the best of all worlds, *all* problems) are found by *testing* at the developer's site before they ever could be experienced by a user. Testing is the process of executing a program with the intent of producing some problem. Once such a problem has been found by testing, the process of tracing down the defect and fixing it is the same as if the problem had been reported by a user (except that problems found by testing, or any other means of quality assurance, are less embarrassing, and generally much cheaper to fix). First comes the problem (from a test or a user), then comes the debugging.

This classical view of testing is called *testing for validation*. It is geared toward uncovering *yet unknown* problems. A great deal of research revolves around the question of how to test programs such that the tests uncover as many problems as possible. We summarize the basics in Section 3.8. In the context of debugging, though, testing also has its place. However, it is geared toward uncovering a *known* problem. Such *testing for debugging* is required at many stages of the debugging process, and thus throughout this book:

- One must *create a test* to *reproduce the problem* (Chapter 4).

- One must rerun the test multiple times to *simplify the problem* (Chapter 5).

- One must rerun the test to *observe the run* (Chapter 8).

- One must rerun the test to *verify whether the fix has been successful* (Section 15.4).

- One must rerun the test before each new release such that the problem (or a similar one) *will not occur in the future*. This is also called *regression testing* (Section 15.6).

As testing occurs so frequently while debugging, it is a good thing to *automate* it as much as possible. In general, by using automation more thorough tests can be achieved with less effort. Automation:

- Allows the reuse of existing tests (for instance, to test a new version of a program)

- Allows one to perform tests that are difficult or impossible to carry out manually (such as massive random tests)

- Makes tests repeatable

- Increases confidence in the software

All of these benefits apply to validation as well as to debugging, such as the previously listed.

Automation not only streamlines the "classical" testing and debugging tasks but enables additional *automated debugging techniques*, such as those discussed in this book.

- Automated tests enable *automated simplification of test cases* (Chapter 5).

- One can use automated tests to *isolate failure causes automatically*, including:

  - Failure-inducing input (Section 13.5)

  - Failure-inducing code changes (Section 13.7)

  - Failure-inducing thread schedules (Section 13.6)

  - Failure-inducing program states (Section 14.4)

```
Ok the following operations cause mozilla to crash consistently
on my machine

-> Start mozilla
-> Go to bugzilla.mozilla.org
-> Select search for bug
-> Print to file setting the bottom and right margins to .50
   (I use the file /var/tmp/netscape.ps)
-> Once it's done printing do the exact same thing again on
   the same file (/var/tmp/netscape.ps)
-> This causes the browser to crash with a segfault
```

EXAMPLE 3.1 MOZILLA problem report #24735.

In this chapter, we will thus focus on how to set up automated tests that support our (automated and nonautomated) debugging tasks. We examine the question:

HOW CAN WE LEVERAGE TESTS TO SUPPORT DEBUGGING?

3.2 CONTROLLING THE PROGRAM

Consider a real-world example, related to the MOZILLA web browser — or more specifically, its HTML layout engine named *Gecko*. In July 1999, two years before the final completion of MOZILLA 1.0, BUGZILLA (the MOZILLA problem database) listed more than 370 open problem reports — problem reports that were not even reproduced. At the same time, test automation was in a bad shape. To test MOZILLA, developers essentially had to visit a number of critical web pages, such as http://www.cnn.com/, and (visually) check whether the layout and functionality was okay.

Example 3.1 shows the problem report we want to turn into an automated test case. Under certain conditions, MOZILLA crashes when printing a page. How do we automate this sequence of actions? In general, an automated test must simulate the *environment* of the program — that is, the test must provide the program's input and assess the program's output. Simulating an environment can be very tricky, though. If the environment involves users who interact with

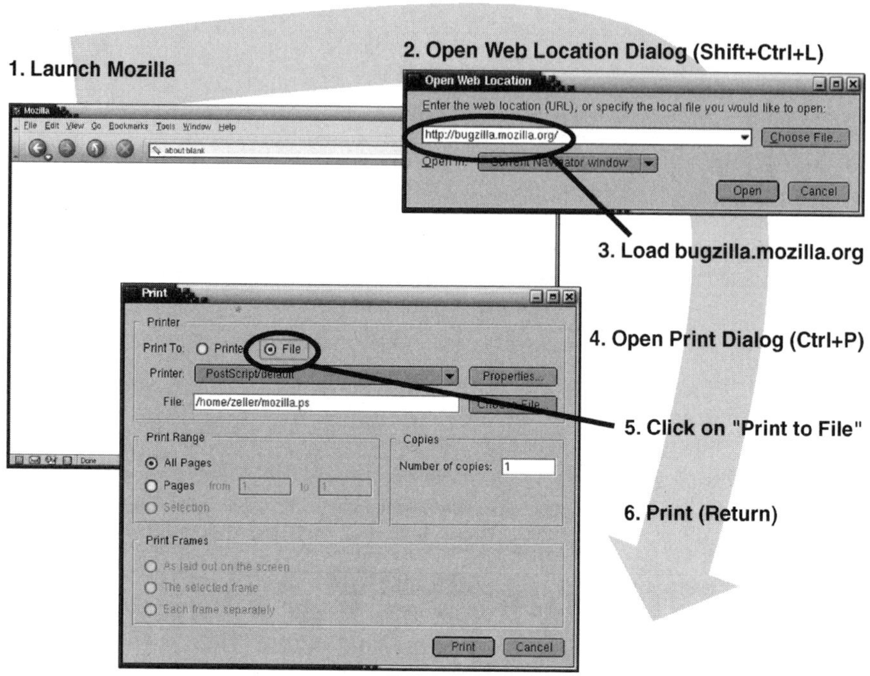

FIGURE 3.1 Making MOZILLA print (and crash). This takes just six easy steps.

the program, the automated test must simulate actual users (including all of their capabilities).

Figure 3.1 shows the steps our user simulation must conduct, which are:

1. Launch MOZILLA.

2. Open the Open Web Location dialog.

3. Load *bugzilla.mozilla.org*.

4. Open the Print dialog.

5. Enter appropriate print settings.

6. Invoke the actual printing.

However, our user simulation must also *synchronize* its actions with the application. For instance, the simulation can "click" in the dialog only after it has popped up. The same applies for the second printing, which can only start after

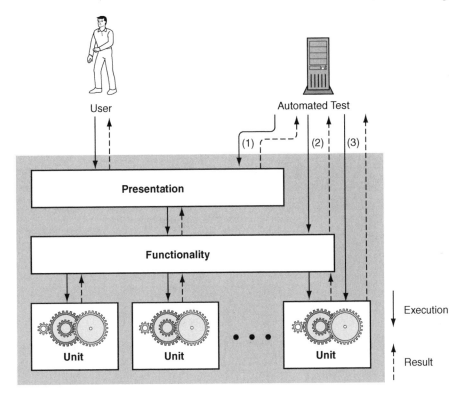

FIGURE 3.2 Testing layers. A program can be tested (1) at the presentation layer, (2) at the functionality layer, or (3) at the unit layer.

the first printing is done. Thus, the user simulation must not only provide input but interpret the output.

Such efforts can be avoided by identifying *alternate interfaces*, where control and assessment are easier to automate. Figure 3.2 shows a typical decomposition of a program into three layers:

- The *presentation layer* handles the interaction with the user (or whatever constitutes the environment of the program).

- The *functionality layer* encapsulates the actual functionality of the program, independent of a specific presentation.

- The *unit layer* splits the functionality across multiple units, cooperating to produce a greater whole.

Whereas the user (and the environment) interact only with the presentation layer, an automated test can use all three layers for automating execution and for retrieving and assessing results. Each layer requires individual techniques, though, and brings its own benefits and drawbacks for testing and debugging. In the next three sections, we shall discuss testing at the individual layers and check for the following features:

- *Ease of execution:* How easy is it to get control over program execution?

- *Ease of interaction:* How easy is it to interact with the program?

- *Ease of result assessment:* How can we check results against expectations?

- *Lifetime of test case:* How robust is my test when it comes to program changes?

3.3 TESTING AT THE PRESENTATION LAYER

Let's start with the presentation layer, where the program interacts with its environment. How does one test at the presentation layer? Basically, one simulates the *input* and monitors the *output.* Depending on the nature of the input and output, this can be done at multiple *abstraction levels.* For a networking device, for instance, we can capture input and output at the *data link layer* (monitoring and sending individual bits between two ends of a physical connection), or at the *transport layer* (monitoring and sending data packets between two machines). The higher the abstraction level, the more details are abstracted away, which makes it easier to simulate interaction. On the other hand, one risks abstracting away the very details that cause a failure.

As a more detailed (and frequent) example of abstraction levels, let's take a look at *user interaction.* User interaction can be simulated at two abstraction levels: at a *low level* (expressing interaction as a sequence of mouse and keyboard events) or at a *higher level,* denoting interaction using graphical user controls of the application.

3.3.1 Low-level Interaction

At the lowest abstraction level, user input becomes a stream of mouse and keyboard events. Such event streams can be *captured* (i.e., recorded from the input devices) and *replayed,* substituting the stream from actual input devices by the previously recorded stream.

```
# 1. Launch mozilla and wait for 2 seconds
exec mozilla &
send_xevents wait 2000


# 2. Open URL dialog (Shift+Control+L)
send_xevents keydn Control_L
send_xevents keydn Shift_L
send_xevents key L
send_xevents keyup Shift_L
send_xevents keyup Control_L
send_xevents wait 500


# 3. Load bugzilla.mozilla.org
#    and wait for 5 seconds
send_xevents @400,100
send_xevents type {http://bugzilla.mozilla.org}
send_xevents key Return
send_xevents wait 5000


# 4. Open Print Dialog (Ctrl+P)
send_xevents @400,100
send_xevents keydn Control_L
send_xevents key P
send_xevents keyup Control_L
send_xevents wait 500


# 5. Click on "Print to File"
send_xevents @550,170 click 1


# 6. Print (Return)
send_xevents key Return
send_xevents wait 5000
```

EXAMPLE 3.2 ANDROID script to make MOZILLA print. This script simulates user inter-action at a low level by means of keyboard and mouse interaction.

As an example, Example 3.2 shows a script recorded by the open-source tool ANDROID to reproduce the MOZILLA interaction shown in Figure 3.1. To make it more user readable, the script has been simplified to the relevant events.

Each of these send_xevents command simulates a user action. The command

```
send_xevents @550,170 click 1
```

tells ANDROID to move the mouse pointer to position (550,170), and then to simulate a click of mouse button 1 (the left mouse button). Likewise, the command key simulates the press of a key, and type is shorthand for typing several keys in a row. The commands keydn and keyup are handy for simulating modifiers such as Shift, Alt, or Ctrl that need to be held down while other keys are pressed.

As nobody wants to read or maintain tests that deal with absolute screen coordinates, such event scripts are largely *write-only*. Furthermore, any recorded information is *fragile*: the slightest change in the user's display or the program's interface makes the recorded scripts obsolete.

To illustrate the fragility, just try to invoke the script *twice* in a row: the second time the script executes, the file to be printed to already exists, and thus MOZILLA wants special confirmation before overwriting the file. This extra dialog, though, is not handled in our script and thus will fail miserably. Other changes that quickly make the script obsolete include a different placement of the MOZILLA main window or its dialogs (all coordinates in the script are absolute) and changes in font size, screen size, layout, user language, or even interaction speed.

If we record and replay nonuser interaction at a low level, such as data flow on a network, any changes to the program or the protocol will also make recorded scripts quickly obsolete. Nonetheless, such recorded information can be very useful for automating user interaction again and again — as long as it is used for one single debugging session in one specific environment.

3.3.2 System-level Interaction

One way of overcoming the problem of fragility (Section 3.3.1) is to control not only the single application but the entire machine. For this purpose, one typically uses a *virtual machine* system that simulates an entire machine as software. The virtual machine FAUmachine, for instance, allows us to simulate many types of input and can even inject faults such as simulated hardware defects. Example 3.3 shows a simple script.

Use of virtual machines for testing and debugging typically requires that a number of well-defined virtual machines be available. Therefore, virtual machines are nice to have if one desires or requires complete control at the system

```
# Power on the machine and wait for 5s
power <= true; wait for 5000;


# Click mouse button 1
m_b1 <= true; wait for 300; m_b1 <= false;


# Click the CDROM change button
cdctrl'shortcut_out_add("/cdrom%change/...");
```

EXAMPLE 3.3 A script for automating execution of a virtual FAUmachine. This script interacts at the system level, simulating the hardware of a real machine.

level. Although a large set of virtual machines requires careful administration, it is still easier to administer and configure virtual rather than real machines.

3.3.3 Higher-level Interaction

A more comfortable way of making user interaction scripts more robust against changes and thus more persistent is to choose a *higher abstraction level* — that is, controlling the application not by means of coordinates but by actual graphical user controls. As an example, consider Example 3.4. It shows a script in the APPLESCRIPT language that makes MOZILLA on Mac OS load and print the page *bugzilla.mozilla.org*. APPLESCRIPT is designed to be readable by end users. The ¬ character lets you split one line of script onto two.

The main difference with the ANDROID script shown in Example 3.2 is that APPLESCRIPT no longer references user controls by position but by *names* such as Open Web Location and *relative numbers* such as menu bar 1. This makes the script much more robust against size or position changes (only the labels and the relative ordering of the user interface controls must remain constant).

Again, such scripts can also be recorded from user interactions. Several capture/replay tools are available that work at the level of named user controls. However, even if we raise the abstraction level to user controls scripts remain fragile: a single renaming or rearrangement of controls causes in all scripts to become obsolete.

```
-- 1. Activate mozilla
tell application "mozilla" to activate

-- 2. Open URL dialog via menu
tell application "System Events"
  tell process "mozilla"
    tell menu bar 1
      tell menu bar item "File"
        click menu item "Open Web Location"
      end tell
    end tell
  end tell
end tell

-- 3. Load bugzilla.mozilla.org
--    and wait for 5 seconds
tell window "Open Web Location"
  tell sheet 1
    set value of text field 1 to ¬
      "http://bugzilla.mozilla.org/"
  end tell
  click button 1
end tell
delay 5
⋮
```

EXAMPLE 3.4 APPLESCRIPT makes MOZILLA print. This script excerpt interacts with MOZILLA at a higher level. It refers to named GUI elements to simulate actions.

3.3.4 Assessing Test Results

Whether we are controlling the application using event streams or user controls, one major problem remains: our simulation must still *examine the program's output*.

- Examining the output is necessary for *synchronization*, as the simulated user may have to wait until a specific action completes. In our MOZILLA script, we circumvented this problem by introducing appropriate delays.

- Examining the program's output is necessary for *result assessment*. Eventually, our test must determine whether the result matches the expectations or not. In our MOZILLA example, this was particularly easy. The crash of a program is relatively easy to detect, but if we had to verify MOZILLA's output on the screen we would have a difficult time processing and assessing this output.

To sum up, the advantage of testing at the presentation layer is that it is always feasible. We can always simulate and automate a user's behavior. However, this is already the only advantage. In general, one should use the presentation layer for testing only:

- If the problem occurs in the presentation

- If the presentation layer is easily used by computers

- If there is no other choice (for instance, because there is no clear separation between presentation and functionality, or because the lower layers are inaccessible for testing)

The rule of thumb is: The friendlier an interface is to humans, the less friendly it is to computers. Therefore, we should have a look at alternative interfaces that are better suited to automation.

3.4 TESTING AT THE FUNCTIONALITY LAYER

Rather than simulate user interaction, it is much preferable to have the program provide an interface that is *designed for automation* — or, more generally, designed for interaction with technical systems. Such an interface may be designed for interaction with programming languages (for instance, the programming language the application itself is written in). However, some programs provide interfacing with *scripting language*, allowing even end users and non-programmers to automate execution in a simple way.

Example 3.5 shows an APPLESCRIPT program that uses the scripting capabilities of the Safari web browser to load a given web page and to print it, mimicking our MOZILLA example. This script uses commands such as

```
set the URL of the front document
```

```
# 1. Load document
tell application "Safari"
  activate
  if not (exists document 1)
    make new document at the beginning of documents
  end if
  set the URL of the front document ¬
    to "http://bugzilla.mozilla.org/"
  delay 5
end tell


# 2. Print it
# No script support for printing, so we go via the GUI
tell application "System Events"
  tell process "safari"
    keystroke "p" using command down
  end tell
end tell
```

EXAMPLE 3.5 Loading a site in Safari using APPLESCRIPT. This script uses Safari's built-in functionality layer to open web pages — except for printing, where one has to resort to simulating user interaction.

which work regardless of what the user interface looks like, and thus make the script unaffected by any changes of the user interface. Note, though, that not every Safari feature is scriptable. To print a page (Step 2 in Example 3.5), we still have to fall back to the presentation layer.

Support for automation at the functionality layer greatly differs by operating environment. In Mac OS, APPLESCRIPT is available for several applications. In Windows, this role is filled by *Visual Basic*. Example 3.6 shows a VBSCRIPT program that loads a file into Internet Explorer (note how this program waits until the page is actually loaded). Under Linux and UNIX, there is no single standard for scripting — no scripting support for MOZILLA, for instance.

Nonetheless, the advent of web components has encouraged further separation of functionality and presentation — thus making automation far easier for future applications. Every major scripting language (such as VBSCRIPT, PERL, PYTHON, and, APPLESCRIPT) can use web component interfaces such as SOAP to interact with local and distributed components and services. Essentially, arbitrary web components can be accessed using arbitrary scripting languages.

```
' Load document
Set IE = CreateObject("InternetExplorer.Application")
IE.navigate "http://bugzilla.mozilla.org/"
IE.visible=1


' Wait until the page is loaded
While IE.Busy
    WScript.Sleep 100
Wend
```

EXAMPLE 3.6 Loading a site in Internet Explorer using VBSCRIPT. The script uses IE's functionality layer to open pages.

You may be tempted to define your own *home-grown* scripting language that is built into the application. In general, however, this is not worth the invest-ment. Sooner or later you will require variables, control structures, and modu-larization — and it is difficult to add these features one at a time. It is far easier to incorporate an existing interpreter for a powerful scripting language such as PYTHON, PERL, or TCL and extend it with application-specific commands. Even more easily, you can turn your application into a .NET component, a JAVA bean, or a CORBA component. All of this makes the functionality available for arbitrary automation purposes and is thus great for automated testing. (Be aware, though, that automation interfaces can be exploited by malicious users. For instance, au-tomation features in Office have frequently been used to send document and e-mail viruses automatically.)

Overall, the big advantage of testing at the functionality layers is that the *results can be easily accessed and evaluated* — something that is difficult to do at a presentation layer for humans. For web components, results typically come in XML format, which is easy to parse and process for all scripting languages. Thus, unless one wants to test individual parts of the program, testing (and debugging) at the functionality level is the way to go.

Unfortunately, all of this requires a clear separation between presentation and functionality. Especially older programs may come as monolithic enti-ties without presentation or functionality layers. In this case, you have three choices.

• You can go through the presentation layer, as discussed in Section 3.3, and suffer all of the problems associated with assessing test results.

- You can do a major redesign to separate presentation and functionality — or at least to reduce dependences between them. We will come back to this idea when discussing designing for debugging (Section 3.7).

- You can decompose the program and access the individual units directly. (This is discussed in the next section.)

3.5   TESTING AT THE UNIT LAYER

Any nontrivial program can be decomposed into a number of individual *units* — that is, subprograms, functions, libraries, modules, abstract data types, objects, classes, packages, components, beans, or whatever decomposition the design and the language provide. These units communicate via *interfaces* — just like the program communicates with its environment.

The idea now is not to automate the execution of the entire program but only *the execution of a specific unit.* This has the advantage that automating the unit in isolation is frequently easier than automating the entire program. The disadvantage, of course, is that you can only automate the behavior of the given unit and thus must count on the unit producing the problem in isolation.

Units are typically not accessible to end users, and thus not necessarily accessible for scripting, as discussed in Section 3.4. However, they are accessible to programmers, using the same means as the enclosing program to access their services — typically, simple invocation of functions and methods in the language of the program.

Whereas units are among the eldest concepts of programming, the concept of automated testing at the unit level has seen a burst of interest only in the last few years. This is due to the big interest in extreme programming, which mandates automated tests as early and often as possible (and notably the creation of a unit test case *before* implementation), and to the fact that massive automated testing has become much more affordable than, say, 20 years ago.

All of these tools provide a *testing framework* that collects a number of individual *unit tests* — a test that covers a single unit. Unit tests are supposed to run automatically; that is, without any user interaction. Upon request, the testing framework runs some or all unit tests and displays a summary of the executed unit tests and their respective outcomes. When a single unit test executes, a testing framework does three things.

- *It* sets up *an environment for embedding the unit.* Frequently, a unit will require services of other units or the operating environment. This part sets up the stage.

- *It* tests *the unit.* Each possible behavior of the unit is covered by a test case, which first performs the operation(s) and then verifies whether the outcome is as expected.

- *It* tears down *the environment again.* This means it brings everything back in the state encountered initially.

Consider an example of how to use unit tests. Assume that as part of a web browser you manage a JAVA class for uniform resource locators (URLs) such as the following.

```
http://www.askigor.org/status.php?id=sample#top
```

A URL class has a constructor that takes a URL as a string. Among others, it provides methods for retrieving the protocol (e.g., `http`), the host (e.g., `www.askigor.org`), the path (e.g., `/status.php`), and the query (e.g., `id=sample`).

Suppose you want to test these methods. Because you are working with a JAVA class, one of the first choices for unit testing is the JUNIT testing framework. JUNIT provides all we want from a testing framework. It allows us to organize and conduct automated tests in a simple yet effective fashion. (In fact, JUNIT has been so successful that its approach has been adopted for more than 100 languages, including CPPUNIT for C++, VBUNIT for VBSCRIPT, PYUNIT for PYTHON, and so on.)

To test the URL class with JUNIT, you create a test case `URLTest` that is a subclass of `TestCase`. The source code `URLTest.java` is shown in Example 3.7. In this template, the `setUp()` method is responsible for setting up the environment for embedding the unit. The `tearDown()` method destroys the environment again. Our environment consists of a rational member variable `askigor_url` containing the URL. This variable can be used in all further tests.

We can add the individual tests to this class. In JUNIT, each test comes in a separate method. We shall add four methods that test for equality and non-equality, respectively, as shown in Example 3.8. The `assertEquals()` method makes the test fail if the two arguments do not equal each other.

We next need a suite that runs all tests, as shown in Example 3.9. By default, any method of the test class whose name begins with the word `test` will be run as a test. For the last step, we have to give the class a main method that invokes

```
import junit.framework.Test;
import junit.framework.TestCase;
import junit.framework.TestSuite;

public class URLTest extends TestCase {

    private URL askigor_url;

    // Create new test
    public URLTest(String name) {
        super(name);
    }

    // Assign a name to this test case
    public String toString() {
        return getName();
    }

    // Setup environment
    // will be called before any testXXX() method
    protected void setUp() {
        askigor_url = new URL("http://www.askigor.org/" +
                                "status.php?id=sample");
    }

    // Release environment
    protected void tearDown() {
        askigor_url = null;
    }
```

EXAMPLE 3.7 URLTest.java — a unit test for URLs.

a GUI for testing. This piece of code is shown in Example 3.10. This concludes the URLTest class.

The main method we have added to the test case allows us to execute it as a stand-alone application. If we do so, we obtain the graphical user interface shown in Figure 3.3. Clicking on Run runs all tests at once. The bar below shows the status. If the bar is green (as in the left-hand window), all tests have

```
// Test for protocol ("http", "ftp", etc.)
public void testProtocol() {
    assertEquals(askigor_url.getProtocol(), "http");
}


// Test for host
public void testHost() {
    int noPort = -1;
    assertEquals(askigor_url.getHost(),
                "www.askigor.org");
    assertEquals(askigor_url.getPort(), noPort);
}


// Test for path
public void testPath() {
    assertEquals(askigor_url.getPath(), "/status.php");
}


// Test for query part
public void testQuery() {
    assertEquals(askigor_url.getQuery(), "id=sample");
}
```

EXAMPLE 3.8 Actual tests in URLTest.java.

```
// Set up a suite of tests
public static TestSuite suite() {
    TestSuite suite =
        new TestSuite(URLTest.class);
    return suite;
}
```

EXAMPLE 3.9 Setting up a test suite in URLTest.java.

been run successfully. If the bar is red (as in the right-hand window), some tests have failed.

The important thing about unit tests is that they run *automatically*; that is, we can assess the unit state with a click of a single button. Recent studies by Saff and Ernst (2004b) show that users write better code faster if the test

```
// Main method: Invokes GUI
  public static void main(String args[]) {
      String[] testCaseName =
          { URLTest.class.getName() };

      // Run using a textual user interface
      // junit.textui.TestRunner.main(testCaseName);

      // Run using a graphical user interface
      junit.swingui.TestRunner.main(testCaseName);
  }
}
```

EXAMPLE 3.10 A main method for URLTest.java.

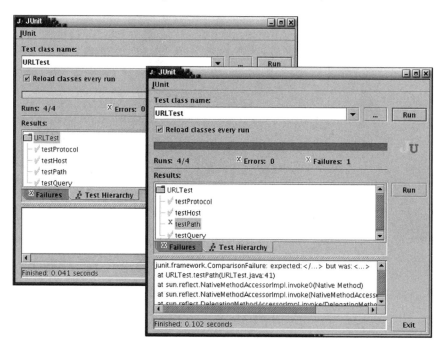

FIGURE 3.3 The JUNIT graphical user interface. The left-hand dialog shows a passing test, the right-hand dialog a failing test—with a failure description in the bottom test field.

runs automatically *each time they save the program* (i.e., not even a button click is needed). This idea of *continuous testing* suggests that you simply cannot test early and often enough.

3.6 ISOLATING UNITS

Automated unit testing of low-level classes such as URL is particularly easy, because such classes do not *depend* on anything. That is, we do not have to import and set up an entire environment just to make the URL class run. In principle, we could also use unit test entire applications such as Mozilla—in a manner similar to testing at the functionality layer (Section 3.4) but using an API rather than a scripting language.

However, all of this automation again requires that the unit in question clearly separate functionality and presentation and make its results available for automatic assessment. This is true for many programs, which thus make it possible for functionality to be examined (and tested and debugged) in isolation.

However, there are programs in which the functionality depends on the presentation, such that it is impossible to separate them. Example 3.11 shows an example. The function print_to_file prints the current web page to a file. To avoid overwriting an existing file, it asks the user for confirmation if the file already exists. From the user's perspective, such protection against data loss is a strict necessity. From the tester's perspective, though, this confirmation makes the functionality depend on the presentation. This introduces a *circular dependence*, as shown in Figure 3.4.

```
// Print current Web page to FILENAME.
void print_to_file(string filename)
{
    if (path_exists(filename))
    {
        // FILENAME exists;
        // ask user to confirm overwrite
        bool confirmed = confirm_loss(filename);
        if (!confirmed)
            return;
    }

    // Proceed printing to FILENAME
    ...
}
```

EXAMPLE 3.11 Functionality depending on presentation.

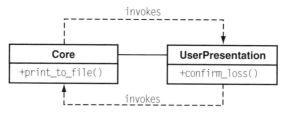

FIGURE 3.4 A circular dependence. The `Core` and `UserPresentation` classes depend on each other and can thus not be tested (or debugged) separately.

- The presentation invokes `print_to_file()`, thus depending on the functionality.

- The functionality invokes `confirm_loss()`, thus depending on the presentation.

As a result, presentation and functionality can no longer be separated from each other. This has a bad impact on testing (and debugging), as we can no longer interact at the functionality layer alone. If a testing program invokes `print_to_file()`, setting up `confirm_loss()` to reply automatically will result in a major hassle. The question is thus: How do we break dependences that keep us from isolating units?

In the case of `confirm_loss()`, we could easily hack it such that the function runs in two modes: the "automated" mode disables confirmation, always returning `true`; the "interactive" mode enables confirmation, querying the user. A much more general solution, though, would be to *parameterize* the `print_to_file()` function such that it could work with arbitrary presentations.

This variant of the `print_to_file()` function is shown in Example 3.12. The idea here is to have a `Presentation` class that, among others, again includes the `confirm_loss()` method. However, `Presentation` need not necessarily be a presentation for the user. Instead, as shown in Figure 3.5, `Presentation` is an interface — an abstract superclass that is instantiated only in subclasses. One of these subclasses (e.g., `UserPresentation`) may be geared toward the user and implement all user interaction. Another subclass (e.g., `AutomatedPresentation`) may be geared toward automation, though, and always return `true` whenever `confirm_loss` is invoked.

What do we get by adopting the inheritance scheme shown in Figure 3.5? We have effectively *broken* the dependence between functionality and presentation — that is, the presentation that is geared toward the user. For testing purposes, we must still provide some functionality we depend on, but this can be encapsulated in a small class such as `AutomatedPresentation`.

```
// Print current Web page to FILENAME.
void print_to_file(string filename,
                  Presentation *presentation)
{
    if (path_exists(filename))
    {
        // FILENAME exists; confirm overwrite
        bool confirmed =
            presentation->confirm_loss(filename);
        if (!confirmed)
            return;
    }

    // Proceed printing to FILENAME
    ...
}
```

EXAMPLE 3.12 Functionality with parameterized presentation.

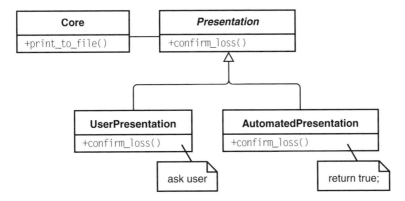

FIGURE 3.5 Depending on abstractions rather than details. Presentation is now an abstract superclass, which can be instantiated either as UserPresentation (with confirmation) or as AutomatedPresentation (without confirmation). The circular dependency between core and presentation is broken.

Overall, the general principle of breaking a dependence is known as the *dependence inversion principle*, which can be summarized as *depending on abstractions rather on details*. Whenever you have some component A depending on some component B, and you want to break this dependence, you perform the following.

1. Introduce an abstract superclass B', and make B a subclass of B'.

2. Set up A such that it depends on the abstract B' rather than on the concrete B.

3. Introduce alternate subclasses of B' that can be used with A such that B is no longer required.

By having A depend on the abstract B' rather than on the concrete B, we can set up arbitrary new subclasses of B without ever having to change A — and we have effectively broken the dependence between A and B.

3.7 DESIGNING FOR DEBUGGING

The principle of reducing dependences by depending on abstractions rather than on details goes a long way. In fact, entire application frameworks can be built this way. Among the most popular examples is the *model-view-controller* architectural pattern, which decouples functionality and presentation at the application level.

To illustrate the model-view-controller pattern, let's imagine we want to build an information system for election day. As illustrated in Figure 3.6, we

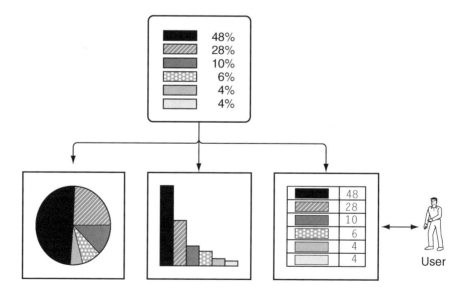

FIGURE 3.6 An information system for election day. The actual data (on top) is displayed in a number of graphical formats, and also manipulated as text.

want to display the election data in a number of graphical formats, including pie and bar charts. We also want to display the data in the form of a spreadsheet, whereby an operator can manipulate and enter the data.

How would one build such a system? The key idea here is again to separate functionality and presentations. In no way do we want the core functionality being dependent on a specific view. The model-view-controller pattern, as illustrated in Figure 3.7, gives us a general solution to this problem. It splits responsibilities into two parts.

- A *model* that holds the core data and provides services that operate on this core data.

- A number of *observers* that register or *attach* to the model and get notified whenever the core data changes.

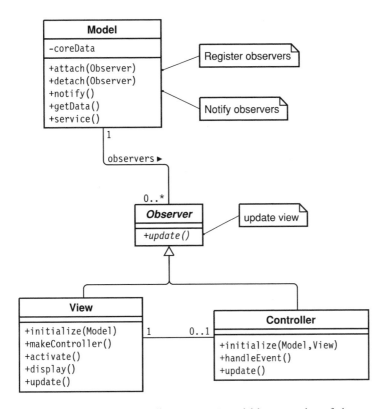

FIGURE 3.7 The model-view-controller pattern. A model has a number of observers, which can be either views or controllers.

Observers, again, are divided into two subclasses.

- A *view* is responsible for displaying the core data in a specific way (such as pie chart views or bar chart views).

- A *controller* handles input events (typically from the user) and invokes the services of the model.

When a user thus interacts with a controller, she will eventually invoke a service that changes the core data. When this happens, all views attached to the model are automatically notified; that is, they can get the data from the model in order to update their displays. This also includes the view of the user, who thus gets visual feedback.

When it comes to testing and debugging, a model-view-controller architecture has several benefits. For testing, one can build and add new controllers that invoke services of the model — for instance, controllers that automate execution of these services. For debugging, one can register special views that automatically log all changes to the model. Finally, every observer and model can be examined and tested in isolation, thus reducing complexity.

As the model-view-controller pattern shows, it is generally advisable to avoid dependences between presentation and functionality. However, any dependence may eventually cause problems in testing and debugging. Just as we want to examine systems that are isolated in our controlled environment (rather than embedded in the user's environment), we want to examine units that are isolated in a controlled environment rather than entangled with the entire system. Isolated units are not only easier to test and debug but easier to understand, reuse, and maintain. Reducing dependences is thus a key issue in software design. Fortunately, all software design methods attempt to minimize dependences between units, using the same two principles.

- *High cohesion:* This is the basic principle that tells what to group into a unit. Those parts of a system that operate on common data (and thus depend on this data) should be grouped together — typically, into some unit as supported by the design or programming language. For instance, object-oriented design groups the state (i.e., data) and the functions that work on this data into classes and objects.

- *Low coupling:* This is the principle that reduces dependences. If two units do *not* operate on common data, they should exchange as little information as possible. This principle is also known as *information hiding*, and is the key for understandable, reusable, and extensible systems. The principle of low coupling also prohibits *circular dependences*, as they couple all involved units.

Applying the principles of strong cohesion and low coupling consistently will reduce the number of dependences in any design. Thus, the `confirm_loss()` invocation (Example 3.11) would be counterintuitive as it violates the principle of low coupling by coupling presentation and functionality more than necessary.

Given the time potentially saved on coding, testing, and debugging, any extra hour spent on improving the design is a good investment. A good design will not only make your system more flexible, more robust, and more reusable but will make it easier to test and to debug. If you want to know more about design, the "Further Reading" section gives a number of useful references.

3.8 PREVENTING UNKNOWN PROBLEMS

So far, this section has been about setting up tests for debugging — that is, how to isolate a unit in a controlled environment. All of this assumes that a problem has already occurred.

Any problem that escapes into the wild (and is experienced by a user) indicates that the product has not been tested (or reviewed, or proven) well enough. Consequently, the quality assurance process must be refined such that the problem in question (and hopefully similar problems) will not occur in the future.

As this is a book about debugging (i.e., the cure of *known* problems), we cannot spend too much space on preventing yet *unknown* problems. This is not to negate that prevention is better than cure. In fact, one might say that by far most of computer science is concerned with preventing problems. But when prevention fails, there is need for a cure, and that is what this book is about. Nonetheless, for your reference, Lists 3.1 and 3.2 capture basic rules of testing and quality assurance.

Quality assurance can never reach perfection. Even if all techniques are applied to the extreme, we will still have programs with surprising behavior. However, as a professional developer, you should know about all of these techniques, and be prepared to suggest them whenever it comes to reducing risk. Making mistakes is hard to avoid but not caring to prevent mistakes is unacceptable.

- *Specify.* A program cannot be correct on its own — it can only be correct with respect to some *specification* that describes its purpose. Attempt precise, or even formal, specifications that cover the entire behavior, including exceptions. A full specification will be a big help in understanding how the system is supposed to work — and hence help you in writing a correct system.

- *Test early.* This principle states that you must not wait with testing until the entire system is assembled. Instead, run test cases as soon as a unit is implemented, and assemble your system out of carefully tested units.

- *Test first.* Write test cases *before* implementing the unit. This is useful because test cases can serve as *specifications.* Although test cases specify only examples, a sufficient number of test cases can make it difficult to implement something else than the most elegant (and correct) solution.

- *Test often.* At the minimum, run your tests with each release of the system. Better yet, run your tests with every change. The sooner you know that there is a defect the smaller the set of accumulated changes that might have caused the defect. Automation helps a lot here.

- *Test enough.* Measure the coverage of your tests. How many statements and branches are actually taken? Instrument your code to gather coverage and design your test cases to achieve sufficient coverage. Use random inputs to cover exceptional and extreme situations.

- *Have others test.* Testing for unknown problems is a *destructive* process. By all means, one must try to uncover a weakness in the program. As people in general prefer being constructive to ripping things apart, this is a difficult psychological situation for most. In particular, it makes an author unsuited to test her or his own code. Therefore, always have someone independent test your program, and be open to criticism.

LIST 3.1 Essential rules for testing.

- *Have others review.* Testing is not the most effective way to catch defects. Reviewing is. No other technique catches so many defects for the same amount of effort. Have someone else review your code and check for possible defects. Think about *pair programming* as a means of increasing the amount of reviews.

- *Check the code.* More and more, computers can detect errors and anomalies in your system. Chapters 7 and 11 give an overview. Running such tools on your code comes at a small cost, but brings greater and greater benefits as computers get faster and faster.

- *Verify.* Several important properties of software systems can today be shown automatically or semiautomatically. If the behavior of your system can be modeled as a finite state machine, *software model checking* comes in handy to prove correctness. That is how Microsoft validates its device drivers.

- *Assert.* If you cannot fully prove correctness, go the simpler way: let the computer do the work and have it check its state at runtime (Chapter 10). Your program may still fail due to a failed assertion, but if all assertions are met the result will be correct with respect to all assertions.

LIST 3.2 More tools and techniques for quality assurance.

3.9 CONCEPTS

✎ *To test for debugging*, one must:

- Create a test to reproduce the problem

- Run the test several times during debugging

- Run the test before new releases to prevent regression

✎ Due to the number of tests needed in debugging, it is thus useful to *automate* as much as possible.

✎ *To automate program execution*, one can access *three layers*.   **HOW TO**

- Presentation layer

- Functionality layer

- Unit layer

The layers differ in ease of execution, ease of interaction, ease of result assessment, and robustness against changes.

HOW TO   ✎ *To test at the presentation layer*, the testing environment must stimulate human activities — either *input devices* (low level) or *user controls* (higher level).

HOW TO   ✎ *To test at the functionality layer*, use an interface designed for automation — typically using specific *scripting languages.*

HOW TO   ✎ *To test at the unit layer*, use the *API of a program unit* to control it and to assess its results.

HOW TO   ✎ *To isolate a unit*, break dependences using the *dependence inversion principle*, making the unit depend on abstractions rather than on details.

HOW TO   ✎ *To design for debugging*, reduce the amount of dependences using the principles of *high cohesion* and *low coupling.*

✎ Design patterns such as *model-view-controller* are useful for reducing dependences.

HOW TO   ✎ *To prevent unknown problems*, one can use a variety of techniques, including the following.

- Testing early, testing often, and testing enough

- Reviewing by others and pair programming

- Having the computer check the code for anomalies and common errors

- Proving correctness formally (using computer support)

3.10 TOOLS

JUNIT

JUNIT as well as unit test tools for other languages can be obtained via its web page at:

        http://www.junit.org/

ANDROID

All scripting languages described in the chapter are also documented online. ANDROID can be found at:

```
http://www.wildopensource.com/larry-projects/android.html
```

APPLESCRIPT

APPLESCRIPT documentation and examples are found at:

```
http://www.apple.com/applescript/
```

Neuburg (2003) is strongly recommended as a guide to APPLESCRIPT.

VBSCRIPT

VBSCRIPT and other Microsoft tools for scripting can be found at:

```
http://msdn.microsoft.com/scripting/
```

Other scripting languages

Other scripting languages suitable for test automation include PYTHON, PERL, TCL, and JAVASCRIPT, all of which are documented by a great deal of information available on the web.

FAUmachine

The virtual machines discussed in this chapter are also publicly available. The FAUmachine is a virtual machine specifically built for testing purposes. Among others, the FAUmachine allows you to control the entire virtual machine via scripts. FAUmachine can be researched at:

```
http://www.faumachine.org/
```

VMWare

At the time of this writing, VMWare was one of the most popular provider of virtual machines. It can be found at:

```
http://www.vmware.com/
```

Virtual PC

Microsoft also offers *Microsoft Virtual PC* for various operating systems, found at:

```
http://www.microsoft.com/virtualpc/
```

3.11   FURTHER READING

- *Testing:* The book by Myers (1979) has been the classic text on testing for more than 25 years. It is still up-to-date, and I recommend it as a first read to anyone who is interested in testing. It also includes a chapter on testing for debugging. If you prefer a hands-on approach, try Kaner et al. (1999).

   The forthcoming book of Pezzè and Young (2005) promises to be an in-depth treatment of all things testing and analysis. Psychological issues, in particular the law that developers are unsuited to testing their own code, are addressed in Weinberg (1971).

- *Automation:* Fewster and Graham (1998) and Dustin et al. (2001) focus on *automated* testing, focusing especially on the management view — such as when and how we should automate which parts of our test suite. A more technical view on automated testing can be found on the web sites devoted to extreme programming and unit testing — in particular

```
http://www.junit.org/
```

for JUNIT and

```
http://www.xprogramming.com/
```

for extreme programming.

- *Design:* If you do not have it already, the *Design Patterns* book by Gamma et al. (1994) contains much wisdom regarding how to structure systems. On the architectural level, the *Pattern-Oriented Software Architecture Series* by Buschmann et al. (1996) and Schmidt et al. (2000) contains several useful patterns. The model-view-controller example is taken from this series.

    The classic all-in-one textbook on object-oriented software design is the book by Meyer (1997). Other classic design books include those by Booch (1994) and Larman (2002). The *dependence inversion principle* was coined by Martin (1996). The article is available online at:

```
http://www.objectmentor.com/
```

3.12 EXERCISES

EXERCISE 3.1. In a few words, describe testing for debugging and for validation. Discuss the differences between these purposes.

EXERCISE 3.2. Discuss the differences between testing at presentation, functionality, and unit layer. Focus on ease of execution, ease of interaction, ease of result assessment, and robustness against changes.

EXERCISE 3.3. Is testing at the presentation layer of a command-line tool the same as functionality testing? Discuss similarities and differences.

EXERCISE 3.4. Use your favorite web browser and try to automate the loading of a web page, interacting at the presentation or the functionality layer.

EXERCISE 3.5. Run the JUNIT test URLtest.java code (Example 3.7). You need a URL class for testing. You can use the URL class that is part of the JAVA 1.4 java.net.URL package, documented at:

```
http://java.sun.com/
```

Simply include import java.net.URL in URLTest.java and you can start running JUNIT.

EXERCISE 3.6. Extend URLTest.java to include tests for other methods of the URL class. Is the documentation precise enough to let you write test cases?

EXERCISE 3.7. In the model-view-controller pattern (Figure 3.7), every observer still depends on a given model. How can you use the dependence inversion principle to break this dependence?

EXERCISE 3.8. When it comes to breaking dependences, there are alternatives to introducing abstract classes. Sketch and discuss

1. the usage of *macros* (C, C++)

2. the usage of *aspects* (Section 8.2.3)

to break the dependence illustrated in Example 3.11.

EXERCISE 3.9. JUNIT works fine to discover defects at the unit level, but fails if a failure is caused by multiple units. Discuss.

Software features that can't be demonstrated by automated tests simply don't exist.

— KENT BECK
Extreme Programming Explained (2000)

REPRODUCING PROBLEMS

T HE FIRST STEP IN DEBUGGING is to *reproduce* the problem in question — that is, to create a test case that causes the program to fail in the specified way. The first reason is to bring it under control, such that it can be observed. The second reason is to verify the success of the fix. This chapter discusses typical strategies for reproducing the operating environment, the history, and the problem symptoms.

4.1 THE FIRST TASK IN DEBUGGING

Once a problem report is in the problem database, or once a test has failed, the problem will eventually be processed by some programmer in order to fix it. The programmer's first task (or, more precisely, the first task of any debugging activity) is to *reproduce the problem* — that is, the problem must occur in the very same way as stated in the original problem report. Reproducing the problem is important for two reasons.

- *To observe the problem:* If you are not able to reproduce the problem, you cannot observe what is going on. This thoroughly limits your ability to reason about the program, as pointed out in Chapter 6. Basically, your only chance is to *deduce* from the program code what *might* have happened to cause the problem.

- *To check whether the problem is fixed:* You may be able to deduce a potential problem cause — and even to design a change that would fix this potential cause. But how do you show that your change actually fixes the problem in question? You can do so only by reproducing the initial scenario with the changed product, and showing that the problem now no longer occurs. Without reproducing the problem, you can never know that the problem has been fixed.

Of course, if the problem occurred in a test in the local environment we are already set and done, because we can reproduce the test at the touch of a button — assuming the test was automated and deterministic. In other cases, and if the problem was reported by a user, we must first *create a test case* that reproduces the problem. This is the key issue in this chapter:

HOW CAN A TEST REPRODUCE A SPECIFIC PROBLEM?

4.2   REPRODUCING THE PROBLEM ENVIRONMENT

Whereas creating test cases per se is well understood (see Chapter 3), reproducing a specific problem can be one of the toughest problems in debugging. The process consists of two main steps.

- Reproducing the *problem environment* — that is, the setting in which the problem occurs.

- Reproducing the *problem history* — the steps necessary to create the problem.

We first focus on reproducing the problem environment. If a problem occurs in a specific environment, the best place to study the problem is exactly this environment. Thus, if Olaf has trouble with the Perfect Publishing Program we should simply knock on Olaf's door and ask him whether we could take a brief look at his machine — or in a more tech-savvy environment ask him for permission to log on to his machine.

Working in the problem environment offers the best chance of reproducing the problem. However, for numerous reasons working in the problem environment typically does not happen.

- *Privacy:* The most important reason is *privacy* — users may simply not wish others to operate their machines; the same goes for large corporations.

- *Ease of development:* To examine the problem, programmers may require a complete development environment, involving diagnostic software such as debuggers, which are not typically found on customer's machines.

- *Cost of maintenance:* Users may depend on their machines being operational. In many cases, you cannot simply take a machine out of production to maintain the software.

- *Travel cost:* When physical access is required, having maintainers move to the user's environment is expensive.

- *Risk of experiments:* Debugging typically involves experiments, and running experiments on a user's machine may cause damage.

Thus, unless the problem environment is already prepared for diagnostic actions your *local environment* involves the least cost in reproducing the problem. For these reasons, as a maintainer you typically attempt to reproduce the problem using as much of the local environment as possible. This is an iterative process, as follows.

1. Attempt to reproduce the problem in *your environment*, using the product release as specified in the problem report (Section 2.2). If the problem occurs, you are done — and you are lucky.

   However, do not cry "success" simply because you experience *a* problem — cry "success" only if you experience *the* problem. Here, "the" problem means the problem exactly as specified in the problem report. Every deviation from the specified symptoms increases the risk of you working on a problem that is different from the user's problem. Thus, be sure to check every single symptom that is specified. If it does not occur in your environment, you may want to refine your efforts.

2. If the problem does not occur yet, adopt more and more circumstances from the problem environment — one after the other. This applies to configuration files, drivers, hardware, or anything else that might possibly influence the execution of the product. Start with those circumstances

   - that are the most likely to cause problems (as inferred from previous problem reports), and

   - that are easy to change (and to be undone).

   For instance, if the problem environment includes a specific set of user preferences first try using this set of preferences. If, however, the problem environment uses LemonyOS 1.0, but you use LemonyOS 1.1, you may want to downgrade your machine to LemonyOS 1.0 only after adopting all less expensive aspects — or better yet have quality assurance keep a LemonyOS 1.0 machine for testing.

3. Adopt one circumstance after the other until

- you could reproduce the problem or

- your environment is identical to the problem environment (as far as specified by the user).

In the latter case, there are two alternatives:

- The first alternative is that because the problem does not occur in your environment it *cannot* have occurred in the problem environment. Consider the fact that the problem report is incomplete or wrong.

- The second alternative is that the problem report is accurate but there still *is* a difference between your environment and the problem environment — because otherwise the problem would occur in your environment as well. Try to find that difference by querying further facts about the problem environment.

In both cases, it is wise to query further facts about the problem environment. As illustrated in Bug Story 4, even otherwise insignificant details can have an impact on whether one can reproduce earlier runs.

This process of getting nearer and nearer to the problem environment has a beneficial side effect: you also isolate some circumstances that are relevant in producing the problem. Let's say the problem environment includes a Helquist graphics card. Your environment does not yet include a Helquist graphics card and the problem does not occur. However, as soon as you add a Helquist graphics card the problem *does* occur. This means that the Helquist graphics card is relevant for reproducing the problem; more precisely, the Helquist graphics card is a *problem cause.* Chapter 13 "Isolating Failure Causes" discusses systematic ways of isolating such causes — manually and automatically.

BUG STORY 4: Mad Laptop

In 2002, I went to a conference to give a laptop demonstration of a complex software system. Before I left, we had taken every precaution that the software would run perfectly. But the evening before the demonstration, I sat in my hotel room and nothing worked. The software would run into time-out errors anytime, everywhere. I phoned my department at home. They had the same software on the same machine and everything worked.

After three hours of trials, I decided to start from scratch. To my amazement, the demo now ran just fine. What had happened? Within these three hours, the battery had run out of power and I had connected my laptop to a power plug. I disconnected the laptop, repeated the demo, and the problem occurred again. It turned out that my laptop ran slower when running on batteries, which saved energy but also introduced the time-out errors. Needless to say, all of our previous tests had been conducted on AC power, and this was how I gave the demo.

4.3 REPRODUCING PROGRAM EXECUTION

Finding an environment in which the problem occurs is not enough. We must also be able to recreate the individual steps that lead to the problem. Let's assume that we have recreated the problem environment, as discussed in Section 4.2. Let's also assume that the problem history, as stated in the problem report (Section 2.2), is accurate and complete. Still, we may not be able to reproduce the problem. In fact, even the user on the original machine may not be able to reproduce the problem.

Why is it that for the same program a problem may or may not occur? The execution of a program is determined by its code (which we assume constant) and its *input*. If the input differs, so does the execution of the program. To reproduce a specific execution, we must thus *reproduce the program input.*

To reproduce an input, the programmer must *observe* it and *control* it. Only when the input is under control does the execution become *deterministic* — that is, the outcome of the execution does not change when repeated. Without such control, the execution becomes *nondeterministic* — that is, the problem may occur or not, regardless of the will of the programmer.

All of this sounds rather trivial when thinking of the program input in a classical sense — that is, data read from a file or a keyboard. Unfortunately, the input of a program can be more than that — in particular, if you take the view

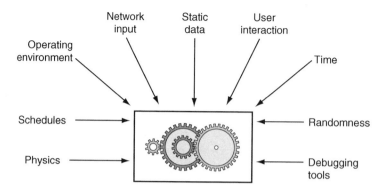

FIGURE 4.1 Input that might influence a program's execution.

that the input comprises anything that influences the execution. The following are possible inputs, as sketched in Figure 4.1.

- *Data:* As stored in files and databases is the least problematic input, as it can easily be reproduced.

- *User inputs:* Can differ in minor details, which may be relevant for a problem.

- *Communications:* Between threads, processes, or machines offer several challenges for reproduction.

- *Time:* Can influence the program execution in various ways.

- *Random numbers:* By definition make every program execution different.

- *Operating environments:* Provide services beyond those listed previously that can heavily interact with the program, all of which may or may not influence the execution.

- *Process and thread schedules:* Normally should not interfere with the program's execution. However, if the program has a defect they may.

Most of these inputs have *intended* effects on the program (which is why they should be reproduced). Other inputs, though, have unintended effects, such as the following inputs.

- *Physics:* Is typically abstracted away at the hardware layer, but cosmic rays, electrical discharges, or quantum effects can influence a program's execution.

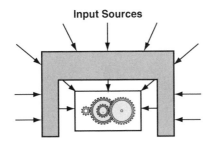

Input Sources

FIGURE 4.2 Controlling a program's input. To control program input, one sets up a control layer between the real input and the input as perceived by the program.

- *Debugging tools:* Typically interfere with the program execution, and thus may uncover but also mask problems.

The general pattern for controlling these inputs is to set up a *control layer* between the real input and the input as perceived by the program, as sketched in Figure 4.2. This control layer *isolates* the program under observation from its environment. The program input becomes controllable, and thus the execution becomes deterministic. Any of the automated techniques discussed in Chapter 3 can be used for actually controlling the program.

In the remainder of this chapter, we will focus on applying this pattern to make a run deterministic, organized by input source. In Section 4.2, we have already discussed how to reproduce the environment. Start with your own environment and reproduce one input source after the other until the problem is reproduced. In the process, you will narrow down the input sources relevant to the problem.

4.3.1 Reproducing Data

Regarding reproduction, data as stored in files and/or databases is seldom an issue. Files and databases can easily be transferred from one machine to another, and can easily be replicated. There are only three issues to be aware of.

- *Get all the data you need.* Be sure to reproduce all data your application accesses and all data under the user's control. This also includes *configuration data* such as registries or configuration files.

  Most of the data required to reproduce the problem is typically already included in the problem report. As discussed in Section 2.2, on reporting problems, it is helpful to set up a specific tool or functionality to collect such data.

- *Get only the data you need.* Some programs operate on enormous amounts of data, which makes it difficult to examine the problem. Chapter 5 discusses how to simplify input data.

- *Take care of privacy issues.* Data under the user's control may contain private or confidential information. Be sure not to find entire hard disks with sensitive information in your mailbox (this has happened!).

4.3.2 Reproducing User Interaction

In the good old days, programs would read their input from data files only, making reproduction an easy task. Modern programs, though, use complex user interfaces, and these make it difficult to observe and control the user's input.

The standard approach to reproducing user interaction is to use a *capture/replay* tool. Such a tool comes in two modes (Figure 4.3).

- *Capturing interaction:* The program executes normally, interacting with its environment. However, the tool *records* all input from the environment to a *script* before forwarding it to the program.

- *Replaying interaction:* The program executes under control of the tool. The tool redirects the program input such that it no longer gets its input from the environment but rather from the previously recorded script. Obviously, this makes the input controllable — and hence allows for reproducible runs.

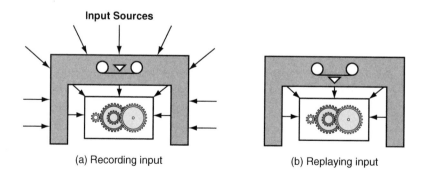

FIGURE 4.3 Capturing and replaying program input. During a normal execution, the controlling layer records the interaction. Later, it replays it.

Technically, a tool realizes capture/replay by intercepting calls to library or system functions providing input. Capture takes place after the execution of the input function. The tool records the returned input and passes it on to the program. During replay, the tool no longer executes the input function. Instead, it returns the previously recorded input.

What does the recorded information look like? In Chapter 3 we saw examples of scripts that automate program interaction. Depending on the layer at which input capturing occurs, the scripts simulate user input either

- as a "low-level" stream of events (Section 3.3.1) or

- as a "higher-level" sequence of interactions with user controls (Section 3.3.3).

Capturing user interaction can also take place at the following two layers.

- As a stream of events, a captured user interaction looks like that shown in Figure 3.4, except that there would be no comments and the script would include real-time aspects (such as waiting for, say, 376 milliseconds until releasing a key).

- As a sequence of interactions with user controls, a captured user interaction looks like that shown in Figure 3.6, except that (again) there would be no comments.

As discussed in Section 3.3, on testing at the presentation level, a script at the "low level" is *fragile*. That is, the slightest change in user interface layout, font size, or even interaction speed will make them unusable. Therefore, a low-level script should not be used beyond a single short-term debugging session.

To make the test reusable, one should at least aim to automate input at the higher level — or test at the functionality layer, as described in Section 3.4. Alas, few tools are available that allow programmers to capture and replay interaction at these layers. For a single testing or debugging session, though, it may already suffice to capture and replay just the basic user interaction in terms of key presses and mouse clicks.

BUG STORY 5: Press Play on Tape

As a student, I worked in a computer store. This was in the mid-1980s, and we had HP calculators, Commodore PETs, and Ataris. One day, a customer walked in and asked for help. He was not able to enter a program on his Commodore 64 home computer. Whenever he entered the first line, the computer would issue a syntax error message. We asked him to show us the problem on a C-64 nearby. He entered the first line of the program and got the message:

```
10 PRINT "HELLO WORLD"
?SYNTAX ERROR
READY
```

We were amazed, and tried to reproduce the problem. However, when one of us would enter the same line it would work properly. Only if the customer entered the line did the error occur. Finally, one of us asked the customer to enter just the number 10. He did so, and got:

```
10
PRESS PLAY ON TAPE
```

Now we understood. We asked the customer, "How do you type ones and zeros?" He replied, "I use a lowercase l and a capital letter O, as on my old typewriter." The customer had just entered lowercase l and capital O instead of ten, and the C-64 interpreted this as an abbreviation for the LOAD command. "Oh, you mean I should use the digit keys instead?" Yes, we said, and off went another happy customer.

4.3.3 Reproducing Communications

The techniques used for capturing and replaying user interaction (Section 4.3.2) can be extended to any type of communication. For instance, specialized tools can capture, inspect, reconstruct, and replay network traffic.

A general problem with such tools is that they may alter the performance of your program and its communications, especially if there is much data to be captured and replayed. (This is not the case with user interactions, which are typically low bandwidth.) The fact that tools alter the performance is not so much a problem in itself, but this change in the environment may mask problems that would occur otherwise (see Section 4.3.9 for the effects of debugging tools).

Note that one does not necessarily have to capture the entire communication since the start of the program. If the program goes into a reproducible state while operating, it suffices to capture (and replay) only the communication since that reproducible state. Databases, for instance, reach such a reproducible state after each transaction.

Failure causes are likelier to be found in the later communications than in earlier communications. Thus, it may frequently suffice to capture just the latest communication (say, the database transactions that are not yet completed). This saves space, does not hamper performance too much, and still may be helpful for reproducing the problem.

4.3.4 Reproducing Time

Many programs require the current time of day for executing correctly. Problems that depend on the time of day are difficult to reproduce and difficult to trace (see Bug Story 6, for example).

If the program is supposed to depend on the time of day, or if there is some indication that the problem depends on the time of the day, one must be able to execute the program under an arbitrary time of day. One way to do so is to change the system time before each execution—but this is cumbersome and error prone. A much more comfortable option, though, is to make time a *configurable item*: the program is set up such that it can be executed with an

BUG STORY 6: Program Only Works on Wednesday (Eisenstadt, 1997)

I once had a program that worked properly only on Wednesdays. The documentation claimed the day of the week was returned in a double word (8 bytes). In fact, Wednesday is nine characters long, and the system routine actually expected 12 bytes of space for the day of the week. Because I was supplying only 8 bytes, it was writing 4 bytes on top of the storage area intended for another purpose. As it turned out, that space was where a y was supposed to be stored for comparison with the user's answer. Six days a week the system would wipe out the y with blanks, but on Wednesdays a y would be stored in its correct place.

arbitrary time of day. This is useful for reproducing problems and very helpful for creating automatic tests (Chapter 3).

As in Section 4.3.2, on reproducing user input, the basic idea here is to obtain *control over input sources* such that they can be reproduced at will. The time of day is just a specific instance of how to obtain such control.

4.3.5 Reproducing Randomness

Specific programs, notably games and cryptographic applications, depend on *randomness*. That is, they are supposed to behave differently in every single execution. Here, nondeterminism is part of the design. That is, the program is set up in such a way as to prohibit reproduction of individual runs.

When testing such applications, such randomness must also be controlled and made reproducible. The most efficient way to do so depends on the source of randomness. If randomness is obtained from a series of pseudorandom numbers, it may suffice to capture (and replay) the initial *seed* of the random number generator. Many games allow one to explicitly specify a seed such that individual executions can be reproduced.

Cryptographic applications typically depend on more than just a pseudo-random number generator. They obtain randomness from several sources (such as user input, network events, thermal noise, or others). These sources must be captured and replayed like input, as discussed in Section 4.3.2. If needed, organize your program such that developers can replace the source of randomness by a deterministic source. (Be cautious about enabling end users to turn randomness off, though — especially in cryptographic applications!)

4.3.6 Reproducing Operating Environments

User interaction, communications, time, and randomness all have one thing in common: a *program interacts with its environment*, using services provided by this environment. Such an operating environment typically consists of further libraries, maybe a virtual machine, an operating system, and eventually the entire world to which the particular machine may be connected.

The entire interaction between a program and its environment is typically handled by the *operating system*. More precisely, the operating system controls all inputs and outputs of a program. Thus, the boundary between program and operating system comes as a natural place at which to monitor, control, and possibly record and replay program executions.

As an example, consider the simple C++ program shown in Example 4.1. When executed, it reads in a password from standard inputs and outputs "access

```
#include <string>
#include <iostream>

using namespace std;

string secret_password = "secret";

int main()
{
    string given_password;

    cout << "Please enter your password: ";
    cin >> given_password;
    if (given_password == secret_password)
        cout << "Access granted." << endl;
    else
        cout << "Access denied." << endl;
}
```

EXAMPLE 4.1 password.C — a simple C++ password requester.

granted" if the correct password is entered. (A real application would at least care not to echo the input.)

What does the interaction between this program and its environment look like? On a Linux box, the STRACE tool monitors the interaction of a program with the operating system by printing out all system calls, their arguments, and their return values. (Similar tools are available on all UNIX-like systems.) After compiling password.C, we run STRACE on the resulting password binary, diverting the STRACE output into a file named LOG.

```
$ c++ -o password password.C
$ strace ./password 2> LOG
Please enter your password: secret
Access granted.
$ _
```

What does the STRACE output look like? Example 4.2 shows an excerpt from the LOG file. The LOG file lists the *system calls* — function invocations by

```
⟨Clutter produced by shared libraries ...⟩
write(1, "Please enter your password: ", 28)  = 28
read(0, "secret\n", 1024)                      = 7
write(1, "Access granted.\n", 16)              = 16
exit_group(0)                                  = ?
```

EXAMPLE 4.2 The STRACE log from password.C (excerpt).

which the program requests services from the operating system. The write() system call, for instance, writes a string to stream number 1, the standard output stream on Linux (and other POSIX environments). STRACE also logs the *data* returned by the system calls. For instance, it reports the return value of write() (the number of written characters). For the following read() call, it reports the actual characters ("secret\n") read. Obviously, a tool such as STRACE is great for monitoring the interaction between a program and its operating system.

STRACE basically works by *diverting* the calls to the operating system to *wrapper functions* that log the incoming and outgoing data. There are various ways of achieving this. For instance, STRACE could link the program with its own "faked" versions of read(), write(), and so on that would all do the logging before and after invoking the "real" read() and write() functions. STRACE goes a more general way, which does not require relinking. On a Linux system, all system calls use one single functionality—a specific *interrupt* routine that transfers control from the program to the system kernel. STRACE diverts this interrupt routine to do the logging.

The same mechanism that STRACE and like tools use for *reporting* the interaction can also be used for *recording* and *replaying* the interaction (actually, this is how recording and replaying input works). For instance, a log as generated by STRACE could be processed by a replay tool. Such a replay tool would no longer invoke the "real" functions but simply have its "fake" functions return the values as found in the STRACE log file.

In Chapter 8 we will learn more about obtaining such logs. In particular, *aspect-oriented programming* (Section 8.2.3) offers elegant and system-independent ways of adding monitoring code to large sets of functions.

However, the true technical problem is less the capturing (or even replaying) of logs than the sheer *amount of data* we have to cope with. As an example, consider a web server that serves 10 requests per second. Say that each of these requests results in a trace log of about 10 kilobytes. Every hour will thus result in $10 \times 3,600 \times 10 \text{ KB} = 360 \text{ MB}$ of trace. A single day will result in 8,640 MB of trace. Given the advances in storage capacity, this may sound feasible. However, you should also consider that whenever you have to reproduce a problem you also have to replay all of this interaction.

An alternative to tracing all of the interaction from scratch is to use *checkpoints*. A checkpoint basically records the entire state of a program such that it can be restored later. This is typically done when the program has reached some *stable state*. In the case of the web server, for instance, this may be a pause between two requests or transactions. To reproduce a problem, it then suffices to restore the latest checkpoint, and then to replay the interaction since that checkpoint.

There is an obvious trade-off here. States are huge (see Figure 1.3, for instance) and capturing states into checkpoints may take time, and thus one must decide when to prefer checkpoints over recorded interaction. Chapter 14 discusses how to capture program states into checkpoints and how to restore them.

4.3.7 Reproducing Schedules

Modern programs typically consist of several concurrent threads or processes. In general, the *schedule* in which these individual parts are executed is defined by the runtime or operating system, thus abstracting away details that would otherwise burden the programmer. Indeed, a program is supposed to behave identically, whatever the schedule is. Consequently, although the schedule is nondeterministic the program execution should stay deterministic and the programmer need not care about parallelism and nondeterminism (if the program is correct, that is).

Nondeterminism introduced by thread or process schedules is among the worst problems to face in debugging. The following is a simple example. The APACHE web server provides a number of authentication mechanisms to make sure that only authorized clients can access specific web pages. One of these authentication mechanisms is the htaccess mechanism. If a directory contains a .htaccess file, the access to this directory is *restricted* — typically to a set of users with passwords stored in a separate .htpasswd file.

To maintain .htpasswd files, APACHE provides a helper program named htpasswd. For instance, the invocation

```
$ htpasswd .htpasswd jsmith
New password: _
```

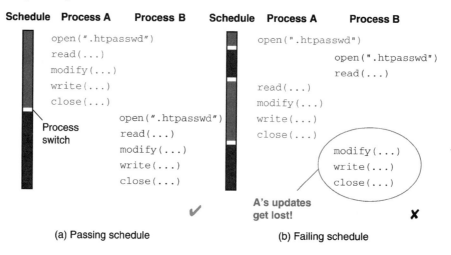

FIGURE 4.4 Differences in schedules may cause problems. If a process switch occurs in the middle of processing a file the second process B may undo updates made by the first process A.

adds or modifies the password for user jsmith. The htpasswd program prompts the user for the password and stores the user name and the encrypted password in the file .htpasswd.

How can htpasswd ever be nondeterministic? The trouble occurs when multiple users (or processes, or threads) are invoking htpasswd at the same time. Normally, each invocation of htpasswd reads the .htpasswd file, modifies it, writes it, and closes it again. Multiple sequential invocations cause no problem, as illustrated in Figure 4.4a.

However, if two htpasswd processes are running in parallel, bad things can happen, as illustrated in Figure 4.4b. Some htpasswd process A begins opens the .htpasswd file. Another process B does so at the same time and reads in the content. Now, process A modifies the content and writes back the .htpasswd file. However, process B does so, too, effectively overwriting and undoing the changes made by A. As long as write accesses to .htpasswd are scarce, it is unlikely that such a schedule would ever occur, but if it does it will be difficult to reproduce the failure.

There are several solutions to the htpasswd problem (none of which the htpasswd program implements at the time of this writing). The htpasswd could *lock* the .htpasswd file and thus protect it against multiple concurrent updates. It may also *retrieve the last update time* when reading the file, and *check it again before writing*. If the update time has changed in between, the file has changed and must be reread again.

Similar problems (with similar solutions) exist for all resources shared across multiple threads or processes. If multiple threads all write into a shared variable, the thread that writes last wins. Again, the solution would be to introduce locks or language-specific synchronization mechanisms, as described in any good textbook on operating systems or parallel processes.

However, all of these are solutions to a *known* problem, but to identify a problem we must first reproduce it. The general solution is to treat a schedule just like another input source, recording it and replaying it at will. However, as with communications (Section 4.3.3, on reproducing communication), the amount of data to collect can greatly affect the performance of a system. Another issue is scalability: recording and replaying the thread schedule of a single program has been shown to be practically feasible. However, recording and replaying an entire set of communicating processes, including the schedules as imposed by the operating system, is still a challenge for today's tools.

As programs should behave identically under all possible thread and process schedules, one may attempt to uncover *differences in execution* as induced by schedule differences. Such differences may be uncovered by program analysis (Chapter 7). For instance, one can verify that all access to shared variables happens in a synchronized fashion. Likewise, massive random testing (Chapter 3) can uncover problems due to differing schedules.

4.3.8 Physical Influences

Nondeterminism, as induced by thread or process schedules, is just one of the aspects of the real world that programmers deliberately abstract away. Why do they abstract these aspects away? Because they are not supposed to influence the execution of the program.

However, there are many ways to influence the machine on which our program executes. Energy impulses, for instance, can cause bits to flip. Such energy impulses can come over power lines or network communications, but also from alpha particles emitted from the earth's crust. (*Cosmic rays,* on the other side, have been shown to not influence programs in any way — except maybe in space-borne computers.) Quantum effects may also account for a certain amount of unpredictability. Real-life bugs can also cause failures (recall the tale of the moth caught in a relay, as told in Bug Story 1).

Although computers are typically designed to withstand physical influence, there is a very small chance that such influences may actually cause the program to fail — and as they are extremely rare, physical influences are difficult to reproduce. However, physical influences are also so rare that they can hardly be blamed for a nonreproducible problem. Yet it is common among programmers to blame, say, cosmic rays for an inexplicable problem, to shrug the shoulders, and go away.

Professional programmers should take such physical influences into account only if all other alternatives have been proven to be irrelevant — and if the physical influences can actually be proven. One exception remains, though: if physical influences are likelier than expected, because the physical environment is different from average, then (and only then) are you allowed to take such causes into account. Thus, if the problem occurs in the hot chamber of some nuclear research facility feel free to have someone check for sources of strong magnetic fields or alpha particles.

4.3.9 Effects of Debugging Tools

Another source that can alter a program's behavior is the *debugging process itself.* In fact, simply observing or examining the problem can cause the problem to disappear — or to be replaced by another problem. Problems that behave in this manner are known as *Heisenbugs* — in analogy to Heisenberg's famous uncertainty principle, which states that you cannot observe position and momentum of a particle at the same time with arbitrary precision (the observation itself alters the situation to be observed).

One major source for Heisenbugs are differences between the debugging (i.e., observation) environment and the production environment, combined with undefined behavior of the program. As a simple example, consider the following short C program.

```
int f() {
    int i;
    return i;
}
```

Note that i is not initialized. Hence, the value of i as returned by f() is undefined. "Undefined" means "undefined by the C standard," which again means that whatever f() returns it all conforms to the C standard. In practice, though, f() will return a definite value on many systems. Multiuser operating systems take care to start processes only with initialized memory (typically zeroed), such that a process may not examine the leftovers of other processes. Hence, in such an environment if f() is the first function being called it is likely to always return zero.

Now consider f() being executed within an interactive debugger (Chapter 8). The debugger has no need to clear the leftovers of earlier processes. In

BUG STORY 7: A `print` Statement Introduces a Heisenbug

In the midst of a debugging session, I inserted a `print` statement such that I could observe what was going on. To my great surprise, the problem no longer occurred after I had inserted the `print` statement. Even more puzzling, after I removed the `print` statement the problem was still gone, although the program had been reverted to its original state. Well, the problem was gone, but I remained suspicious.

When the problem resurfaced on our production machine, I went on investigating what had gone on. It turned out that there *was* a difference between the original and the reverted program: the executables were different. The problem was caused by a bug in the initial linker: a symbol had been resolved to a bad address. To insert the `print` statement, though, an alternate *incremental linker* had been used — and using this incremental linker fixed the problem.

particular, if you run the program multiple times, `f()` may return a random leftover from a previous run of the program, which may or may not be zero. Hence, running the program in a debugger alters the program's behavior — which may result in the original problem being masked by another problem, or (worse) the problem not occurring anymore at all.

If you experience a Heisenbug, think about *undefined behavior* in your program. Undefined behavior is almost always caused by a defect. In particular, consider the following.

- Check the data flow of your program to identify uninitialized variables (Section 7.5, on code smells).

- Use system assertions to identify memory that is read before being written (Section 10.8, on system assertions).

Some languages are more prone to Heisenbugs than others (in particular, languages, where undefined behavior is part of the semantics, such as C and C++). In more modern languages, such as JAVA and C#, almost every single aspect of the program execution is well defined, including forced initialization of variables. Furthermore, these languages come with *managed memory*, giving every memory access a predictable outcome.

- *Bohr bug (from quantum physics):* A repeatable bug — one that manifests reliably under a possibly unknown but well-defined set of conditions.

- *Heisenbug (from Heisenberg's Uncertainty Principle in quantum physics):* A bug that disappears or alters its behavior when one attempts to probe or isolate it.

- *Mandelbug (from the Mandelbrot set):* A bug whose underlying causes are so complex and obscure as to make its behavior appear chaotic or even nondeterministic. This term implies that the speaker thinks it is a Bohr bug, rather than a Heisenbug.

- *Schroedinbug (MIT: from the Schrödinger's Cat thought experiment in quantum physics):* A design or implementation bug in a program that does not manifest until someone reading source or using the program in an unusual way notices that it never should have worked, at which point the program promptly stops working for everybody until fixed.

LIST 4.1 Jargon about reproducible and less-reproducible problems (Raymond, 1996).

You do not necessarily need a debugger to trigger a Heisenbug (any of the debugging techniques discussed in this book can trigger differences in behavior) among the most obvious issues is that examining a program (interactively or not) can introduce *timing issues*, as discussed in Section 4.3.4. Recompilation for debugging might trigger bugs in the tool chain. Even something as innocuous as a `print` statement can alter the behavior of a program (Bug Story 7). The debugging tools, of course, may themselves be buggy, and this can lead programmers far astray from the actual problem cause.

For these reasons, whenever there is the least suspicion the problem may be a Heisenbug it is always useful to *double check* and to observe the program by at least two independent means. In addition to Heisenbugs, computer jargon also introduced Schroedinbugs, Bohr bugs, and others (List 4.1 lists them all).

4.4 REPRODUCING SYSTEM INTERACTION

As seen in the previous section, the interface between a program and its environment becomes more and more difficult to control the tighter the program is *coupled* to its environment. In other words, the more information program and environment exchange and the more the program depends on this information, the more difficult it will be to reproduce a given problem.

One way to overcome this issue is to replay not only the program but its environment — in fact, to record and replay every single aspect of the physical machine executing the program. To do so, *virtual machines* (as discussed in Section 3.3.2) come in handy.

The REVIRT system uses a virtual machine called UMLinux (not to be confounded with the similarly named User-Mode-Linux) to record and replay all interaction of a virtual machine. It uses a specially modified guest operating system to reduce the overhead of virtualization. Compared to the computation directly on the host, UMLinux virtualization adds an overhead of 58% to execution time. REVIRT recording adds another overhead of 8%. This indicates that virtual machines are feasible one-size-fits-all solutions when it comes to control, record, and replay program executions — if such a machine is available for the problem at hand. The single major drawback is that the recorded scripts are difficult to read, let alone maintain.

4.5 FOCUSING ON UNITS

Another way of dealing with the coupling between program and environment is to search for *alternative interfaces* that may be controlled, recorded, and replayed. In Section 3.5 we saw how to control individual *units* of the program — that is, subprograms, functions, libraries, modules, abstract data types, objects, classes, packages, components, beans, or whatever decomposition the design and the language provide.

The idea now is not to reproduce the execution of the entire program but only *the execution of a specific unit.* This has the advantage that controlling the unit in isolation may be easier than controlling the entire program. The disadvantage, of course, is that you can only reproduce the behavior of the given unit — and thus must count on the unit producing the problem in isolation.

4.5.1 Setting Up a Control Layer

The basic scheme for controlling a single unit is sketched in Figure 4.5. Again, we set up a layer that isolates the unit from its other units. This *unit control layer* can be used to monitor, record, and replay the input.

A control layer is a generalization of the STRACE tool (discussed in Section 4.3.6). Rather than setting up a layer between program and environment

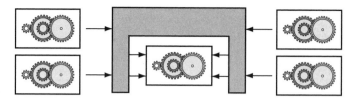

FIGURE 4.5 Controlling a unit's interaction. Setting up a layer for a single unit controls its interaction with the other units.

(operating system), we attempt to isolate arbitrary program units from their environment (the remainder of the program). This technique is typically used to isolate *bottom-level* units — that is, units

- whose services are being used frequently by higher-level units and

- who do not rely on services provided by other units.

Most such bottom-level units are concerned with elementary services such as storage and communication. To reproduce a problem in such a bottom-level unit, it is usually easier to record and replay the interaction at the unit boundary rather than reproducing the entire behavior of the application that uses the unit. The following are some examples.

- *Databases:* To reproduce a problem in a database, record and replay the SQL transactions as issued by an application — rather than reexecuting the entire application.

- *Compilers:* To reproduce a problem in a compiler, record and restore the intermediate data structures — rather than reexecuting the entire front end.

- *Networking:* To reproduce a networking problem, record and replay the basic communication calls as issued by the application — rather than reexecuting the entire application.

4.5.2 A Control Example

As an example of a unit control layer, imagine a simple C++ class that realizes a *mapping* from strings to integers, as follows.

```
class Map {
public:
```

```
    virtual void add(string key, int value);
    virtual void del(string key);
    virtual int lookup(string key);
};
```

Our aim is to create a control layer that *logs* all input and output of such a map. We also want to use the log to *reproduce* the interaction between the map and the other units. That is, we need a means of reading the log and invoking the appropriate Map methods.

A very simple way of creating such means is to create the log as a stand-alone *program file*. If, for instance, first add("onions", 4) and then del("truffels") is called, and finally lookup("onions") is called, the log file should read as follows.

```
#include "Map.h"
#include <assert>

int main() {
    Map map;
    map.add("onions", 4);
    map.del("truffels");
    assert (map.lookup("onions") == 4);
    return 0;
}
```

This does not look like the log files you are used to, right? This log file can be compiled and executed — and thus reproduces the interaction of a Map object with its environment. Note that we use an assertion both to log and to verify the output of the lookup method. This way, the resulting log can also be used for regression testing.

To implement the logging functions, we have to overwrite the original Map methods. In an object-oriented language such as C++, a simple way of doing so is to create a *subclass* of Map with redefined methods. (A more elegant alternative would be *aspects*, discussed in Section 8.2.3.)

```
class ControlledMap: public Map {
public:
    typedef Map super;

    virtual void add(string key, int value);
    virtual void del(string key);
    virtual int lookup(string key);
```

```
        ControlledMap();              // Constructor
        ~ControlledMap();             // Destructor
};
```

Each of the `ControlledMap` methods actually invokes the method of the `Map` superclass, but also logs the invocation to the `clog` stream. As an example, consider the `add()` method, as follows.

```
void ControlledMap::add(string key, int value)
{
    clog << "map.add(\"" << key << "\", "
        << value << ");" << endl;
    Map::add(key, value);
}
```

We do the same for the deletion method:

```
void ControlledMap::del(string key)
{
    clog << "map.del(\"" << key << "\");" << endl;
    Map::del(key);
}
```

For the `lookup` methods, we also log the return value and enclose the whole into an assertion.

```
virtual int ControlledMap::lookup(string key)
{
    clog << "assert (map.lookup(\"" << key << "\") == ";
    int ret = Map::lookup(key);
    clog << ret << ");" << endl;
    return ret;
}
```

All three methods have a slight problem: if the key contains a character that cannot be enclosed literally in a C++ string, the resulting program will not compile. A better implementation would thus take care to translate such characters properly.

The constructor and destructors of `ControlledMap`, called when a `ControlledMap` object is created and deleted (respectively), add some framework to the `clog` stream such that the output becomes a stand-alone compilation unit:

```
ControlledMap::ControlledMap()
{
    clog << "#include \"Map.h\"" << endl
         << "#include <assert>" << endl
         << "" << endl
         << "int main() {" << endl
         << "    Map map;" << endl;
}

ControlledMap::~ControlledMap()
{
    clog << "    return 0;" << endl;
         << "}" << endl;
}
```

How do we use this layer? We simply replace `Map` with `ControlledMap` for some object in the program and thus have all interaction logged to `clog`. By diverting the log into a program file, we can always reproduce all `Map` interaction simply by compiling and executing the program file. As a side effect, the resulting program files can also be used as *test cases* and thus protect against regression. Such recorded test cases are more abstract than recorded user interaction (Section 4.3.2 on reproducing input), and are thus more valuable for long-term use (integrating them into unit test tools such as JUNIT is straightforward).

4.5.3 Mock Objects

In the `ControlledMap` example, we have seen how to set up an object such that it records all of its interaction. In addition to recording, though, we could also set up an object such that it *replays* a previously recorded interaction. This way, we could *replace* an original object with a *mock object* — an object that does nothing but *simulate* the original object by replaying previously recorded interaction. This basic idea is illustrated in Figure 4.6. During capture, a special tool logs all interactions between the original object and its clients. Upon replay, a mock object replaces the original object, expecting and replaying the previously recorded interaction.

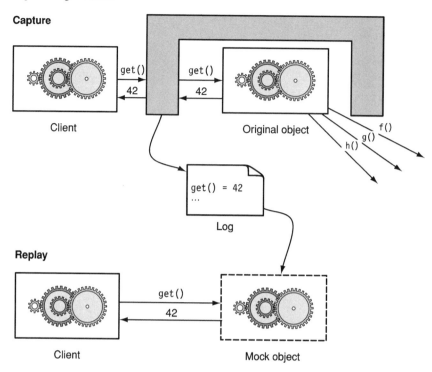

FIGURE 4.6 Replaying unit interaction with mock objects. Upon replay, the mock object replays the behavior of the original object.

Assume we have a `MockMap` available, which is able to replay interactions recorded earlier by `ControlledMap`. Replaying the interaction from Section 4.5.2, such a `MockMap` object would:

- Expect a call `add("onions", 4)` and do nothing

- Expect a call `del("truffels")` and do nothing

- Expect a call `lookup("onions")` and return 4

Note that the `MockMap` does not actually store items; it simply faithfully replays the earlier behavior. For a simple container such as a map, this does not make that much of a difference. For complex items that are difficult to move from one setting to another, however, a mock object can make a huge difference. As an example, consider a *database* installed at a user's site. To reproduce a problem, you normally need to install and replicate the user's database. This problem can be addressed by turning the database into a capture/replay mock object, as follows.

1. We record the database interaction at the user's site.

2. We then forward the mock object (rather than the database) to the developer.

3. Using the mock object, the developer can reproduce and examine the original run — without going into the hassle of reproducing the entire environment.

Creating mock objects *manually* can be a large amount of programming work, especially for objects with complex interfaces. Recently, though, tools have begun to emerge that allow us to turn arbitrary objects into mock objects. These tools automatically examine the object interfaces and add recording and playback facilities. The tools also take care of the following issues.

- *Return values:* The tool must generate mock objects for *returned values*. A query to a database typically returns a query result, which comes as an object. If the database is turned into a mock object, the query must also return a mock result.

- *Outgoing calls:* The tool must capture and replay *outgoing* calls as well (that is, the mock object calls other objects using previously recorded calls). A mock object for a database, for instance, may call back methods of other objects as soon as a query result is available. Such outgoing calls must also be recorded.

- *Arguments:* The tool must provide mock objects for *arguments* of outgoing calls. In the previous example, a method called back by a mock database must be provided with (mock) arguments.

- *Variables:* The tool must monitor direct read and write access to object variables, such that these accesses can also be mocked.

At the time of this writing, such capture/replay mock objects are still research prototypes. However, the approach can be applied to arbitrary objects (or units) and thus nicely generalizes to all problems recording and reproducing unit behavior.

4.5.4 Controlling More Interaction

A layer as sketched in the previous examples monitors and reproduces only function calls. However, there may be more ways in which the unit depends on its environment. If a unit works in isolation, but not within the application, there must be some *interaction* that is not yet adequately monitored.

- *Variables:* Some units provide variables the application can access to alter the unit's behavior, or to retrieve query results. Such *implicit communication* via variables must also be monitored and controlled, which requires a lot of work unless you use a capture/replay mock tool (as discussed in Section 4.5.3).

- *Other units:* Some units depend on other units, which may also be controlled by the application. Be sure to capture and restore the state of these units as well. If needed, break the dependence (Section 3.6, on isolating units).

- *Time:* Some units (or more precisely, some problems within units) depend on a specific amount of time that must elapse between function calls. If needed, you may wish to record and replay these time intervals.

Obviously, the more possibilities there are for an application to alter the behavior of a unit the more difficult it becomes to isolate the unit from the application. At this point, it becomes clear how a good program design (as discussed in Section 3.7) has a positive impact on debugging efforts. The less information is being exchanged between units, and the less dependences there are between units, the easier it becomes to control and reproduce unit behavior. Thus, a good design not only makes a program easier to understand, maintain, restructure, and reuse but to debug.

4.6 CONCEPTS

✎ Once a problem is tracked, the next step is to *reproduce* it in *your environment.*

HOW TO ✎ *To reproduce a problem:*

- Reproduce its environment (Section 4.2)

- Reproduce the execution (Section 4.3 and later)

✎ *To reproduce the problem environment:*   **HOW TO**

- Start with *your environment*

- Adopt one circumstance of the *problem environment* after the other

For details, see Section 4.2.

✎ *To reproduce the problem execution*, place a *control layer* between the pro-   **HOW TO**
gram's input and the input as perceived by the program (Figure 4.2). Such
a control layer can be used to monitor, control, capture, and replay the program's input.

✎ Technically, one realizes a control layer by intercepting calls to input functions.

✎ Inputs that can be (and frequently must be) controlled include:

- Data (Section 4.3.1)

- User inputs (Section 4.3.2)

- Communications (Section 4.3.3)

- Time (Section 4.3.4)

- Randomness (Section 4.3.5)

- Operating environment (Section 4.3.6)

- Process schedules (Section 4.3.7)

✎ Physics (Section 4.3.8) and debugging tools (Section 4.3.9) can influence a
program's behavior in unintended ways.

✎ Executing on a *virtual machine* gives the best possibilities for recording and
replaying interaction.

✎ *To reproduce unit behavior*, place a *control layer* between the unit's input and   **HOW TO**
the input as perceived by the unit (Figure 4.5).

✎ *Mock objects* can provide a general means of recording and replaying the
interaction of arbitrary units.

4.7 TOOLS

WINRUNNER

Tools that record and replay user input are commonly used for testing. The WINRUNNER and XRUNNER tools provide record/replay facilities for Windows and UNIX. These are found at:

> http://www.mercuryinteractive.com/

ANDROID

The ANDROID open-source GUI testing tool is available at:

> http://www.wildopensource.com/larry-projects/android.html

REVIRT

The REVIRT system by Dunlap et al. (2002) allows you to record and replay the interaction of an entire machine. This is found at:

> http://www.eecs.umich.edu/CoVirt/

Checkpointing Tools

Regarding *checkpointing*, a variety of research tools are available. Such tools allow "freezing" a running process such that it can be resumed later, even on a different machine. For details, see:

> http://www.checkpointing.org/

4.8 FURTHER READING

When it comes to capturing and replaying more than just user interaction, tools are less in a product than in a research prototype stage. Ronsse et al. (2003) give an excellent introduction to the field of making program executions deterministic by recording and replaying their interaction with the environment. They also give pointers on how to replay message passing and shared memory.

Choi and Srinivasan (1998) and Konuru et al. (2000) describe the DEJAVU tool that allows for deterministic replay of multithreaded and even distributed JAVA applications. Among others, DEJAVU records and replays input as well as thread schedules. Mock objects for capturing and replaying object interaction are discussed by Saff and Ernst (2004a).

4.9 EXERCISES

EXERCISE 4.1. Use ANDROID (or similar tool) to record and replay a user session with a web browser. Can you use the script on a different machine or a different window manager?

EXERCISE 4.2. A recorded user interaction script typically simply records the *delays* between events, rather than *synchronizing* with the program output. An example of synchronization might be waiting for a dialog window to appear before continuing to simulate input. Discuss the advantages and disadvantages of synchronization.

EXERCISE 4.3. Use STRACE (or similar tool) to monitor the interaction of `ls` (or similar simple command). For each of the calls reported:

1. Look it up in the manual.

2. Estimate the effort for recording and replaying the information passed.

Start with calls you know (say, `open`, `close`, `read`, and `write`) and proceed to lesser known calls.

EXERCISE 4.4. Extend the unit capture scheme of Section 4.5.2 such that the generated log becomes a test case for a unit test framework such as CPPUNIT or JUNIT.

EXERCISE 4.5. Which events should be recorded to create a capture/replay tool for:

- Random numbers and time events?

- Kernel interaction?

How can program design support use of this capture/replay tool?

EXERCISE 4.6. "If I cannot reproduce a problem, it must be the user's fault." Discuss this statement, given a program with nondeterministic behavior and an environment that is difficult to reproduce.

EXERCISE 4.7. "Not every infection of a program state needs to stem from a defect. There could be a bit flip in a memory cell, due to an energy impulse, that caused the infection." Discuss.

Here also are huge men having horns four feet long,
and there are serpents also of such magnitude
that they can eat an ox whole.

— MAP INSCRIPTION,
Biblioteca Apostolica Vaticana (1430)

For every fact, there is an *infinity* of hypotheses.

— ROBERT PIRSIG,
Zen and the Art of Motorcycle Maintenance (1974)

## CHAPTER 5

SIMPLIFYING PROBLEMS

O NCE WE HAVE REPRODUCED A PROBLEM, we must *simplify* it — that is, we must find out which circumstances are not relevant for the problem and can thus be omitted. This process results in a test case that contains only the relevant circumstances. In the best case, a simplified test case report immediately pinpoints the defect. In this chapter, we introduce *delta debugging*, an automated debugging method that simplifies test cases automatically.

5.1 SIMPLIFYING THE PROBLEM

After one has reproduced a problem, the next step in debugging is to find out what is relevant and what is not. Does the problem really depend on the entire 10,000 lines of input? Is it really necessary to replay all of these interaction steps? Does the failure occur only if this exact schedule of events takes place? Do I really need this long sequence of recorded method calls?

This stage of debugging is known as *simplifying,* meaning to turn a detailed problem report into a simple *test case.* A test case contains the *relevant* details only. A detail of the problem report is relevant if it is *required* to make the problem occur. It is *irrelevant* if the problem occurs whether the detail is present or not.

Why is simplification important? As an analogy, consider a simple *flight test.* An airplane crashes a few seconds after taking off. To find out what happened, we repeat the flight in a simulator.

Even if we do not have a clue about how planes work, we can still find out what is relevant and what not — by repeating the flight over and over again under *changed circumstances.* For instance, we might take out the passenger seats and find that the plane still crashes. We might take out the coffee machine and the plane still crashes. We might take out the engines and — oops, the plane does not move off the runway. Obviously, the engines are important!

Eventually, only the relevant "simplified" skeleton remains, including a (simulated) test pilot, the wings, the runway, the fuel, and the engines. Each part of this skeleton is relevant for reproducing the crash.

To explain how the crash came to be, we need every single part of this skeleton. However, the value of simplification is less in the remaining parts but rather in all parts that have been taken away — all of the irrelevant details (such as the coffee machine) that did not contribute to the crash. The general process for simplifying a problem report follows a simple rule:

For every circumstance of the problem, check whether it is relevant for the problem to occur. If it is not, remove it from the problem report or the test case in question.

A *circumstance* is any aspect that may influence the problem — in short, the same circumstances one needs to reproduce the problem (Chapter 4 "Reproducing Problems"). In particular, these are:

- Aspects of the problem environment

- Individual steps in the problem history

How does one check whether a circumstance is relevant? You do this *experimenting*. That is, you omit the circumstance and try to reproduce the problem. If the problem no longer occurs, the circumstance is relevant. If the problem still occurs, the circumstance is irrelevant. As McConnell (1993) puts it:

The goal of simplifying the test case is to make it so simple that changing any aspect of it changes the behavior of the error.

This is exactly our key question:

HOW DO WE SIMPLIFY TEST CASES SYSTEMATICALLY AND AUTOMATICALLY?

5.2   THE GECKO BUGATHON

Simplification of test cases is not an academic problem. Consider a real-world example, related to the MOZILLA web browser — or more specifically, its HTML

```
<td align=left valign=top>
<SELECT NAME="op_sys" MULTIPLE SIZE=7>
<OPTION VALUE="All">All<OPTION VALUE="Windows 3.1">Windows 3.1<OPTION
VALUE="Windows 95">Windows 95<OPTION VALUE="Windows 98">Windows 98<OP-
TION VALUE="Windows ME">Windows ME<OPTION VALUE="Windows 2000">Windows
2000<OPTION VALUE="Windows NT">Windows NT<OPTION VALUE="Mac System 7">Mac
System 7<OPTION VALUE="Mac System 7.5">Mac System 7.5<OPTION VALUE="Mac
System 7.6.1">Mac System 7.6.1<OPTION VALUE="Mac System 8.0">Mac Sys-
tem 8.0<OPTION VALUE="Mac System 8.5">Mac System 8.5<OPTION VALUE="Mac
System 8.6">Mac System 8.6<OPTION VALUE="Mac System 9.x">Mac System
9.x<OPTION VALUE="MacOS X">MacOS X<OPTION VALUE="Linux">Linux<OPTION
VALUE="BSDI">BSDI<OPTION VALUE="FreeBSD">FreeBSD<OPTION
VALUE="NetBSD">NetBSD<OPTION VALUE="OpenBSD">OpenBSD<OPTION
VALUE="AIX">AIX<OPTION VALUE="BeOS">BeOS<OPTION VALUE="HP-UX">HP-
UX<OPTION VALUE="IRIX">IRIX<OPTION VALUE="Neutrino">Neutrino<OPTION
VALUE="OpenVMS">OpenVMS<OPTION VALUE="OS/2">OS/2<OPTION
VALUE="OSF/1">OSF/1<OPTION VALUE="Solaris">Solaris<OPTION
VALUE="SunOS">SunOS<OPTION VALUE="other">other</SELECT>
</td>
<td align=left valign=top>
<SELECT NAME="priority" MULTIPLE SIZE=7>
<OPTION VALUE="-">-<OPTION VALUE="P1">P1<OPTION VALUE="P2">P2<OPTION
VALUE="P3">P3<OPTION VALUE="P4">P4<OPTION VALUE="P5">P5</SELECT>
</td>
<td align=left valign=top>
<SELECT NAME="bug_severity" MULTIPLE SIZE=7>
<OPTION VALUE="blocker">blocker<OPTION VALUE="critical">critical<OPTION
VALUE="major">major<OPTION VALUE="normal">normal<OPTION
VALUE="minor">minor<OPTION VALUE="trivial">trivial<OPTION
VALUE="enhancement">enhancement</SELECT>
</tr>
</table>
```

EXAMPLE 5.1 Printing this HTML page (excerpt) makes MOZILLA crash.

layout engine named *Gecko*. In July 1999, two years before the final completion of MOZILLA 1.0, BUGZILLA — the MOZILLA problem database — listed more than 370 open problem reports — problem reports that were not even reproduced.

In Example 3.1 we have already seen one of these open problem reports, reported by a MOZILLA user in 1999. This problem report is already close to perfection: it is short, reproducible, and precise. It can also easily be automated, as discussed in Chapter 3 "Making Programs Fail." The problem, though, is that the web page in question — the page at http://bugzilla.mozilla.org — was 896 lines of quite obfuscated HTML code (shown in Example 5.1). Loading this HTML code into Gecko and printing it caused a fatal failure. Something in this HTML input made MOZILLA fail — but what?

Obviously, reading this HTML code does not give us any hints about possible failure causes. If we were MOZILLA programmers, what we want here is the *simplest HTML input* that still produces the failure — and hopefully pinpoints the failure cause.

A simplified test case not only helps in finding failure causes, though. There are at least three further good reasons for simplifying.

- *A simplified test case is easier to communicate.* The simpler a test case, the less time it takes to write it down, to read its description, and to reproduce it. In addition, you know that the remaining details are all relevant because the irrelevant details have been taken away. In our example, is it relevant that the margins be set to .50? If the failure occurs nonetheless, we can leave out this detail.

- *A simplified test case facilitates debugging.* Typically, a simplified test case means less input (and thus smaller program states to examine) and less interaction with the environment (and thus shorter program runs to understand). Obviously, if the HTML code in Example 5.1 can be simplified to a small number of HTML tags, the state of Gecko would be much easier to examine. In the best case, the HTML tag could even directly lead to the error.

- *Simplified test cases identify duplicate problem reports.* As discussed in Section 2.8, duplicate problem reports can fill up your problem database. Simplified test cases typically *subsume* several duplicate problem reports that differ only in irrelevant details. If we know that some specific HTML tag causes printing to fail, we can search for this HTML tag in other problem reports, marking them as duplicates.

Despite these benefits, new problem reports now came in quicker than MOZILLA programmers could possibly simplify them or even look at them. With this queue growing further, the MOZILLA engineers "faced imminent doom."

But then, Eric Krock, MOZILLA product manager, had a clever idea: Why not have *volunteers* simplify test cases? Thus, Krock started what became the *Gecko BugAThon*: volunteers would help the MOZILLA programmers by creating simplified test cases. To simplify test cases, you do not have to be a programmer. All you need is a *text editor* (as shown in List 5.1). The entire process boils down to removing parts of the page and periodically rerunning MOZILLA until all remaining input is relevant.

As an incentive, Krock offered *rewards* for simplified test cases. For five problem reports turned into simplified test cases, a volunteer would be invited to the launch party. For 10 test cases, he or she would also get an attractive *Gecko stuffed animal*, and 20 test cases would earn her or him a T-shirt signed by the grateful engineers. This simple scheme worked out very well, because of the large number of enthusiastic volunteers on the web the very first night a number of volunteers earned their stuffed animal by staying up late and simplifying test cases.

5.3 MANUAL SIMPLIFICATION

How would a MOZILLA volunteer proceed in an actual example? Let's apply the instructions in List 5.1 on the HTML input in Example 5.1. We use a method sketched by Kernighan and Pike (1999):

Proceed by binary search. Throw away half the input and see if the output is still wrong; if not, go back to the previous state and discard the other half of the input.

This *divide-and-conquer* process is sketched in Figure 5.1.

- Download the web page that shows the bug to your local machine.

- Using a text editor (such as Notepad on Windows, SimpleText on the Mac, or vi or emacs on UNIX), start removing HTML markup, CSS rules, and lines of JavaScript from the page. Start by commenting out parts of the page (using `<!-- -->`) that seem unrelated to the bug. Every few minutes, check the page to make sure it still reproduces the bug. Code not required to reproduce the bug can be safely removed.

- You will do well if you use an editor supporting multiple levels of Undo, and better if you use an HTML-editing tool that supports preview to an external browser.

- When you have cut away as much HTML, CSS, and JavaScript as you can — and cutting away any more causes the bug to disappear — you are done.

LIST 5.1 Instructions for simplifying HTML pages manually. *(Source: mozilla.org.)*

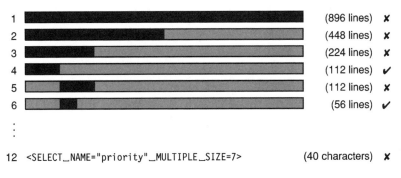

FIGURE 5.1 Simplifying the HTML input from Example 5.1.

1. The gray bar stands for the HTML input — initially 896 lines that cause MOZILLA to fail (✘).

2. Using a text editor, we cut away the second half of the input (shown in light gray), leaving only the first half (dark gray), and repeat the test with this 418-line input. MOZILLA still crashes (✘).

3. Again, we cut away the second half, leaving only 224 lines. Still, MOZILLA crashes.

4. When we again cut away the second half, leaving only 112 lines, MOZILLA just works (✔).

5. We undo the earlier cut and cut away the first half instead. When being fed with these 112 lines, MOZILLA again crashes.

6. We continue simplifying the input.

7. After 12 tests, one single line with a <SELECT> tag is left:

    ```
    <SELECT␣NAME="priority"␣MULTIPLE␣SIZE=7>
    ```

    (This HTML line in `http://bugzilla.mozilla.org/` is used to have users input the *problem priority* of a report.)

We have now simplified the problem report from 896 lines to one single line. Further testing shows that the tag attributes are irrelevant, too, and thus all we need to cause the problem is an input of <SELECT>.

Having simplified this problem is very beneficial. In particular, it helps in:

- *Communication:* All one needs is the three-word summary "Printing <SELECT> crashes"

- *Debugging:* A MOZILLA programmer can immediately focus to the piece of code that handles printing of <SELECT> tags

- *Duplicates:* A Bugzilla maintainer can scan the database for other problems with printing, and if <SELECT> is part of the respective HTML input chances are that they are all duplicates of each other

5.4 AUTOMATIC SIMPLIFICATION

Manual simplification, as demonstrated in Section 5.3, has important benefits. However, these come at a price:

- *Simplification is tedious.* You have to run tests manually all over again.

- *Simplification is boring.* It is a rather mechanical activity without great intellectual challenge.

As with so many other tedious and boring activities, one may wonder whether it would not be possible to *automate* the simplification process. And indeed, it can. Once again, we illustrate the basic idea using the MOZILLA example:

- We set up an *automatic test* that determines whether MOZILLA fails to print on some specific input.

- We implement a *strategy* that realizes the binary search strategy mentioned earlier, running the test on some subset of the HTML page.

Setting up an automatic test for MOZILLA is not too difficult, applying the basic strategies from Chapter 4 "Reproducing Problems": We have MOZILLA read its input from file (rather than from the network), and use record/replay to automate the user interaction from Example 3.1. The test can thus be realized as follows:

1. Launch MOZILLA.

2. Use Capture and Replay to:

    - Load the HTML page into MOZILLA

    - Set printing settings as described in the problem report

    - Print the page

3. Wait for a certain amount of time to see whether:

    - MOZILLA crashes — that is, the test fails (✘)

    - whether it is still alive — that is, the test passes (✔)

4. If MOZILLA should not start, or if it fails for some other reason, our test returns **?**.

Let's consider the second part: to design an *automatic simplification strategy* using such an automatic test. As a starting point, we simply adapt the "binary search" strategy from Section 5.3:

1. Cut away half the input and check if the test returns **✗**. If so, continue the process with the remaining half.

2. Otherwise, go back to the previous state and discard the other half of the input.

This simple description has a drawback: What do we do if *neither half* fails the test — that is, testing the first half passes and testing the second half passes as well? As an example, consider Example 5.2, where we attempt to simplify the remaining HTML line by *characters*. Again, input that has been cut away is shown in gray characters. Neither first nor second half is valid HTML, and thus MOZILLA interprets the input as text and the test does not fail.

A simple binary search does not suffice any longer, in that we are not searching for a single character but for a *subset* of the input. In this example, the subset we are searching for is the string <SELECT>, spread across the two input halves.

How do we deal with this situation? The answer is not to cut away *halves* of the input, but *smaller parts* — quarters, for instance. Thus, instead of cutting away the first half we cut away the first quarter, the second quarter, and so on.

This process is illustrated in Example 5.3, continuing the example from Example 5.2. Removing the first quarter (Step 4, the first 10 characters) still does not cause the problem to occur, but removing the second quarter (Step 5, characters 11–20) is successful. MOZILLA fails.

1	**<SELECT_NAME="priority"_MULTIPLE_SIZE=7>**	⟨40 characters⟩	✗
2	<SELECT_NAME="priori**ty"_MULTIPLE_SIZE=7>**	⟨20 characters⟩	✔
3	**<SELECT_NAME="priori**ty"_MULTIPLE_SIZE=7>	⟨20 characters⟩	✔

EXAMPLE 5.2 Simplifying a single line.

4	<SELECT_NA**ME="priority"_MULTIPLE_SIZE=7>**	⟨30 characters⟩	✔
5	**<SELECT_NA**ME="priori**ty"_MULTIPLE_SIZE=7>**	⟨30 characters⟩	✗
6	**<SELECT_NA**ME="priority"_MULTI**PLE_SIZE=7>**	⟨20 characters⟩	✗
7	**<SELECT_NA**ME="priority"_MULTIPLE_SIZE=7>	⟨10 characters⟩	✔

EXAMPLE 5.3 Simplifying by quarters.

Now that we have a failure on a simplified input, should we go back to cutting away halves or should we continue with quarters? One could argue that we should at least test all subsets at the given granularity. Thus, we continue removing quarters (Step 6) until the last one (Step 7).

If removing neither quarter makes the test fail, we continue with eighths, and then sixteenths, and so on. Eventually, we will thus come down to a point where we remove single characters — and end up in an input where removing any character causes the problem to disappear (a single <SELECT> tag). Thus, our automatic simplification strategy has eventually cut away everything that is irrelevant for producing the problem — and has done so only by trial and error, without any knowledge of the program or the input.

5.5 A SIMPLIFICATION ALGORITHM

Let's now write down a general algorithm that realizes the automatic strategy sketched in Section 5.4. We have some test function $test(c)$ that takes some input c and determines whether the failure in question occurs (✘, "fail") or not (✔, "pass") or whether something different happens (?, "unresolved").

Assume we have some failure-inducing input $c_\mathbf{x}$ that we can split into subsets. If we split $c_\mathbf{x}$ into two subsets c_1 and c_2, three things can happen:

- *Removing first half fails.* If $test\,(c_\mathbf{x} \setminus c_1) = ✘$, we can continue with $c_\mathbf{x}' = c_\mathbf{x} \setminus c_1$. ($c_\mathbf{x}'$ is the value for $c_\mathbf{x}$ in the next iteration.)

- *Removing second half fails.* Otherwise, if $test\,(c_\mathbf{x} \setminus c_2) = ✘$, we can continue with $c_\mathbf{x}' = c_\mathbf{x} \setminus c_2$.

- *Increase granularity.* Otherwise, we must increase the granularity and split $c_\mathbf{x}$ into four (eight, sixteen, and so on) subsets.

To accommodate the last case, we must generalize our description to an arbitrary number of subsets n. If we split $c_\mathbf{x}$ into n subsets c_1 to c_n, we get:

- *Some removal fails.* If $test\,(c_\mathbf{x} \setminus c_i) = ✘$ holds for some $i \in \{1, \ldots, n\}$, continue with $c_\mathbf{x}' = c_\mathbf{x} \setminus c_i$ and $n' = \max(n - 1, 2)$.

- *Increase granularity.* Otherwise, continue with $c_\mathbf{x}' = c_\mathbf{x}$ and $n' = 2n$. If $c_\mathbf{x}$ cannot be split into more subsets, we are done.

Let's generalize this further. Data input is just one way to determine a program's execution. In Chapter 4 "Reproducing Problems," we saw the influence of other circumstances such as time, communications, or thread schedules. We call such a set of circumstances that influence program behavior a *configuration*.

Our aim is now to find a *minimal set of circumstances* under which the failure occurs. That is, we want to *minimize a failure-inducing configuration* (to minimize the "failing" configuration $c_{\textbf{X}}$). In the MOZILLA case, the HTML input is such a configuration — a set of circumstances that determine MOZILLA 's execution — and we want to minimize this HTML input as far as possible.

This generalization ends up in the *ddmin* algorithm shown in List 5.2, as proposed by Zeller and Hildebrandt (2002). Its core, the *ddmin'* function, gets two arguments: the configuration (input) to be simplified (denoted as $c_{\textbf{X}}'$) and the granularity n. Depending on test results, *ddmin'* invokes itself recursively with a smaller $c_{\textbf{X}}'$ ("some removal fails"), invokes itself recursively with double granularity ("increase granularity"), or ends the recursion.

ddmin is an instance of *delta debugging* — a general approach to isolate failure causes by narrowing down differences (*deltas*) between runs. (More precisely,

---

Let a program's execution be determined by a set of circumstances called a *configuration*. The set of all circumstances is denoted by $\mathcal{C}$.

Let $test : 2^{\mathcal{C}} \rightarrow \{\textbf{X}, \textbf{✔}, \textbf{?}\}$ be a testing function that determines for a configuration $c \subseteq \mathcal{C}$ whether some given failure occurs ($\textbf{X}$) or not ($\textbf{✔}$) or whether the test is unresolved ($\textbf{?}$).

Let $c_{\textbf{X}}$ be a "failing" configuration with $c_{\textbf{X}} \subseteq \mathcal{C}$ such that $test(c_{\textbf{X}}) = \textbf{X}$, and let the test pass if no circumstances are present [i.e., $test(\emptyset) = \textbf{✔}$].

The *minimizing delta debugging algorithm ddmin* $(c_{\textbf{X}})$ minimizes the failure-inducing configuration $c_{\textbf{X}}$. It returns a configuration $c_{\textbf{X}}' = ddmin(c_{\textbf{X}})$ such that $c_{\textbf{X}}' \subseteq c_{\textbf{X}}$ and $test(c_{\textbf{X}}') = \textbf{X}$ hold and $c_{\textbf{X}}'$ is a *relevant configuration* — that is, no single circumstance of $c_{\textbf{X}}'$ can be removed from $c_{\textbf{X}}'$ to make the failure disappear.

The *ddmin* algorithm is defined as $ddmin(c_{\textbf{X}}) = ddmin'(c_{\textbf{X}}', 2)$ with

$ddmin'(c_{\textbf{X}}', n)$

$$
= \begin{cases}
c_{\textbf{X}}' & \text{if } |c_{\textbf{X}}'| = 1 \\
ddmin'(c_{\textbf{X}}' \setminus c_i, \max(n-1, 2)) & \text{else if } \exists i \in \{1..n\} \cdot test(c_{\textbf{X}}' \setminus c_i) = \textbf{X} \\
& \quad (\text{"some removal fails"}) \\
ddmin'(c_{\textbf{X}}', \min(2n, |c_{\textbf{X}}'|)) & \text{else if } n < |c_{\textbf{X}}'| \text{ ("increase granularity")} \\
c_{\textbf{X}}' & \text{otherwise}
\end{cases}
$$

where $c_{\textbf{X}}' = c_1 \cup c_2 \cup \cdots \cup c_n$ such that $\forall c_i, c_j \cdot c_i \cap c_j = \emptyset \wedge |c_i| \approx |c_j|$ holds.
The recursion invariant (and thus precondition) for *ddmin'* is $test(c_{\textbf{X}}') = \textbf{X} \ \wedge n \leq |c_{\textbf{X}}'|$.

LIST 5.2 The *ddmin* algorithm in a nutshell.

ddmin is a "minimizing" variant of delta debugging.) Delta debugging again is an instance of *adaptive testing*—a series of tests in which each test depends on the results of earlier tests.

Let's turn the abstract *ddmin* algorithm into a concrete implementation. Example 5.4 shows a PYTHON implementation of *ddmin*, in which *ddmin*'s tail recursion and existential quantifiers have been changed into nested loops. The implementation relies on a function split(l, n), which splits a list l into n

```python
def ddmin(circumstances, test):
    """Return a sublist of CIRCUMSTANCES that is a
       relevant configuration with respect to TEST."""

    assert test([]) == PASS
    assert test(circumstances) == FAIL

    n = 2      # Initial granularity

    while len(circumstances) >= 2:
        subsets = split(circumstances, n)
        assert len(subsets) == n

        some_complement_is_failing = 0
        for subset in subsets:
            complement = listminus(circumstances, subset)

            if test(complement) == FAIL:
                circumstances = complement
                n = max(n - 1, 2)
                some_complement_is_failing = 1
                break

        if not some_complement_is_failing:
            if n == len(circumstances):
                break
            n = min(n * 2, len(circumstances))
    return circumstances
```

EXAMPLE 5.4 A PYTHON implementation of the *ddmin* algorithm.

```python
def split(circumstances, n):
    """Split a configuration CIRCUMSTANCES into N subsets;
       return the list of subsets"""

    subsets = []    # Result
    start = 0       # Start of next subset
    for i in range(0, n):
        len_subset = int((len(circumstances) - start) /
                         float(n - i) + 0.5)
        subset = circumstances[start:start + len_subset]
        subsets.append(subset)
        start = start + len(subset)

    assert len(subsets) == n
    for s in subsets:
        assert len(s) > 0

    return subsets
```

EXAMPLE 5.5   A PYTHON implementation of the split() function.

sublists of roughly equal size (Example 5.5). The function listminus(c1, c2) returns a list of all elements that are in the list c1 but not in the list c2 (Example 5.6). The constants PASS, FAIL, and UNRESOLVED stand for ✔, ✗, and ?, respectively.

The while and if constructions have the usual meaning (as in C-like languages, the break statement leaves the enclosing loop). The assert statements document the preconditions and loop invariants.

In addition to these functions, we need an implementation of the test() function. Example 5.7 shows a (simplified) version of the test() function used by Zeller and Hildebrandt (2002) on a LINUX system. Essentially, it invokes a MOZILLA process and checks its outcome. If it exited normally (indicated by a zero exit status), test() returns ✔ (PASS). If it crashed (in UNIX: "terminated by a signal 11"), test() returns ✗ (FAIL), and if anything else happens, test() returns ? (UNRESOLVED).

The full-fledged implementation (not listed here) additionally replays recorded user interaction to trigger the failure (Chapter 4 "Reproducing Problems"). It also instruments a debugger (Chapter 8 "Observing Facts") to check

```python
def listminus(c1, c2):
    """Return all elements of C1 that are not in C2.
       Assumes elements of C1 are hashable."""

    # The hash map S2 has an entry for each element in C2
    s2 = {}
    for delta in c2:
        s2[delta] = 1

    # Check elements in C1 whether they are in S2
    c = []
    for delta in c1:
        if not s2.has_key(delta):
            c.append(delta)

    return c
```

EXAMPLE 5.6 A PYTHON implementation of the `listminus()` function.

the *backtrace*—the stack of functions active at the moment of the crash—and returns FAIL only if the found backtrace is identical to the backtrace of the original failure (that is, the program crashes at the same place in the same way).

What happens if we actually run this PYTHON implementation? Example 5.8 shows all tests conducted by delta debugging. The initial tests are run as sketched in Section 5.4—cutting away large chunks of input first, and smaller chunks later. At test 33, *ddmin* has actually reached the relevant input <SELECT>. The remaining tests demonstrate that every single character in <SELECT> is relevant for the failure to occur.

This property—every remaining circumstance in $c'_{\mathbf{x}} = ddmin(c_{\mathbf{x}})$ being relevant—is a general property of *ddmin*. Such a configuration is called *relevant configuration* or a *1-minimal configuration* (see Definition A.11 for details). It can be easily proven (Proposition A.12) that every configuration returned by *ddmin* is relevant because *ddmin* can return $c'_{\mathbf{x}}$ only after it tried removing every single element and the failure did not occur for any such configuration.

```python
def test(c):
    # Create Mozilla input file
    write_html(c, "input.html")

    parent = os.fork()
    if parent < 0:
        # fork() failed - no more processes
        sys.exit(1)

    elif not parent:
        # Invoke Mozilla
        # TODO: Replay user interaction, too
        os.execv("/usr/bin/mozilla",
                 ["mozilla", "input.html"])

    # Wait for Mozilla to complete
    childpid, status = os.waitpid(parent, 0)
    if os.WIFEXITED(status):
        exit_status = os.WEXITSTATUS(status)
        if exit_status == 0:
            return PASS     # Exited normally

    if os.WIFSIGNALED(status):
        caught_signal = os.WTERMSIG(status)
        if caught_signal == 11:
            # TODO: Check backtrace, too
            return FAIL     # Crashed w/ signal 11

    return UNRESOLVED
```

EXAMPLE 5.7 A (simplified) PYTHON implementation of the test() function.

One should note, though, that $c'_{\mathbf{x}}$ is not necessarily the *minimal* configuration for which the failure still occurs. To find that out, an algorithm would have to test every subset of $c'_{\mathbf{x}}$ — that is, $2^{|c'_{\mathbf{x}}|}$ tests.

Input: **`<SELECT_NAME="priority"_MULTIPLE_SIZE=7>`** ⟨40 characters⟩ ✗
`<SELECT_NAME="priority"_MULTIPLE_SIZE=7>` ⟨0 characters⟩ ✓

1   `<SELECT_NAME="priority"_MULTIPLE_SIZE=7>`⟨20⟩✓
2   `<SELECT_NAME="priority"_MULTIPLE_SIZE=7>`⟨20⟩✓
3   `<SELECT_NAME="priority"_MULTIPLE_SIZE=7>`⟨30⟩✓
4   `<SELECT_NAME="priority"_MULTIPLE_SIZE=7>`⟨30⟩✗
5   `<SELECT_NAME="priority"_MULTIPLE_SIZE=7>`⟨20⟩✓
6   `<SELECT_NAME="priority"_MULTIPLE_SIZE=7>`⟨20⟩✗
7   `<SELECT_NAME="priority"_MULTIPLE_SIZE=7>`⟨10⟩✓
8   `<SELECT_NAME="priority"_MULTIPLE_SIZE=7>`⟨10⟩✓
9   `<SELECT_NAME="priority"_MULTIPLE_SIZE=7>`⟨15⟩✓
10 `<SELECT_NAME="priority"_MULTIPLE_SIZE=7>`⟨15⟩✓
11 `<SELECT_NAME="priority"_MULTIPLE_SIZE=7>`⟨15⟩✗
12 `<SELECT_NAME="priority"_MULTIPLE_SIZE=7>`⟨10⟩✓
13 `<SELECT_NAME="priority"_MULTIPLE_SIZE=7>`⟨10⟩✓
14 `<SELECT_NAME="priority"_MULTIPLE_SIZE=7>`⟨10⟩✓
15 `<SELECT_NAME="priority"_MULTIPLE_SIZE=7>`⟨12⟩✓
16 `<SELECT_NAME="priority"_MULTIPLE_SIZE=7>`⟨13⟩✓
17 `<SELECT_NAME="priority"_MULTIPLE_SIZE=7>`⟨12⟩✓
18 `<SELECT_NAME="priority"_MULTIPLE_SIZE=7>`⟨13⟩✗
19 `<SELECT_NAME="priority"_MULTIPLE_SIZE=7>`⟨10⟩✓
20 `<SELECT_NAME="priority"_MULTIPLE_SIZE=7>`⟨10⟩✓
21 `<SELECT_NAME="priority"_MULTIPLE_SIZE=7>`⟨11⟩✓
22 `<SELECT_NAME="priority"_MULTIPLE_SIZE=7>`⟨10⟩✗
23 `<SELECT_NAME="priority"_MULTIPLE_SIZE=7>`⟨7⟩✓
24 `<SELECT_NAME="priority"_MULTIPLE_SIZE=7>`⟨8⟩✓
25 `<SELECT_NAME="priority"_MULTIPLE_SIZE=7>`⟨7⟩✓
26 `<SELECT_NAME="priority"_MULTIPLE_SIZE=7>`⟨8⟩✓
27 `<SELECT_NAME="priority"_MULTIPLE_SIZE=7>`⟨9⟩✓
28 `<SELECT_NAME="priority"_MULTIPLE_SIZE=7>`⟨9⟩✓
29 `<SELECT_NAME="priority"_MULTIPLE_SIZE=7>`⟨9⟩✓
30 `<SELECT_NAME="priority"_MULTIPLE_SIZE=7>`⟨9⟩✓
31 `<SELECT_NAME="priority"_MULTIPLE_SIZE=7>`⟨8⟩✓
32 `<SELECT_NAME="priority"_MULTIPLE_SIZE=7>`⟨9⟩✓
33 `<SELECT_NAME="priority"_MULTIPLE_SIZE=7>`⟨8⟩✗
34 `<SELECT_NAME="priority"_MULTIPLE_SIZE=7>`⟨7⟩✓
35 `<SELECT_NAME="priority"_MULTIPLE_SIZE=7>`⟨7⟩✓
36 `<SELECT_NAME="priority"_MULTIPLE_SIZE=7>`⟨7⟩✓
37 `<SELECT_NAME="priority"_MULTIPLE_SIZE=7>`⟨7⟩✓
38 `<SELECT_NAME="priority"_MULTIPLE_SIZE=7>`⟨7⟩✓
39 `<SELECT_NAME="priority"_MULTIPLE_SIZE=7>`⟨6⟩✓
40 `<SELECT_NAME="priority"_MULTIPLE_SIZE=7>`⟨7⟩✓
41 `<SELECT_NAME="priority"_MULTIPLE_SIZE=7>`⟨7⟩✓
42 `<SELECT_NAME="priority"_MULTIPLE_SIZE=7>`⟨7⟩✓
43 `<SELECT_NAME="priority"_MULTIPLE_SIZE=7>`⟨7⟩✓
44 `<SELECT_NAME="priority"_MULTIPLE_SIZE=7>`⟨7⟩✓
45 `<SELECT_NAME="priority"_MULTIPLE_SIZE=7>`⟨7⟩✓
46 `<SELECT_NAME="priority"_MULTIPLE_SIZE=7>`⟨7⟩✓
47 `<SELECT_NAME="priority"_MULTIPLE_SIZE=7>`⟨7⟩✓
48 `<SELECT_NAME="priority"_MULTIPLE_SIZE=7>`⟨7⟩✓

Result: **`<SELECT>`**

EXAMPLE 5.8 Simplifying by characters.

5.6 SIMPLIFYING USER INTERACTION

Delta debugging can be applied to all inputs, as described in Chapter 4 "Reproducing Problems." For instance, one can use it to simplify *user input* — leaving only the relevant key strokes and mouse movements in the script. This is especially useful if it is used anyway to reproduce the failure, as in the case of the MOZILLA crash.

To reproduce the failure, Zeller and Hildebrandt recorded 95 user events, such as pressing keys or buttons and moving the mouse. Replaying these 95 events reproduced the failure — but are they all necessary?

Figure 5.2 shows the progress of *ddmin* applied to these 95 events. The (logarithmic) Y axis shows the number of events $|c'_\mathbf{x}|$ left to be simplified; the (linear) X axis shows the number of tests executed so far. After 82 tests, *ddmin* has simplified the user interaction to only three events:

- Press the *P* key while the *Alt* modifier key is held. (Invoke the *Print* dialog.)

- Press the *left mouse button* on the *Print* button without a modifier. (Arm the *Print* button.)

- Release the *left mouse button*. (Start printing.)

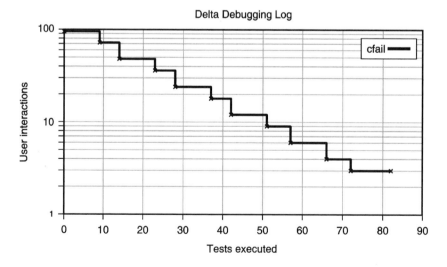

FIGURE 5.2 Simplifying MOZILLA user interactions. After 82 tests, *ddmin* has determined three events out of 95 that are required to produce the failure: Pressing Alt+P, pressing the mouse button, and releasing it again.

Irrelevant user actions include moving the mouse pointer, selecting the *Print to File* option, altering the default file name, setting the print margins to *.50*, and releasing the *P* key before clicking on *Print* (all of this is irrelevant in producing the failure). (It *is* relevant, though, that the mouse button be pressed before it is released.)

In addition to input in general, delta debugging can be applied to circumstances as they occur during the program run or during the program development. Chapter 13 "Isolating Failure Causes" discusses how to generalize delta debugging to automatically find actual causes in input, code changes, or schedules. Chapter 14 "Isolating Cause-Effect Chains" extends this to isolating cause-effect chains within program runs.

5.7 RANDOM INPUT SIMPLIFIED

Another application of automated simplification is to use it in conjunction with *random testing.* The basic idea is to generate large random inputs that trigger a failure and then to simplify the input to reveal the relevant part.

In a classical experiment, Miller et al. (1990) examined the robustness of UNIX utilities and services by sending them *fuzz input* — a large number of random characters. The studies showed that in the worst case 40% of the basic programs crashed or went into infinite loops when being fed with fuzz input.

Zeller and Hildebrandt subjected a number of UNIX utilities to fuzz input of up to a million characters until they showed a failure — and then used *ddmin* to simplify the failure-inducing input. The first group of programs showed obvious *buffer overrun* problems:

- FLEX (fast lexical analyzer generator), the most robust utility, crashed on sequences of 2,121 or more nonnewline and non-NUL characters.

- UL (underlining filter) crashed on sequences of 516 or more printable nonnewline characters.

- UNITS (convert quantities) crashed on sequences of 77 or more 8-bit characters.

The second group of programs appeared vulnerable to *random commands*:

- The document formatters NROFF and TROFF crashed

- on *malformed commands* such as \D^J%0F and

- on *8-bit input* such as $\hat{A}$ (ASCII code 194).

• CRTPLOT crashed on one-letter inputs t and f.

All of these simplified test cases can directly be associated to a piece of code that handles these inputs — and thus to the defect in question.

5.8 SIMPLIFYING FASTER

As Zeller and Hildebrandt report, the number of tests required increased with the length of the simplified input. Whereas the NROFF and TROFF tests typically required about 100 to 200 test runs, the FLEX tests required 11,000 to 17,960 test runs. Although a single test run need not take more than a few hundredths of a second, this raises the question on how to reduce the number of test cases and to improve the speed.

As shown in Example 5.8, simplifying a configuration $c_{\mathbf{x}}$ with *ddmin* requires at least $|c'_{\mathbf{x}}|$ tests, as every single circumstance in the resulting $c'_{\mathbf{x}}$ must be tested once. In the worst case, the number of tests can even be quadratic with respect to $|c_{\mathbf{x}}|$, resulting in a maximum number of tests $t = (|c_{\mathbf{x}}|^2 + 7|c_{\mathbf{x}}|)/2$ (for details, see Proposition A.13). Although this is a quite pathological example, we should strive to get simplification done as quickly as possible.

5.8.1 Caching

The *ddmin* algorithm does not guarantee that each configuration is tested only once. Hence, our simple ddmin() implementation in Example 5.4 may invoke the test function multiple times for the same configuration. In Example 5.8, for instance, the six tests runs 41 through 45 and 48 have been executed before. By using a cache to store test outcomes, one could return the earlier test outcome whenever a test is repeated.

5.8.2 Stop Early

Why does it take so long to simplify the FLEX input? Figure 5.3 shows the first 500 steps of the *ddmin* algorithm. You can easily see that the size quickly decreases, but after about 50 tests progress is very slow (and continues this way for the next 10,500 tests).

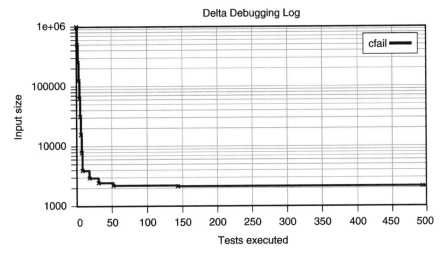

FIGURE 5.3 Simplifying FLEX input. Initially, *ddmin* quickly decreases the size of the input, but then simplifying shows no significant progress.

Normally, there is no need to try to squeeze the very last character out of an input. One can simply stop the simplification process:

- When a certain granularity has been reached ("We don't care about removing single characters")

- When no progress has been made ("In the last 100 iterations, the size of the input has been reduced by 1% only")

- When a certain amount of time has elapsed ("One hour of automatic simplification suffices")

In the case of FLEX, any of these heuristics could stop minimization early.

5.8.3 Syntactic Simplification

One effective way of speeding up simplification is to simplify not by characters but by *larger entities*. As shown in Figure 5.1, simplifying the HTML input by *lines* requires but 12 tests to get down to a single line. And indeed, if only *one* circumstance (i.e., one line) is failure-inducing it can be shown that *ddmin* is as efficient as a binary search (Proposition A.14).

This idea of *grouping* circumstances can be taken further by simplifying input not at the *lexical* level (i.e., characters, words, or lines) but at a *syntactical*

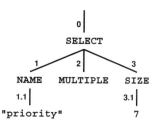

FIGURE 5.4 A HTML tree. Simplifying such a tree structure rather than plain text yields better performance.

level — that is, simplifying while preserving the syntactic structure of the input. The basic idea of syntactic simplification is to turn the input into a tree (formally, a *syntax tree*) and to simplify the tree rather than the input string. An HTML or XML tree representing our MOZILLA one-line example, for instance, would look like that shown in Figure 5.4.

To simplify such a tree, we make every *node* a *circumstance*. Our initial failing configuration thus contains six nodes rather than 40 characters. The *test* function accepting a configuration would remove missing nodes from the HTML tree (rather than cutting away chunks of the input string), and create an HTML input from the remaining tree and feed it to MOZILLA.

However, what would *test* do if asked by *ddmin* to test an *infeasible configuration*? In Figure 5.4, for instance, we cannot remove node 1, NAME, without also removing its child node 1.1, "priority". Vice versa, HTML rules dictate that the NAME attribute must have a value. The "priority" node is thus mandatory.

To cope with such syntactic and semantic constraints, the *test* function should be set up to simply return **?** ("unresolved") whenever a configuration is impossible to achieve. That is, *test* does not run MOZILLA, but immediately returns **?** such that *ddmin* selects the next alternative. Furthermore, the splitting of a configuration into subsets can be set up to take constraints into account — for instance, by also keeping nodes that are in the same subtree in the same subset.

Figure 5.5 shows the tests actually carried out within the *ddmin* run. Our initial configuration is $c_\textbf{x} = \{0, 1, 1.1, 2, 3, 3.1\}$, standing for "all nodes are present."

ddmin tries the configuration $\{2, 3, 3.1\}$, which is infeasible. Removing the second half works and gets us $c'_\textbf{x} = \{0, 1, 1.1\}$. In the next iteration, the configuration $\{1, 1.1\}$ is infeasible, but $\{0\}$ is fine. *ddmin* is done, having required just two actual tests to simplify the HTML input.

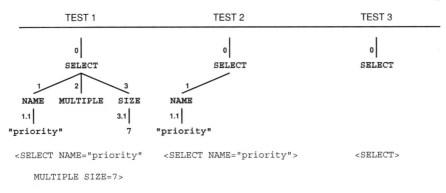

FIGURE 5.5 Simplifying an HTML tree in three steps.

```
<SELECT␣NAME="priority"␣MULTIPLE␣SIZE=7>   ⟨40 characters⟩   ✗
<SELECT␣NAME="priority"␣MULTIPLE␣SIZE=7>   ⟨39 characters⟩   ✓
```

EXAMPLE 5.9 A failure-inducing difference. The initial < sign is isolated as failure cause.

5.8.4 Isolate Differences, Not Circumstances

Instead of simplifying *all* circumstances, one can also simplify a *difference* between a configuration that works and a configuration that fails. The following is an example that illustrates this idea. Example 5.9 again shows two MOZILLA inputs: one that makes MOZILLA fail and one that makes it pass. Neither of these two inputs is simplified. However, their *difference* has been simplified to just one character — the leading < sign. If the < sign is missing, MOZILLA interprets the input as ordinary text instead of as an HTML tag. Hence, whether the < is part of the input or not determines whether MOZILLA fails or not.

Why would one want to simplify differences? There are two answers.

- *Focusing:* As we will see in Chapter 12 "Causes and Effects," a difference between a configuration that works and a configuration that fails is a *failure cause* — and this failure cause is more precise the smaller the difference is. Hence, a small difference can pinpoint the problem cause in a common context.

  As an example of a common context, think about simplifying user interactions. Minimizing user interaction may still end up in 1,000 interactions or so, all required to set up the context in which the failure occurs. Isolating a difference, though, will reveal a (minimal) difference that decides the final outcome: "If the user had not selected this option, the test would have passed."

- *Efficiency:* Differences can be simplified faster than entire configurations. This is so because each passing test can be exploited to reduce the difference. Using minimization, only failing tests help in minimizing the configuration. As an example of efficiency, an algorithm that isolates the single < difference requires only five tests (compared to the 48 tests in Example 5.8).

More on the isolation of failure causes automatically, as well as a discussion of the involved algorithms and techniques, can be found in Chapter 13 "Isolating Failure Causes."

5.9 CONCEPTS

- The aim of simplification is to create a simple *test case* from a detailed problem report (Section 5.1).

- Simplified test cases (Section 5.2):

  - Are easier to communicate

  - Facilitate debugging

  - Identify duplicate problem reports

HOW TO
- *To simplify a test case,* remove all irrelevant circumstances. A circumstance is irrelevant if the problem occurs regardless of whether the circumstance is present or not (Section 5.3).

HOW TO
- *To automate simplification,* set up:

  - An *automated test* that checks whether the problem occurs

  - A *strategy* that determines the relevant circumstances

  One such strategy is the *ddmin delta debugging algorithm* (Section 5.4).

- Circumstances to be simplified include not only the program input as data but all circumstances that might affect the program's outcome—for instance, user interactions (Section 5.6).

✎ Simplification can be combined with *random testing* to reveal the failure-inducing parts of the input.

✎ *To speed up automatic simplification*, employ one or more of the following. **HOW TO**

- Make use of caching

- Stop early

- Simplify at a syntactic or semantic level

- Isolate failure-inducing differences rather than circumstances

These techniques are described in Section 5.8.

5.10 TOOLS

Delta Debugging

A full PYTHON implementation of *ddmin* is available at:

http://www.st.cs.uni-sb.de/dd/

Simplification Library

Daniel S. Wilkerson of the University of California at Berkeley has another implementation of *ddmin*. This is found at:

http://freshmeat.net/projects/delta/

5.11 FURTHER READING

Manual simplification of test cases is a long-known programming (or debugging) technique. I recommend Kernighan and Pike (1999) for anyone who wants further depth on the subject. McConnell (1993) also highlights the importance of simplifying a test case as the first step in debugging.

The principle of *divide-and-conquer* is often attributed to the Romans ("divide et impera") as a governing principle. Its first explicit usage as a political maxime was by the Florentine political philosopher Niccolò Machiavelli (1469–1527), denouncing the motto of Louis XI of France in dealing with his nobles.

As far as I know, the work of Zeller and Hildebrandt (2002) was the first general approach to automatic test case simplification. Details on delta debugging applied to program input are listed here. The article also includes a set of case studies, including an in-depth examination of the MOZILLA example. Ralf Hildebrandt and I had much fun conducting this research. I hope you'll have some fun reading the article.

Note that the *ddmin* algorithm as described in Zeller and Hildebrandt (2002) slightly differs from the version presented here. The "old" *ddmin* algorithm had an additional check whether one of the subsets c_i would fail — that is, $test(c_i) = ✘$ holds — and if so would reduce $c'_✘$ to c_i. This extra test has shown few benefits in practice, which is why it is not included here.

The Gecko BugAThon is still going on, and you can still contribute — automatically or manually. Have a look at:

```
http://www.mozilla.org/newlayout/bugathon.html
```

5.12 EXERCISES

For some of the following exercises, you need PYTHON or JAVA:

- Using PYTHON, you can start immediately, using the code examples in this chapter. PYTHON interpreters are available at:

  ```
  http://www.python.org/
  ```

- Using JAVA, you can use the JAVA class in Example 5.10 as a starting point. All it needs are `split()` and `listminus()` functions as those defined for PYTHON. The `test()` function is designed to be overloaded in a problem-specific subclass.

- If you know neither PYTHON nor JAVA, adapt the code to a language of your choice.

EXERCISE 5.1. The function `bool geegg(string s)` returns

```
import java.util.LinkedList;
import java.util.List;
import java.util.Iterator;

public class DD {
    // Outcome
    public static final int FAIL       = -1;
    public static final int PASS       = +1;
    public static final int UNRESOLVED = 0;

    // Return a - b
    public static List minus(List a, List b) { ... }

    // test function - to be overloaded in subclasses
    public int test(List config) { return UNRESOLVED; }

    // Split C into N sublists
    public static List split(List c, int n) { ... }

    // ddmin algorithm
    // Return a sublist of CIRCUMSTANCES that is a relevant
    // configuration with respect to TEST.
    public List ddmin(List circumstances_) {
        List circumstances = circumstances_;

        assert test(new LinkedList()) == PASS;
        assert test(circumstances) == FAIL;

        int n = 2;

        while (circumstances.size() >= 2) {
            List subsets = split(circumstances, n);
            assert subsets.size() == n;

            boolean some_complement_is_failing = false;
            for (int i = 0; i < subsets.size(); i++) {
                List subset = (List)subsets.get(i);
                List complement = minus(circumstances, subset);

                if (test(complement) == FAIL) {
                    circumstances = complement;
                    n = Math.max(n - 1, 2);
                    some_complement_is_failing = true;
                    break;
                }
            }

            if (!some_complement_is_failing) {
                if (n == circumstances.size())
                    break;
                n = Math.min(n * 2, circumstances.size());
            }
        }

        return circumstances;
    }
}
```

EXAMPLE 5.10 A delta debugging class in JAVA.

- true if the string s contains three g characters or more or

- true if s contains two e characters or more and

- false otherwise.

For instance, geegg("good eggs tomorrow") returns true, geegg("no eggs today") returns false.

Apply the *ddmin* algorithm on the 16-character input

```
a-debugging-exam
```

to find a 1-minimal input that still causes geegg() to return true. Record the individual inputs and test outcomes.

EXERCISE 5.2. As recent versions of MOZILLA tend to be much more stable, we shall simulate the "old" MOZILLA behavior using a test function. Implement a PYTHON or JAVA test() function that accepts a list of characters. If this character list contains <SELECT>, have it return FAIL, and PASS otherwise.

EXERCISE 5.3. Use your test() function to minimize the problem report in Figure 3.1 manually and systematically. How many executions of test() do you need?

EXERCISE 5.4. Using test(), split(), and listminus(), use your implementation of *ddmin* to simplify the problem report in Figure 3.1 automatically. If you simplify by lines, how many tests do you need?

EXERCISE 5.5. Repeat Exercise 5.4, simplifying the remaining line by characters.

EXERCISE 5.6. Repeat Exercise 5.4, simplifying syntactically. Use an XML parser to read in the HTML input. Use syntactic simplification as sketched in Section 5.8.3.

EXERCISE 5.7. Design an input and a test() function such that *ddmin* requires a maximum of test runs. [Hint: see Zeller and Hildebrandt (2002) for the discussion of worst-case behavior.]

EXERCISE 5.8. Design a split() function for plain text that attempts to keep paragraphs, lines, and words together as long as possible.

EXERCISE 5.9. The *ddmin* algorithm only finds one possible 1-minimal input (i.e., an input where removing any single character makes the the failure disappear). Sketch an extension of `ddmin()` that finds *all* possible 1-minimal inputs. Sketch its complexity.

EXERCISE 5.10. Isolating a minimal failure-inducing difference using only a *test* function has exponential complexity. Prove this claim.

Perfection is achieved not when you have nothing more to add, but when there is nothing left to take away.

— (ATTRIBUTED TO) ANTOINE DE SAINT-EXUPÉRY

## CHAPTER 6

SCIENTIFIC DEBUGGING

ONCE WE HAVE REPRODUCED AND SIMPLIFIED the problem, we must understand how the failure came to be. The process of obtaining a theory that explains some aspect of the universe is known as *scientific method*. It is also the appropriate process for obtaining problem diagnostics. We introduce the basic techniques for creating and verifying hypotheses, for making experiments, for conducting the process in a systematic fashion, and for making the debugging process explicit.

6.1 HOW TO BECOME A DEBUGGING GURU

Some people are true *debugging gurus*. They look at the code and point their finger at the screen and tell you: "Did you try X?" You try X and, voilà!, the failure is gone. Such *intuition* comes from experience with earlier errors — one's own errors or other people's errors — and the more experience you have the easier it is to identify potential error causes and set up accurate hypotheses. Thus, the good news is that you too will eventually become a debugging guru — if you live long enough to suffer through all of the failures it takes to gather this experience.

We can speed up this process by training our reasoning. How can we systematically find out why a program fails? And how can we do so without vague concepts of "intuition," "sharp thinking," and so on? What we want is a method of finding an explanation for the failure — a method that:

- *does not require a priori knowledge* (that is, we need no experience from earlier errors)

- *works in a systematic and reproducible fashion* such that we can be sure to eventually find the cause and reproduce it at will.

The key question for this chapter is thus:

> HOW DO WE SYSTEMATICALLY FIND AN EXPLANATION FOR A FAILURE?

6.2 THE SCIENTIFIC METHOD

If a program fails, this behavior is initially just as surprising and inexplicable as any newly discovered aspect of the universe. Having a program fail also means that our abstraction fails. We can no longer rely on our model of the program, but rather must explore the program independently from the model. In other words, we must approach the failing program as if it were a *natural phenomenon.*

In the natural sciences, there is an established method for developing or examining a theory that explains (and eventually predicts) such an aspect. It is called *scientific method* because it is supposed to summarize the way (natural) scientists work when establishing some theory about the universe. In this very general form, the scientific method proceeds roughly as follows.

1. Observe (or have someone else observe) some aspect of the universe.

2. Invent a tentative description, called a *hypothesis,* that is consistent with the observation.

3. Use the hypothesis to make *predictions.*

4. Test those predictions by *experiments* or further *observations* and modify the hypothesis in the light of your results.

5. Repeat steps 3 and 4 until there are no discrepancies between hypothesis and experiment and/or observation.

When all discrepancies are gone, the hypothesis becomes a *theory.* In popular usage, a theory is just a synonym for a vague guess. For an experimental scientist, though, a theory is a conceptual framework that explains earlier observations and predicts future observations—such as relativity theory or plate tectonics, for instance.

In our context, we do not need the scientific method in its full glory, nor do we want to end up with grand unified theories for everything. We should be perfectly happy if we have a specific instance for finding the causes of program failures. In this debugging context, the scientific method operates as follows.

1. Observe a failure (i.e., as described in the problem description).

2. Invent a *hypothesis* as to the failure cause that is consistent with the observations.

3. Use the hypothesis to make *predictions*.

4. Test the hypothesis by *experiments* and further *observations*:

    • If the experiment satisfies the predictions, refine the hypothesis.

    • If the experiment does not satisfy the predictions, create an alternate hypothesis.

5. Repeat steps 3 and 4 until the hypothesis can no longer be refined.

The entire process is illustrated in Figure 6.1. Again, what you eventually get is a theory about how the failure came to be:

• It explains earlier observations (including the failure).

• It predicts future observations (for instance, that the failure no longer appears after applying a fix).

In our context, such a theory is called a *diagnosis*.

6.3 APPLYING THE SCIENTIFIC METHOD

How is the scientific method used in practice? As an example in this chapter, consider the sample program as discussed in Chapter 1 "How Failures Come to Be." The sample program is supposed to sort its command-line arguments, but some defect causes it to fail under certain circumstances:

```
$ sample 11 14
Output: 0 11
$ _
```

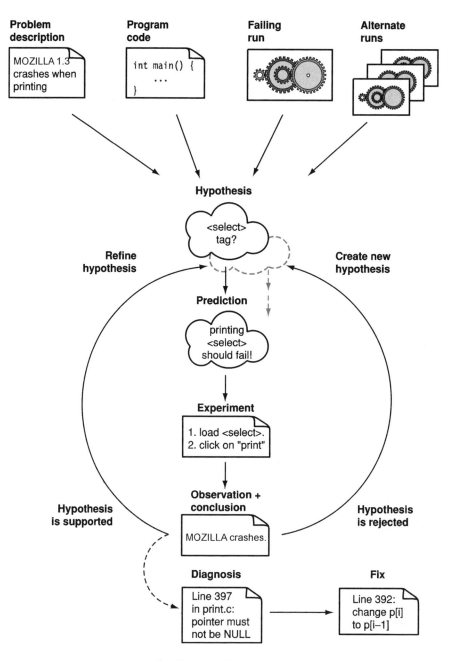

FIGURE 6.1 The scientific method of debugging.

In Section 1.4 we saw how to find the defect in the sample program — but in a rather *ad hoc* or unsystematic way. Let's now retell this debugging story using the concepts of scientific method.

6.3.1 Debugging sample — Preparation

We start with *writing down the problem*: what happened in the failing run and how it failed to meet our expectations. This easily fits within the scientific method scheme by setting up an initial hypothesis "The program works," which is then rejected. This way, we have observed the failure, which is the first step in the scientific method.

- *Hypothesis:* The sample program works.

- *Prediction:* The output of sample 11 14 is "11 14".

- *Experiment:* We run sample as previously.

- *Observation:* The output of sample 11 14 is "0 11".

- *Conclusion:* The hypothesis is *rejected*.

6.3.2 Debugging sample — Hypothesis 1

We begin with a little verification step: Is the zero value reported by sample caused by a zero value in the program state? Looking at Example 1.1, lines 38 through 41, it should be obvious that the first value printed (the zero) should be the value of a[0]. It is unlikely that this output code has a defect. Nonetheless, if it does we can spend hours and hours on the wrong trail. Therefore, we set up the hypothesis that a[0] is actually zero.

- *Hypothesis:* The execution causes a[0] to be zero.

- *Prediction:* a[0] = 0 should hold at line 37.

- *Experiment:* Using a debugger, observe a[0] at line 37.

- *Observation:* a[0] = 0 holds as predicted.

- *Conclusion:* The hypothesis is confirmed.

(What does "using a debugger" mean in practice? See Section 8.3.1 to find out.)

6.3.3 Debugging `sample` — Hypothesis 2

Now we must determine where the infection in a[0] comes from. We assume that shell_sort() causes the infection.

- *Hypothesis:* The infection does not take place until shell_sort().

- *Prediction:* The state should be sane at the beginning of shell_sort() — that is, a[] = [11, 14] and size = 2 should hold at line 6.

- *Experiment:* Observe a[] and size.

- *Observation:* We find that a[] = [11, 14, 0], size = 3 hold.

- *Conclusion:* The hypothesis is *rejected.*

6.3.4 Debugging `sample` — Hypothesis 3

Assuming we have only one infection site, the infection does *not* take place within shell_sort(). Instead, shell_sort() gets bad arguments. We assume that these arguments cause the failure.

- *Hypothesis:* Invocation of shell_sort() with size = 3 causes the failure.

- *Prediction:* If we correct size manually, the run should be successful — the output should be "11 14".

- *Experiment:* Using a debugger, we:

  1. Stop execution at shell_sort() (line 6).

  2. Set size from 3 to 2.

  3. Resume execution.

- *Observation:* As predicted.

- *Conclusion:* The hypothesis is confirmed.

6.3.5 Debugging `sample` — Hypothesis 4

The value of size can only come from the invocation of shell_sort() in line 36 — that is, the argc argument. As argc is the size of the array *plus 1,* we change the invocation.

- *Hypothesis:* Invocation of `shell_sort()` with `size` = `argc` (instead of `size` = `argc - 1`) causes the failure.

- *Prediction:* If we change `argc` to `argc - 1`, the "Changing argc to argc -1" run should be successful. That is, the output should be `"11 14"`.

- *Experiment:* In line 36, change `argc` to `argc - 1` and recompile.

- *Observation:* As predicted.

- *Conclusion:* The hypothesis is confirmed.

After four iterations of the scientific method, we have finally refined our hypothesis to a theory; the diagnosis "Invocation of `shell_sort()` with `argc` causes the failure." We have proven this by showing the two alternatives:

- With the invocation `argc`, the failure occurs.

- With the invocation `argc - 1`, the failure no longer occurs.

Hence, we have shown that the invocation with `argc` caused the failure. As a side effect, we have generated a *fix*—namely, replacing `argc` with `argc - 1` in line 36.

Note that we have not yet shown that the change induces *correctness*—that is, `sample` may still contain other defects. In particular, in programs more complex than `sample` we would now have to validate that this fix does not introduce new problems (Chapter 15 "Fixing the Defect" has more on this issue). In the case of `sample`, though, you can do such a validation by referring to a higher authority: Being the author of this book, I claim that with the fix applied there is no way `sample` could ever sort incorrectly. Take my word.

6.4 EXPLICIT DEBUGGING

In Section 6.3 we saw how to use the scientific method to establish the failure cause. You may have noticed that the process steps were quite *explicit*: we explicitly stated the hypotheses we were examining, and we explicitly set up experiments that supported or rejected the hypotheses.

Being explicit is an important means toward understanding the problem at hand, starting with the problem statement. Every time you encounter a problem, write it down or tell it to a friend. Just *stating* the problem in whatever way makes you rethink your assumptions — and often reveals the essential clues to the solution. The following is an amusing implementation, as reported by Kernighan and Pike (1999):

> One university center kept a Teddy bear near the help desk. Students with mysterious bugs were required to explain them to the bear before they could speak to a human counselor.

Unfortunately, most programmers are implicit about the problem statement, and even more so within the debugging process (they keep everything in their mind). But this is a dangerous thing to do. As an analogy, consider a *Mastermind game* (Figure 6.2). Your opponent has chosen a secret code, and you have a number of guesses. For each guess, your opponent tells you the number of tokens in your guess that had the right color or were in the right position.

FIGURE 6.2 A Mastermind game.

If you have ever played Mastermind and won, you have probably applied the scientific method.

However, as you may recall from your Mastermind experiences, you must remember all earlier experiments and their outcomes, in that this way you can keep track of all confirmed and rejected hypotheses. In a Mastermind game, this is easy, as the guesses and their outcomes are recorded on the board. In debugging, though, many programmers do not explicitly keep track of experiments and outcomes, which is equivalent to *playing Mastermind in memory.* In fact, forcing yourself to remember all experiments and outcomes prevents you from going to sleep until the bug is eventually fixed. Debugging this way, a "master mind" is not enough — you also need a "master memory."

6.5 KEEPING A LOGBOOK

A straightforward way of making debugging explicit and relieving memory stress is to write down all hypotheses and observations — that is, *keep a logbook.* Such a logbook can be either on paper or in some electronic form. Keeping a logbook may appear cumbersome at first, but with a well-kept logbook you do not have to keep all experiments and outcomes in memory. You can always quit work and resume next morning.

In *Zen and the Art of Motorcycle Maintenance*, Robert M. Pirsig writes about the virtue of a logbook in cycle maintenance:

Everything gets written down, formally, so that you know at all times where you are, where you've been, where you're going, and where you want to get. In scientific work and electronics technology this is necessary because otherwise the problems get so complex you get lost in them and confused and forget what you know and what you don't know and have to give up.

And beware — this quote applies to *motorcycle maintenance.* Real programs are typically much more complex than motorcycles. For a motorcycle maintainer, it would probably appear amazing that people would debug programs *without* keeping logbooks.

And how should a logbook be kept? Unless you want to share your logbook with someone else, feel free to use any format you like. However, your notes should include the following points, as applied in Section 6.3.

- *Statement* of the problem (a problem report, as in Chapter 2 "Tracking Problems," or, easier, a report identifier)

- *Hypotheses* as to the cause of the problem

Hypothesis	Prediction	Experiment	Observation	Conclusion
Infection in shell_sort()	At shell_sort() (Line 6), expect a[] = [11, 14] and size = 2	Observe a[] and size[]	a[] = [11,14,0] and size = 3	*rejected*
Invocation of shell_sort() with size = 3 causes failure	Setting size = 2 should make sample work	Set size = 2 using debugger	As predicted	*confirmed*

FIGURE 6.3 A debugging logbook (excerpt).

- *Predictions* of the hypotheses

- *Experiments* designed to test the predictions

- *Observed results* of the experiments

- *Conclusions* from the results of the experiments

An example of such a logbook is shown in Figure 6.3, recapitulating hypotheses 2 and 3 of Section 6.3. Again, quoting Robert Pirsig:

This is similar to the formal arrangement of many college and high-school lab notebooks, but the purpose here is no longer just busywork. The purpose now is precise guidance of thoughts that will fail if they are not accurate.

6.6 DEBUGGING QUICK-AND-DIRTY

Not every problem needs the full strength of the scientific method or the formal content of a logbook. Simple problems should be solved in a simple manner — without going through the explicit process. If we find a problem we suppose to be simple, the gambler in us will head for the lighter process. Why bother with formalities? Just think hard and solve the problem.

The problem with such an implicit "quick-and-dirty" process is to know when to use it. It is not always easy to tell in advance whether a problem is simple or not. Therefore, it is useful to set up a *time limit*. If after 10 minutes of quick-and-dirty debugging you still have not found the defect, go for the scientific method instead and write down the problem statement in the logbook.

Then, straighten out your head by making everything formal and exact — and feel free to take a break whenever necessary.

6.7 ALGORITHMIC DEBUGGING

Another way of organizing the debugging process is to *automate* it — at least partially. The idea of *algorithmic debugging* (also called *declarative debugging*) is to have a tool that guides the user along the debugging process *interactively*. It does so by asking the user about possible infection sources:

1. Assume an incorrect result R has the origins $O_1, O_2, \ldots, O_n$.

2. For each of the origins O_i, algorithmic debugging enquires whether the origin O_i is correct or not.

3. If one of the origins O_i is incorrect, algorithmic debugging restarts at step 1 with $R = O_i$.

4. Otherwise, all origins O_i are correct. Then, the infection must have originated at the place where R was computed from the origins. The process terminates.

Let's illustrate algorithmic debugging via an example. Example 6.1 shows a PYTHON sorting function: sort(L) is supposed to return a sorted copy of the list L. Unfortunately, sort() does not work properly: sort([2, 1, 3]) returns [3, 1, 2] rather than [1, 2, 3].

Our sort() function is based on *insertion sort*. It thus relies on a function insert(X, L), which returns a list where X is inserted between the elements of L: insert(2, [1, 3]) should return [1, 2, 3].

Figure 6.4 summarizes the execution of sort([2, 1, 3]) (a line stands for functions being invoked). Each invocation of sort(L) first calls itself for the tail of L and then calls insert() to insert the first element of L into the freshly sorted list.

The execution tree shown in Figure 6.4 now becomes the base for the algorithmic debugging process. Assume we have a tool that implements algorithmic debugging for PYTHON , working on the console. Such a tool would first ask us whether the end result is correct, which we decline:

sort([2, 1, 3]) = [3, 1, 2]? **no**

```
def insert(elem, list):
    """Return a copy of LIST with ELEM sorted in"""
    if len(list) == 0:
        return [elem]

    head = list[0]
    tail = list[1:]
    if elem <= head:
        return list + [elem]

    return [head] + insert(elem, tail)

def sort(list):
    """Return a sorted copy of LIST"""
    if len(list) <= 1:
        return list

    head = list[0]
    tail = list[1:]
    return insert(head, sort(tail))
```

EXAMPLE 6.1 A buggy insertion sort program.

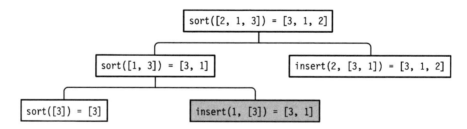

FIGURE 6.4 Execution tree of the sorting function in Example 6.1. Each computation of a function (top) relies on further function calls (below).

The error can originate either from sort([1, 3]) or the subsequent insert() call. Algorithmic debugging starts querying about the first origin:

sort([1, 3]) = [3, 1]? **no**

Again, the error could originate from the earlier sort([3]) call. Is the result correct?

```
sort([3]) = [3]? yes
```

Because the call sort([3]) = [3] was fine but sort([1, 3]) = [3, 1] is wrong, the error could have originated in the insert() call. It actually does, because insert(1, [3]) should return [1, 3], and not [3, 1]:

```
insert(1, [3]) = [3, 1]? no
```

As insert(1, [3]) invokes no further functions, we have isolated the defect. The infection originates at the call insert(1, [3]) = [3, 1] (shown in gray). Our algorithmic debugging tool reports:

```
An error has been localized in the body of insert().
```

We can even narrow down the infection to the code executing in the call insert(1, [3]). This leaves us with the return statement:

```
if elem <= head:
    return list + [elem]
```

This statement is wrong. If the element to be inserted is smaller than the head of the list, it should be inserted at the beginning rather than at the end. The statement thus must read:

```
if elem <= head:
    return [elem] + list
```

This fixes the sort() function from Example 6.1. With this fix applied, it sorts just fine.

The general idea of having an algorithm drive the debugging process is applicable to arbitrary debugging techniques. Wherever we search an error — and need to rely on human input to decide what is correct, right, or true — algorithmic debugging can drive the search in a systematic way. Unfortunately, algorithmic debugging has not been demonstrated to be effective for real-world applications:

- *The process does not scale.* In a large imperative program, there are millions and millions of functions being executed. Many of these functions communicate via shared data structures, rather than simple arguments and returned values. Worse yet, the data structures being accessed are far too huge to be checked manually. Imagine debugging a compiler: "Are these 4 megabytes of executable code correct? (yes/no)?"

For these reasons, algorithmic debugging works best for functional and logical programming languages. Functional and logical programs have few or no side effects — that is, there is no shared state that is updated, and the user does not have to check the entire program state. For logical languages such as PROLOG , an execution tree (Figure 6.4) becomes a proof tree, which is part of every program execution.

- *Programmers prefer driving to being driven.* The algorithmic debugging process, as implemented in early tools, is extremely rigid. Many programmers do not like being instrumented in such a mechanical way. Making the process user friendly in the sense that it provides *assistance* to programmers (rather than having the programmer assist the tool) is an open research issue.

  It is conceivable that future tools, combined with the analysis techniques defined in this book, will provide guidance to the programmer by asking the right questions. In particular, one can think of programmers providing specifications of particular function properties — specifications that can then be reused for narrowing down the incorrect part.

All of these problems disappear if we replace the programmer being queried by an *oracle* — an automatic device that tells correctness from noncorrectness. To determine its result, such an oracle would use an external specification. In this book, however, we assume that there is no such specification (except from the final test outcome) — at least not in a form a mechanical device could make use of it. Therefore, scientific method still needs human interaction.

6.8   DERIVING A HYPOTHESIS

Scientific method gives us a general process for turning a hypothesis into a theory — or, more specifically, an initial guess into a diagnosis. But still, within each iteration of the scientific method we must come up with a new hypothesis. This is the creative part of debugging: thinking about the many ways a failure could have come to be. This creative part is more than just mechanically enumerating possible origins, as in algorithmic debugging.

Unfortunately, being creative is not enough: we must also be *effective*. The better our hypotheses the less iterations we need and the faster the diagnosis is done. To be effective, we need to leverage as many knowledge sources as possible. These are the *ingredients of debugging*, as shown in Figure 6.1.

● *The description of the problem:* Without a concise description of the problem, you will not be able to tell whether the problem is solved or not. A simplified problem report also helps. In Chapter 2 "Tracking Problems" we saw examples of such descriptions, and discussed the issues of tracking problems. Chapter 5 "Simplifying Problems" provided details on the simplification of problem reports.

● *The program code:* The program code is the common abstraction across all possible program runs, including the failing run. It is the basis for almost all debugging techniques.

   Without knowledge about the internals of the program, you can only observe concrete runs (if any) without ever referring to the common abstraction. Lack of program code makes understanding (and thus debugging) much more difficult. As you cannot recreate the program from code, you must *work around defects,* which is far less satisfactory than fixing the code itself.

   As an example, consider the sort() algorithmic debugging session in Section 6.7. In principle, we (as users) could have run the session without knowing the source code. To determine whether a result is correct or not, all we need is a specification. However, the tool itself must have access to the code (Example 6.1) in order to trace and instrument the individual function calls. Chapter 7 "Deducing Errors" discusses techniques for reasoning from the (abstract) program code to the (concrete) program run — including the failing run.

● *The failing run:* The program code allows you to *speculate* about what may be going on in a concrete failing run. If you actually *execute* the program such that the problem is reproduced, you can observe actual *facts* about the concrete run. Such facts include the code being executed and the program state as it evolves. These observation techniques are the bread and butter of debugging.

   Again, debugging the sort() code in Example 6.1 becomes much easier once one can talk about a concrete (failing) run. In principle, one could do without observation. This is fine for proving abstract properties but bad for debugging concrete problems.

Chapter 8 "Observing Facts" discusses techniques with which programmers can observe concrete runs. Chapter 10 "Asserting Expectations" extends these techniques to have the computer detect violations automatically.

- *Alternate runs:* A single run of a nontrivial program contains a great deal of information, and thus we need a means of focusing on specific aspects of the execution. In debugging, we are most interested in *anomalies* — those aspects of the failing run that *differ* from "normal" passing runs. For this purpose, we must know which "normal" runs exist, what their common features are, and how these differ in the failing run.

  In the sort() example, algorithmic debugging has used alternate runs of individual functions to narrow down the defect. From the fact that sort([3]) worked, and sort([1, 3]) failed, algorithmic debugging could deduce that the error must have originated in the insert() call taking place between the two sort() calls.

  In practice, we seldom have a specification available to tell us whether some aspect of a run is correct or not. Yet, with a sufficient number of alternate runs we can classify what is "normal" or not. Chapter 11 "Detecting Anomalies" discusses automated techniques for detecting and expressing commonalities and anomalies across multiple runs.

- *Earlier hypotheses:* Depending on the outcome of a scientific method experiment, one must either *refine* or *reject* a hypothesis. In fact, every new hypothesis must

  - *include* all earlier hypotheses that passed (whose predictions were satisfied) and

  - *exclude* all hypotheses that failed (whose predictions were not satisfied).

Any new hypothesis must also explain all earlier *observations,* regardless of whether the experiment succeeded or failed — and it should be different enough from earlier hypotheses to quickly advance toward the target. Again, the algorithmic debugging session is a straightforward example of how the results of earlier tests (i.e., answers given by the user) drive the scientific method and thus the debugging process. The final diagnosis of insert() having a defect fits all passed hypotheses and explains all earlier observations.

To automate the process, we would like to reuse earlier hypotheses without asking the user for assistance. If a hypothesis is about a cause (such as a failure cause), the search for the actual cause can be conducted systematically by narrowing the difference between a passing and a failing scenario. These techniques can be automated and applied to program runs. Chapter 13 "Isolating Failure Causes" discusses automating the search for failure-inducing circumstances. Chapter 14 "Isolating Cause-Effect Chains" does the same for program states.

6.9 REASONING ABOUT PROGRAMS

Depending on the ingredients that come into play, humans use different reasoning techniques to learn about programs. These techniques form a *hierarchy,* as shown in Figure 6.5.

- *Deduction:* Deduction is reasoning from the general to the particular. It lies at the core of all reasoning techniques. In program analysis, deduction is used for reasoning from the program code (or other abstractions) to concrete runs — especially for deducing what can or cannot happen. These deductions take the form of mathematical proofs. If the abstraction is true, so are the deduced properties. Because deduction does not require any knowledge about the concrete, it is not required that the program in question actually be executed.

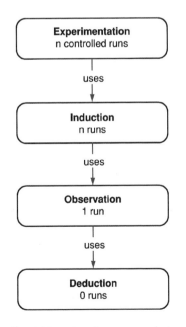

FIGURE 6.5 A hierarchy of program analysis techniques.

In this book, we call any technique *static analysis* if it infers findings without executing the program — that is, the technique is based on deduction alone. In contrast, *dynamic analysis* techniques use actual executions.

As Nethercote (2004) points out, this distinction of whether a program is executed or not may be misleading. In particular, this raises the issue of what exactly is meant by "execution." Instead, he suggests that *static techniques predict approximations of a program's future; dynamic analysis remembers approximations of a program's past.* Because in debugging we are typically concerned about the past, most interesting debugging techniques fall into the "dynamic" categories, which we discuss next.

- *Observation:* Observation allows the programmer to inspect arbitrary aspects of an individual program run. Because an actual run is required, the associated techniques are called *dynamic.* Observation brings in actual *facts* of a program execution. Unless the observation process is flawed, these facts cannot be denied.

  In this book, we call a technique *observational* if it generates findings or approximations from a *single execution* of the program. Most observational techniques make use of the program code in some form or another and thus also rely on deduction.

- *Induction:* Induction is reasoning from the particular to the general. In program analysis, induction is used to *summarize* multiple program runs (e.g., a test suite or random testing) to some abstraction that holds for all considered program runs. In this context, a "program" may also be a piece of code that is invoked multiple times from within a program — that is, some function or loop body.

  In this book, we call a technique *inductive* if it generates findings from *multiple executions* of the program. By definition, every inductive technique makes use of observation.

- *Experimentation:* Searching for the cause of a failure using scientific method (Chapter 6 "Scientific Debugging") requires a series of *experiments*, refining and rejecting hypotheses until a precise diagnosis is isolated. This implies multiple program runs that are *controlled* by the reasoning process.

  In this book, we call a technique *experimental* if it generates findings from *multiple executions* of the program that are *controlled* by the technique. By definition, every experimental technique uses induction and thus observation.

In the following chapters, we examine the most important of these techniques. We start with Chapter 7 "Deducing Errors," deducing hypotheses from the program code without actually executing the program. Chapter 8 "Observing Facts," Chapter 9 "Tracking Origins," and Chapter 10 "Asserting Expectations" focuses on observational techniques. Chapter 11 "Detecting Anomalies" discusses inductive techniques. Finally, Chapter 13 "Isolating Failure Causes" and Chapter 14 "Isolating Cause-Effect Chains" introduce experimental techniques.

6.10 CONCEPTS

✎ *To isolate a failure cause*, use *scientific method* (Section 6.2):   **HOW TO**

   1. Observe a failure (i.e., as described in the problem description).

   2. Invent a *hypothesis* as to the failure cause that is consistent with the observations.

   3. Use the hypothesis to make *predictions.*

   4. Test the hypothesis by *experiments* and further *observations:*

      • If the experiment satisfies the predictions, refine the hypothesis.

      • If the experiment does not satisfy the predictions, create an alternate hypothesis.

   5. Repeat steps 3 and 4 until the hypothesis can no longer be refined.

✎ *To understand the problem at hand*, make it explicit. Write it down or talk to   **HOW TO**
   a friend (Section 6.4).

✎ *To avoid endless debugging sessions*, make the individual steps explicit. Keep   **HOW TO**
   a logbook (Section 6.5).

✎ *To locate an error in a functional or logical program*, consider algorithmic   **HOW TO**
   debugging.

✎ Algorithmic debugging drives the debugging process by proposing hypotheses about error origins, which the user (or some oracle) must individually judge.

✎ *To debug quick-and-dirty*, think hard and solve the problem — but as soon   **HOW TO**
   you exceed some time limit go the formal way (Section 6.6).

✎ *To derive a hypothesis*, consider: **HOW TO**

- The problem description

- The program code

- The failing run

- Alternate runs

- Earlier hypotheses

See Section 6.8 for details.

HOW TO   ✎ *To reason about programs*, one can use four different techniques:

- Deduction (zero runs)

- Observation (one single run)

- Induction (multiple runs)

- Experimentation (multiple controlled runs)

All of these are discussed in further chapters.

6.11 FURTHER READING

Algorithmic debugging as a semiautomation of scientific method was conceived by Shapiro (1982) for logical programming languages such as PROLOG. In 1992, Fritzson et al. extended the approach to imperative languages, using program slicing (Section 7.4) to determine data dependences, and demonstrated the feasibility on a subset of PASCAL. The algorithmic debugging example session is based on Fritzson et al. (1992). In 1997, Naish generalized algorithmic debugging to the more general concept of declarative debugging.

Whereas the *scientific method* is the basis of all experimental science, it is rarely discussed or used in computer science. The reason is that computer science is concerned with artifacts, which are supposed to be fully under control and fully understood. However, as an unexpected failure occurs the artifact must be explored just like some natural phenomenon. For an early but still excellent book on experimental and statistical methods for data reduction, see *An Introduction to Scientific Research* by Wilson (1952). A more general book from the same period that remains useful today is *The Art of Scientific Investigation* by Beveridge (1957).

For philosophy of science, the undisputed classic is the work of Popper (1959), who coined the term *falsifiability* as the characteristic method of scientific investigation and inference. For Popper, any theory is scientific only if it is refutable by a conceivable event — which is why experiments play such a role in obtaining diagnoses.

The definitions of cause and effect in this book are called based on *counterfactuals,* because they rely on assumptions about nonfacts. The first counterfactual definition of causes and effects is attributed to Hume (1748): "If the first object [the cause] had not been, the second [the effect] never had existed." The best-known counterfactual theory of causation was elaborated by Lewis (1973), refined in 1986.

Causality is a vividly discussed philosophical field. Other than the counterfactual definitions, the most important alternatives are definitions based on *regularity* and *probabilism*. I recommend Zalta (2002) for a survey.

6.12 EXERCISES

EXERCISE 6.1. "We have reached a state where many programs are just as unpredictable as natural phenomena." Discuss.

EXERCISE 6.2. Using the logbook format (Section 6.5), describe the individual steps of the algorithmic debugging run in Section 6.7. Which are the hypotheses, predictions, and experiments?

EXERCISE 6.3. Simplification of tests, as discussed in Chapter 5 "Simplifying Problems," can be seen as an application of the scientific method. What are the hypotheses, predictions, and tests being used?

EXERCISE 6.4. Set up a logbook *form sheet* with entries such as "Prediction," "Observation," and so on such that programmers only need to fill in the gaps. Give them to fellows and collect their opinions.

EXERCISE 6.5. "I want to *archive* logbook entries, such that in case a similar problem occurs I may find hints on which hypotheses to use and which experiments to conduct." Discuss.

– How do they know the load limit on bridges, Dad?
– They drive bigger and bigger trucks over the bridge until it breaks.
  Then they weigh the last truck and rebuild the bridge.

— BILL WATTERSON,
Calvin and Hobbes (1997)

## CHAPTER 7

DEDUCING ERRORS

I N THIS CHAPTER, WE BEGIN EXPLORING THE TECHNIQUES for creating hypotheses introduced in Chapter 6. We start with *deduction* techniques — reasoning from the *abstract* program code to the *concrete* program run. In particular, we present *program slicing*, an automated means of determining possible origins of a variable value. Using program slicing, one can effectively narrow down the number of possible infection sites.

7.1 ISOLATING VALUE ORIGINS

Oops! We have observed something that should not happen — the program has reached some state it never should have reached. How did it get into this state? Kernighan and Pike (1999) give a hint:

Something impossible occurred, and the only solid information is that it really did occur. So we must think backwards from the result to discover the reasons.

What does "thinking backwards" mean here? One of the main applications of program code during debugging is to identify *relevant statements* that *could* have caused the failure — and, in the same step, to identify the *irrelevant statements* that *could not* have caused the failure in any way. This allows the programmer to neglect the irrelevant statements — and to focus on the relevant ones instead. These relevant statements are found by following back the *possible origins* of the result — that is, "thinking backward." As an example of relevant and irrelevant statements, consider the following piece of BASIC code.

```
10 INPUT X
20 Y = 0
```

```
30 X = Y
40 PRINT "X = ", X
```

This piece of code outputs the value of X, which is always a zero value. Where does this value come from? We can trace our way backward from the printing statement in line 40 and find that X's value was assigned from Y (line 30), which in turn got its zero value in line 20. The input to X in line 10 (and anything else that might be inserted before line 20) is irrelevant for the value of X in line 40.

Applying this relevant/irrelevant scheme, we can effectively narrow down our search space — simply by focusing on the relevant values and neglecting the irrelevant ones. This is sketched in Figure 1.5. During the execution of a program, only a few values (marked with exclamation points) can possibly influence the failing state. Knowing these relevant values can be crucial for effective debugging.

How does one determine whether a value (or a statement that generates this value) is relevant for a failure or not? To do so, we need not execute the program. We can do so by pure *deduction* — that is, reasoning from the abstract (program code) to what might happen in the concrete (run). By deducing from the code, we can abstract over *all* (or at least several) runs to determine properties that hold for all runs (for instance, properties about relevant and irrelevant values). The key question is:

> WHAT GENERAL ERRORS CAN WE DEDUCE FROM CODE ALONE?

7.2 UNDERSTANDING CONTROL FLOW

Deducing from program code is more than just sitting in front of the code and trying to understand it. A few basic principles can effectively guide the search for relevant values — and incidentally, these principles are the same for seasoned programmers as for automated analysis tools.

As an ongoing example, consider the fibo.c program shown in Example 7.1. This program displays the first nine members of the *Fibonacci sequence* $1, 1, 2, 3, 5, 8, \ldots$, in which each element is the sum of its two predecessors. Formally, the nth element of the Fibonacci sequence is defined as

$$fib(n) = \begin{cases} 1 & \text{for } n = 0 \vee n = 1 \\ fib(n-1) + fib(n-2) & \text{otherwise.} \end{cases}$$

Unfortunately, the implementation in Example 7.1 has a defect. Its output is:

```
$ gcc -o fibo fibo.c
$ ./fibo
fib(9)=55
fib(8)=34
fib(7)=21
fib(6)=13
fib(5)=8
fib(4)=5
fib(3)=3
fib(2)=2
fib(1)=134513905
$ _
```

As we see, the value of fib(1) is wrong. fib(1) should be 1 instead of the arbitrary value reported here.

How does the bad return value of fib(1) come to be? As an experienced programmer, you can probably identify the problem in half a minute or less (just read the source code in Example 7.1). Let's try, though, to do this in a little more systematic fashion — after all, we want our process to scale and we eventually want to automate parts of it.

The first thing to reason about when tracking value origins through source code is to identify those regions of code that could have influenced the value *simply because they were executed*. In our example, this is particularly easy. We only need to consider the code of the fib() function, as the defect occurs between its call and its return.

Because earlier statements may influence later statements (but not vice versa), we must now examine the *order* in which the statements were executed. We end up in a *control flow graph*, as shown in Figure 7.1. Such a graph is built as follows.

- Each statement of a program is mapped to a *node*. (In compiler construction — the origin of control flow graphs — statements that must follow each other are combined into nodes called *basic blocks*. In Figure 7.1, for instance, nodes 1 through 3 and 5 through 8 would form basic blocks.)

- Edges connecting the nodes represent the possible *control flow* between the statements — a possible execution sequence of statements. An edge from a

```
 1   /* fibo.c -- Fibonacci C program to be debugged */
 2
 3   #include <stdio.h>
 4
 5   int fib(int n)
 6   {
 7       int f, f0 = 1, f1 = 1;
 8
 9       while (n > 1) {
10           n = n - 1;
11           f = f0 + f1;
12           f0 = f1;
13           f1 = f;
14       }
15
16       return f;
17   }
18
19   int main()
20   {
21       int n = 9;
22
23       while (n > 0)
24       {
25           printf("fib(%d)=%d\n", n, fib(n));
26           n = n - 1;
27       }
28
29       return 0;
30   }
```

EXAMPLE 7.1 fibo.c prints out Fibonacci numbers — except for one.

statement A to a statement B means that during execution statement B may immediately be executed after statement A.

- An entry and exit node represent the beginning and the end of the program or function.

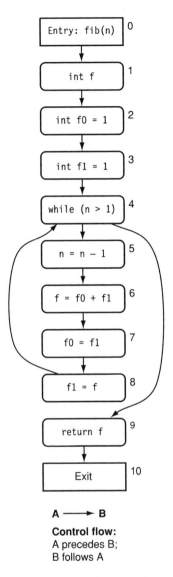

FIGURE 7.1 The fib() control flow graph.

In Figure 7.1, for instance, you can see that after f1 = f (Statement 8), we always have to check the loop condition (Statement 4) before possibly returning from fib() (Statements 9 and 10).

For structured programming languages such as C, a control flow graph (such as that shown in Figure 7.1) is straightforward to produce. All one needs is a

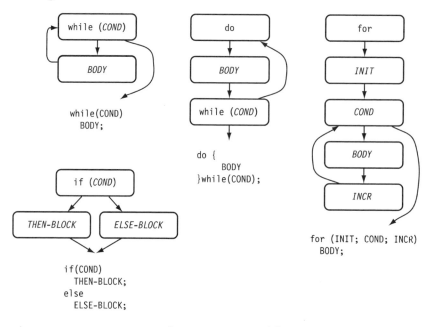

FIGURE 7.2 Some common control flow patterns.

pattern for each control structure, as sketched in Figure 7.2. The actual control flow graph for a program is composed from such patterns.

There are situations, though, where the control flow cannot be determined from such patterns. All of these impose difficult situations for debugging. List 7.1 outlines the most important caveats you should be aware of.

7.3 TRACKING DEPENDENCES

The control flow graph is the basis for all deduction about programs, as it shows how information propagates along the sequence of statements. Let's go a little more into detail here. Exactly how do individual statements affect the information flow? And how are statements affected by the information flow?

7.3.1 Effects of Statements

To contribute to the computation, every statement of the program must (at least potentially) affect the information flow in some way. We distinguish two types of effects.

- *Jumps and gotos.* A jump or *goto* is an unconditional transfer of control; goto 50 means to resume execution at line or label 50. Unconstrained gotos can make reasoning about programs much more difficult — in particular if they involve jumps into loop or function bodies. (In technical terms, this may make the control flow graph *unstructured* or *irreducible*.) Fortunately, most programmers (and languages) avoid goto statements as a whole or use them only to jump to the end of a block.

- *Indirect jumps.* Even more complicated than a goto to a specific line is a *computed* goto, also known as an indirect jump. A statement such as goto X transfers control to the statement or address as stored in the variable X.

  Unconstrained indirect jumps make reasoning about control flow very difficult because in principle they can be followed by an arbitrary statement. Fortunately, indirect jumps are almost exclusively used for dynamic function dispatch. The address of a function is taken from some table and then used for invocation. Languages such as C and C++ provide such mechanisms as *function pointers*.

- *Dynamic dispatch.* A very constrained form of indirect jumps is found in object-oriented languages. A call such as shape.draw() invokes the draw() method of the object referenced by shape. The actual destination of the call is resolved at runtime, depending on the class of the object. If the object is a rectangle, then Rectangle.draw() is called. If it is a circle, then Circle.draw() is called.

  Dynamic dispatch is a powerful tool, but also a frequent source of misunderstanding when reasoning about program code. For every method call, one must be aware of the possible destinations.

- *Exceptions.* By throwing an *exception*, a function can transfer control back to its caller, which either must handle the exception or rethrow it to its respective caller. (Instead of the caller, a surrounding block may also handle or rethrow the exception.)

  In the presence of exceptions, one must be aware that control may never reach the "official" end of a function but be transferred directly to the caller. Be sure that an exception does not go by unnoticed, such that you know that it has occurred.

LIST 7.1 Control flow caveats.

- *Write:* A statement can *change the program state* (i.e., assign a value to a variable). For example, the statement v1 = 1 writes a value to the variable v1.

  The "program state" considered here is a very general term. For instance, printing some text on an output device changes the state of the device. Sending a message across the network changes the state of attached devices. To some extent, the "program state" thus becomes the state of the world. Therefore, it is useful to limit the considered state—for instance, to the hardware boundaries.

- *Control:* A statement may *change the program counter*—that is, determine which statement is to be executed next. In Figure 7.1, the while statement determines whether the next statement is either 5 or 9. Obviously, we are only talking about *conditional* changes to the program counter here—that is, statements that have at least two possible successors in the control flow graph, dependent on the program state.

  In principle, one may consider the program counter as part of the program state. In practice, though, locations in the program state and locations in the program code are treated conceptually as separate dimensions of space and time. Figure 1.1 uses this distinction to represent the intuition about what is happening in a program run.

7.3.2 Affected Statements

Affecting the information flow by writing state or controlling execution represents the *active* side of how a statement affects the information flow. However, statements are also *passively* affected by other statements.

- *Read:* A statement can *read the program state* (i.e., read a value from a variable). For example, the statement v2 = v1 + 1 reads a value from the variable v1. Consequently, the effect of the statement is affected by the state of v1.

  Just as in writing state, the "program state" considered here is a very general term. For instance, reading some text from an input device reads the state of the device. Reading a message across the network reads the state of attached devices.

- *Execution:* To have any effect, a statement must be *executed*. Consequently, if the execution of a statement B is potentially controlled by another statement A, then B is affected by A.

TABLE 7.1 Effects of the `fib()` statements. Each statement read or writes a variable, or controls whether other statements are executed

	Statement	Reads	Writes	Controls
0	`fib(n)`		n	1–10
1	`int f`		f	
2	`f0 = 1`		f0	
3	`f1 = 1`		f1	
4	`while (n > 1)`	n		5–8
5	`n = n - 1`	n	n	
6	`f = f0 + f1`	f0, f1	f	
7	`f0 = f1`	f1	f0	
8	`f1 = f`	f	f1	
9	`return f`	f	⟨return value⟩	

For each statement S of a program, we can determine what part of the state is being read or written by S (as deduced from the actual program code), and which other statements are controlled by S (as deduced from the control flow graph). As an example, consider Table 7.1, which lists the actions of the statements in the `fib()` program.

7.3.3 Statement Dependences

Given the effects of statements as well as the statements thereby affected, we can construct *dependences* between statements, showing how they influence each other. We distinguish two types of dependences.

- *Data dependence:* A statement B is *data dependent* on a statement A if

  - A writes some variable V (or more generally, part of the program state) that is being read by B and

  - there is at least one path in the control flow graph from A to B in which V is not being written by some other statement.

  In other words, the outcome of A can influence the data read by B.

  Figure 7.3 shows the data dependences in the `fib()` program. By following the dashed arrows on the right-hand side, one can determine where the data being written by some statement is being read by another statement. For instance, the variable `f0` being written by Statement 2, `f0 = 1`, is read in Statement 6, `f = f0 + f1`.

- *Control dependence:* A statement B is *control dependent* on a statement A if B's execution is potentially controlled by A. In other words, the outcome of A determines whether B is executed.

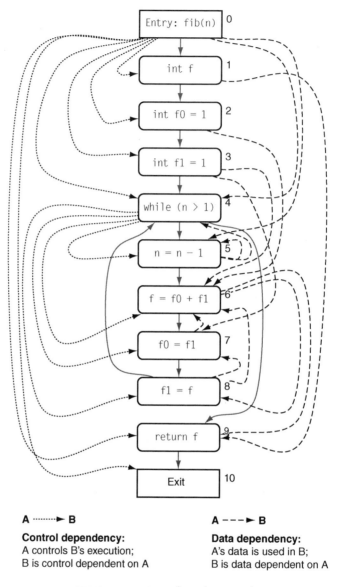

A ·······▶ **B**
Control dependency:
A controls B's execution;
B is control dependent on A

A ---▶ **B**
Data dependency:
A's data is used in B;
B is data dependent on A

FIGURE 7.3 fib() dependence graph.

The dotted arrows on the left-hand side of Figure 7.3 show the control dependences in fib(). Each statement of the body of the while loop is dependent on entering the loop (and thus dependent on the head of the while loop). All other statements are dependent on the entry of the function (as it determines whether the body is actually executed).

The control and data dependences of a program, as shown in Figure 7.3, form a graph — the *program dependence graph*. This graph is the basis for a number of program analysis techniques, as it reflects all influences within a program.

7.3.4 Following Dependences

Following the control and data dependences in the program dependence graph, one can determine which statements influence which other statements — in terms of data, control, or both. In particular, one can answer two important questions.

- *Where does this value go to?* Given a statement S writing a variable V, we can determine the impact of S by checking which other statements are dependent on S — and which other statements are dependent on these. Let's follow the dependences to see what happens when we call fib(). In Figure 7.3, the value of n is being used in the while head (Statement 4) as well as in the while body (Statement 4). Because the while head also controls the assignments to f, f0, and f1 (Statements 6 through 8), the value of n also determines the values of f, f0, and f1 — and eventually, the returned value f. This is how fib() is supposed to work.

- *Where does this value come from?* Given a statement S reading a variable V, we can determine the statements that possibly influenced V by following back the dependences of S. Let's now follow the dependences to see where the arbitrary value returned by fib(1) comes from. In Figure 7.3, consider the return value f in Statement 9. The value of f can come from two sources. It can be computed in Statement 6 from f0 and f1 (and, following their control dependences, eventually n). However, it also can come from Statement 1, which is the declaration of f. In the C language, a local variable is not initialized and hence may hold an arbitrary value. It is exactly this value that is returned if the while body is not executed. In other words, this is the arbitrary value returned by fib(1).

7.3.5 Leveraging Dependences

Following dependences through programs is a common technique for finding out the origins of values. But from where does one get the dependences?

Typically, programmers *implicitly* determine dependences while reading the code. Assessing the effect of each statement is part of understanding the program. Studies have shown that programmers effectively follow dependences

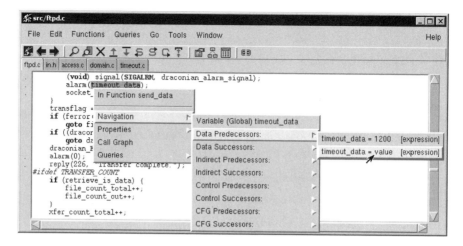

FIGURE 7.4 Following dependences in CODESURFER. For each variable, one can query the predecessors and successors along the dependence graph.

while debugging, either in a *forward* fashion to assess the impact of a statement or in a *backward* fashion to find out which other parts of the program might have influenced a statement. As Weiser (1982) puts it: "When debugging, programmers view programs in ways that need not conform to the programs' textual or modular structures." Thus, dependences become an important guide for *navigating through the code.*

Obtaining *explicit* dependences such that they can be leveraged in tools is also feasible and is part of several advanced program analysis tools. Figure 7.4 shows a screen-shot of the CODESURFER tool, one of the most advanced program analysis tools available. Rather than visualizing dependences as in Figure 7.3, CODESURFER allows programmers to explore the dependences interactively by navigating to predecessors and successors according to data and control dependences.

7.4 SLICING PROGRAMS

Using dependences, one can check for specific defect patterns and focus on specific *subsets* of the program being debugged (the subset that may have influenced a specific statement or the subset that may be influenced by a specific statement). Such a subset is called a *slice,* and the corresponding operation is called *slicing.*

7.4.1 Forward Slices

By following all dependences from a given statement A, one eventually reaches *all statements whose read variables or whose execution could ever be influenced by* A. This set of statements is called a *program slice*, or more specifically the *forward slice* of $S^F(A)$. Formally, it consists of all statements that (transitively) depend on A:

$$S^F(A) = \{B|A \rightarrow^+ B\}$$

In a slice $S^F(A)$, the originating statement A is called the *slicing criterion.*

As an example for a forward slice, consider Figure 7.3. The forward slice originating at Statement 2, f0 = 1, first includes Statement 6, f = f0 + f1. Via f, the slice also includes Statement 8, f1 = f, and Statement 9, return f. Via f1, the slice finally also includes Statement 7, f0 = f1. Overall, the forward slice $S^F(2)$ is thus $S^F(2) = \{2, 6, 7, 8, 9\}$.

More important than the statements included in a slice are the statements *not* included in a slice, in that these can be in no way affected by the original statement. In our case, the statements excluded are not just the Statements 0 and 1 (hardly surprising, as they are always executed *before* Statement 2) but Statements 4 and 5 — the head of the while loop. In other words, the execution of the while loop is independent of the initial value of f0.

7.4.2 Backward Slices

The term *forward slice* implies that there is also a backward slice. To compute the backward slice of B, one proceeds *backward* along the dependences. Thus, we can determine all statements that could have influenced B. This is most useful in determining where the program state at execution of B could have come from. Formally, the backward slice $S^B(B)$ is computed as

$$S^B(B) = \{A|A \rightarrow^* B\}.$$

Again, B is called the *slicing criterion* of $S^B(B)$.

As an example for a backward slice, again consider Figure 7.3. The backward slice of Statement 9, return f, first includes Statement 1, int f, and Statement 6, f = f0 + f1. Because Statement 6 is control dependent on the while loop, the slice also includes Statement 4, while (n > 1), and Statement 5, n = n + 1, on which Statement 4 is data dependent. Because f0 and f1 are computed in Statements 7 and 8 and are initialized in Statements 2 and 3, all of these statements also become part of the backward slice — which means that the slice includes *all statements* of fib(), or $S^B(9) = \{0, 1, 2, 3, 4, 5, 6, 7, 8, 9\}$.

Having *all* statements being included in the backward slice of a returned value is quite typical. After all, if some statement would *not* contribute to the computation this would be a code smell, as discussed in Section 7.5. However, if a function computes *multiple values* a backward slice for one of these values may well result in a true subset. As an example, consider the program in Example 7.2a, which computes the sum and the product of the range of integers $[a, b]$. The backward slice of write(mul), shown in Example 7.2b slices away all those parts that compute sum and cannot influence the computation or output of mul in any way.

7.4.3 Slice Operations

To further focus on specific behavior, one can *combine* several slices. Typical operations on slices include the following.

- *Chops:* The intersection between a forward and a backward slice is called a *chop*. Chops are useful for finding out *how* some statement A (originating the forward slice) influences another statement B (originating the backward slice).

    In the fib() program from Figure 7.3, for instance, a chop from Statement 3 to Statement 7 also includes Statements 6 and 8, thus denoting all possible paths by which the initial value of f1 could have influenced f0.

- *Backbones:* The *intersection* between two slices is called a *backbone slice*, or backbone for short. A backbone is useful for finding out those parts of an application that contribute to the computation of several values.

    As an example, consider the program shown in Example 7.2. The backbone of the two backward slices of write(sum) and write(mul) consists of those statements included in both slices — namely, a = read(), b = read(), while (a <= b), and a = a + 1.

    As the name suggests, backbones are central parts of the computation. In debugging, finding a backbone is most useful if one has multiple infected values at different places and wants to determine a possible common origin.

- *Dices:* The *difference* between two slices is called a *dice*. A dice is useful for finding out how the backward slice of some variable differs from the backward slice of some other variable.

    Again, consider the program shown in Example 7.2. If we subtract the backward slice of write(sum) from the backward slice of write(mul) (shown in the figure), all that remains is the initialization mul = 1 and the assignment mul = mul * a.

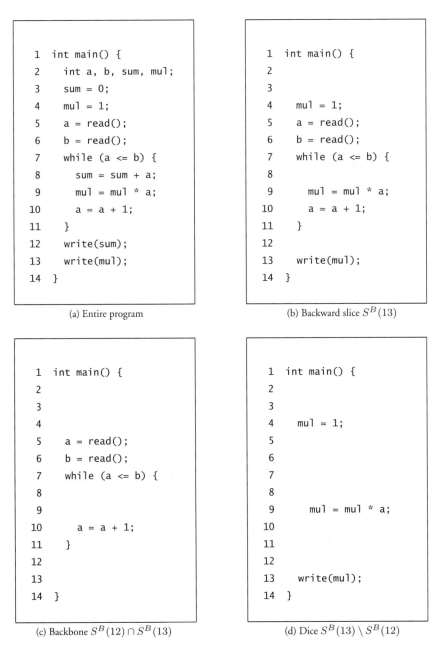

```
 1   int main() {
 2     int a, b, sum, mul;
 3     sum = 0;
 4     mul = 1;
 5     a = read();
 6     b = read();
 7     while (a <= b) {
 8       sum = sum + a;
 9       mul = mul * a;
10       a = a + 1;
11     }
12     write(sum);
13     write(mul);
14   }
```

(a) Entire program

```
 1   int main() {
 2
 3
 4     mul = 1;
 5     a = read();
 6     b = read();
 7     while (a <= b) {
 8
 9       mul = mul * a;
10       a = a + 1;
11     }
12
13     write(mul);
14   }
```

(b) Backward slice $S^B(13)$

```
 1   int main() {
 2
 3
 4
 5     a = read();
 6     b = read();
 7     while (a <= b) {
 8
 9
10       a = a + 1;
11     }
12
13
14   }
```

(c) Backbone $S^B(12) \cap S^B(13)$

```
 1   int main() {
 2
 3
 4     mul = 1;
 5
 6
 7
 8
 9       mul = mul * a;
10
11
12
13     write(mul);
14   }
```

(d) Dice $S^B(13) \setminus S^B(12)$

EXAMPLE 7.2 Slicing away irrelevant program parts.

Dices are most useful if one knows that a program is "largely correct" — that is, most of the values it computes are correct but some are not. By subtracting the backward slices of the correct variables from the backward slices of the infected variables one can focus on those statements that only contribute to the infected values — that is, those statements likely to cause the failure.

7.4.4 Leveraging Slices

Just like dependences, slices can be leveraged in programming environments, allowing programmers to explore slices and to explicitly ignore those parts of a program that are irrelevant for a specific behavior. As an example, consider the CODESURFER screen shot shown in Example 7.2, showing the program from Example 7.2a. The programmer has selected Statement 13, write(mul), as the slicing criterion and has chosen to view its backward slice. CODESURFER highlights all statements that are part of the backward slice. As in Example 7.2b, it turns out that the computation of sum has no influence whatsoever on the computation of mul.

In addition to displaying slices, CODESURFER can perform slice operations (as discussed in Section 7.4.3). This allows the programmer to further focus on possible failure origins.

7.4.5 Executable Slices

Comparing the backward slice as determined by CODESURFER with the slice as shown in Example 7.2b, you may notice a small difference: the CODESURFER slice also includes the declarations of a, b, and mul, whereas Example 7.2b does not. Could it be that CODESURFER determines dependences we do not know about?

The reason CODESURFER (Figure 7.5) includes the declarations in the slice is not that anything would depend on these declarations. (If something would, this would be an error, as discussed in Section 7.5.) CODESURFER includes these declarations because it attempts to make the slice *executable*. That is, the slice should be an "independent program guaranteed to represent faithfully the original program within the domain of the specified subset of behavior" (i.e., the state of the program as read by the slicing criterion). Because the program needs to be executable, all variables have to be declared, regardless of whether the declarations are actually part of some dependence or not. In our examples, though, we do not require the slice to be executable. Hence, we omit declarations if they are not involved in any dependence.

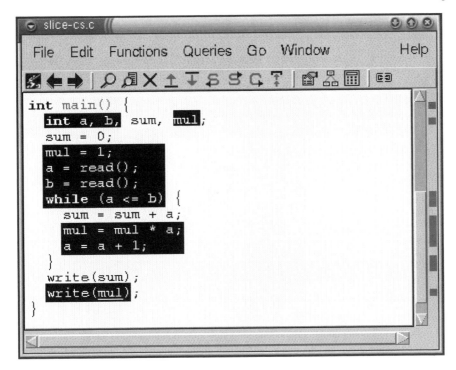

FIGURE 7.5 A program slice in CODESURFER. All statements that are part of the slice are highlighted.

7.5 DEDUCING CODE SMELLS

In Section 7.3.4 we saw how a data dependence from the uninitialized variable f caused the fib() program to fail. In general, we can assume that *any* read from an uninitialized variable is a bad idea, and we may thus easily qualify any such attempt as an error. In fact, a number of common errors can be directly detected from the dependence graph — that is, deduced from the program code alone.

- *Reading uninitialized variables:* Uninitialized variables, such as f in fib(), are a common source of errors. In terms of dependences, declarations such as int f should have no influence on any other statement. If they do, this should be considered an error.

  Compilers routinely determine variable usage and dependences when they *optimize* the generated code. Hence, they can easily report if some variable appears to be used although not initialized:

```
$ gcc -Wall -O fibo.c
fibo.c: In function 'fib':
fibo.c:7: warning: 'f' might be used uninitialized
           in this function
$ _
```

(The -O option turns on optimization, and the -Wall option turns on most warnings.) As the wording suggests, the compiler may err in reporting a variable as being used. This is illustrated by the following example.

```
int go;
switch (color) {
    case RED:
    case AMBER:
        go = 0;
        break;
    case GREEN:
        go = 1;
        break;
}
if (go) { ... }
```

Here, go is initialized if color is one of RED, AMBER, or GREEN. If color has another value, though, go will remain uninitialized. The compiler is unable to determine automatically whether color may take another value. Nonetheless, the compiler emits a warning such that the programmer can take a look at the code.

- *Unused values:* If some variable is written, but never read, this is likely to be an error. In the dependence graph, a write into such a variable translates into a statement on which no other statement is data dependent — in other words, a statement without any effect.

  Compilers (and derived program analysis tools) can also warn against unused values. However, as there are many ways to access a variable that may go unnoticed by the compiler (including access of other modules to global variables, access via pointers, and so on) the feature is typically limited to local variables.

- *Unreachable code:* If some code is never executed, this is likely to be an error. In the dependence graph, this translates into a statement that is not control dependent on any other statement.

In many simple cases, compilers can warn against unreachable code. Consider the following example.

```
if (w >= 0)
    printf("w is non-negative\n");
else if (w > 0)
    printf("w is positive\n");
```

The second `printf()` will never be executed because its condition is subsumed by the first condition. Its execution is dependent on no other statement. The compiler, being smart enough to notice the subsumption, issues a warning such as:

```
$ gcc -Wunreachable-code -O noop.c
noop.c:4: warning: will never be executed
$ _
```

Why do we have to enable warnings about unreachable code explicitly? The reason is that during debugging programmers frequently insert statements to observe the behavior (Chapter 8 "Observing Facts") or to check their expectations (Chapter 10 "Asserting Expectations"). Such statements may be written in such a way that executing them would show the presence of a failure. The following is an example.

```
switch (color) {
    case RED:
    case AMBER:
        go = 0;
        break;
    case GREEN:
        go = 1;
        break;
    default:
        printf("This can't happen\n");
        exit(1);
}
```

If the compiler reports that the `printf` statement is unreachable, this is actually a good sign. (At the same time, the warning about go used before initialization should also go away.)

If one of these conditions occurs, this typically is an error in the program in question. At the least it is a *code smell* that should be verified before the code goes into production.

So far, the code smells we have seen are all related to dependences concerning the usage of variables. In addition to these *general* dependences there are dependences that are specific to some language feature or runtime library — and again, such dependences can be leveraged to detect errors.

- *Memory leaks:* In languages without garbage collection, such as C or C++, the programmer is responsible for deallocating dynamic memory. If the last reference to a chunk of dynamic memory is lost, the chunk can no longer be deallocated (a *memory leak* occurs). Example 7.3 shows a C function that has a memory leak at return 0. The reference p to the memory allocated in line 4 is lost.

  Just as we tracked the effects of statements on variables in Table 7.1, we can track the effects of statements on dynamic memory. For each statement, we check whether it allocates, uses, or deallocates a chunk. We also check whether the reference to the chunk is still *live* — that is, accessible by other statements — and we can identify statements where a reference becomes *lost*, such as overwriting an existing reference or returning from a function in which the reference was declared a local variable. If there is a path in the control flow graph from an allocation to a statement where a chunk becomes

```
1   /* Allocate and read in SIZE integers */
2   int *readbuf(int size)
3   {
4       int *p = malloc(size * sizeof(int));
5       for (int i = 0; i < size; i++)
6       {
7           p[i] = readint();
8           if (p[i] == 0)
9               return 0;  // end-of-file
10      }
11
12      return p;
13  }
```

EXAMPLE 7.3 A potential memory leak. Upon premature return, memory pointed to by p is not deallocated.

dead without going through a deallocation first, this is a memory leak. In Example 7.3, such a path goes from line 4 to line 9.

• *Interface misuse:* In addition to memory, one can think of other resources that must be explicitly deallocated when they are no longer in use. As an example, consider *streams*. An input/output stream is first opened, but must be closed when it is no longer used. Checking for such conditions uses the same mechanisms as memory leaks. If there is a path in the control flow graph from a stream opening to a statement where the stream reference becomes dead without going through a closing first, this is an error. Similar techniques apply to resources such as locks, sockets, devices, and so on.

• *Null pointers:* In the same style as memory leaks, we can check whether a pointer being null may be accidentally referenced. This happens if there is a path from a statement in which a null pointer p is being initialized to a statement in which p is dereferenced without going through some assignment to p.

   In Example 7.3, for instance, the `malloc()` function may return a null pointer if no more memory is available. Consequently, in the expression `p[i]` the pointer p may be null, resulting in a potential runtime failure. Therefore, this error can be detected automatically. The code should be changed such that `malloc()` returning a null pointer ends in a user-friendly diagnosis.

Given a control flow graph, and basic data and control dependences, a tool that checks for such common errors is not too difficult to build. Some advanced compilers even have such built-in functionality. However, there are also external tools that are especially built for detecting code smells. As an example, consider the FINDBUGS tool for JAVA programs. FINDBUGS scans JAVA bytecode for *defect patterns* — that is, common programming errors (as those listed previously) — and highlights potential problems, as shown in Figure 7.6. Table 7.2 lists some of the most common defect patterns detected by FINDBUGS.

   Tools such as FINDBUGS are highly useful in detecting code smells before they end up in production code. One should keep in mind, though, that these tools can report *false positives* — that is, they can report possible influences where indeed there are not. The FINDBUGS authors, for instance, list a false positive rate of 50%, meaning that only every second smell reported by FINDBUGS is indeed an error. Programmers are well advised, though, to rewrite even those smells that are not errors — simply because this way they will not shown up in the next diagnostic.

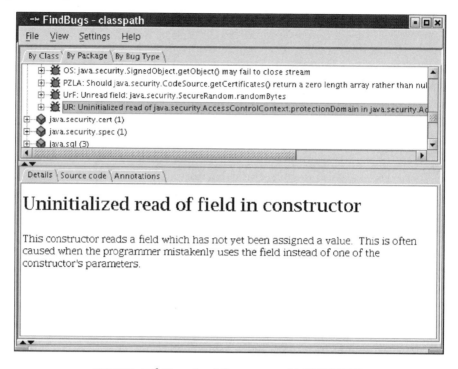

FIGURE 7.6 Detecting defect patterns with FINDBUGS.

TABLE 7.2 Some defect patterns detected by FINDBUGS.

Class implements `Cloneable` but does not define or use `clone` method
Method might ignore exception
Null pointer dereference in method
Class defines `equal()`; should it be `equals()`?
Method may fail to close database resource
Method may fail to close stream
Method ignores return value
Unread field
Unused field
Unwritten field
Private method is never called

In general, whenever a failure occurs it is good practice to use a static checker such as FINDBUGS (or the compiler with all warnings enabled) to rule out common defect patterns as a failure cause. In addition, if one has a concrete failure to deal with one can also apply checking tools that search for common issues in this particular run — such as memory issues or violation of invariants. These dynamic tools are discussed in Chapter 10 "Asserting Expectations."

7.6 LIMITS OF STATIC ANALYSIS

As discussed in Section 7.5, a tool such as FINDBUGS has a false positive rate of 50%. Why can't we rewrite tools such as FINDBUGS to have *no* false positives at all?

The reason for the imprecision of FINDBUGS (or CODESURFER, or any tool using static analysis) is that there are a number of language constructs that make computing precise data dependences difficult, if not impossible. For instance, given a statement A that writes a[i], and a following statement B that reads a[j], how can one know whether A may influence B? To answer this question requires finding out whether i = j can ever hold. Although it may be possible to answer a *specific* question such as this, in general such questions are instances of Turing's halting problem and thus undecidable.

Note that this limitation is not necessarily prone to machines. Humans suffer the very same problem. The following is an example showing the limits of static analysis. In the following piece of code, is x being used uninitialized or not?

```
int x;
for(i=j=k=1;--j||k;k=j?i%j?k:k-j:(j=i+=2));
write(x);
```

The answer is: nobody knows. The for loop terminates if and only if i holds an odd *perfect number*, an integer that is the sum of its proper positive divisors (28 is a perfect number because $28 = 1 + 2 + 4 + 7 + 14$). In that nobody knows today whether odd perfect numbers exist, it is unknown whether the write(x) statement will ever be executed — and neither humans nor machines have a straightforward way of deciding this.

[In practice, though, we may well treat write(x) as unreachable. It is known that an odd perfect number must be greater than 10^{300}, and thus we must prepare for at least 10^{600} loop iterations. In addition, write(x) is either unreachable or uses an uninitialized variable, and thus an error anyway — and this ambiguity is something a tool *could* determine.]

As a consequence, static analysis tools must resort to *conservative approximations* — for instance, an approximation saying that *any* write to the array a[] may influence *any* read from the array a[]. Although this approximation may result in more data dependences than strictly necessary, it at least ensures that no data dependence is falsely omitted. List 7.2 outlines the most important language constructs that require approximations.

- *Indirect Access.* To determine that a write to a variable V influences a later read of this variable requires that V be precisely determined. If V is a location that is determined at runtime, however, one has to resort to *approximations.*

  As a typical example, consider *array accesses.* If some statement writes into a[i], one has to determine the possible values of i in order to track precise dependences. These possible values can be approximated by following back the dependences of i (assuming they all lead to constants) or by *symbolic evaluation* of i. (Humans, of course, may have better means of abstracting possible values of i.)

- *Pointers.* Writing to a location referenced by a pointer or reference P requires that one know the locations P may point to or reference. This type of analysis is known as *points-to analysis,* which is a common part of optimizing compilers. A simple and common automated strategy is to assume that a pointer P may point to all objects whose addresses have been taken in the program code (again, human reasoning is usually more precise).

- *Functions.* Including function calls in the analysis results in dependences between the arguments at the call sites (the *context*) and the formal parameters at the function entries. If a function is called from multiple sites in a program, one can choose to inline the function body at each call site, resulting in precise dependences. This approach fails, though, for large numbers of functions. It is also infeasible for recursive functions.

  A viable alternative is to introduce *summary edges* at call sites that represent the transitive dependences of the function in question. Such summaries also introduce imprecision.

- *More Features.* Other features that make computing dependences difficult include *object orientation* and *concurrency.*

LIST 7.2 Data flow caveats.

The drawback of such approximations is that dependences are difficult to track. In the sample program discussed in Chapters 1 "How Failures Come to Be" and 6 "Scientific Debugging," tracking the origins of a[0] stops short at the shell_sort() function, which writes into every element of a[]. Therefore, all one can deduce at this point is that the content of a[] was responsible for the value of a[0]. Consequently, any member of a[] may influence a[0].

If one is really paranoid about conservative approximation, static analysis results in virtually no results for many real-life programs. If a stray pointer may access noninitialized memory, and if an array index may go out of bounds, anything can happen — meaning that conservative approximation returns "I don't know" for any program property. Likewise, if a function is unavailable to analysis (due to lack of source code, for instance), calling such a function also stops static analysis on the spot. Anything can happen after the function is done. However, even if there were no conservative approximation deduction brings a number of risks simply by being based on *abstraction*.

- *Risk of code mismatch:* Using source code to deduce facts in a concrete program run requires that the run actually be created from this very source code. Otherwise, bad mismatches can happen (see List 7.3).

- *Risk of abstracting away:* To actually execute the source code, one requires a compiler, an operating system, a runtime library, or other tools. When deducing from source code, one cannot take all of this "real world" into account. One assumes that the environment of the source code operates properly. More precisely, one assumes semantics of the program code that hold regardless of the environment. In rare instances, though, failures can be caused by a defect in the environment — and therefore, deducing an error from source code will be impossible.

- *Risk of imprecision:* In Figure 7.3 we saw that an ordinary program already has much data and many control dependences, such that any slice quickly encompasses large parts of the program. In the presence of data flow caveats (List 7.2), slices become even larger, as conservative approximation is required to make sure no dependence is lost. On average, a static slice encompasses about 30% of the program code — which is a significant reduction but still a huge amount of code.

The risk of code mismatch can be easily taken care of by establishing precise configuration management. Abstracting away is a risk inherent to any type of pure deduction. The risk of imprecision, though, can be addressed by two mechanisms.

- *Verification:* If one can constrain the possible program states, it is possible to increase the precision of deduction. As an example, consider the following code.

```
p = &y;
if (x > 0)
    y = x;
```

- *Source mismatch.* Whenever processing source code, one must make sure that the source code being read actually corresponds to the program being executed. For released programs, this means to use version control, as discussed in Section 2.9. For a local program, be sure not to confound the locations (Bug Story 8). Using incremental construction (using tools such as *make*), be sure that all compilations are up-to-date.

- *Macros and preprocessors.* A *preprocessor* is a program that manipulates program text before it is being fed to the compiler. In Example 7.1, for instance, the #include statement in line 3 makes the C preprocessor insert the contents of the stdio.h header.

  Preprocessors can be tricky because they may introduce uncommon behavior. For instance, a *macro definition* such as #define int long causes all subsequent int types to be read in as long types. Programmers typically make macros explicit to ease understanding. Modern programming languages avoid the usage of preprocessors.

- *Undefined behavior.* Some programming languages deliberately do not specify the semantics of some constructs. Instead, each compiler can choose its own implementation. In C, for instance, the value range of a char is not defined. It may be anything from an 8-bit to a 128-bit value or even larger.

  Issues with undefined behavior typically arise when a program is ported to a new environment or a new compiler. Being aware of undefined behavior helps to identify errors quickly.

- *Aspects.* An *aspect* is a piece of code that is added (or *woven*) to specific parts of a program — for instance, an aspect that prints out "set() has been called" at the beginning of every set() method.

  Aspects are great tools for logging and debugging. We will cover these uses in Section 8.2.3. However, as adding an aspect to a program can cause arbitrary changes in behavior aspects can also seriously hamper our ability to understand the code.

LIST 7.3 Source code caveats.

```
if (y > 0)
    p = &x;
```

Where can the pointer p point to after this code? It is trivial to prove that the condition x > 0 and the assignment y = x imply y > 0. Hence, if we know that x > 0 holds we can ensure that p points to x. Such constraints can be

BUG STORY 8: Stubborn Hello

In the beginning of my programming career, I was writing a simple program called `hello` that would output `Hello, world!` to the UNIX console. My program worked fine, but as I changed the text to `Bonjour, monde!` and compiled it, `hello` would still output `Hello, world!`. Regardless of what I did, the text would remain fixed.

A friend then explained to me that by typing `hello` at the prompt, I was invoking the preinstalled GNU `hello` program instead of my own. He reported similar problems with a program of his own called `test` — conflicting with the built-in `test` command. I quickly learned to type `./test`, `./sort`, `./hello`, and so on to start my own programs from my directory.

computed, accumulated, and resolved across the code, thereby increasing precision. In Chapter 10 "Asserting Expectations," we shall see how such conditions can be expressed as assertions and verified at runtime as well as deduced at compile time.

- *Observation:* Rather than deducing facts from source code that hold for *all* runs, one can combine deduction with facts observed from concrete program runs — notably from the one run that fails. Not only does this give concrete findings about the failure in question, as a side effect observation also removes the risk of abstracting away.

7.7 CONCEPTS

✎ *To isolate value origins*, follow back the dependences from the statement in question (Section 7.3).   **HOW TO**

✎ Dependences can uncover *code smells* — in particular common errors such as use of uninitialized variables, unused values, or unreachable code.

✎ Before debugging, get rid of code smells reported by automated detection tools (such as the compiler).

✎ *To slice a program*, follow dependences from a statement S to determine all statements that: **HOW TO**

- Could be influenced by S (*forward slice*)

- Could influence S (*backward slice*)

✎ Using deduction alone includes a number of risks, including the risk of code mismatch, the risk of abstracting away relevant details, and the risk of imprecision.

✎ Any type of deduction is limited by the halting problem and must thus resort to conservative approximation.

7.8 TOOLS

CODESURFER

CODESURFER is considered among the most advanced static analysis tools available. It is available free of charge to faculty members (if you are a student, ask your advisor). All others must purchase a license. CODESURFER is available at:

```
http://www.codesurfer.com/
```

FINDBUGS

The FINDBUGS tool was developed by Hovemeyer and Pugh (2004). It is open source. Its project page is found at:

```
http://findbugs.sf.net/
```

7.9 FURTHER READING

Weiser (1982) was the first to discover that programmers mentally ignore statements that cannot have an influence on a statement in which an erroneous state is discovered. In this paper, Weiser also coined the term *program slicing*.

The original approach by Weiser (1984) was based on data flow equations. The same year, Ottenstein and Ottenstein (1984) introduced the notion of the program dependence graph. Indeed, all later slicing approaches used a graph-based representation of program dependences.

Since these pioneer works, several researchers have extended the concept. Tip (1995) still summarizes today's state of the art in slicing. Regarding the usefulness of slices, Binkley and Harman (2003) examined slice sizes in 43 C programs and found that the average slice size was under 30% of the original program.

Besides Hovemeyer and Pugh, several researchers have worked on using static analysis to detect defect patterns. I specifically recommend the work of Dawson Engler's group on analyzing the Linux kernel. Chelf (2004) gives a survey.

The basic techniques for analyzing source code — especially scanning, parsing, and detecting the effects of statements — are all part of compiler construction. As an introduction, I recommend Aho et al. (1986) as well as the series of *Modern Compiler Implementation* by Andrew Appel. Advanced readers may like to look at Muchnik (1997).

Christian Morgenstern's poem "The Impossible Fact" is taken from Morgenstern (1964).

7.10 EXERCISES

EXERCISE 7.1. For the program shown in Example 7.2a, write down:

1. The control flow graph, as in Figure 7.1

2. The effects of the statements, as in Table 7.1

3. The control dependences, as in Figure 7.3

4. The data dependences, as in Figure 7.3

EXERCISE 7.2. Sketch a mechanism based on the control flow graph and dependences that ensures that after a call to free(x) the value x is no longer used.

EXERCISE 7.3. For the defect patterns in Table 7.2, explain what type of program representation (call flow graph, data dependence graph, source code) is needed to compute these smells.

EXERCISE 7.4. (Xie and Engler, 2002) describe an analysis technique for catching defects in code. The idea is that *redundant operations* commonly flag correctness errors. Xie and Engler applied their technique on the source code of the Linux kernel and found errors such as the following.

- *Idempotent operations:* Such as when a variable is assigned to itself — for instance, in the following code, where the programmer makes a mistake while copying the structure sa to the structure da.

```
/* 2.4.1/net/appletalk/aarp.c:aarp_rcv() */
/* We need to make a copy of the entry. */
da.s_node = sa.s_node;
da.s_net = da.s_net;
```

- *Redundant assignments:* Where a value assigned to a variable is not subsequently used — such as the value assigned to err in the following code.

```
/* 2.4.1/net/decnet/af_decnet.c:dn_wait_run() */
do {
    ...
    if (signal_pending(current)) {
        err = -ERESTARTSYS;
        break;
    }
    SOCK_SLEEP_PRE(sk);
    if (scp->state != DN_RUN)
        schedule();
    SOCK_SLEEP_POST(sk);
} while (scp->state != DN_RUN);
return 0;
```

- *Dead code:* Which is never executed — such as the following code, where the insertion of a logging statement causes the function to always return (note the misleading indentation).

```
/* 2.4.1/drivers/net/arcnet/arc-rimi.c:arcrimi_found() */
/* reserve the irq */
if (request_irq(dev->irq, &arcnet_interrupt ...))
                BUGMSG(D_NORMAL,
                    "Can't get IRQ %d!\n", dev->irq);
    return -ENODEV;
```

⟨Following code is never executed⟩

1. For each of the previous categories, sketch how dependences can be used to detect them.

2. Are these defects still present in the current Linux kernel? When were they fixed?

EXERCISE 7.5. What problems can you imagine that arise for users of deduction from code mismatch?

EXERCISE 7.6. A *dice* can highlight those program statements computing an infected variable that cannot have an influence on a correct variable. How should a conservative approximation of indirect access look for a slice of a correct and a slice of an infected variable?

Palmström, old, an aimless rover,
walking in the wrong direction
at a busy intersection
is run over.

"How," he says, his life restoring
and with pluck his death ignoring,
"can an accident like this
ever happen? What's amiss?"

"Did the state administration
fail in motor transportation?
Did police ignore the need
for reducing driving speed?"

"Isn't there a prohibition,
barring motorized transmission
of the living to the dead?
Was the driver right who sped . . . ?"

Tightly swathed in dampened tissues
he explores the legal issues,
and it soon is clear as air:
Cars were not permitted there!

And he comes to the conclusion:
His mishap was an illusion,
for, he reasons pointedly,
that which must not, can not be.

— CHRISTIAN MORGENSTERN,
The Impossible Fact (1905)

## CHAPTER 8

OBSERVING FACTS

A LTHOUGH DEDUCTION TECHNIQUES do not take concrete runs into account, observation determines *facts* about what has happened in a concrete run. In this chapter, we look under the hood of the actual program execution and introduce widespread techniques for examining program executions and program states. These techniques include classical logging, interactive debuggers, and postmortem debugging, as well as eye-opening visualization and summarization techniques.

8.1 OBSERVING STATE

Deduction alone, as discussed in Chapter 7 "Deducing Errors," is good for telling what *might* happen. To find out what is *actually* happening in a concrete failing run, though, we cannot rely on deduction alone. We must take a look at the actual facts — that is, *observe* what is going on — and judge whether the values are infected or not. The following are some general principles of observation.

- *Do not interfere.* Whatever you observe should be an effect of the original run — rather than an effect of your observation. Otherwise, you will have a difficult time reasoning about the original run. That is, you have a Heisenbug (Section 4.3.9). Any observation technique should take care to alter the original run as little as possible.

- *Know what and when to observe.* As discussed in Section 1.3, a program run is a long succession of huge program states, which is impossible to observe and comprehend as a whole. Observation is effective only if you know:

  - Which part of the state to observe (what)

  - At which moments during execution to observe (when)

- *Proceed systematically.* Rather than observing values at random, let your search be guided by scientific method (Chapter 6 "Scientific Debugging"). Always be aware of the current hypothesis, the observations predicted by the hypothesis, and how the actual observations contribute to the hypothesis.

In the remainder of this chapter, we shall take a look at some common techniques for observing what is going on in a run. These techniques can be used "as is" by humans, but they can also be leveraged by automated debugging techniques. Here, we ask:

> HOW CAN WE OBSERVE A PROGRAM RUN?

8.2 LOGGING EXECUTION

To observe facts about a run, we must make the facts accessible to the programmer. The simplest way of doing so is to have the program output the facts as desired — for instance, by inserting appropriate *logging statements* in the code. For instance, if a programmer wants to know the value of `size` in the function `shell_sort()` she simply inserts a logging statement at the beginning of `shell_sort()`, as follows.

```
printf("size = %d\n", size);
```

Whenever this statement executes, a line such as

```
size = 3
```

will appear on the output device. Several outputs like this constitute a *debugging log* — a list of events that took place during the execution.

This technique of observation is perhaps best known as *printf debugging* — from `printf()`, the function that in C outputs strings and values. [Although C and printf() slowly become obsolete, the term *printf debugging* lives on — and JAVA-inspired alternatives such as *system-err-println debugging* are just not catchy enough. Feel free to replace *printf* by the name of your favorite output function.] It is always available in some form. Even if a program might not log on a console-like device, there always must be some effect that can be observed by the programmer — even if it is just a blinking LED. Being always available (and extremely easy to teach), it is also the most widespread debugging technique. In addition, requiring no infrastructure other than a means of making the log available to the programmer it is also the most basic technique. Although printf debugging is easy to use, it has several drawbacks as an observation technique.

- *Cluttered code:* Because logging statements serve no other purpose than debugging, they do not help us in understanding the code. The main message a logging statement conveys is that the procedure in question was in need of debugging. Therefore, programmers frequently remove logging statements once the observation is done.

- *Cluttered output:* Logging statements can produce a great deal of output, depending on the number of events and variables traced. If the debugging log is interleaved with the ordinary output, both can be difficult to separate properly. (This problem is best solved by using a designated output channel for debugging logs.)

- *Slowdown:* A huge amount of logging — in particular, to some slow device — can slow down the program. In addition to the obvious performance problem, this changes the program under test and introduces the risk of Heisenbugs (Section 4.3.9).

- *Loss of data:* For performance reasons, output is typically *buffered* before actually being written to the output device. In the event of a program crash, this buffered output is lost. Using ordinary (buffered) output for logging thus hides what happened in the last few events before the crash. One can either use an unbuffered channel for logging (introducing a slowdown, as described previously) or make sure that the program flushes its buffered logs in case of a crash.

Taking care of all of these issues in a single output statement is quite a hassle. Therefore, it is better to use *dedicated logging techniques* that allow far better customization. In particular, we would like to do the following.

- *Use standard formats:* Standard formats make it easy to search and filter logs for:

  - Specific *code locations* ("prefix each line with the current file or function")

  - Specific *events* ("prefix each line with time")

  - Specific *data* ("output all dates in Y-M-D format")

- *Make logging optional:* For performance reasons, logging is typically turned off in production code as well as in code not under consideration for debugging.

- *Allow for variable granularity:* Depending on the problem you are working on, it may be helpful to focus on specific levels of detail. Focusing only on specific events also improves performance.

- *Be persistent:* One should be enabled to reuse or reenable logging even when the debugging session is completed—just in case a similar problem resurfaces.

8.2.1 Logging Functions

The easiest way of customizing logging is to use or design a function that is built for logging purposes only—a *logging function.* For instance, one could introduce a function named dprintf() that would behave as printf(), but forward its output to a debugging channel (rather than standard output) and allow the output to be turned off. For instance, one could use

```
dprintf("size = %d", size);
```

to output the variable size to the debugging log, possibly prefixed with common information such as date or time, or a simple marker indicating the type of output:

```
DEBUG: size = 3
```

In addition, a function such as dprintf() can be easily set up not to generate any output at all, which is useful for production code. In practice, though, a programmer would not want to rely exclusively on such a debugging function — particularly if the logging code is to survive the current debugging session. The reason is performance. Even if dprintf() does nothing at all, the mere cost of computing the arguments and calling the function may be a penalty if it occurs often.

Languages with a *preprocessor* (such as C and C++) offer a more cost-effective way of realizing logging. The idea is to use a *logging macro* — a piece of code that expands to a logging statement or a no-op, depending on settings made at compilation. The following is a simple example of a LOG() macro that takes printf() arguments in parentheses.

```
LOG(("size = %d", size));
```

The macro LOG() is easily defined as being based on dprintf() [or printf(), or any other suitable logging function]:

```
#define LOG(args) dprintf args
```

The effect of this macro definition is that LOG(args) is being replaced by dprintf args in the subsequent code. Thus, the statement

```
LOG(("size = %d", size));
```

expands into

```
dprintf("size = %d", size);
```

The main benefit of writing LOG() rather than dprintf() is that a macro can be set up to expand into nothing:

```
#define LOG(args) ((void) 0)
```

Thus, all LOG() statements get expanded to a no-op — a statement without any effect. Not even the arguments will be evaluated. Therefore, LOG() statements may even contain calls to some expensive function, as in

```
LOG(("number_of_files = %d", count_files(directory)));
```

If LOG() is defined to be a no-op, count_files() will not be called — in contrast to the argument to a no-op function.

The choice between turning logging on or off is typically made at compile time. For instance, defining a preprocessor variable (say, NDEBUG for "no debugging") during compilation may turn logging off.

```
#if !defined(NDEBUG)
#define LOG(args) dprintf args
#else
#define LOG(args) ((void) 0)
#endif
```

In addition to performance benefits, macros bring a second advantage over functions: they can convey information about *their own location*. In C and C++, the macros __FILE__ and __LINE__ expand to the name of the current source file and the current source line, respectively. This can be used in a macro definition such as the following.

```
#define LOG(args) do { \
    dprintf("%s:%d: ", __FILE__, __LINE__); \
    dprintf args; \
    dprintf("\n"); } while (0)
```

[The do ... while loop makes the macro body a single statement, for having code such as if (debug) LOG(var); work the intended way.] If we insert a LOG() macro in line 8 of sample.c, its logging output will automatically be prefixed with the location information, as in

```
sample.c:8: size = 3
```

This feature of reporting the location in a macro makes it easy to trace back the log line to its origin (such as sample.c:8 in the previous example). It can also be leveraged to *filter* logs at runtime. For instance, one could set up a function named do_we_log_this(file) that returns true if file is to be logged (by looking up some configuration resource such as an environment variable). Then, we could introduce a conditional LOG() using:

```
#define LOG(args) do { \
    if (do_we_log_this(__FILE__)) { \
        dprintf("%s:%d: ", __FILE__, __LINE__); \
        dprintf args; \
        dprintf("\n"); \
    } } while (0)
```

It is easy to see how these pieces fall into place to produce a set of macros and functions that allow for easy logging of arbitrary state — using standard formats, with optional logging, and variable granularity. With a bit of discipline, such logging code can even become persistent and remain in the source code. Thus, later programmers can observe the specified events just by turning on some configuration option.

Logging functions are not just useful for making logging optional; they can also help standardize the output of large data structures. Assume we have a very basic linked list, defined as:

```
struct list {
    int elem;               // List element
    struct list *next;      // Next node, or NULL
};
```

We can create a variant of the LOG() macro to log the content of a linked list:

```
#define LOG_LIST(list) do { \
    if (do_we_log_this(__FILE__)) { \
        dprintf("%s:%d: ", __FILE__, __LINE__); \
        dprintf("%s = ", #list); \
        print_list(list); \
        dprintf("\n"); \
    } } while (0)
```

In a C macro, the expression #VAR expands to a string containing the macro argument VAR. We use this to log the variable name. If we invoke the macro as LOG_LIST(my_list), then #list becomes "my_list" and the log starts with "my_list = ". The print_list function invoked does a simple traversal of the list, printing its elements:

```
void print_list(struct list *l)
{
    int number_of_elems = 0;
    printf("[");

    while (l != NULL)
    {
        if (++number_of_elems > 1)
            printf(", ");
        printf("%d", l->elem);
        l = l->next;
    }
```

```
        printf("]");
    }
```

Overall, LOG_LIST(my_list) thus logs something such as:

```
    list.c:47: my_list = [1, 10, 100, 1000, 10000]
```

Any large program contains functions to output central data structures in a human-readable form. In C++, such functions typically overload the << operator such that they can write to arbitrary output streams. In JAVA, the standard is to provide a toString() method, which returns a human-readable string for the object.

8.2.2 Logging Frameworks

Although many projects include their own home-grown logging facilities, there are also *standard libraries* for logging, providing a wealth of functionality seldom present in individual projects. As an example, consider the LOG4J framework, a popular logging framework for JAVA programs (also available for C, C++, C#, PERL, PYTHON, RUBY, and EIFFEL).

The core idea of LOG4J is to assign each class in an application an individual or common *logger*. A logger is a component that takes a request for logging and logs it. Each logger has a *level*, from DEBUG (messages of low importance) over INFO, WARN, and ERROR to FATAL (very important messages). Messages for each of these levels are logged by invoking the corresponding logger methods (debug(), info(), ..., fatal()).

Example 8.1 shows an example of how to use a logger, using the universal UGLI interface. The TestLogging class initializes a logging category, named after the class in which it is instantiated. Then, we can use the logger methods to log individual messages. The TestLogging class, when executed, creates a log starting with:

```
        Start of main()
        A log message with level set to INFO
        A log message with level set to WARN
        A log message with level set to ERROR
        A log message with level set to FATAL
        Calling init()
        *** System Environment As Seen By Java ***
        *** Format: PROPERTY = VALUE ***
```

```
import org.apache.ugli.ULogger;
import org.apache.ugli.LoggerFactory;

// How to use log4j
public class TestLogging {

    // Initialize a logger.
    final ULogger logger = LoggerFactory.getLogger(TestLogging.class);

    // Try a few logging methods
    public static void main(String args[]) {
        logger.debug("Start of main()");
        logger.info ("A log message with level set to INFO");
        logger.warn ("A log message with level set to WARN");
        logger.error("A log message with level set to ERROR");
        logger.fatal("A log message with level set to FATAL");

        new TestLogging().init();
    }

    // Try some more logging methods
    public void init() {
        java.util.Properties prop = System.getProperties();
        java.util.Enumeration enum = prop.propertyNames();

        logger.info("*** System Environment As Seen By Java ***");
        logger.debug("*** Format: PROPERTY = VALUE ***");

        while (enum.hasMoreElements()) {
            String key = (String) enum.nextElement();
            logger.info(key + " = " + System.getProperty(key));
        }
    }
}
```

EXAMPLE 8.1 A sample test file using LOG4J.

```
java.runtime.name = Java(TM) 2 Runtime Environment, Standard Edition
sun.boot.library.path = /System/Library/.../1.4.2/Libraries
java.vm.version = 1.4.2-38
```

⋮

The interesting thing about LOG4J is that one can customize every aspect of
the log. In particular, one can define specific *logging levels* for individual classes.
For instance, one can set up LOG4J such that for the application only messages
of level ERROR and higher are shown — except for a specific class, for which we
want all messages of DEBUG and higher. Furthermore, one can set up specific

appenders, which direct the log to a particular output (files, console, database, mail, servers). This can be done in a particular *layout.*

All of this can be defined at runtime using configuration files. The following configuration file defines a specific layout, where *conversion patterns* such as %d or %t insert the current time of function before the actual message (%m).

```
# Set root logger level to DEBUG and its only appender to A1.
log4j.rootLogger=DEBUG, A1


# A1 is set to be a ConsoleAppender.
log4j.appender.A1=org.apache.log4j.ConsoleAppender


# A1 uses PatternLayout.
log4j.appender.A1.layout=org.apache.log4j.PatternLayout
log4j.appender.A1.layout.ConversionPattern=%d [%t] %-5p %c %x - %m%n
```

This configuration pattern changes the format of the layout to:

```
2005-02-06 20:47:31,508 [main] DEBUG  TestLogging - Start of main()
2005-02-06 20:47:31,529 [main] INFO   TestLogging - A log message
                                                    with level set to INFO
⋮
```

Because such log files can become painfully long, LOG4J comes with an analysis tool called CHAINSAW that helps to explore these logs. As seen in the screen shot in Figure 8.1, searching for specific events, levels, or messages is straightforward.

LOG4J is a very powerful logging package that includes everything but the kitchen sink. Despite its functionality, it is easy to set up initially, and with a little bit of planning scales up to very large applications. There is every reason to replace printf(), System.out.println(), and similar output methods with the appropriate logger calls from LOG4J and like packages for other languages.

8.2.3 Logging with Aspects

Despite their benefits, logging statements still clutter the source code. The concern of logging is separate from the concern of computation—which is why most programmers prefer to remove logging statements once the debugging session is done. Some languages, though, offer an alternative: rather than intertwining actual computation and logging they treat these two concerns as sep-

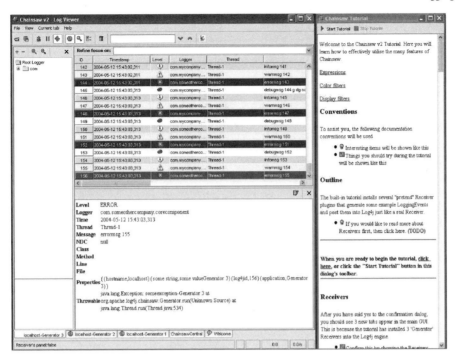

FIGURE 8.1 Exploring logs with CHAINSAW. Events can be sorted, filtered, and shown in detail.

arate entities called *aspects*. Each aspect holds only the code for its individual concern. A logging aspect thus holds the logging code in one syntactical entity called an *advice*.

The following is a small example. Suppose we have some `Article` class with a `buy()` method:

```
class Article {
    public void buy() {
        // Code
    }
}
```

We want to log the execution of `buy()`, but without actually changing the method. We first write an advice—a simple piece of code logging that `buy()` was called.

```
{
    System.out.println("Calling Article.buy()");
```

```
        }
```

Alternatively, we do this as a LOG4J aficionado (Section 8.2.2):

```
{
    logger.debug("Calling Article.buy()");
}
```

In the ASPECTJ language, we now have to specify the *location* at which this advice is to be executed. This is done using a *point cut* — a set of locations (*join points*) at which the previously cited advice is to be woven into the code. We name this point cut buyMethod():

```
pointcut buyMethod():
    call(public void Article.buy());
```

The advice and the point cut are combined in an *aspect* — for instance, an aspect named LogBuy:

```
public aspect LogBuy {
    pointcut buyMethod():
        call(public void Article.buy());
    before(): buyMethod() {
        System.out.println ("Calling Article.buy()")
    }
}
```

The word before() means that the advice is to be executed *before* the actual call. We can also specify some advice to be executed after the call has completed:

```
public aspect LogBuy {
    pointcut buyMethod():
        call(public void Article.buy());
    before(): buyMethod() {
        System.out.println ("Entering Article.buy()")
    }
    after(): buyMethod() {
        System.out.println ("Leaving Article.buy()")
    }
}
```

Such an aspect can now be *woven into* the original code, resulting in an executable that is roughly equivalent to:

```
class Article {
    public void buy() {
        System.out.println("Entering Article.buy()");
        original_buy();
        System.out.println("Leaving Article.buy()");
    }
    public void original_buy() {
        // Original code of Article.buy()
    }
}
```

Note, though, that this transformation takes place at the executable level (no source code is ever produced or changed). This weaving is done by the ASPECTJ compiler ajc, which substitutes the original JAVA compiler:

```
$ ajc LogBuy.aj Shop.java
$ java Shop
Entering Article.buy()
Leaving Article.buy()
Entering Article.buy()
Leaving Article.buy()
    ⋮
$ _
```

Weaving in an aspect, though, is *optional* — that is, aspects such as LogBuy can also be left away, effectively turning all logging off. Using the ASPECTJ compiler without any aspects is equivalent to using the JAVA compiler alone.

Nonetheless, you may wonder about whether specifying the aspect is worth the hassle. After all, we need a lot of fixture just to insert small advices into the code. The interesting thing about aspects, however, is that the same advice may be woven in at *multiple locations* in the program. For instance, we can specify a point cut that encompasses *all methods* of the Article class:

```
pointcut allMethods():
    call(public * Article.*(..));
```

As usual, a star is a wildcard for arbitrary names and qualifiers. Such a point cut can now be used to log multiple methods, all in one place. The variable thisJoinPoint can be used to log the name of the current method:

```
public aspect LogArticle {
    pointcut allMethods():
        call(public * Article.*(..));
    before(): allMethods() {
        System.out.println ("Entering " + thisJoinPoint);
    }
    after(): allMethods() {
        System.out.println ("Leaving " + thisJoinPoint);
    }
}
```

Using wildcards and other pattern expressions for class and method names, such aspects can be easily extended to log an even greater number of methods — or even every single method of the entire program.

Just logging that some method was called is rarely enough. One also wants to log the program state at the event. This is done by integrating the current object and its parameters into the point cut such that they can be accessed in the advice. As an example, imagine we want to log all moves of a Line object — that is, all invocations of the Line.setPX() and Line.setPY() methods. We define a point cut that encompasses these join points and assigns names to the object and the argument. These names can then be used in the advice:

```
public aspect LogMoves {
    pointcut setP(Line a_line, Point p):
        call(void a_line.setP*(p));

    after(Line a_line, Point p): setP(a_line, p) {
        System.out.println(a_line +
                            " moved to " + p + ".");
    }
}
```

These examples should suffice to demonstrate the power of aspects when it comes to observing facts in the program run. Aspects do not clutter the code, and they encourage standard formats, are optional, can be enabled at will, and can easily be reused. The only concern is that logging aspects must not interfere with the actual computation. (Note also that the general idea of having aspects not interfere with each other may also be central for your future aspect-oriented designs.)

8.2.4 Logging at the Binary Level

Aspects, as discussed in Section 8.2.3, require the source code of the program to be logged, and are not available for every language. An alternative is to add logging code not at the source code level but at the binary level — that is, we instrument binary code rather than source code.

The PIN framework provided by Intel is a tool for the instrumentation of Linux binary executables for x86 and other Intel processors. PIN allows arbitrary C or C++ code to be injected at arbitrary places in the executable. It provides a rich API that allows us to access context information such as register content, symbol, and debug information. Conceptionally, you can think of PIN as aspects at the binary level.

In PIN, the actual analysis tools come as so-called PIN tools. They contain the mechanism that decides where and what code to insert (in aspect terminology, a *join point*), as well as the code to be executed at the insertion points (in aspect terminology, the *advice*).

Example 8.2 shows the source code of a simple PIN tool. Running this tool on a binary program creates a trace of all executed instructions — for instance, for the directory listing program /bin/ls:

```
$ cd pin-2.0/ManualExamples
$ make itrace
$ ../Bin/pin -t itrace -- /bin/ls
atrace.C      inscount0.C  _insprofiler.C  itrace.o      staticcount.C...
$ _
```

The trace of all instructions is stored in the file itrace.out:

```
$ head itrace.out      # output first 10 lines
0x40000c20
0x40000c22
0x40000c70
0x40000c71
0x40000c73
0x40000c74
0x40000c75
0x40000c76
```

```
// itrace.C - generate an instruction trace

#include <stdio.h>
#include "pin.H"

FILE * trace;

// This function is called before every instruction
// is executed and prints the IP
VOID printip(VOID *ip) { fprintf(trace, "%p\n", ip); }

// Pin calls this function every time
// a new instruction is encountered
VOID Instruction(INS ins, VOID *v)
{
    // Insert a call to printip before every instruction,
    // and pass it the IP
    INS_InsertCall(ins, IPOINT_BEFORE, (AFUNPTR)printip,
                   IARG_INST_PTR, IARG_END);
}

// This function is called when the application exits
VOID Fini(INT32 code, VOID *v)
{
    fprintf(trace, "#eof\n");
    fclose(trace);
}

// argc, argv are the entire command line,
// including pin -t <toolname> -- ...
int main(int argc, char * argv[])
{
    trace = fopen("itrace.out", "w");

    // Initialize pin
    PIN_Init(argc, argv);

    // Register Instruction to be called to
    // instrument instructions
    INS_AddInstrumentFunction(Instruction, 0);

    // Register Fini to be called when the
    // application exits
    PIN_AddFiniFunction(Fini, 0);

    // Start the program, never returns
    PIN_StartProgram();

    return 0;
}
```

EXAMPLE 8.2 Logging executed instructions (Cohn and Muth, 2004).

```
0x40000c79
0x40011d9b
$ _
```

Overall, 501,585 instructions were executed:

```
$ wc -l itrace.out    # count lines in itrace.out
501585
$ _
```

How does this work? Let's take a look at the code shown in Example 8.2. The main work is done in three functions.

- The advice to be executed for each instruction is stored in the function printip(). The parameter ip holds the current instruction address.

- The function Instruction() executes every time a new instruction I is encountered. It inserts printip() as a function to be executed before I.

- In main(), the Instruction() function is registered as a function to instrument instructions.

In addition to operating at the instruction level, the PIN framework also offers means of instrumenting functions (you can retrieve the address of a function, and add advice code to function calls or returns). Thus, it is not too difficult to log a trace of executed functions rather than instructions. Remember the STRACE tool from Section 4.3.6, logging the interaction between a program and the operating system? With PIN, you can set up your own logging tool.

8.3 USING DEBUGGERS

The logging techniques discussed in Section 8.2 all require writing and integrating code into the program to be debugged, which takes some time — especially if you consider that the program has to be rerun (and frequently rebuilt) to execute the additional logging code. An alternative mechanism is to use an *external observation tool* that hooks into the execution of the program and observes (and possibly manipulates) the state at specific moments in time — without changing the original program code in any way. This approach has a number of benefits.

- *Getting started fast:* An observation tool can be started right away, without any change to the source code or recompilation.

- *Flexible observation:* It is possible to observe arbitrary aspects of the program execution. Typically, one can even change the aspect during execution.

- *Transient sessions:* Observation tools are good for single shots at debugging, with interaction leading to quick results.

The most important observation tools are known as *debuggers* — not because they actually remove bugs but because they are being used almost exclusively for debugging programs. Debuggers provide three functionalities to help you observe actual executions.

- Execute the program and make it stop on specified conditions

- Observe the state of the stopped program

- Change the state of the stopped program

An example is one of the most powerful debuggers, the GNU debugger (GDB). GDB is an interactive program controlled via a command line. Although your favorite debugger probably comes with a graphical user interface, GDB's command line allows you to focus on the bare debugger functionality — applied on the `sample` program (Example 1.1).

8.3.1 A Debugging Session

As discussed earlier, the `sample` program is supposed to sort its arguments. However, it has a defect. When invoked with arguments 11 and 14, the output contains a zero:

```
$ sample 11 14
Output: 0 11
$ _
```

To examine this program run in a debugger, we must first prepare the program for debugging (which seasoned programmers do by default). This means to have the compiler include *debugging information* in the generated executable: locations, names, and types of all variables and functions from the source code. The debugger needs this information in order to find out where a particular item is stored. For GDB, debugging information is included by compiling the program with the -g option:

```
$ gcc -g -o sample sample.c
$ _
```

Next, we must load the program into the debugger. (Some debuggers also allow you to attach them to an already-running process.) In the case of GDB, this is done by invoking GDB with the executable as an argument:

```
$ gdb sample
GNU gdb 6.1, Copyright 2004 Free Software Foundation, Inc. ...
(gdb) _
```

The string (gdb) is GDB's prompt, at which it accepts a number of commands. At the time of writing, there were 135 different commands built into GDB. However, a few suffice to get acquainted. At first, we must decide *where to stop the program* such that its state can be examined. Following Hypothesis 1 from Section 6.3, we first predict that a[0] = 0 should hold when line 38 is being executed. Therefore, we set a *breakpoint* that will make sample's execution stop at line 38, using the GDB break command:

```
(gdb) break 37
Breakpoint 1 at 0x1d04: file sample.c, line 38.
(gdb) _
```

Technically, a breakpoint translates into an *interrupt instruction* that GDB inserts into the executable at the breakpoint location. When execution reaches the breakpoint, the interrupt instruction makes the program stop and returns control to GDB. Now we can actually run the program with the failure-inducing arguments, using GDB's run command:

```
(gdb) run 11 14
Starting program: sample 11 14

Breakpoint 1, main (argc=3, argv=0xbffff9f0) at sample.c:38
37              printf("Output: ");
(gdb) _
```

The program has stopped at line 38. Now we can examine the values of individual variables, using GDB's print command:

```
(gdb) print a[0]
$1 = 0
(gdb) _
```

GDB reports that the value of a[0] is 0, which confirms the initial hypothesis. (As a courtesy, GDB has saved the printed value in a pseudovariable $1 such that we can reuse it later — if we run out of zeroes, that is.)

From here, we could now step through the execution, querying variables as we like. GDB provides a step and a next command that both execute the current line and then stop again. The difference between the two is when the current line is a function call: step will go to the first line of the called function, whereas next will execute the called function as a whole and remain within the current function.

Instead of stepping through a program without any specific target, it is better to formulate a hypothesis and to verify this hypothesis explicitly. Hypothesis 2 from Section 6.3 was that at the beginning of shell_sort, a[] = [11, 14], and size = 2 should hold. The following shows how we can verify this in GDB.

```
(gdb) break shell_sort
Breakpoint 2 at 0x1b00: file sample.c, line 9.
(gdb) run
The program being debugged has been started already.
Start it from the beginning? (y or n) y
Starting program: sample 11 14

Breakpoint 2, shell_sort (a=0x100140, size=3) at sample.c:9
9               int h = 1;
(gdb) print a[0]
$2 = 11
(gdb) p a[1]
$3 = 14
(gdb) p a[2]
$4 = 0
(gdb) _
```

(Note that we can simply type run without arguments to reuse the previous arguments, and that we can abbreviate common commands such as print to their first letter p.) It turns out that size = 3 holds. Therefore, hypothesis 2 is rejected.

Hypothesis 3 from Section 6.3 states that changing size from 3 to 2 should make the run successful. We do so using GDB's set command and use continue to resume execution:

```
(gdb) set size = 2
(gdb) continue
Continuing.

Breakpoint 1, main (argc=3, argv=0xbffff9f0) at sample.c:38
37          printf("Output: ");
(gdb) _
```

Oops — our first breakpoint is still active. We delete it and finally resume execution, abbreviating continue to c:

```
(gdb) delete 1
(gdb) c
Continuing.
Output: 11 14

Program exited normally.
(gdb) _
```

Hypothesis 3 is confirmed. We have narrowed down the failure cause to one single variable: size. Where does it get its value from? We restart the program and use where to show the *backtrace* — the stack of functions that are currently active:

```
(gdb) run
Starting program: sample 11 14

Breakpoint 2, shell_sort (a=0x100140, size=3) at sample.c:9
9               int h = 1;
(gdb) where
#0  shell_sort (a=0x100140, size=3) at sample.c:9
#1  0x00001d04 in main (argc=3, argv=0xbffff9f0) at sample.c:36
(gdb) _
```

It turns out that shell_sort() (Frame #0) was invoked by main() (Frame #1). To check the local variables of main(), we must select its *stack frame* — Frame #1 — using the frame command:

```
(gdb) frame 1
#1  0x00001d04 in main (argc=3, argv=0xbffff9f0) at sample.c:36
35              shell_sort(a, argc);
(gdb) _
```

This is the place from which `shell_sort()` was invoked, and this is the place we have to fix — by changing `argc` to `argc - 1` (Hypothesis 4 from Section 6.3). Many debuggers are incorporated into an editor such that one can change the code on the fly. GDB does not support this, though. Thus, we must fix `sample.c` with an external editor, recompile it, and rerun it:

```
$ sample 11 14
Output: 11 14
$ _
```

Our hypothesis about the failure cause is now refined to a theory. At the same time, we have fixed the defect — all in a five-minute debugger session. We have seen how to:

- Execute the program (`run`) and make it stop on specified conditions (`break`)

- Observe the state of the stopped program (`print`), possibly selecting a frame (`where` and `frame`)

- Resume execution until the next stop (`continue`) or the next line (`next`, `step`)

- Change the state of the stopped program (`set`)

This is the basic debugger functionality, as realized in GDB and almost every other debugger. In the remainder of this section, we discuss other useful functionality.

8.3.2 Controlling Execution

A debugger allows you to control almost every aspect of the environment in which your program executes. This includes:

- Setting of environment and configuration variables:

  ```
  (gdb) set environment USER smith
  ```

```
(gdb) _
```

- Setting of signals and interrupts:

```
(gdb) handle SIGINT ignore        # ignore interrupt
(gdb) _
```

- Hardware-specific settings such as register content:

```
(gdb) set $pc = main      # resume execution at main
(gdb) _
```

8.3.3 Postmortem Debugging

Several operating systems can be set up such that when a program crashes they dump its memory content to a special file. This memory dump (called a *core dump* on UNIX or a *Dr. Watson file* on Windows) can be read in by a debugger such that you may examine the state of the program at the moment it crashed.

The most important hint of a memory dump is the *backtrace*, as it records the functions executing at the time of the crash. Suppose your fourier program crashes on a bus error. The default message gives no clue about what might have happened:

```
$ fourier input.txt
Bus error (core dumped)
$ _
```

Loading the memory dump (called core on UNIX machines) into the debugger reveals what has happened. Using where, we can take a look at the backtrace. print reveals the null pointer a being dereferenced:

```
$ gdb fourier core
GNU gdb 6.1, Copyright 2004 Free Software Foundation, Inc. ...
Core was generated by './fourier'.
0x00001d8c in init_fourier (a=0x0, x=0) at fourier.c:4
4            a[0] = x;
(gdb) where
#0  0x00001d8c in init_fourier (a=0x0, x=0) at fourier.c:4
#1  0x00001de8 in main (argc=2, argv=0xbffff9e8) at fourier.c:12
(gdb) print a
$1 = (int *)0x0
(gdb) _
```

Even if a program does not leave a memory dump, repeating the run from within the debugger yields the same results — which is why seasoned programmers always test their programs within a debugger.

8.3.4 Logging Data

Some debuggers allow us to execute *commands* automatically. In GDB, for instance, when a breakpoint has been reached it can execute a prerecorded sequence of commands. This can be useful for having breakpoints enable and disable each other, and for realizing *logging of variables* from within the debugger.

In GDB, using the commands command we have a breakpoint print the value of a variable (using the GDB printf command) and then continue execution. The first command silent instructs GDB not to report a reached breakpoint.

```
(gdb) break 33
Breakpoint 1 at file sample.c, line 33.
(gdb) commands
Type commands for when breakpoint 1 is hit,
one per line.  End with a line saying just "end".
>silent
>printf "a[%d] = %d\n", i, a[i]
>continue
>end
(gdb) _
```

When executing the program, the value of i is logged just as if we had entered an appropriate printf command in the source code:

```
(gdb) run
Starting program: sample 7 8 9
a[0] = 7
a[1] = 8
a[2] = 9
...
```

8.3.5 Invoking Functions

Many debuggers allow us to invoke functions of the debugged program. This is frequently used to invoke specific logging functions, as discussed in Section 8.2.1.

```
(gdb) call print_list(my_list)
[1, 10, 100, 1000, 10000]
(gdb) _
```

In GDB, functions can be invoked as parts of expressions:

```
(gdb) print proc.wired_memory() + proc.active_memory()
2578438
(gdb) _
```

Invoking functions can interfere with normal execution of the program. For instance, any side effect of an invoked function affects the program being debugged.

```
(gdb) call clear_list(my_list)
(gdb) call print_list(my_list)
[]
(gdb) _
```

Some side effects are quite confusing, though. For instance, if executing the function reaches a breakpoint execution will stop at the breakpoint. In such a case, what has happened to the original execution? How do we finish execution of our own invocation, and how do we resume the original execution? Even worse: what happens if the invoked function causes a crash? How do we ensure the original program is not affected? Because of such potential problems, it is wise to invoke only simple functions that do not interfere with the original execution.

8.3.6 Fix and Continue

Some debuggers, integrated within a development environment, allow you to alter the code of the program while it is executing. This way, you can verify whether a fix is successful without having to alter the state explicitly, and without resuming execution from scratch. Be aware, though, that such fixes should be limited to very simple changes. Anything greater creates a mismatch between source code and executable.

8.3.7 Embedded Debuggers

Traditionally, a debugger invokes the program to be debugged. However, one may also set up a system such that it invokes a debugger (or similar interactive facility) on itself. In an interpreted language such as PYTHON, for instance, you can have a program invoke the interactive interpreter, which allows you to explore all of the program's state at will. The following is a very simple piece of code that invokes the interpreter in the middle of a loop by invoking the PYTHON code.interact() function with the local scope.

```python
import code

for i in range(1, 10):
    print i,
    if i == 5:
        print
        code.interact("Mini Debugger - use Ctrl-D to exit",
                        None, locals())
```

If you execute this code, you obtain:

```
$ python embedded.py
1 2 3 4 5
Mini Debugger - use Ctrl-D to exit
>>> _
```

In the interpreter, you can enter arbitrary expressions, which are then evaluated. You can also invoke and evaluate arbitrary functions.

```
>>> print i
5
>>> import math
>>> math.sqrt(4)
2.0
>>> _
```

Note, though, that changes to local variables may not affect the (cached) instances in the remainder of the execution. Thus, if you enter i = 1 the i in the main loop may remain unchanged. Once you are done exploring the state, leaving the interpreter will resume execution of the program.

```
>>> (Ctrl-D)
6 7 8 9
$ _
```

Such an embedded interactive debugging facility can be triggered by inserting appropriate calls in the code, by enabling it from the outside, or upon specific failure conditions. Be aware, though, that this facility is not enabled in production code. Otherwise, bad guys will have fun gaining complete control over your system.

8.3.8 Debugger Caveats

Despite the functionality provided by a debugger, one should keep in mind that interactive debuggers have a certain toy-like quality. That is, it is simply fascinating for the creator to see his or her program in action and to exercise total control. This can easily distract from solving the problem at hand. Even when working with an interactive debugger, one should always be explicit about the current hypothesis, and the steps required to validate it, as described in Chapter 6 "Scientific Debugging." Debuggers can be excellent tools — but only when combined with good thinking.

8.4 QUERYING EVENTS

Most hypotheses about a program can be tied to a specific *location* within the program, as in "at line 38, a[0] = 0 should hold." This location is the place at which logging code can be inserted, at which aspects can be woven in, and at which a debugger user sets a breakpoint to stop execution.

However, some hypotheses cannot be attached to such a precise location. In fact, the location may well be the subject of a query itself. Just imagine you find some variable (say, Printer.errno) being set to a specific value at the end of a program run. You could now follow back Printer.errno's dependences, as discussed in Chapter 7 "Deducing Errors," and observe each of the locations in which Printer.errno may be set. You will find, though, that in the presence of pointers there will probably be several such locations, and checking them all is a tedious activity. What one needs in this situation is a means of having the program stop at a location that is implied by a condition (e.g., "the location at which `Printer.errno` is set").

Using an aspect (Section 8.2.3), this is a fairly easy task. All one needs to do is to define a point cut `set(Printer.errno)` that includes all locations in which the `Printer.errno` is set:

```
public aspect LogErrno {
  pointcut setErrno():
    set(Printer.errno);

  before(): setErrno() {
    System.out.println("Old value:" + Printer.errno);
  }
  after(): setErrno() {
    System.out.println("New value:" + Printer.errno);
  }
}
```

It is fairly easy to refine this aspect further — for instance, to log `Printer.errno` only if it gets a specific value.

8.4.1 Watchpoints

Using languages without aspect support such as C, though, we must resort to *debuggers* to catch assignments to specific variables. GDB provides a feature called *data breakpoints* or *watchpoints* to catch the specific moment in time in which a given condition comes true. For instance, in the `sample` program to catch the moment in which a[0] is assigned use:

```
(gdb) watch a[0]
Watchpoint 3: a[0]
(gdb) _
```

Having created this watchpoint (which must be done when a[0] actually exists), GDB will check for each subsequent machine instruction whether the value of a[0] has changed. If so, GDB will stop program execution:

```
(gdb) continue
Watchpoint 3: a[0]
```

```
Old value = 11
New value = 0
shell_sort (a=0x100140, size=3) at sample.c:15
15                  for (i = h; i < size; i++)
(gdb) _
```

Execution has stopped at the statement *after* the value of a[0] has changed. The most recent executed statement is at the end of the for loop, a[j] = v—and this is where a[0] got its zero value from.

Watchpoints are expensive. Because the debugger must verify the value of the watched expression after each instruction, a watchpoint implies a switch between the debugged processes and the debugger process for each instruction step. This slows down program execution by a factor of 1,000 or more. Fortunately, some processors provide *hardware watchpoints* that can automatically monitor a small number of locations for changes without degrading performance. Debuggers such as GDB can make use of such hardware facilities to provide a limited number of hardware-assisted watchpoints.

If your program restricts access to specific data via accessor functions [such as setX() and getX() methods in a class], it is much easier to set up a breakpoint in these accessor functions. Languages with managed memory, such as JAVA, ensure that no external piece of the program can modify or access data without going through the public interface of the encapsulating class. In languages with unmanaged memory, such as C or C++, protection is limited. It is conceivable that an external piece of the program accesses data directly—either on purpose or by accident (say, via a stray pointer). To catch the culprit, watchpoints can come in as a last resort.

In some cases, one might be interested in having a program stop upon a specific condition *and* at a specific location. In this case, a *conditional* breakpoint comes in handy—a breakpoint that stops only under certain conditions. The following is a simple example.

```
(gdb) break 37 if a[0] == 0
Breakpoint 4 at 0x1d04: file sample.c, line 37.
(gdb) _
```

Here, the breakpoint stops the program only if the given condition is met. This is useful when checking for specific infections—such as a[0] being zero, in this example.

TABLE 8.1 Attributes in COCA

Events		Data	
Attribute	*Meaning*	*Attribute*	*Meaning*
type	function/return …	**name**	Variable name
port	enter/exit	**type**	Type
func	Function name	**val**	Value
chrono	Time stamp	**addr**	Address
cdepth	Call stack	**size**	Size in memory
line	Current line	**linedecl**	Declaration line
file	Current file	**filedecl**	Declaration file

8.4.2 Uniform Event Queries

The distinction among watchpoints, breakpoints, and conditional breakpoints is purely motivated by the technique by which these concepts are implemented. One might as well *generalize* these concepts to have *a uniform query mechanism* that stops program execution as soon as a specific condition is met — a condition that may involve the current execution position as arbitrary aspects of the program state. One such attempt was realized by the COCA debugger — a front end to GDB that provides a uniform query for arbitrary events during execution.

In COCA, events and data are characterized by *attributes* (outlined in Table 8.1). These attributes can be used in *queries* to obtain all events or data where the query would be satisfied. A query typically consists of two parts.

- *Time:* A query fget(*attributes*) denotes the subset of the execution time in which the given attributes hold. The query fget(func=shell_sort), for instance, denotes all events in which the current function is shell_sort.

- *Space:* A query current_data(*attributes*) denotes the subset of the execution data in which the given attributes hold. For example, a query current_data(type=int) denotes all data whose type is int.

If time is not specified, the query refers to the data at the current execution position.

Within the specification of time and space, *logical variables* (starting with an uppercase letter) can be used to *match* specific events. Any events that match will then be returned as a result of the query. (Readers familiar with PROLOG may recognize this style of query.) Thus, a full query at COCA's prompt might look as follows.

Which variable currently has a value of 42?

```
[coca] current_var(Name, val=42).
Name = x0
Name = x1
[coca] _
```

Which variables are zero during execution of shell_sort()?

```
[coca] fget(func=shell_sort and line=Ln),
        current_var(Name, val=0).
Name = a[2]   Ln = ⟨int i, j;⟩
Name = v      Ln = ⟨int v = a[i]⟩
Name = a[0]   Ln = ⟨a[j] = v⟩
[coca] _
```

When did a[2] become zero?

```
[coca] fget(line=Ln),
        current_var(a, val=array(-,-,0,...)).
Ln = ⟨a = malloc(...)⟩
[coca] _
```

Internally, COCA translates all of these queries into appropriate GDB commands:

- `fget()` sets appropriate breakpoints and executes the program.

- `current_var()` queries the set of variables.

Although a single query can generate several GDB commands, the general performance issues of data queries persist. A general query such as

```
fget(func=shell_sort), current_var(a[0], val=0)
```

still requires a watchpoint to capture the moments in which `a[0]` was zero.

Overall, event and data queries as realized in COCA provide a far more general (and far more versatile) interface than the basic debugger breakpoint and watchpoint commands. One should keep in mind, though, that queries over a wide range of events may take a surprisingly long time to execute, because they must rely on slow watchpoints — a surprise that does not take place when programmers must "manually" translate their experiment into appropriate breakpoint and watchpoint commands.

A different situation occurs, though, when the language in question is *interpreted* — because then the interpreter can easily be extended to monitor the execution for specific conditions. The Java virtual machine (JVM), for instance, has an interface for *monitoring* the access of object attributes. It can interrupt the execution whenever some specific attribute is read or written. Because the JVM is realized in software, there are no limits on the number of monitors, and the performance loss is not as dramatic compared with debugger watchpoints.

8.5   VISUALIZING STATE

The observation techniques discussed so far all have relied on pure *textual* output of program states and variables. The following is an example of a tree node as it is being output by GDB and other debuggers.

```
*tree = {value = 7, _name = 0x8049e88 "Ada",
  _left = 0x804d7d8, _right = 0x0,
  left_thread = false, right_thread = false,
  date = {day_of_week = Thu, day = 1, month = 1,
    year = 1970,
    _vptr. = 0x8049f78 ⟨Date virtual table⟩},
  static shared = 4711}
```

Although textual output is useful for keeping track of scalar values, it is hardly useful when it comes to tracking *relationships* between objects — especially inclusions and references. In the previous structure, which are the elements of the date substructure, for instance? Would you spot whether two pointers have the same address and thus reference the same object?

To improve the understanding of data structures, some debuggers allow us to *visualize* these relationships. The GNU Data Display Debugger, or DDD for short, is a graphical front end for GDB and other debuggers that provides such a visualization (Figure 8.2).

DDD visualizes such data as a box whose elements can be unfolded at the user's will (Figure 8.3). This allows the user to focus on specific parts of the data without cluttering the screen with irrelevant data.

DDD displays each individual datum as a single box. However, if a box originates from another box DDD creates an arrow from the origin to the target. This normally happens if the user dereferences a pointer. A pointer arc points from the origin (the pointer address) to the target (the dereferenced element).

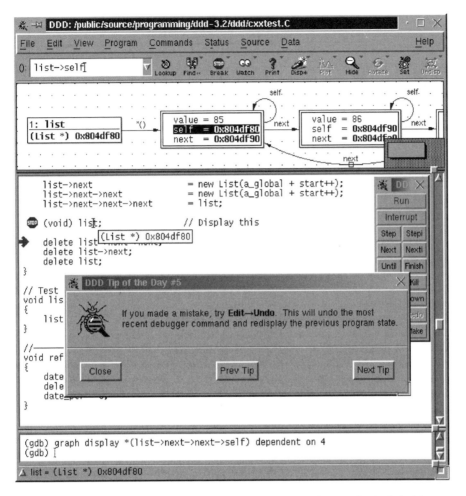

FIGURE 8.2 The DDD debugger. In the top window, DDD has visualized a linked list.

This allows for simple exploration and visualization of complex data structures (Figure 8.4).

In addition to visualizing data structures and relationships, DDD can plot numerical values as charts, and even plot the history of individual variables. Such plots summarize multiple values into a single visualization, and make it easier for programmers to detect uncommon state.

All of these visualizations are limited, though, by the programmer's ability to comprehend and compare large amounts of data. If one already knows the properties of some infection (such as "there is a cycle somewhere in the tree"), it can be easier to have the computer search for these properties rather than

```
1: *tree
{...}        1: *tree
             value       = 7           1: *tree
             _name       = 0x8049       value       = 7
             _left       = 0x804d       _name       = 0x8049e88 "Ada"
             _right      = 0x0          _left       = 0x804d7d8
             left_thread = false        _right      = 0x0
             right_thread = false       left_thread = false
             date        = {...}        right_thread = false
             shared      = 4711
                                                    day_of_week = Thu
                                                    day         = 1
                                        date   =    month       = 1
                                                    year        = 1970
                                                    _vptr.      = 0x8049f78 <Date virtual table>

                                        shared      = 4711
```

FIGURE 8.3 Unfolding data structures in DDD.

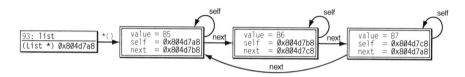

```
93: list        *()    value = 85    next    value = 86    next    value = 87
(List *) 0x804d7a8      self  = 0x804d7a8     self  = 0x804d7b8     self  = 0x804d7c8
                       next  = 0x804d7b8     next  = 0x804d7c8     next  = 0x804d7a8
                                          next
```

FIGURE 8.4 A linked list in DDD.

scanning huge amounts of data manually. We will come back to this idea in Chapter 10 "Asserting Expectations."

8.6 CONCEPTS

✎ When observing state, do not interfere. Know what and when to observe, and proceed systematically.

HOW TO ✎ *To observe state*, use:

- Logging functions (Section 8.2.1)

- Aspects (Section 8.2.3)

- A debugger (Section 8.3)

✎ Logging statements ("printf debugging") are easy to use, but tend to clutter the code and the output.

HOW TO ✎ *To encapsulate and reuse debugging code*, use a dedicated logging framework or aspects.

✎ Dedicated logging functions can be set up such that they can be turned off without impacting performance. With enough discipline, they can even remain in the production code.

✎ Aspects offer an elegant way of keeping all logging code in one place and applying the same logging code to multiple places.

✎ Debuggers allow flexible and quick observation of arbitrary events. Reuse of logging code is difficult, though.

✎ *To observe the final state of a crashing program*, use a debugger to observe the postmortem memory dump. If that is not available, repeat the run in a debugger.

HOW TO

✎ Advanced debuggers allow flexible querying of events (Section 8.4) and visualization of program data (Section 8.5).

8.7 TOOLS

LOG4J

The development of LOG4J started in 1996, and has seen countless enhancements and incarnations before it became the popular package it is today. Everything about LOG4J, as well as its ports to other languages, can be found at:

```
http://logging.apache.org/
```

ASPECTJ

ASPECTJ was introduced by Kiczales et al. (2001). Its web page has several resources to aspect-oriented programming. It can be found at:

```
http://www.eclipse.org/aspectj/
```

PIN

The PIN tool for dynamic binary instrumentation is available at:

```
http://rogue.colorado.edu/Pin/
```

The site also contains online manuals and documentation.

BCEL

For JAVA, binary instrumentation is available through BCEL, the Byte Code Engineering Library. It allows arbitrary manipulation of JAVA byte code, including inserting code to be executed before and after function calls. This can be found at:

```
http://jakarta.apache.org/bcel/
```

GDB

GDB was developed by Stallman and Pesch (1994), mimicking Sun's DBX interactive debugger. Its web page is found at:

```
http://www.gnu.org/software/gdb/
```

DDD

DDD was built by Zeller and Lütkehaus (1996) as a front end to GDB. Since then, it has been extended to various other command-line debuggers. The DDD manual was written by Zeller (2000), available from its web page at:

```
http://www.gnu.org/software/ddd/
```

JAVA SPIDER

Although DDD also supports JDB, the JAVA command-line debugger, I would not recommend it for debugging JAVA programs. If you are interested in visualizing JAVA state, have a look at the JAVA SPIDER tool by Erich Gamma and Ken Beck. This may be found at:

```
http://sourceforge.net/projects/javaspider/
```

JAVA SPIDER is publicly available as a plug-in for the ECLIPSE programming environment.

eDOBS

The eDOBS project by Geiger and Zündorf (2002) uses UML diagrams for visualization. It thus raises the level of abstraction from plain programming structures to the level of UML object diagrams. This is especially useful in large-scale program understanding. This can be found at:

```
http://www.se.eecs.uni-kassel.de/se/index.php?edobs
```

eDOBS also comes as an ECLIPSE plug-in.

8.8 FURTHER READING

To learn how debuggers, such as GDB work, the book by Rosenberg (1996) gives an insight about the basic algorithms, data structures, and architecture of interactive debuggers.

GDB allows efficient watchpoints only with hardware support. As Wahbe (1992) points out, efficient watchpoints need not necessarily be implemented in hardware, and suggests a software solution. His technique modifies the code of the debuggee to monitor the instructions that might affect the watched data—with acceptable performance for most debugging applications.

COCA was developed by Ducassé (1999). An efficient querying concept for JAVA, using JAVA class instrumentation, is described in the book by Lencevicius (2000).

8.9 EXERCISES

EXERCISE 8.1. Use DDD to debug `sample` (Section 1.1):

1. Set breakpoints at lines 31, 35, and 37 by pressing the right button of your mouse in that line at the left border of the source window and selecting Set Breakpoint from the resultant context menu.

2. Run the program by selecting Program → Run from the menu. Insert your failure-producing arguments and select Run.

3. The program should have stopped at line 31. Display the content of array a: In the argument field, insert a[0]@5 and click on the display button. (Replace 5 with an appropriate number of array fields.) Display argv in the same way.

   To obtain a display of variables i and argc, it may be easier to hover with the mouse pointer above a variable name in the source window and use the context menu obtained with the right mouse button.

4. Select Program → Continue (or click on the Cont button on the small navigation window).

5. The program should have stopped at line 35. Click on the continue button.

6. The program should have stopped at line 37. Click on the continue button.

7. The program should run to the end. To restart the program, you can simply click on "Run again" (or on Run in the small navigation window).

Inspect the content of the variables at each breakpoint. Which variables have changed? When does the state become infected?

EXERCISE 8.2. Insert logging macros into the sample program (Section 1.1). Make your logging macros optional at compile time. Can you determine the behavior of the shell_sort() function with the log output only?

EXERCISE 8.3. In the exercises of Chapter 5 "Simplifying Problems," we used a JAVA implementation of the delta debugging algorithm (Example 5.10) to simplify inputs. In this exercise, we shall use observation methods to trace the run.

1. Use LOG4J to create a trace. Log all invocations of all methods.

2. Using appropriate logging levels, allow users to follow the execution of:

   • Each test (i.e., a test is being carried out)

   • Each progress (i.e., the input size has been reduced)

   • Start and end of delta debugging only (showing the final result)

3. Use aspects to create a trace on the console.

- Log all invocations of all methods. Use separate aspects for different methods.

- Extend your example to use LOG4J.

4. Modify the example in Example 8.2 such that it computes an execution *profile*—that is, it records for each instruction how often it was executed.

EXERCISE 8.4. You would like to examine a program run as soon as one of the following holds:

A   Function foo() is reached

B   Variable a[0] is equal to 2

C   foo() is reached and a[0] is equal to 2

D   foo() is reached or a[0] is equal to 2

E   foo() is reached and at least one of a[0], a[1], ..., a[99] is equal to 2

F   All of a[0], a[1], ..., a[99] are equal to 2

Assume that the processor has no special debugging support, except for changing individual machine instructions into interrupt instructions.

1. Sort these queries according to the execution speed of the examined program. Start with the fastest.

2. Sketch processor support that can make these queries more efficient.

3. Sketch possible code instrumentation (e.g., adding new code at compilation time) which makes these queries more efficient.

EXERCISE 8.5. When stopping a program, the current *backtrace* is a summary of how your program got where it is. It is a sequence of *frames,* where each frame holds the execution context of a called function. The backtrace starts with the currently executing frame (frame 0), followed by its caller (frame 1), and on up the stack. The following is an example of a backtrace, showing the innermost three frames.

```
#0  m4_traceon (obs=0x24eb0, argc=1, argv=0x2b8c8)
    at builtin.c:993
```

```
#1  0x6e38 in expand_macro (sym=0x2b600) at macro.c:242
#2  0x6840 in expand_token (obs=0x0, t=177664, td=0xf7fffb08)
        at macro.c:71
```

Suppose you have a given backtrace as an array of function names. For instance:

```
backtrace[0] == "m4_traceon"
backtrace[1] == "expand_macro"
backtrace[2] == "expand_token"
```

Your task is to instrument a debugger such that the program being examined stops as soon as a specific backtrace or its superset is reached. In this backtrace, the program should stop as soon as m4_traceon is reached while expand_macro is active, where expand_macro was reached while expand_token was active. To instrument the debugger, you can use the following functions.

- set_breakpoint(*function*, ENTER/EXIT|) sets a breakpoint such that execution stops when entering/exiting the function *function*. It returns a unique number for each created breakpoint.

- delete_breakpoint(*bp_nr*) deletes the breakpoint number *bp_nr*.

- continue() starts or resumes execution until the next breakpoint is reached. It returns the number of the reached breakpoint.

Example: To make the program stop as soon as "m4_traceon" is entered, use the following.

```
m4_bp = set_breakpoint("m4_traceon", ENTER);
do {
    bp = continue();
} while (bp != m4_bp);
delete_breakpoint(m4_bp);
```

Design an algorithm in C-like pseudocode that uses the previous functions to make a program stop at a specific backtrace. Be sure to comment your work.

EXERCISE 8.6. Mystery time! When being executed on Mac OS, the bigbang program shown in Example 8.3 is reported to hang up after issuing the result (rather than terminating normally):

```
1   #include <iostream>
2   using namespace std;
3
4   #include "Element.h"
5   #include "Container.h"
6
7     bool mode = true;  // (1)
8
9   int main (int argc, char *argv[]) {
10        Element *a = new Element(1);
11        Element *b = new Element(2);
12        a->setPeer(b);
13        b->setPeer(a);
14        a->doSomeStuff();
15
16        Container *c = new Container(10, mode);
17        // c->add(b); // (2)
18        c->add(a);
19        c->add(b);
20
21        cout << "result is: " << c->processElements() << '\n';
22
23        delete c;
24        return 0;
25  }
```

EXAMPLE 8.3 The bigbang program. The Container class is defined in Example 8.4. The Element class is shown in Example 8.5.

```
$ bigbang
result is: 2
⟨Interrupting execution⟩
$ _
```

What's wrong with this program?

1. Use logging functions to log the program state. Use a dedicated method for each class.

```
1  #ifndef MY_CONTAINER_H
2  #define MY_CONTAINER_H
3
4  #include "Element.h"
5
6  class Container {
7  private:
8      bool deleteElements;
9      int size;
10     Element **elements;
11
12 public:
13     Container(int sz, bool del)
14       : size(sz), deleteElements(del)
15     {
16         elements = new Element *[size];
17         for (int i = 0; i < size; i++)
18             elements[i] = 0;
19     }
20     int processElements() {
21         int sum = 0;
22         for (int i = 0; i < size; i++)
23             if (elements[i])
24                 sum += elements[i]->getData();
25
26         return sum;
27     }
28     bool add(Element* e) {
29         for (int i = 0; i < size; i++)
30             if (elements[i] == 0) {
31                 elements[i] = e;
32                 return true;
33             }
34
35         return false;
36     }
37     virtual ~Container () {
38         if (deleteElements)
39             for (int i = 0; i < size; i++)
40                 delete elements[i];
41
42         delete elements;
43     }
44 };
45 #endif
```

EXAMPLE 8.4 The Container.h file for the bigbang program.

2. Use GDB or another interactive debugger to examine the run.

3. Use DDD to visualize the relationships between the individual elements.

    Document all of your steps in a logbook (Section 6.5).

```
1   #ifndef MY_ELEMENT_H
2   #define MY_ELEMENT_H
3
4   class Element {
5       int data;
6       Element *peer;
7
8   public:
9       Element (int d)
10        : data(d), peer(0)
11      {}
12
13      int getData ()            { return data; }
14      void setPeer (Element *p) { peer = p; }
15      void resetPeer ()         { peer = 0; }
16
17      void doSomeStuff () {
18          if (peer != 0) {
19              delete peer;
20              resetPeer();
21          }
22      }
23
24      virtual ~Element () {
25          if (peer != 0 && peer->peer == this) {
26              peer->resetPeer();
27          }
28      }
29  };
30
31  #endif
```

EXAMPLE 8.5 The Element.h file for the bigbang program.

"If a program can't rewrite its own code", he asked, "what good is it?"

— ED NATHER
The Story of Mel (1983)

CHAPTER 9

TRACKING ORIGINS

O NCE WE HAVE OBSERVED AN INFECTION during debugging, we need to discover its origin. In this chapter, we discuss *omniscient debugging*, a technique that records an entire execution history such that the user can explore arbitrary moments in time without ever restarting the program. Furthermore, we explore *dynamic slicing,* a technique that tracks the origins of specific values.

9.1 REASONING BACKWARDS

A common issue with observation tools, as discussed in Chapter 8 "Observing Facts," is that they execute the program *forward* in time, whereas the programmer must reason *backward* in time. Applied to interactive debugging tools, this means that the programmer must carefully approach the moment in time where the infection is observable. As soon as the infection is found, he must restart the program and stop at some earlier moment in time to explore the previous state.

Restoring the steps to get to the earlier state can be pretty time consuming—and if we go just one step too far, the program must be restarted anew. One key issue for (human) debuggers is thus how to ease the task of discovering the *origin* of a value, and how to keep a *memory* of what was going on during the run. Here, we ask:

> WHERE DOES THIS VALUE COME FROM?

9.2 EXPLORING EXECUTION HISTORY

So you want to support the programmer in examining the history? One first idea would be to have a means of undoing the last execution steps. An even better idea is to *explore the entire execution history backward.* In other words, we *record* the execution — every single change to every single aspect of the state.

This radical idea has been realized under the name of *omniscient debugging* in a number of recent debuggers. Rather than accessing the program while it is running, an omniscient debugger first executes the program and then records it. Once the run is complete, the omniscient debugger loads the recording and makes it available for observation.

Figure 9.1 shows the ODB debugger for JAVA, a prototype that pioneered and proved the concept. At the center of ODB, one can see the traditional source code window, highlighting the current execution position. The other windows show more of the program state, such as current threads, the stack content, variable values, the console output, and so on.

Using the arrow buttons above the source code window, one can step through the program's execution. In contrast to ordinary debuggers, though,

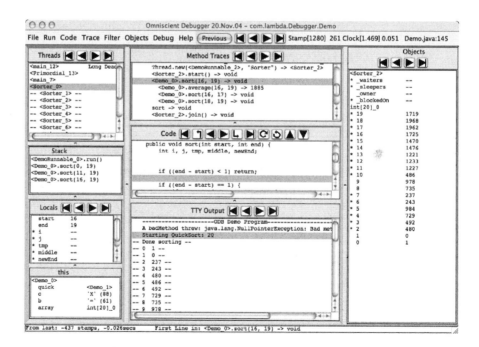

FIGURE 9.1 Exploring execution history in ODB. Users can navigate backward and forward through the execution, and along events related to variables, statements, and outputs.

ODB also features buttons to step *backward* through the execution. As one walks back in time, all windows are synchronized properly. If you step before an assignment, the variable value shown will go back to the earlier value, and if you step before an output statement the appropriate output will disappear from the console.

In addition to stepping backward and forward along program lines, one can step back and forth between *time stamps* specific to the individual windows. In the code window, each moment of line execution has a time stamp (nothing special here). In the data window, though, time stamps correspond to *value changes* of the displayed variables. To find out when array[] was last changed, you can select array[] in the window listing the variable values, and then use the buttons above that window to walk back and forth in the value history. Variables whose value has changed from the previously shown time stamp are highlighted with a leading *.

Each time an earlier point in the execution history is reached, the other windows synchronize as well. Therefore, one sees the previous value and the line that assigned the value, as well as every other aspect of the current state. In addition to stepping through events, the programmer can issue *event queries* (as discussed in Section 8.4.2) and thus directly jump to specific events. (In contrast to COCA, though, ODB does not need to renew the execution, which makes querying much faster.) A typical debugging session using ODB proceeds as follows.

1. Start with the failure, as reported in the console window. Clicking on the output will lead to the moment in time the output was produced — that is, the output statement will be shown in the code window.

2. Step backward, searching the infection at each point.

3. Follow the infection back to the defect.

The main drawback, of course, is that recording all state changes is expensive. First, recording adds a certain overhead, such that a typical program will be slowed down by a factor of 10 or more. Second, recording needs memory — a lot of it. ODB generates data at the rate of 100 MB per second, meaning that a 2-GB address space will fill up in 20 seconds. To deal with the memory issue, one can

•   record specific events only (such as the last second before the failure, or whatever fits into memory),

- record specific parts of the system only (we do not care what is going on in the runtime library), or

- use a compressed storage of the individual events.

All in all, though, the advantages far outweigh the disadvantages. Using omniscient debugging, the programmer has random access to every moment in time and every aspect of the execution, without ever needing to restart the program — a tremendous advantage over ordinary interactive debuggers. It is not unlikely that omniscient debugging will become a standard feature of future interactive debuggers.

9.3 DYNAMIC SLICING

Although omniscient debugging is handy for accessing every aspect of a program execution, the programmer still has to figure out how the individual values came to be. This is where *dependences* come in handy, as discussed in Chapter 7 "Deducing Errors." If we know that the bad value of variable A can only come from variable B at some earlier moment in time, we can immediately focus on B. A good programmer would thus use both observation (of the program run) and deduction (from the program code) to quickly progress toward the defect.

Chapter 7 "Deducing Errors" treated dependences in an abstract way — that is, we have explored dependences as they hold for arbitrary runs of the program. When debugging, we have a concrete failing run at hand, and we would like to know the *dependences for this concrete run* in order to trace back origins.

This is where the technique of *dynamic slicing* comes in handy. Like a static slice, a dynamic slice encompasses a part of the program — that is, the part of the program that could have influenced (or could be influenced by) a specific variable at some point. However, a dynamic slice does not hold for *all* possible runs but for one single *concrete* run.

As an example of a static versus a dynamic slice, consider the program shown in Example 9.1. The static backward slice (a) of s, being output in line 15, encompasses the entire program (try it!). The dynamic slice in b applies to the run in which n and a are read in as 2 and 0, respectively. Note that a large number of statements has no effect on the final value of s. The dynamic slice for the run is more precise than the static slice for the entire program.

How can a slice as shown in Example 9.1 be computed? To compute a dynamic slice, one requires a *trace* — a list of statements in the order they were exe-

```
1 n = read();                    1 n = read(); // 2
2 a = read();                    2 a = read(); // 0
3 x = 1;                         3 x = 1;
4 b = a + x;                     4 b = a + x;
5 a = a + 1;                     5 a = a + 1;
6 i = 1;                         6 i = 1;
7 s = 0;                         7 s = 0;
8 while (i <= n) {               8 while (i <= n) {
9      if (b > 0)                9      if (b > 0)
10         if (a > 1)            10         if (a > 1)
11             x = 2;            11             x = 2;
12     s = s + x;                12     s = s + x;
13     i = i + 1;                13     i = i + 1;
14 }                             14 }
15 write(s);                     15 write(s);
```

(a) Static slice for s   (b) Dynamic slice for s

EXAMPLE 9.1 Static and dynamic slices.

Trace	Write	Read	Dynamic Slice
1 n = read();	n		
2 a = read();	a		
3 x = 1;	x		
4 b = a + x;	b	a, x	**2, 3**
5 a = a + 1;	a	a	**2**
6 i = 1;	i		
7 s = 0;	s		
8 while (i <= n) {	p8	i, n	**6, 1**
9 if (b > 0)	p9	b, p8	**2, 3, 6, 1, 4, 8**
10 if (a > 1)	p10	a, p9	**2, 3, 6, 1, 4, 8, 5, 9**
12 s = s + x;	s	s, x, p8	**6, 1, 7, 3, 8**
13 i = i + 1;	i	i, p8	**6, 1, 8**
8 while (i <= n) {	p8	i, n	6, 1, **8, 13**
9 if (b > 0)	p9	b, p8	2, 3, 6, 1, 4, 8, **13**
10 if (a > 1)	p10	a, p9	2, 3, 6, 1, 4, 8, 5, 9, **13**
12 s = s + x;	s	s, x, p8	6, 1, 7, 3, 8, **13, 12**
13 i = i + 1;	i	i, p8	6, 1, 8, **13**
8 while (i <= n) {	p8	i, n	6, 1, 8, **13**
15 write(s);	o15	s	**6, 1, 7, 3, 8, 13, 12**

EXAMPLE 9.2 Computing a dynamic slice from a trace.

cuted during the concrete run. Such a trace is either created by *instrumenting* the program — that is, having the compiler or another tool embed special tracing commands — or by running the program in an interpreter. The leftmost column of Example 9.2 shows the trace of statements from the run n = 2, a = 0 in Example 9.1b.

In this trace, one records the variables that were read and written — just as in Table 7.1, except that now the effects are recorded for each statement as it is executed. In addition, one introduces a *predicate pseudovariable* for each predicate that controls execution (such as p8 for the predicate i <= n in line 8). Each of these pseudovariables is "written" by the statement that control execution and "read" by the statements that are controlled. Example 9.2 shows the effects of the individual statements.

From these effects, one can now compute dynamic slices by following the read/write dependences. The following is a method that computes all dynamic slices for all written values at once.

1. For each write w to a variable, assign an empty dynamic slice.

$$DynSlice(w) = \emptyset$$

2. Proceed forward through the trace (or execute the program, generating the trace). Whenever a value w is written, consider all variables r_i read in that statement. For each r_i, consider the line $line(r_i)$ where r_i was last written, as well as its dynamic slice $DynSlice(r_i)$. Compute the union of these lines and slices and assign it to the write of w.

$$DynSlice(w) = \bigcup_i (DynSlice(r_i) \cup \{line(r_i)\})$$

As an example, consider the dynamic slice of line 4, $DynSlice(4)$. In line 4, b = a + x, variable b is written and variables a and x are read, last written in lines 2 and 3, respectively. Therefore, the dynamic slice of b in line 4 is the union of

-   the dynamic slice of a in line 2 (empty),

-   the dynamic slice of x in line 3 (empty), and

-   lines 2 and 3.

Formally, this reads:

$$\begin{aligned}
DynSlice(4) &= DynSlice(2) \cup \{2\} \cup DynSlice(3) \cup \{3\} \\
&= \emptyset \cup \{2\} \cup \emptyset \cup \{3\} \\
&= \{2, 3\}
\end{aligned}$$

3. At the end of the execution, all definitions will be assigned a slice that holds all origins of all values.

As an example, consider the right-hand column in Example 9.2, showing the dynamic slices as they are computed along the trace. (Values in bold indicate new additions to the slices.) The last line shows the dynamic backward slice for s in the statement write(s). These are exactly the lines highlighted in Example 9.2.

On average, dynamic slices are far more precise than static slices. In a concrete run, all locations of all variables — including those in *computed* expressions such as a[i] or *p — are known, eliminating conservative approximation. Likewise, in a concrete run paths that were not taken need not be taken into account.

All in all, this makes dynamic slices smaller than static slices. Whereas a static backward slice typically encompasses 30% of a program's statements, a dynamic slice only encompasses 5% of the executed statements (note that the *executed* statements also form a subset of all statements). The increased precision comes at a price, though.

- *Overhead:* Dynamic slices depend on a trace of the program, which is difficult to obtain efficiently. Although we need not record the entire value history (as in omniscient debugging), we still need to record which statements were taken in which order.

- *Lack of generality:* Dynamic slices only apply to a single run of the program, and thus cannot be reused for other runs (in contrast to program dependence graphs and static slices, which are valid for all runs).

9.4 LEVERAGING ORIGINS

How can dynamic slices be used in a debugger? This was explored by Ko and Myers (2004) in the WHYLINE system. WHYLINE stands for "**W**orkspace that **H**elps **Y**ou **L**ink **I**nstructions to **N**umbers and **E**vents." It is a debugger whereby programmers can ask questions about why things happened, and why other things did not happen. In short, it is a debugger whereby you can ask: "Why did my program fail?"

The WHYLINE has been designed for the ALICE language — a simple language in which three-dimensional objects can be defined and manipulated. ALICE is designed for novices learning programming. In the programming environment, users select and compose ALICE statements interactively rather than

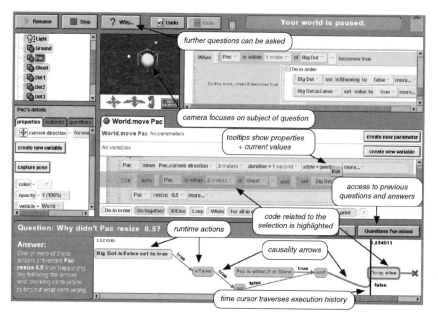

FIGURE 9.2 Asking "Why didn't" questions in the WHYLINE (Ko and Myers, 2004).

entering them as text. Nonetheless, ALICE is just as powerful as any other programming language.

In Figure 9.2, we see a screen shot from a student's debugging session. In a PACMAN program, the protagonist Pac has collided with a ghost, but does not shrink as it should. The student uses the WHYLINE for debugging the program. In the center window, we see the code that should resize Pac by 0.5.

```
if both Pac is within 2 meters of Ghost and
    not Big Dot.isEaten:
    Pac resize 0.5
```

However, this resizing code is not being executed. To find out why the branch is not taken, the student has clicked on the Why button. From a menu (Figure 9.3), she has opted to ask why Pac resize 0.5 was not executed.

The WHYLINE's answer is shown at the bottom of Figure 9.2. The diagnosis comes as a chain of dependences ending at the else branch (), consisting of the following events.

1. Big Dot.isEaten is set to true.

2. Therefore, the isEaten variable is true.

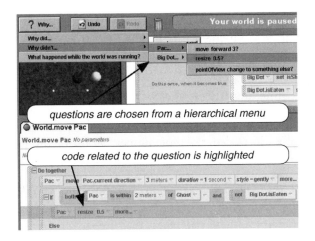

FIGURE 9.3 Selecting a question in the WHYLINE (Ko and Myers, 2004). At the bottom, the diagnosis shows why a specific piece of code was not executed.

3. The negation not (from the previous code) is false.

4. Although Pac is within 2 meters of Ghost is true,

5. the and conjunction (from the previous code) evaluates to false,

6. and therefore the else clause is taken.

The student can further explore this diagnosis by scrubbing a time cursor over the dependency chain and thus access arbitrary moments in time, just as in omniscient debugging. When she moves the cursor over the Big Dot.isEaten set to true bubble, the code window shows the code in which the Big Dot.isEaten variable is set.

All of this is just correct behavior. It turns out that Pac did not resize simply because he had eaten a big dot before, making him immune against ghost attacks. (Rather than Pac being resized, one should see the ghost being eaten!)

How does the WHYLINE compute its diagnosis? The answer is simple: all the WHYLINE does is to compute a *dynamic backward slice* of the queried property. More precisely, the following are the strategies that WHYLINE uses.

- *"Why did" questions:* For a *why did* question, the WHYLINE shows the *dynamic backward slice* from the queried statement S. That is, it would show all statements P is dependent upon. The slice is limited to two such statements. If needed, the programmer can query again about a specific statement.

As an example, consider the slices shown in Example 9.1 and the question "Why did s = 2 in line 15?" The WHYLINE strategy would point to

– "s = 1" from line 12 (s = s + x), the direct origin of s, as well as

– "i = 2" from line 8 (i <= n), which controls execution of line 12.

[Instead of line 8, the WHYLINE strategy could also point to line 3 (x = 1), the origin of x.] If needed, the programmer can further explore the origins by querying why one of these statements was executed.

- *"Why didn't" questions:* For a *why didn't* question, the WHYLINE would use the *static backward slice* of the statement S and by following back the control dependences retrieve those statements that directly prevented execution. It then performs the *why did* question on each.

  As an example, let's ask the question "Why didn't x = 2 in line 11?" Following the static dependences, we have three control dependences from line 11 to lines 8, 9, and 10, respectively. Assume the WHYLINE asks the *why did* question only for the closest one, line 10 (if (a > 1)). As an answer, it would then present

  – "a = 1" from line 5 (a = a + 1), as well as

  – "b = 1" from line 9 (if (b > 0)), the statement directly controlling line 5.

Again, the programmer could interactively query the WHYLINE about how these values came to be.

Overall, the WHYLINE demonstrates what can be done in a modern debugger. It incorporates random access in time (as in omniscient debugging) as well as static and dynamic slicing to trace origins. By limiting the slice length, it prevents the programmer from having to deal with too many possible origins, and allows exploration along the dependences. Finally, it shows how to package it all in a nice user interface, avoiding the use of program analysis jargon such as "dependences" or "slices." A study conducted by Ko and Myers (2004) showed that the WHYLINE would reduce debugging time by nearly a factor of 8, highlighting the potential of modern debugging environments. If only the WHYLINE were available for my favorite programming language!

9.5 TRACKING DOWN INFECTIONS

Even with all of the advanced observation tools discussed in this chapter, we still need a strategy for using them systematically. The following is a *general strategy* that combines observation and dependences to narrow down arbitrary infection sites — that is, a strategy for *locating arbitrary defects*.

1. Start with the infected value as reported by the failure. In the `sample` program (Example 1.1), this would be `a[0]`.

2. Follow back the dependences to potential origins. This can be done using

    *   static dependences, as discussed in Chapter 7 "Deducing Errors," or

    *   dynamic dependences, as discussed in Section 9.3.

    Following the data dependences in `sample`, we can trace back the value of `a[0]` to other values in `a[]` as well as to `size`.

3. Observe the origins and judge whether the individual origins are infected or not. In the `sample` run, we find that `size` is infected (it has the wrong value).

4. If you find an earlier infected value, repeat steps 2 and 3 to track its origins. In `sample`, the value of `size` depends on `argc` (and only on `argc`).

5. When you find an infected value V where all values that V depends on are sane, you have found the infection site — in other words, the defect. `argc` is sane, but `size` is not. Hence, the infection must have taken place at the assignment of `argc` to `size` — at the function call to `shell_sort()`.

6. Fix the defect, and verify that the failure no longer occurs. This ensures that you have found the defect that caused the failure in question.

This strategy is in fact an application of scientific method (Chapter 6 "Scientific Debugging") that creates hypotheses along the dependences, and uses observation to assess possible origins. It also guarantees that you *will* find the infection site, just by observation and judgment. It even works when dependences are imprecise or even unknown in such cases, there is more to observe and more to judge, of course.

However, the amount of data to be observed and to be judged can still be enormous. We must still ease the task. In particular, we can:

- Help the programmer *judge* whether some origin is infected. This can be done using *assertion* techniques, discussed in Chapter 10 "Asserting Expectations."

- Help the programmer *focus* on specific origins. Such origins include *anomalies* (discussed in Chapter 11 "Detecting Anomalies") and actual *failure causes* (discussed in Chapter 13 "Isolating Failure Causes" and Chapter 14 "Isolating Cause-Effect Chains").

Stay tuned — there is more to come.

9.6 CONCEPTS

HOW TO   ✎ *To explore execution history*, use an *omniscient debugger*, which records the entire execution of a program and grants random access to every aspect of the execution.

HOW TO   ✎ *To isolate value origins for a specific run*, use *dynamic slicing*.

✎ Dynamic slices apply only to a single run of the program, but are far more precise than static slices.

✎ The best available interactive debuggers leverage omniscient debugging, static slicing, and dynamic slicing to provide diagnoses about why things happen and why they do not.

HOW TO   ✎ *To track down an infection*, follow back the dependences and observe the origins, repeating the process for infected origins (Section 7.3).

9.7 TOOLS

ODB

Of the tools mentioned in this chapter, only ODB is available publicly. The ODB debugger was developed by Lewis (2003), who also coined the term *omniscient debugging*. ODB is available at:

```
http://www.lambdacs.com/debugger/debugger.html
```

Commercial implementations of omniscient debugging include Visicomp's RETROVUE and Omnicore's CODEGUIDE.

9.8 FURTHER READING

Dynamic slicing was invented independently by Korel and Laski (1990) and by Agrawal and Horgan (1990). The computation method in this chapter follows Gyimóthy et al. (1999). Still, the main challenge of dynamic slicing is *efficiency*. Zhang and Gupta (2004) offer several interesting approaches to the subject, as well as an extensive overview on the literature.

An interesting variant of dynamic slicing is *critical slicing,* as realized by DeMillo et al. (1996) in the SPYDER debugger. Critical slicing is based on the idea of removing individual statements from the program and to leave only those statements relevant to the error. As DeMillo et al. (1996) point out, this reduces the average program by 64%.

The WHYLINE was presented by Ko and Myers (2004). The extended version by Ko and Myers (2005) gives great insights on how to make a debugger user friendly — especially for people with little programming experience.

9.9 EXERCISES

EXERCISE 9.1. In the exercises of Chapter 5 "Simplifying Problems," we used a JAVA implementation of the delta debugging algorithm (Example 5.10) to simplify inputs. Download and use ODB to debug the run.

EXERCISE 9.2. Compute the dynamic slices for the run `sample 11 14` for the `sample` program (Example 1.1).

EXERCISE 9.3. Using the WHYLINE strategies, answer the following questions for the run `sample 11 14`.

- Why is a[0] = 0 at line 38?

- Why is line 22 not executed in the first iteration of the `for` loop in line 16?

EXERCISE 9.4. The following program is supposed to determine the greatest common divisor.

```
01    int gcd(int a, int b)
02    {
03        int d = b;              S  D1  D2  △
04        int r = a % b;          S  D1  D2  △
05
06        while(r > 0)            S  D1  D2  △
07        {
08            int n = d;          S  D1  D2  △
09            d = r;              S  D1  D2  △
10            r = n / d;          S  D1  D2  △
11        }
12
13        return d;               S  D1  D2  △
14    }
```

This program has a defect: gcd(2, 6) returns 3, but 3 is not a divisor of 2. The defect is in line 10: it should read r = n % d.

1. Determine the static backward slice of d (in line 13). Check $\boxed{S}$ for all statements that are part of the slice.

2. Determine the dynamic backward slice of d in the run gcd(2, 6). Check $\boxed{D1}$ for all statements that are part of the slice.

3. Determine the dynamic backward slice of d in the run gcd(0, 5). Check $\boxed{D2}$ for all statements that are part of the slice.

4. Determine the difference between the slices in steps 2 and 3. Check $\boxed{\triangle}$ for all statements that are part of the difference.

5. "A difference as obtained in step 4 always contains the faulty statement." Give a program and two slices that contradict this claim.

Life can only be understood backwards,
but it must be lived forwards.

— SØREN AABYE KIERKEGAARD,
Diary (1843)

## CHAPTER 10

ASSERTING EXPECTATIONS

OBSERVATION ALONE IS NOT ENOUGH FOR DEBUGGING. One must *compare* the observed facts with the expected program behavior. In this chapter, we discuss how to automate such comparisons, using well-known *assertion* techniques. We also show how to ensure the sanity of important system components such as memory.

10.1 AUTOMATING OBSERVATION

Observing what is going on in a program can be a burden for a programmer. First, there are many states and events that can and must be observed. Second, for each new run (or each new defect) the same items must be observed again. The burden is not so much the observation itself but the act of *judging* whether the observed state is sane or not — which of course multiplies with the amount of data observed.

In the past, where computing time was expensive, having such judging done by humans was commonplace (see Bug Story 9, for instance). Given our current wealth of computing power, though, it becomes more and more reasonable to *shift the burden of observation over to the computer* — that is, to have the computer check whether the program state is still sane, or whether an infection has occurred. This is the same approach as in automated testing (Chapter 3 "Making Programs Fail"). Rather than observe and judge for ourselves, we have the program test its own state continuously.

The first advantage of automated observation is *scalability.* In contrast to manual observation, where we can only examine a small number of variable values during execution (Figure 10.1a), having the computer observe and judge

BUG STORY 9: Examining a Lot of Data (Kidder, 1981)

Holberger drives into Westborough. The sun is in his eyes this morning, and he wonders in a detached sort of way where it will be hitting his windshield when they finish this job. Debugging Eagle has the feel of a career in itself. Holberger isn't thinking about any one problem, but about all the various problems at once, as he walks into the lab. What greets him there surprises him. He shows it by smiling wryly. A great heap of paper lies on the floor, a continuous sheet of computer paper streaming out of the carriage at Gollum's system console. Stretched out, the sheet would run across the room and back again several times. You could fit a fairly detailed description of American history from the Civil War to the present on it. Veres sits in this midst of this chaos, the picture of a scholar. He's examined it all. He turns to Holberger.
"I found it," he says.

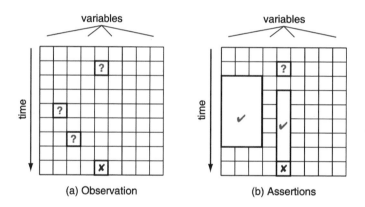

FIGURE 10.1 Observation versus assertion. Whereas observation is limited to small probes in space and time, assertions can automatically cover a large area.

allows us to check large parts of the execution automatically (Figure 10.1a). Each automated observation acts like an *infection detector*, catching infections before they can propagate and obscure their origins. This effectively narrows down possible infection sites, and thus speeds up debugging.

The second advantage is, of course, *persistence*. Once we have specified the properties of a sane state, we can reuse this specification over and over again. This not only includes debugging but documentation and general program understanding. Of all debugging techniques, expressing and checking what a program is supposed to do is probably the best long-term investment in code quality. Let's thus explore some common assertion techniques. Here, we ask:

> ### HOW DO WE AUTOMATE OBSERVATION?

10.2 BASIC ASSERTIONS

To have the program ensure its sane state automatically is deceptively simple. The basic idea is to insert appropriate code that *checks for infections*. For instance, to ensure that a divisor is nonzero, one could write:

```
if (divisor == 0) {
    printf("Division by zero!");
    abort();    // or some other exceptional behavior
}
```

Such infection-handling code has been used since the dawn of computing. It is common and useful — and yet somewhat clumsy. As discussed in Section 8.2, it is wise to explicitly separate code concerned with debugging from the normal program code. One way to do so is to have a special function that explicitly checks for a specific condition. The common name of such a function is assert(x), with the functionality that it aborts execution if x should be false.

```
assert (divisor != 0);
```

The assert function could be implemented in a straightforward way, as in:

```
void assert (int x)
{
    if (!x)
    {
        printf("Assertion failed!\n");
        abort();
    }
}
```

In practice, though, simply having assertions marked as such does not suffice. Just as with logging functions (Section 8.2.1), we want to be able to turn assertions off, and we want them to report diagnostic information — at least more than just "Assertion failed."

```
$ my-program
divide.c:37: assertion 'divisor != 0' failed
Abort (core dumped)
$ _
```

The techniques that realize these features in logging functions can easily be used for assertions. The following is a typical definition of assert for C++ programs.

```
#ifndef NDEBUG
#define assert(ex) \
((ex) ? 1 : (std::cerr << __FILE__ << ":" << __LINE__ \
                        << ": assertion '" #ex "' failed\n", \
                        abort(), 0))
#else
#define assert(x) ((void) 0)
#endif
```

This definition uses the __FILE__ and __LINE__ macros to report the location of the assertion in the source file. It also uses the "stringize" mechanism of the C preprocessor to output the assertion that actually failed (#ex). Finally, by setting the NDEBUG preprocessor variable the assertion can be turned off (it compiles to a no-op).

Other languages come with assertions built into the language. In JAVA, assertions are specified using the assert keyword. They work just like the C++ macro, but throw an exception rather than aborting the program. Note that in the JAVA interpreter java assertions are turned off by default. They must be enabled explicitly using the -enableassertions option.

How does one use assertions during debugging? The basic idea of assertions is to have the computer do the observation. Hence, assertions can be spread across the code just like logging functions. The principles of observation, as discussed in Section 8.1, still apply. Assertions should not interfere with the actual run (and hence have no side effects), and should be used *systematically* rather than sprinkled randomly across the code. This brings us to two major (systematic) uses of assertions in debugging.

- *Data invariants* that ensure data integrity

- *Pre- and postconditions* that ensure function correctness

10.3 ASSERTING INVARIANTS

The most important use of assertions in debugging is to ensure *data invariants*—properties that must hold throughout the entire execution. As an example, consider a C++ class Time that manages times of the day—say, a time such as "5pm, 40 minutes, and 20 seconds" or brief, 17:40:20. We do not care about how time is actually represented internally (that is the secret of the class), but we know that it provides an interface that allows us to access the individual components of the current time.

```
class Time {
public:
    int hour();     // 0..23
    int minutes();  // 0..59
    int seconds();  // 0..60 (including leap seconds)

    void set_hour(int h);
    ...
}
```

In the case of Time, a sane state is a valid time from 00:00:00 to 23:59:60. From the client view, this is an invariant that holds for all Time objects for all times. In practice, this means that the invariant should hold at the beginning and end of each public method. For this purpose, we can easily write an assertion at the end of the set_hour() method. This ensures that whatever set_hour() does the invariant is not violated.

```
void Time::set_hour(int h)
{
    // precondition
    assert(0 <= hour() && hour() <= 23) &&
           (0 <= minutes() && minutes() <= 59) &&
           (0 <= seconds() && seconds() <= 60);
    ...

    // postcondition
    assert(0 <= hour() && hour() <= 23) &&
           (0 <= minutes() && minutes() <= 59) &&
           (0 <= seconds() && seconds() <= 60);
}
```

(Note that we use the public interface of Time, rather than accessing the internals. This way, we can check three more functions.)

With these assertions, we can ensure that no set_hour() invocation will ever make a Time object inconsistent. The violated assertion would immediately flag the infection. However, putting such a three-line assertion at the beginning and end of each Time method induces redundancy and makes the code difficult to read. A more elegant way is to introduce a specific *helper function*, which checks the sanity of a Time object.

```
bool Time::sane()
{
    return (0 <= hour() && hour() <= 23) &&
           (0 <= minutes() && minutes() <= 59) &&
           (0 <= seconds() && seconds() <= 60);
}
```

sane() is more than just a helper function. sane(), being true, is an *invariant* of the Time object. It should always hold before and after each public function. We can now ensure that this invariant holds for the current Time object whenever some method is called — for instance, at the beginning and end of set_hour() — and thus ensure that the method did not infect the object state.

```
void Time::set_hour(int h)
{
    assert(sane()); // precondition

    // Actual code goes here

    assert(sane()); // postcondition
}
```

If one of these assertions now fails, we can immediately narrow down our hypothesis on the location of the defect.

- If the precondition is violated, the infection must have taken place before set_hour().

- If the postcondition is violated, the infection must have taken place within set_hour().

- If the postcondition holds, the infection cannot have taken place in set_hour().

To have the entire class continuously checked for sanity, all one needs to do is to wrap each public method that changes the state into two assertions — both checking the sanity as described previously. This ensures that any infection that takes place in these methods is properly caught — and if all assertions pass, we can rule out Time as an infection site.

If data structures get more complex, the invariants become more complex, too — but also ensure more properties. Example 10.1 shows an excerpt of a class invariant of a JAVA red/black tree — the base of the JAVA TreeMap class. Every property of the tree is checked in an individual helper function. The sane() method calls them all together. If anything ever goes wrong in a red/black tree, this sane() invariant will catch it.

Ideally, we would set up our class with assert(sane()) statements at the beginning and end of each public method. Unfortunately, this clutters the code somewhat. To reduce clutter, we can use an aspect (Section 8.2.3). For the red/black tree in Example 10.1, one single aspect can ensure that the invariant holds before and after each modifying method (add ... or del...).

```
public aspect RedBlackTreeSanity {
    pointcut modify():
        call(void RedBlackTree.add*(..)) ||
        call(void RedBlackTree.del*(..));

    before(): modify() {
        assert(sane());
    }

    after(): modify() {
        assert(sane());
    }
}
```

By applying or not applying the aspect, one can easily turn the assertions on and off — for all red/black tree methods now and in the future.

Once one has a function that checks data invariants, one can also invoke it in an interactive debugger to check data sanity on the fly. A conditional breakpoint in GDB such as

```
(gdb) break 'Time::set_hour(int)' if !sane()
```

```
boolean sane() {
    assert(rootHasNoParent());
    assert(rootIsBlack());
    assert(redNodesHaveOnlyBlackChildren());
    assert(equalNumberOfBlackNodesOnSubtrees());
    assert(treeIsAcyclic());
    assert(parentsAreConsistent());

    return true;
}


boolean redNodesHaveOnlyBlackChildren() {
    workList = new LinkedList();
    workList.add(rootNode());
    while (!workList.isEmpty()) {
        Node current = (Node)workList.removeFirst();
        Node cl = current.left;
        Node cr = current.right;
        if (current.color == RED) {
            assert (cl == null || cl.color == BLACK);
            assert (cr == null || cr.color == BLACK);
        }
        if (cl != null) workList.add(cl);
        if (cr != null) workList.add(cr);
    }

    return true;
}


boolean rootHasNoParent() { ... }
```

EXAMPLE 10.1 Ensuring the invariant of a red/black tree.

```
Breakpoint 3 at 0x2dcf: file Time.C, line 45.
(gdb) _
```

acts like an assertion. It will interrupt execution as soon as the breakpoint condition holds at the specified location — that is, the Time invariant is violated. This even works if the assertions have been disabled.

10.4 ASSERTING CORRECTNESS

In addition to data invariants, the major use of assertions in debugging is to *ensure that some function does the right thing*. In the set_hour() example, for instance, we can assert that set_hour() does not result in an invalid Time state. However, how do we know that set_hour(h) is correct — that is, that it sets the hour to h?

Such properties are expressed as *postconditions* — conditions over the state that must hold at the end of the function. As an example, consider a divide function for computing a *quotient* and a *remainder* from a *dividend* and a *divisor*. For such a function, the precondition is $divisor \neq 0$, whereas the postcondition is $quotient \times divisor + remainder = dividend$. Again, a postcondition can be translated into an assertion

```
assert (quotient * divisor + remainder == dividend);
```

at the end of the divide function code to check whether the computed quotient and divisor values are actually correct. In our set_hour() example, this reads:

```
void Time::set_hour(int h)
{
    // Actual code goes here

    assert(hour() == h);   // postcondition
}
```

Whereas a postcondition applies to the state that holds at the end of a function, a *precondition* expresses conditions over the state that must hold at the *beginning* of a function. For instance, to make our divide function work properly the *divisor* must not be zero. This condition is again expressed as an assertion

```
assert(divisor != 0);
```

at the beginning of the divide function. The following is the precondition for set_hour().

```
void Time::set_hour(int h)
{
    assert(0 <= h && h <= 23);
```

```
    // Actual code goes here
}
```

For complex data structures, specifying a pre- or postcondition may require the use of *helper functions* that check for the individual properties. For instance, if a sequence is to be sorted we need a helper function that checks whether the postcondition is satisfied.

```
void Sequence::sort()
{
    // Actual code goes here

    assert(is_sorted());
}
```

Helper functions used in postconditions usually make useful public methods.

```
void Container::insert(Item x)
{
    // Actual code goes here

    assert(has(x));
}
```

And, of course, *invariants* (as discussed in Section 10.3) are essential pre- and postconditions.

```
void Heap::merge(Heap another_heap)
{
    assert(sane());
    assert(another_heap.sane());

    // Actual code goes here

    assert(sane());
}
```

Sometimes, a postcondition involves *earlier state* — that is, state that occurred at the beginning of the function. In the case of the set_hour(h) function, for instance, we might want to specify that set_hour(h) only sets the hours (i.e., it does not change the minutes or the seconds). Asserting this requires us to save the original values at the beginning, such that we can compare against them at the end.

```
void Time::set_hour(int h)
{
    int old_minutes = minutes();
    int old_seconds = seconds();
    assert(sane());

    // Actual code goes here

    assert(sane());
    assert(hour() == h);
    assert(minutes() == old_minutes &&
            seconds() == old_seconds);
}
```

This works fine, but is somewhat cumbersome. In particular, if we turn off the assertions we end up with two unused variables, which will result in a compiler warning (see Section 7.5 on code smells).

In other languages, specifying pre- and postconditions is much more elegant. The EIFFEL language incorporates the concept of *design by contract,* where a contract is a set of preconditions that must be met by the caller (the *client*) and a set of postconditions that are guaranteed by the callee (the *supplier*). In EIFFEL, a contract regarding set_hour() would be specified as:

```
set_hour (h: INTEGER) is
        -- Set the hour from 'h'
    require
        sane_h: 0 <= h and h <= 23
    ensure
        hour_set: hour = h
        minute_unchanged: minutes = old minutes
        second_unchanged: seconds = old seconds
```

These conditions are again checked at runtime, just like assertions (although a true EIFFEL aficionado would shudder at the low-level nature of assertions). Note that the contract is part of the interface description (in contrast to assert calls). It is thus visible to the client and thus serves as documentation. In addition to require and ensure, EIFFEL provides an invariant keyword whose condition is checked before and after every invocation of a public method.

10.5 ASSERTIONS AS SPECIFICATIONS

The EIFFEL example in Section 10.4 can already serve as a *specification* of what the function should do. In short, the assertions become part of the *interface*. A user of the set_hour() function must satisfy its precondition. A supplier of the set_hour() function must satisfy the postcondition under the assumption the precondition holds. (The invariants, if any, must also hold.) This idea of assertions, written using program code, that serve as specifications is something quite recent. In the past, program specifications were of two forms.

- *Natural language:* The great majority of all specifications are written in natural language: "set_hour(h) sets the current hour to h, where h is an integer in the range 0–23." This style of specification is easy to read by humans, but is difficult to make complete and unambiguous. Furthermore, compliance with a natural-language specification cannot be validated automatically.

- *Formal systems:* The most complete and unambiguous language we have is mathematics, and discrete mathematics is the basis for the several specification languages, such as Z. Figure 10.2 shows a Z specification for the Date class and its set_hour() method. It is easy to recognize the invariants as well as the (intermixed) pre- and postconditions. Such a specification is obviously far more precise than the natural-language version.

  However, validating that the program code satisfies the specification is difficult. It requires us to prove that the concrete code requires no more than the abstract specification and that it provides no less than the specification. Such formal proofs can be tedious, and must be redone after each change to the code. (On the other hand, once your code is proven correct there would be no reason to change it again — unless the requirements change.)

However, both approaches have in common that specification and code are *separated* — leading to huge efforts when it comes to mapping one onto the

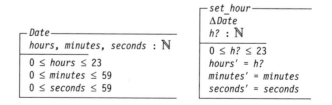

FIGURE 10.2 A Z specification for Date and set_hour(). The specification states the invariants that hold for Date as well as the pre- and postconditions for set_hour().

other. In contrast, EIFFEL-style specifications (and, more generally, all assertions) integrate the specification within the code. Thus, they allow us to *validate* correctness simply by running the program. For every program run where the assertions hold, the assertions guarantee the correctness of the result. For the large bulk of mainstream software, this is already largely sufficient. (There are some programs, though, where a failing assertion is not an option. A computer controlling an airbag, for instance, simply *must* produce a result in a specific time frame. For such dependable systems, we must still prove program correctness for all runs.)

10.6 FROM ASSERTIONS TO VERIFICATION

The success of specification languages largely depends on their expressive power as well as the quantity and quality of available tools. A language that excels in both areas is JML, the Java Modeling Language. JML assertions are written as special comments in the JAVA code, recognized by JML tools alone and ignored by ordinary JAVA compilers. Using requires and ensures keywords, one can specify the pre- and postconditions of an individual JAVA method in EIFFEL style.

```
/*@ requires 0 <= h && h <= 23
  @ ensures  hours() == h &&
  @          minutes() == \old(minutes()) &&
  @          seconds() == \old(seconds())
  @*/
void Time::set_hour(int h) ...
```

As in this example, assertions are written as ordinary Boolean JAVA expressions together with some extra operators such as \old, which stands for the value of the variable at the moment the method was entered. Using JMLC, the JML compiler, such a specification can be translated into assertions that are then checked at runtime.

JML assertions are more than syntactic sugar around ordinary assertions, though. For one thing, they can serve as specifications. What does the following fragment of JML specify?

```
/*@ requires x >= 0.0;
  @ ensures JMLDouble
  @         .approximatelyEqualTo
```

```
@              (x, \result * \result, eps);
@*/
```

Example 10.2 shows a more complex JML example — a specification for a debit card. Note the use of invariants (`invariant`) to assert data sanity (as in EIFFEL, the invariant is checked before and after every invocation of a public method), the use of quantifiers (`\forall`) to express conditions that span multiple variables, and the specification of exceptional behavior (`signals`).

Again, JMLC translates all of these conditions into runtime assertions and thus ensures that no violation passes by unnoticed. However, there is even more to gain from JML, such as the following.

```
public class Purse {
  final int MAX_BALANCE;
  int balance;
  //@ invariant  0 <= balance && balance <= MAX_BALANCE;

  byte[] pin;
  /*@ invariant pin != null && pin.length == 4 &&
    @              (\forall int i; 0 <= i && i < 4;
    @                          0 <= byte[i] && byte[i] <= 9)
    @*/

  /*@ requires    amount >= 0;
    @ assignable balance;
    @ ensures     balance == \old(balance) - amount &&
    @             \result == balance;
    @ signals     (PurseException) balance == \old(balance);
    @*/

  int debit(int amount) throws PurseException {
  ...
  }
}
```

EXAMPLE 10.2 A debit card specified in JML (Burdy et al., 2003).

- *Documentation:* The JMLDOC documentation generator produces HTML containing both JAVADOC comments and JML specifications. This is a great help for browsing and publishing JML specifications.

- *Unit testing:* JMLUNIT combines the JML compiler JMLC with JUNIT (Chapter 3 "Making Programs Fail") such that one can test units against JML specifications.

- *Invariant generation:* The DAIKON invariant detection tool (Chapter 11 "Detecting Anomalies") can report detected invariants in JML format, thus allowing simple integration with JML.

- *Static checking:* The ESC/Java static checker checks simple JML specifications statically, using the deduction techniques laid out in Chapter 7 "Deducing Errors." In particular, it can leverage specified invariants to detect potential null pointer exceptions or out-of-bound array indexes.

- *Verification:* JML specifications can be translated into proof obligations for various theorem provers. The more that properties are explicitly specified the easier it is to prove them.

Finally, the extended use of assertions also improves the software process, as assertions establish a contract between developers — or, more generally, between clients and suppliers of software. As the contract is unambiguous and complete, it allows for blame assignment. Rather than discussing who is wrong, one can immediately focus on making the program conform to its specification. Overall, few techniques are as helpful for debugging as assertions, and no other technique has as many additional benefits. For every program, there is every reason to use assertions lavishly.

By definition, specifications guarantee correctness. However, they do not protect against *surprises* — simply because the specification does not match what is actually desired. The accident of a Lufthansa A320 (see Bug Story 10) in Warsaw is a tragic example of a situation in which everything performed according to the specification — a specification that was in error and had to be altered after the accident. Therefore, be sure to have all of your assertions (and specifications) *carefully reviewed*. Do not fall into the trap of adapting your code to a faulty specification.

BUG STORY 10: The Lufthansa A320 Accident in Warsaw

On September 14, 1993, a Lufthansa A320 landed at Warsaw airport in a thunderstorm. The landing appeared to be normal and smooth, albeit somewhat fast. The pilots were unable to activate any of the braking mechanisms (spoilers, reverse thrust, wheel brakes) for 9 seconds after touchdown, at which point the spoilers and reverse thrust deployed. The wheel brakes finally became effective 13 seconds after touchdown. The aircraft was by this time way too far along the runway to stop before the runway end. It ran off the end, and over an earth bank near the end of the runway, before stopping. The first officer died in the accident, as did a passenger who was overcome by smoke from the burning aircraft.

The investigation of the accident found that the aircraft logics prohibited actuation of reverse thrust unless the shock absorbers were compressed at *both* main landing gears. At Warsaw, due to windshear the shock absorbers of one landing gear were not compressed sufficiently. The aircraft software would not allow actuation of reverse thrust, in compliance with its specification.

As a consequence, Lufthansa had concluded there was a problem with the specification, and was talking with Airbus on a change in the braking logic to reduce the weight-on-wheels load criterion from 12 metric tons to 2 metric tons. In the meantime, Lufthansa required their pilots to land relatively hard in such weather and runway conditions, thus compressing the shock absorbers and "fooling" the specification.

10.7 REFERENCE RUNS

In some cases, the correct behavior of a program P_1 is not specified explicitly but by *reference* to another program P_0, whose behavior is defined as "correct." This means that P_1 is supposed to behave like P_0 in some central aspect, or even in every aspect. List 10.1 outlines a number of situations in which this happens. The most common is that P_1 is a new revision or variant of the original P_0.

Reference programs are mainly used as *oracles* — that is, as universal devices that tell us what is correct, right, or true. For instance, consider *testing*. Any testing method needs to assess whether the result produced by a program is correct or not. Using a reference program P_0, one can simply *compare* against the result of the reference program. This is a common scenario for *regression testing*. We feed P_0 and P_1 with the same input. Any unexpected difference in

- *The program has been modified.* After a change to the program, we want to preserve the original behavior. The old version of the program thus becomes the reference version P_0, and the central behavior of the new version P_1 must not differ from P_0's.

  As an example, consider a program P_0 where a security leak has been detected. Before you release a patched version P_1, you would like to ensure that P_1 behaves like P_0 in every aspect — except for the security leak, of course.

- *The environment has changed.* After a larger change to the environment, we want to ensure that the old behavior is also present in the new environment. Therefore, P_0 becomes the program in the old environment, and P_1 is the program in the new environment.

  The most famous example of this situation is the year 2000 problem, where several programs had to deal with the coming of the new century. If a system in the simulated year 2000 to the current year 1999 showed any differences (except for the date, that is), the system would have a defect.

- *The program has been ported.* After moving a program from one machine to another, we want to ensure that the program P_1 on the new machine behaves like P_0 on the old machine. System architectures and environments have many differences that can impact the program's behavior. In addition to all of the possible influences listed in Chapter 4 "Reproducing Problems," changes in data representation, memory organization, or simply different versions of the used libraries and tools can all induce differing, and sometimes incorrect, behavior.

- *The program has been cloned.* The program P_1 may be a complete reimplementation of P_0 — for instance, because the source code of P_1 is not (or no longer) available, or because one needs a component P_1 that acts like P_0 for the purpose of interoperability.

  Suppose I wanted to write a PERL compiler — that is, a tool that translates PERL programs into machine code. To ensure correctness of my compiler, I have to compare the behavior of the compiled programs with their behavior when being executed by the original PERL interpreter. (Actually, this is how PERL 's semantics are defined: by referring to the implementation of the PERL interpreter.)

LIST 10.1 Sources of reference runs.

output is a potential error — or at least an anomaly to keep in mind for further investigation.

During *debugging*, we frequently need to tell whether some program state is infected or not. Having a reference program P_0 as an oracle, we can compare its state against the debugged program P_1 — and again, any difference is a potential infection or anomaly.

Typically, such a comparison is done by having two interactive debuggers run in parallel, with the programmer comparing the individual results. This is a tedious and error-prone process. A better alternative is to *automate* the comparison. This concept has been explored under the name of *relative debugging* — that is, debugging a program relative to a reference version. The key idea of relative debugging is to execute P_0 and P_1 *in parallel* — and flagging any difference between the program states.

As an example, Figure 10.3 shows the relative debugger GUARD, debugging a JAVA Polygon program under two JAVA virtual machines: the reference P_0 (using JVM 1.3) and its variant P_1, using JVM 1.5. Both processes can be stepped through individually. However, specific variables (such as perimeter) can be set up to be compared.

How does GUARD know when and where to compare variable values? This is specified by the programmer. Essentially, the programmer sets up a *relative assertion* — an assertion that two variables have the same value at a specific location. For instance, the GUARD assertion

```
assert p1::perimeter@Polygon.java:65 == p0::perimeter@Polygon.java:65
```

ensures that in process p1 the value of the variable perimeter at the location polygon.java:65 is equal to the value of the same variable at the same location in process p0. GUARD evaluates every relative assertion as execution reaches the locations, and flags an error if it is violated — very much like the GDB assertion in Section 10.3.

The Comparison Results window shows the result of this comparison. In the first step, the perimeter variable was identical in both programs. In the second step, though, GUARD found a difference (the relative assertion has failed). The perimeter values differ by 1.13. Because JVM 1.3 is the reference, the JVM 1.5 variant is wrong here.

In practice, the two programs being compared may differ in more than just their control flow. Their data structures may also be organized differently. For instance, one implementation may choose to store elements in a tree, whereas another chooses a hash table. Therefore, GUARD lets the user define individual comparison functions that can compare using a common abstraction, such as sets.

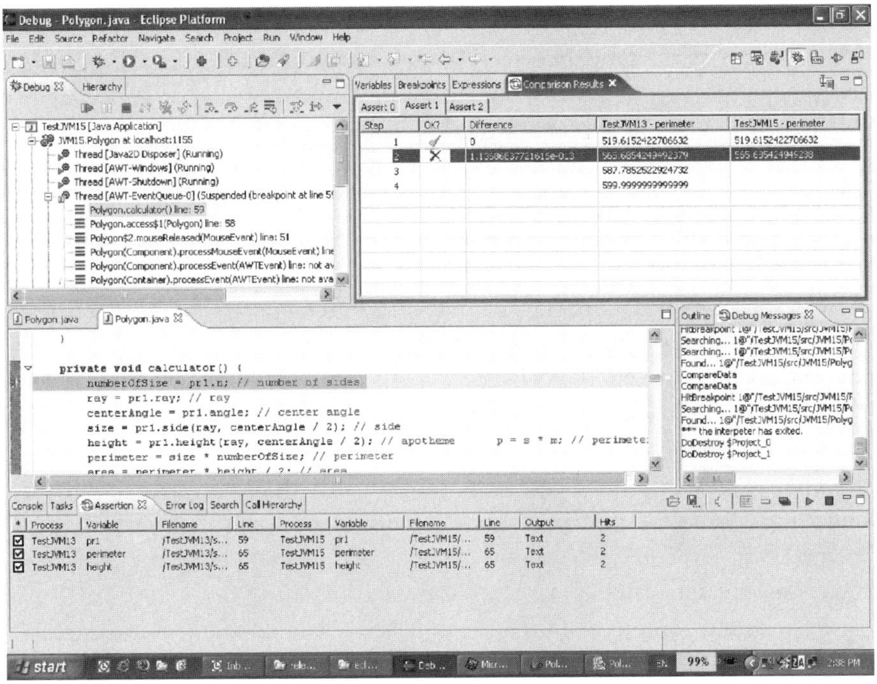

FIGURE 10.3 The GUARD relative debugger. The assertion window highlights differences between the states of two program runs.

All in all, relative debugging exploits the existence of a reference run in a classical interactive debugging session. The more of the state and the run covered by relative assertions the easier it will be to catch infections early. Best results are achieved when porting an otherwise identical program from one environment to another.

10.8 SYSTEM ASSERTIONS

Some properties of a program must hold *during the entire execution.* Good operating systems take care that a program does not access or change the data of other processes, that mathematical exceptions do not go by unnoticed, and that a program stays within the limits set by its privileges. One could think of these properties as *invariants* that are continuously checked at runtime.

In addition to increasing security for the user, such properties are immensely useful for debugging, as they limit the scope of the search. Assume I experience some memory error on a machine where the individual processes are not clearly separated. In such a case, I must extend my search to all processes that ran in conjunction with my program — a situation that is difficult to reproduce and to debug.

Even within a single process, though, it is advisable to have certain properties that are guaranteed during the entire run. The most important of these properties is the *integrity of the program data.* If the fundamental techniques for accessing memory no longer work, it becomes difficult to isolate individual failure causes.

In C and C++ programs, misuse of the *heap* memory is a common source of errors. In C and C++, the heap is a source for memory. This is the place where new objects are allocated. If an object is no longer required, the appropriate heap memory must be deallocated (or *freed*) explicitly. The memory thus becomes available for other objects.

The programmer must take care, though, that deallocated memory is no longer used. In addition, deallocated memory must not be deallocated again. Both actions result in *time bombs* — faults that manifest themselves only millions of instructions later and are thus difficult to isolate.

Fortunately, a number of useful tools help validate the state of the heap. It is a good idea always to have these tools ready during development, and to apply them at the slightest suspicion. It makes little sense to reason about individual variable values if the structure of the heap is not sound. The catch of these tools is that they increase memory and time requirements and thus cannot be used in production code.

10.8.1 Validating the Heap with MALLOC_CHECK

Using the GNU C runtime library (default on Linux systems), one can avoid common errors related to heap use simply by setting an environment variable called MALLOC_CHECK_. For instance, one can detect multiple deallocation of heap memory:

```
$ MALLOC_CHECK_=2 myprogram myargs
free() called on area that was already free'd()
Aborted (core dumped)
$ _
```

The core file generated at program abort can be read in by a debugger, such that one is directly led to the location where free() was called the second time. This postmortem debugging was discussed in Section 8.3.3.

10.8.2 Avoiding Buffer Overflows with ELECTRICFENCE

The ELECTRICFENCE library effectively prohibits buffer overflows. Its basic idea is to allocate arrays in memory such that each array is preceded and followed by a nonexisting memory area — the actual "electric fence." If the program attempts to access this area (i.e., an overflow occurred), the operating system aborts the program.

Using ELECTRICFENCE, one can quickly narrow down the overflowing array in sample (Example 1.1). We compile sample using the efence library and call the resulting sample-with-efence program with two arguments. As soon as a[2] is accessed, the program is aborted.

```
$ gcc -g -o sample-with-efence sample.c -lefence
$ ./sample-with-efence 11 14
Electric Fence 2.1
Segmentation fault (core dumped)
$ _
```

Again, the core file can be read in by a debugger — unless one runs sample-with-efence directly within the debugger.

10.8.3 Detecting Memory Errors with VALGRIND

VALGRIND (named after the holy entrance to Valhalla, the home of Odin) provides the functionality of ELECTRICFENCE, plus a little more. VALGRIND detects:

- Read access to noninitialized memory

- Write or read access to nonallocated memory

- Write or read access across array boundaries

- Write or read access in specific stack areas

- Detection of memory leaks (areas that were allocated but never deallocated)

If we apply VALGRIND to the sample program from Example 1.1, we obtain a message stating that sample accesses memory in an illegal manner. This access takes place in shell_sort (line 18), called by main and __libc_start_main.

```
$ valgrind sample 11 14
Invalid read of size 4
   at 0x804851F: shell_sort (sample.c:18)
   by 0x8048646: main (sample.c:35)
   by 0x40220A50: __libc_start_main (in /lib/libc-2.3.so)
   by 0x80483D0: (within /home/zeller/sample)
```

The remaining message gives some details about the invalid memory area. It is close to the memory area allocated by main (line 32)—the memory area malloc'ed for a[0 ... 1].

```
   Address 0x40EE902C is 0 bytes after a block alloc'd
   at 0x4015D414: malloc (vg_clientfuncs.c:103)
   by 0x80485D9: main (sample.c:32)
   by 0x40220A50: __libc_start_main (in /lib/libc-2.3.so)
   by 0x80483D0: (within /home/zeller/sample)
$ _
```

How does this work? VALGRIND is built around an *interpreter* for x86 machine code instructions. It interprets the machine instructions of the program to be debugged, and keeps track of the used memory in so-called *shadow memory*.

- Each memory bit is associated with a controlling *value bit* (V-bit). Each V-bit is initially unset. VALGRIND sets it as soon as the associated memory bit is being written.

- In addition, each byte is associated with an *allocated bit* (A-bit), which is set if the corresponding byte is currently allocated. When some memory area is deallocated, VALGRIND clears the A-bits.

Whenever the program tries to read some memory whose A-bits or V-bits are not set, VALGRIND flags an error.

Figure 10.4 shows the situation in which VALGRIND generates the previous error message for the sample program: a[0] and a[1] are allocated and initialized—their A- and V-bits set (shown in gray). In contrast, a[2] is neither allocated nor initialized. Accessing it causes VALGRIND to issue an error message.

Using VALGRIND is not without drawbacks. The code size can increase up to 12 times, and execution times can increase up to 25 times. Memory usage doubles due to shadow memory. A more efficient way is not to interpret the machine code but to *instrument it*—that is, to include extra code at memory

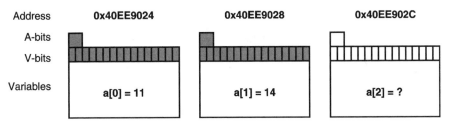

FIGURE 10.4 A- and V-bits in VALGRIND. A-bits are set if the associated byte is allocated; V-bits are set if the associated bit has been written.

accesses to update and check shadow memory. This approach is realized in the PURIFY tool, which detects the same class of errors as VALGRIND but in a more effective way. Programs instrumented with PURIFY have a typical slowdown factor of only 5 to 10. (PURIFY also comes with a nice GUI as well as phone support from IBM.)

The relatively low overhead is in general acceptable for debugging purposes. Most of the Linux KDE project, for instance, is checked with VALGRIND. PURIFY has a long record of successfully checking arbitrary programs. Experienced programmers routinely validate the heap integrity with VALGRIND, PURIFY, or similar tools—just for easy elimination of a failure source and an extra ounce of confidence.

There is one point where VALGRIND is different from PURIFY and other memory checkers. VALGRIND acts as a general *framework*, where VALGRIND *plug-ins* can execute arbitrary code while the original program is interpreted. This allows for much more than just memory check. In fact, memory checking is just one of VALGRIND's plug-ins. For instance, it is easy to write a VALGRIND plug-in that logs the current execution position, in a fashion similar to PIN (Section 8.2.4). The DAIKON tool, discussed in Section 11.5, uses a specialized VALGRIND plug-in to capture execution traces of Linux binaries.

10.8.4 Language Extensions

At this point, one may wonder why we might bother with system assertions at all. Shouldn't one simply switch to a programming language in which such problems do not occur? Indeed, languages with managed memory and garbage collection, such as JAVA or C#, do not suffer from the memory problems described in this section. A more conservative migration path from low-level languages is to use a *safer dialect* of an existing programming language. Such a dialect brings *extensions* that allow programmers to specify further properties of language entities. These extensions can then be checked (at runtime, but also statically) to catch errors early.

As an example, consider CYCLONE, a safer dialect of the C programming language. CYCLONE's central extension to C is the concept of *special pointers*; that is, C pointers with special properties. For instance, in CYCLONE one can declare a pointer that can never be NULL by using @ instead of *. The getc() function, retrieving a character from a file, is thus declared as

```
int getc (FILE @);
```

Calling getc() with a potentially NULL pointer results in a runtime check being triggered: If getc() is called with a NULL pointer, the runtime check will terminate the program rather than having getc() fail in an uncontrolled fashion. In addition, the CYCLONE compiler will give a warning about having inserted such a runtime check.

```
extern FILE *f;
char c = getc (f); // warning: NULL check inserted
```

Another interesting CYCLONE feature is *fat pointers* — pointers that not only record a location but bound information (such as the size of the area being pointed to). Such a pointer is declared by using ? instead of *. Using fat pointers, a function such as strlen(), determining the length of a string, can be declared as

```
int strlen (const char? s);
```

In contrast to the original strlen() function, the CYCLONE implementation need not scan the string for a terminating NUL character. Instead, it can access the bounds of the string s using s.size. This also implies that, unlike the original C variant, the CYCLONE version will not scan past the end of strings that lack a NUL terminator. All memory accesses via a fat pointer will be automatically bounds checked at runtime. If a violation can be detected at compile time already, the CYCLONE compiler will flag an error.

To detect errors at compile time, CYCLONE imposes a number of restrictions on C programs (List 10.2) — restrictions that effectively deal with the caveats outlined in Figure 7.3 and that still enable CYCLONE to support low-level programming. All in all, a few extensions suffice to make C-style programming almost as safe as programming in JAVA or other high-level languages and to prevent memory misuse as described in this section.

- `NULL` checks are inserted to prevent segmentation faults.

- Pointer arithmetic is restricted.

- Pointers must be initialized before use.

- Dangling pointers are prevented through region analysis and limitations on `free()`.

- Only "safe" casts and unions are allowed.

- `goto` into scopes is disallowed.

- `switch` labels in different scopes are disallowed.

- Pointer-returning functions must execute `return`.

- `setjmp()` and `longjmp()` are not supported.

LIST 10.2 Restrictions imposed by CYCLONE to preserve safety (Jim et al., 2002).

10.9 CHECKING PRODUCTION CODE

We have now seen that the computer can automate much of the observation for us, and that large parts of the program state can be checked during execution. This is helpful in debugging and increases our confidence in the program. When it comes to *releasing* the program, though, should we still have all checks enabled? First, the following are some checks that should *never* be turned off.

- *Critical results:* If your program computes a result that people's lives, health, or money depends on, it is a good idea to validate the result using some additional computation. As a lesser alternative, one may also use n-*version programming*; that is, one computes the result a second time (using an alternate implementation or algorithm) and compares the results automatically.

  Obviously, an assertion is not the best way of checking critical results, in that an assertion can be turned off—and you do not want to turn off warnings on critical results.

- *External conditions:* Any conditions that are not within our control must be checked for integrity. This especially holds for external input, which must be verified to satisfy all syntactic and semantic constraints. In case of error, the user must be notified.

  Again, an assertion is not the right way to check external conditions. Think of an assertion that checks whether the length of the input stays within the buffer length, for instance. Turning off such an assertion results in a security leak. Furthermore, the input to a program is typically under the control of the user, and when the user makes a mistake it is better to tell him "A PIN has exactly four digits" rather than to have the program abort with a message such as `assertion 'length == 4' failed`.

What do we do with the other assertions in production code, though? The following are some arguments to consider.

- *The more active assertions there are the greater the chances of catching infections.* Because not every infection need result in a failure, assertions increase your chances of detecting defects that would otherwise go by unnoticed. Therefore, assertions should remain turned on.

- *The sooner a program fails the easier it is to track the defect.* The larger the distance between defect and failure the more difficult it is to track the infection chain. The more active assertions there are the sooner an infection will be caught, which significantly eases debugging. This idea of making code "fail fast" is an argument for leaving assertions turned on.

- *Defects that escape into the field are the most difficult to track.* Remember that failures that occur at the user's site are often difficult to reproduce (Chapter 4 "Reproducing Problems"). Failing assertions can give the essential clues on how the infection spread.

- *By default, failing assertions are not user friendly.* The message from a failing assertion may be helpful for programmers but will appear cryptic to most users — and the fact that the program simply aborts (which is the default) is not what you would call a helpful behavior.

    However, this is not yet a reason to turn off assertions. An unnoticed incorrect behavior is far more dangerous than a noticed aborted behavior. When something bad may happen, do not shoot the messenger (and turn assertions off), but make sure the program *gracefully fails*. For instance, a global exception handler could state that a fatal error occurred and offer some means of recovery.

- *Assertions impact performance.* This argument is true, but should be considered with respect to the benefits of assertions. As with every performance issue, one must first detect how much performance is actually lost. Only if this amount is intolerable one should specifically check for *where* the performance is lost.

    An assertion executed several times as an invariant, for instance, may impact performance far more than a single postcondition executed once at the end of a complex function. Regarding performance, it is thus a wise strategy to turn off those assertions that do have an impact on performance (as proven by earlier measurements) and to leave on those assertions that prohibit a widespread infection — for instance, those assertions that control the integrity of a result (unless already checked as a critical result).

Note that the current trend in software development is to trade performance for runtime safety wherever possible. JAVA and .NET have introduced the concept of *managed code* and *managed data*, whereby the integrity of both code and data is constantly monitored and verified. Given the security issues in our networked world, and given the continuing explosion of computing power, the cost of checking as much as possible becomes more and more irrelevant when compared to the risk of not checking enough. Eventually, *proving correctness* may turn out to be a strategy for optimization. If it can be proven an assertion always holds, it can easily be eliminated.

10.10 CONCEPTS

- *To automate observation*, use assertions.

  `HOW TO`

- Assertions catch infections before they can propagate through the program state and cover their origins.

- Like observation statements, assertions must not interfere with the actual computation.

- *To use assertions*, check preconditions, data invariants, and postconditions.

  `HOW TO`

  - *Preconditions* document the requirements for calling a function. A successful check means the requirements are met.

  - *Data invariants* specify properties over data that hold before and after each public function that operates on that data. A successful check means sane data.

  - *Postconditions* describe the effects of a function. A successful check means correctness of the result.

- Assertions can serve as specifications (as in EIFFEL or JML) and thus document interfaces.

✎ In contrast to "external" specification languages, assertions are interwoven with the code and can be easily checked at runtime.

✎ Rich specification languages such as JML provide a smooth transition from assertions (checked at runtime) to static checking and verification (checked at compile time).

HOW TO ✎ *To check a program against a reference program*, use relative debugging.

HOW TO ✎ *To check memory integrity*, use specialized tools to detect errors in memory management. Such tools should be applied before all other methods of debugging.

✎ The most sophisticated tools detect memory misuse by tracking memory usage via *shadow memory*.

HOW TO ✎ *To prevent memory errors in a low-level language*, consider using a safer dialect such as CYCLONE for the C language.

✎ Use assertions to make your code fail as fast as possible. This increases the chances of catching infections. It also shortens the chain from defect to failure.

✎ Assertions cause a performance loss. You gain benefits for debugging, though, and avoid risks of erroneous computing—advantages that frequently outweigh the costs. Therefore, leave lightweight assertions on in production code—offering a user-friendly recovery from failed assertions.

✎ Do not use assertions for critical results or external conditions. Use hard-coded error handling instead.

10.11 TOOLS

JML

The Iowa State University JML tools include the JML compiler (JMLC), the JMLUNIT unit testing program, and the JMLDOC documentation generator. All are publicly available at:

http://www.jmlspecs.org/

ESC/Java

The ESC/Java tool combines static checking with JML. The version that fully supports JML is ESC/Java version 2, developed by David Cok and Joe Kiniry. ESC/Java version 2 is available at:

```
http://www.sos.cs.ru.nl/research/escjava/
```

GUARD

The GUARD relative debugger was presented by Sosič and Abramson (1997), who also pioneered the concept of relative debugging. Their web site contains more on the concept as well as the debugger. This is found at:

```
http://www.csse.monash.edu.au/~davida/guard/
```

VALGRIND

The VALGRIND tool for Linux is part of Linux distributions for x86 processors. It is available at:

```
http://valgrind.kde.org/
```

PURIFY

PURIFY, marketed by IBM, is also available for Solaris and Windows. Information on PURIFY is available at:

```
http://www.ibm.com/
```

INSURE++

INSURE++ is a commercial tool that detects memory problems by instrumenting C and C++ source code. It is therefore available on a number of platforms. It may be found at:

```
http://www.parasoft.com/
```

CYCLONE

The CYCLONE dialect was developed by Jim et al. (2002). An open-source compiler for Linux can be downloaded at:

> `http://www.research.att.com/projects/cyclone/`

CCURED

The CCURED language by Necula et al. (2002) takes an approach similar to that of CYCLONE, but moves control from the programmer to the system. For this purpose, it has to extend data representations by *metadata* to enable even better dynamic bookkeeping. Such metadata would, for instance, record how pointers are supposed to be used. Condit et al. (2003) describe the use of CCURED on real-world software such as network daemons. CCURED, as well as an online demo, are available at:

> `http://manju.cs.berkeley.edu/ccured/`

10.12   FURTHER READING

Assertions are as old as computers. It is reported that even John von Neumann used them. To see interesting discussions on the use of assertions, have a look at the "People, Projects, and Patterns" WIKI at `http://c2.com/cgi/wiki`. You can contribute, too! The following are some starting points.

- `http://c2.com/cgi/wiki?WhatAreAssertions`

- `http://c2.com/cgi/wiki?UseAssertions`

- `http://c2.com/cgi/wiki?DoNotUseAssertions`

Although people generally believe that assertions are a good thing, there is only one study that has actually conducted controlled experiments to validate this claim. Müller et al. (2002) found that assertions indeed do increase liability and understandability of programs, although requiring a larger programming effort. (Müller et al. did not research the use of assertions for debugging, though.)

The EIFFEL language realized the idea of design by contract pioneered by Meyer (1997). EIFFEL software and voluminous training material are available at:

> http://www.eiffel.com/

To learn more about the *Z* specification language, I recommend *The Way of Z* by Jacky (1996). Few other books on formal methods come close in clarity, precision, and completeness.

JML was originally developed by Leavens et al. (1999). Since then, it has turned into a cooperative effort of dozens of researchers. Burdy et al. (2003) give an overview of JML tools and applications. Leavens and Cheon (2004) give a tutorial on how to use JML as a design-by-contract tool. These papers are available on the JML home page at:

> http://www.jmlspecs.org/

Once one has specified an invariant of a data structure, one can detect any violation. Demsky and Rinard (2003) go one step further and suggest *automatic repair* of data structures with given invariants.

The SPEC# language (spoken "spec sharp") by Barnett et al. (2004) is an extension of C#, providing non-NULL types (as in CYCLONE) as well as method contracts (as in JML). It is being used at Microsoft to improve safety. See the project home page at:

> http://research.microsoft.com/SpecSharp/

ESC/Java was developed at the Compaq Systems Research Center by a large group of researchers. To get started with extended static checking in general, see the project home page at:

> http://research.compaq.com/SRC/esc/

The VALGRIND tool was initially developed by Julian Seward, and later extended to a framework by Nicholas Nethercote. The paper of Nethercote and Seward (2003) gives several details about the framework.

The concept of having software fail fast is discussed by Shore (2004), using several code examples to illustrate the use of assertions and exception handlers.

Checking the integrity of all input is an important factor in building secure software. See Viega and McGraw (2001) for an introduction to the subject.

N-*version programming* is a lesser alternative to checking results, because there are serious doubts whether it works. For details, see Knight and Leveson (1986) and Leveson et al. (1990).

Bug Story 10, on the A320 accident, was compiled from "Report of the Main Commission Aircraft Accident Investigation Warsaw," and information from Peter Ladkin, posted to the risks digest (vol. 15, issue 30) in December of 1993. The report is available, along with other accident reports, at:

```
http://sunnyday.mit.edu/accidents/
```

10.13 EXERCISES

EXERCISE 10.1. Why can an assertion such as assert(sane()) be used at the beginning and end of public functions but not necessarily at other places?

EXERCISE 10.2. What happens if sane() is called from hour()? How can you improve the sane() function?

EXERCISE 10.3. Write assertions for the bigbang program shown in Figure 8.2:

1. As invariants for the Element and Container classes

2. As pre- and postconditions for each public method, checking (among others) that the invariants still hold

Do you catch the infection using these assertions? If so, how? If not, why not?

EXERCISE 10.4. Consider the public interface of the JAVA TreeMap class. Design an aspect that adds assert(sane()) to the beginning and end of each public function. Optimize the aspect such that post-method checks are only issued for methods that can change the state.

EXERCISE 10.5. Assume we had a function that could tell us whether the state is sane [say, state_is_sane()]. To search a defect, all we would have to do is insert assertions

```
assert (state_is_sane());
```

into the program to narrow down the infection site by simple binary search, which could even be automated. However, if we had such a function we would not have to search the defect anyway. Why?

EXERCISE 10.6. Assume the program state consists only of objects whose sanity is guaranteed by (invariant) assertions. Can we assume that the entire state is sane?

EXERCISE 10.7. Rather than writing an assertion such as

```
assert (0 <= h && h <= 23);
```

I can use GDB to check the following condition.

```
(gdb) break 'Time::set_hour(int)' if h < 0 || h > 23
Breakpoint 3 at 0x2dcf: file Time.C, line 45.
(gdb) _
```

Discuss the pros and cons of this technique.

EXERCISE 10.8. Consider the BinaryTree class shown in Example 10.3. Write some aspects for the following tasks.

1. A logging aspect that logs every entry and every exit of a method from the BinaryTree class. This aspect shall log which method is entered or left.

2. A logging aspect that displays every setting of the left or the right child of a BinaryTree.

EXERCISE 10.9. For the BinaryTree class shown in Example 10.3, write some JML invariants that hold for a tree node per the following.

- The key is a nonnegative number.

- The keys of all left children are less than or equal to the node's key. The keys of all right children are greater than or equal to the node's key.

- The data object is not empty.

```
 1  class BinaryTree {
 2      private int key;
 3      private Object value;
 4      private BinaryTree right;
 5      private BinaryTree left;
 6
 7      public BinaryTree(int _key,Object _value) {
 8          key   = _key;
 9          value = _value;
10          right = left = null;
11      }
12
13      // Lookup a node with a specific key
14      public Object lookup(int _key) {
15          BinaryTree descend;
16          if (_key == key)
17              return value;
18          if (_key < key)
19              descend = left;
20          else
21              descend = right;
22          if (descend == null)
23              return null;
24          return descend.lookup(_key);
25      }
26
27      // Insert a node with a certain key and value
28      public void insert(int _key, Object _value) {
29          if (_key <= key)
30              if (left == null)
31                  left = new BinaryTree(_key,_value);
32              else
33                  left.insert(_key,_value);
34          else
35              if (right == null)
36                  right = new BinaryTree(_key,_value);
37              else
38                  right.insert(_key,_value);
39      }
40
41      // Delete a node with a certain key
42      public boolean delete (int key) {
43          // ...
44          return true;
45      }
46  }
```

EXAMPLE 10.3 The BinaryTree.java program.

EXERCISE 10.10. Sketch JML assertions for the insert method of BinaryTree (Example 10.3) that guarantee the following conditions.

- The inserted object is not null.

- The key and the object are not altered during insertion.

- The children of this node contain one further instance of the inserted key/object pair after insertion.

EXERCISE 10.11. Consider the following three pieces of code, which sum up the elements in an array a[]. First, a PYTHON version:

```
a = read_elems()
sum = 0
for elem in a.elems():
    sum = sum + elem
```

A C version:

```
read_elems(a);
sum = 0;
for (int i = 0; i < n; i++)
    sum += a[i];
```

And finally, a JAVA version:

```
a = read_elems();
sum = 0;
for (Iterator it = a.iterator(); it.hasNext(); )
    sum += it.next();
```

In all three versions, we have a variable sum that at the end of the loop holds the sum of all elements in a[]. Using relative debugging, which assertions can you set up?

EXERCISE 10.12. What are the respective benefits of relative assertions versus standard assertions?

EXERCISE 10.13. Some possible points for a program examination are as follows.

A   Function foo() is reached.

B   Variable z[0] is equal to 2.

C   Function foo() is reached and variable z[0] is equal to 2.

D   Function foo() is reached or variable z[0] is equal to 2.

E   Function foo() is reached and at least one of z[0], z[1], ..., z[99] is equal to 2.

F   All of z[0], z[1], ..., z[99] are equal to 2.

Assume that the processor has no special debugging support, except for changing individual machine instructions into interrupt instructions.

1. Sort these queries according to the execution speed of the examined program from fastest to slowest.

2. Sketch processor support that can make these queries more efficient.

3. Sketch possible code instrumentation (e.g., adding new code at compilation time) to make these queries more efficient.

EXERCISE 10.14. Use VALGRIND (or similar heap checker) to check bigbang (Example 8.3) for memory problems.

EXERCISE 10.15. We observe a union in a C program — a data structure in which all members start at the same address and in which only one member is actually used.

```
union node_value {
  char c;   // 1 byte
  int  i;   // 4 bytes
  double d; // 8 bytes
}
```

Your goal is to disambiguate the union — that is, to decide which of the members c, i, or d is actually being used. Discuss means of doing so at the moment of execution, using VALGRIND 's bits. Which bits do you use for which purpose?

EXERCISE 10.16. Design a global exception handler that catches failing assertions and gives user-friendly directions on how to handle the situation. [Hint: See Shore (2004) for a discussion.]

One other obvious way to conserve programmer time
is to teach machines how to do more
of the low-level work of programming.

— ERIC S. RAYMOND
The Art of UNIX Programming (1999)

## CHAPTER 11

DETECTING ANOMALIES

ALTHOUGH ONE PROGRAM RUN CAN TELL you quite a great deal, having multiple runs to compare offers several opportunities for locating *commonalities* and *anomalies* — anomalies that frequently help to locate defects. In this chapter, we discuss how to detect anomalies in code coverage and anomalies in data accesses. We also demonstrate how to infer invariants from multiple test runs automatically, in order to flag later invariant violations. All of these anomalies are good candidates for infection sites.

11.1 CAPTURING NORMAL BEHAVIOR

If we have a full specification of a program's behavior, we can easily narrow down an infection (as discussed in Chapter 10 "Asserting Expectations"). So why not simply use assertions all the way through? The following are some reasons.

- Assertions take time to write, especially in otherwise unspecified or undocumented code.

- Assertions over temporal properties ["Don't call `close()` unless you have called `open()`"] or control flow ("If you've taken this branch, you can't take this other branch") are difficult to specify.

- For practical purposes, assertions cannot cover all properties of the entire state at all times — because this would imply a specification as complex as the original program (and just as likely to contain defects). Hence, there will always be gaps between assertions that must be explored.

All of these limits come from the fact that assertions verify against *correct* behavior, which has to be specified by humans. However, there is an alternative: rather than having assertions compare against the correct behavior we could also have assertions compare against *normal* behavior, and thus detect behavior that is *abnormal* (i.e., deviates from the average in some way). Such behavior is characterized by certain *properties* of the program run, such as the following.

- *Code coverage:* Code that is executed in ("abnormal") failing runs but not in ("normal") passing runs

- *Call sequences:* Sequences of function calls that occur only in ("abnormal") failing runs

- *Variable values:* Variables that take certain ("abnormal") values in failing runs only

Of course, knowing about *abnormal* behavior is not as useful as knowing about *incorrect* behavior. Incorrect behavior implies a defect, whereas abnormal behavior implies — well, formally nothing, just abnormal behavior. However, abnormal behavior is often a good *indicator* of defects, meaning that abnormal properties of a program run are more likely to indicate defects than normal properties of the run. Consequently, it is wise to first search for anomalies and then to focus on anomalies for further observation or assertion.

So, how does one capture normal behavior of a program? This is done using *induction* techniques — inferring an *abstraction* from multiple concrete events. In our case, the concrete events are program runs. The abstractions are general rules that apply to the runs taken into account. Typically, such techniques are applied on runs that pass a given test, generating abstractions for "normal" runs. A run that fails that test is then examined for those properties where these abstractions are not met, resulting in anomalies that should be focused on.

In this chapter, we explore a number of automated techniques that use induction to infer abstractions from runs — and then leverage these abstractions to detect anomalies and potential defects. Many of these techniques are fairly recent, and are hence not necessarily ready for industrial prime time. Nonetheless, they should serve as food for thought on how debugging can be further automated. Here, we ask:

HOW CAN WE FIND OUT WHERE A FAILING RUN DEVIATES FROM PASSING RUNS?

11.2 COMPARING COVERAGE

One of the simplest methods for detecting anomalies operates per the following logic.

1. Every failure is caused by an infection, which again is caused by a defect.

2. The defect must be *executed* in order to start the infection.

3. Hence, code that is executed only in failing runs is more likely to contain the defect than code that is always executed.

To explore this hypothesis, we need a means of checking whether code has been executed or not. This can easily be done using *coverage tools*, which instrument code such that the execution keeps track of all lines being executed. Such coverage tools are typically used for assessing the quality of a test suite. A test suite should execute each statement at least once, because otherwise a defect may not be executed. (More advanced *coverage criteria* demand that each transition in the control flow graph be executed at least once.) In our case, though, we want to use such coverage tools to compare the coverage of a passing and a failing run.

As an ongoing example, consider the piece of code shown in Example 11.1, computing the middle value of three numbers. This program works nicely on a number of inputs.

```
$ ./middle 3 3 5
middle: 3
$ _
```

It fails, though, on specific inputs — the middle number of 2, 1, and 3 is 2, not 1.

```
$ ./middle 2 1 3
middle: 1
$ _
```

We can now examine the code coverage of these runs, as well as a few more, shown in Example 11.2. Each column stands for a run (with the input values at the top), and each circle stands for a line being executed in the run. The return statement in line 15, for instance, has been executed in every single run, whereas the assignment m = y in line 8 has been executed in both test cases 3 3 5 and 2 1 3 (shown previously).

```
 1   // Return the middle of x, y, z
 2   int middle(int x, int y, int z) {
 3       int m = z;
 4       if (y < z) {
 5           if (x < y)
 6               m = y;
 7           else if (x < z)
 8                   m = y;
 9       } else {
10           if (x > y)
11                   m = y;
12           else if (x > z)
13                   m = x;
14       }
15       return m;
16   }
17
18   // Test driver
19   int main(int arc, char *argv[])
20   {
21       int x = atoi(argv[1]);
22       int y = atoi(argv[2]);
23       int z = atoi(argv[3]);
24       int m = middle(x, y, z);
25
26       printf("middle: %d\n", m);
27
28       return 0;
29   }
```

EXAMPLE 11.1 The middle program returns the middle number of three.

This line is somewhat special, too. Every statement that has been executed in the failing run 2 1 3 has also been executed in passing runs. However, line 8 has been executed in only *one* passing test, whereas all other lines have been executed in at least two passing tests. Assuming that a statement is more normal the more often it is executed in passing runs (which indicates it has a low chance of starting an infection), line 8 is the least normal one.

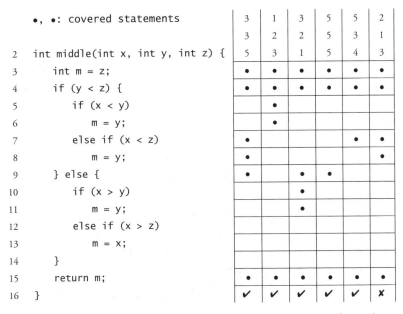

•, •: covered statements	3	1	3	5	5	2
	3	2	2	5	3	1
2 int middle(int x, int y, int z) {	5	3	1	5	4	3
3 int m = z;	•	•	•	•	•	•
4 if (y < z) {	•	•	•	•	•	•
5 if (x < y)		•				
6 m = y;		•				
7 else if (x < z)	•				•	•
8 m = y;	•					•
9 } else {	•		•	•		
10 if (x > y)			•			
11 m = y;			•			
12 else if (x > z)						
13 m = x;						
14 }						
15 return m;	•	•	•	•	•	•
16 }	✔	✔	✔	✔	✔	✘

EXAMPLE 11.2 Comparing coverage of multiple test runs (Jones et al., 2002).

(You may also have noticed that lines 12 and 13 are never executed—neither in the failing nor in the passing run. Is this an anomaly we are looking for? No, because the same effect applies in passing as well as in failing runs.)

If we actually focus on line 8 as an anomaly, we could take a look at the conditions under which line 8 is being executed. These are $y < z$ (line 4), $x \geq y$ (line 5), and $x < z$ (line 7). In other words, $y \leq x < z$ holds. Thus, the middle value is x, and in line 8, m should be assigned x rather than y. Line 8, the greatest anomaly regarding coverage, is indeed the defect that causes the failure.

Such coverage information can be visualized to guide the user in detecting anomalies. Figure 11.1 shows TARANTULA, a tool for visualizing coverage anomalies. In TARANTULA, each nonblank character of the code is shown as a pixel. Each line is assigned a color hue and a brightness, indicating the *anomaly level*.

- *Color:* The redder a statement the higher the percentage of failing test cases in the test cases that executed this statement. In Example 11.2, line 8 would get the highest amount of red, as 50% of the test cases that executed this statement failed. Lines 5, 6, and 9 through 11, though, would appear in green, as they were only executed in passing test cases.

- *Brightness:* The brighter a statement the higher the percentage of test cases executing this statement in all test cases.

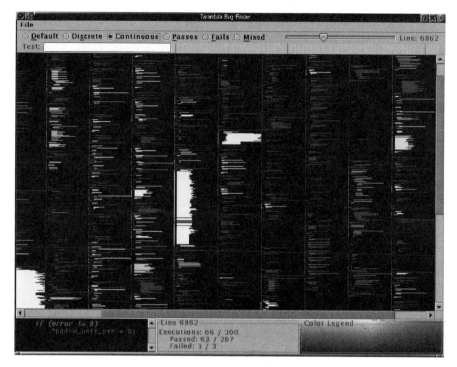

FIGURE 11.1 Visualizing coverage anomalies with TARANTULA (Jones et al., 2002). Each line of code is assigned a specific color. The "redder" a statement the stronger its execution correlates with failure.

In Example 11.2, of lines 5 through 11 line 9 would obtain the highest brightness, as it was executed in the most test cases.

What a TARANTULA user would be searching for, then, is bright red lines — statements that are executed in failing test cases only. In the best of all worlds, only a few of these lines would show up — limiting the number of lines to be examined. In a case study, Jones et al. (2002) showed that an anomaly does not necessarily indicate a defect, but that a defect is frequently an anomaly.

- For some defects, the percentage of abnormal code was as low as 3%. That is, starting the search at the most abnormal category, the programmer would find the defect after looking at 3% of the code.

- The most abnormal category (the 20% "reddest") contained at most 20% of the code. That is, comparing coverage actually yields small significant differences.

- 18 of the 20 defects were correctly classified in the most abnormal category — that is, the one containing 20% (at most) of the code.

Thus, in this particular case study focusing on the abnormal statements allowed programmers to ignore 80% of the code or more. Yet, one can still improve this. In past years, researchers have focused on the following extensions to coverage comparison.

- *Nearest neighbor:* Rather than comparing against a combination of all passing runs, it may be wiser to compare only against one passing run — the so-called "nearest neighbor." This nearest neighbor is the passing run whose coverage is most similar to the failing run. Obviously, the few remaining differences are those that are most strongly correlated with failure — and thus likely to point to the defect.

  In a case study, Renieris and Reiss (2003) found that the "nearest neighbor" approach predicts defect locations better than any other method based on coverage. In 17% of all test runs of the so-called *Siemens* test suite, the defect location could be narrowed down to 10% or less of the code. (In Chapter 14 "Isolating Cause-Effect Chains," we shall see how to improve on this result.)

- *Sequences:* As coverage comparison points out, the code of a single method can be correlated with failure. Some failures, though, occur only through a *sequence* of method calls tied to a *specific object.* As an example, consider streams in JAVA. If a stream is not explicitly closed after use, its destructor will eventually close it. However, if too many files are left open before the garbage collector destroys the unused streams, file handles will run out and a failure will occur. This problem is indicated by a sequence of method calls. If the last access [say, read()] is followed by finalize() [but not close()], we have a defect.

  In a case study, Dallmeier et al. (2005) applied this technique on a test suite based on the JAVA *NanoXML* parser. They found that sequences of calls always predicted defects better than simply comparing coverage. Overall, the technique pinpointed the defective class in 36% of all test runs, with the same low cost as capturing and comparing coverage.

As all of these figures were obtained on a small set of test programs, they do not generalize to larger programs. Nonetheless, these test programs serve as *benchmarks.* If a specific technique works better on a benchmark, it is likely to perform better on other programs. In the future, we will see more and more advanced coverage-comparison tools, demonstrating their advantage on benchmarks as well as on real-life programs.

11.3 STATISTICAL DEBUGGING

In addition to simple coverage, there are other aspects to collect from actual runs. One interesting aspect is exceptional behavior of functions — as indicated by exceptions being raised or unusual values being returned. If such events frequently occur together with failures, we might have important anomalies that point us to the defect.

The following is an example of how such a technique works, developed by Liblit et al. (2003). Release 1.2 of the CCRYPT encryption tool has a defect: when it comes to overwriting a file, CCRYPT asks the user for confirmation. If the user responds with EOF instead of yes or no, CCRYPT crashes.

Liblit et al. attempted to use remote sampling to isolate the defect. They instrumented CCRYPT such that at each call site of a function it would maintain three counters for positive, negative, or zero values returned by the function. (In C functions such arithmetic sign values often differentiate whether the call was successful or not.) When CCRYPT terminated, they would be able to tell how often each function had returned a positive, negative, or zero value. This data from 570 call sites, or $570 \times 3 = 1,710$ counters, would then be collected for statistical evaluation.

To gather data from actual runs, Liblit et al. generated 2,990 *random runs* from random present or absent files, randomized command-line flags, and randomized user responses (including occasional EOF conditions). These runs were classified into *failing* (crashing) and *passing* runs.

Liblit et al. would then examine the counters. Just as when comparing coverage (Section 11.2), they would search for functions executed only in failing runs, but never in passing runs — or more specifically, for functions returning a specific value category only in failing runs. In other words, the appropriate counter is positive for all failing runs, but always zero for passing runs.

It turns out that in the 2,990 CCRYPT test runs only two out of the 1,170 counters satisfy the following conditions.

- `traverse.c:320: file_exists()` > 0

- `traverse.c:122: xreadline()` $== 0$

In other words, the failure occurs if and only if these two conditions are met: `file_exists()` returns true, because a file (to be overwritten) exists, and `xreadline()` returns null, because the user did not provide any input.

Such a result is an *anomaly* because it occurs only in failing runs. It is not a defect, though, because both return values are perfectly legal. However, using this knowledge we can easily follow the forward dependences from the call sites and see where the returned values are used — and we will quickly find that CCRYPT does not expect `xreadline()` to return null.

If we use real user input rather than random strings, we should even expect some runs where a file exists [i.e., `file_exists() > 0` holds] but where the user provides a valid input (such as yes), resulting in `xreadline() \neq 0$ and a passing run. This would imply that the predicate `file_exists() > 0` is true for at least one passing run — and hence only `xreadline() == 0` would remain as the single anomaly correlated with the failure.

11.4 COLLECTING DATA IN THE FIELD

Detecting anomalies from actual executions may require a large set of runs, which is why these are typically *generated* randomly. A far better approach, though, is to use data *collected in the field* — that is, from executions at users' sites.

- The number of executions at users' sites is typically *far higher* than the number of executions during testing.

- Real-life executions produce a greater *variety*. In the CCRYPT example, for instance, the typical behavior of entering "yes" or "no" at a prompt was not covered by the random input.

- In our networked world, collecting and gathering data can easily be automated, as well as the analysis.

- Gathering information from users' runs gives a firsthand indication about how the software is being used — information otherwise difficult to obtain.

- As a side effect, the makers of a software product learn which features are most frequently used and which are not — an important factor when determining the impact of a problem (Section 2.4).

In principle, there is no limit to the information that can be collected. *Exceptional behavior* such as crashes is certainly valuable to the provider (see Section 2.2). However, to statistically correlate such exceptional behavior with other aspects of the program run one may also want to monitor function execution or data values.

It is not wise to log everything, though. Two issues have to be considered.

- *Privacy:* Users have a right to privacy, and are very conscious of privacy issues. Section 2.2 has details on these issues and how to address them.

- *Performance:* Collecting data impacts the local performance of the system. In addition, forwarding large amounts of collected data over the network entails costs. To improve performance, one can *focus* on a specific part of the product — for instance, collect data only from a few components rather than the entire system. Instead of collecting *all* data, one can also *sample* the logs such that each user executes only a small fraction of the collecting statements.

This sampling approach is actually quite effective. In the CCRYPT example from Section 11.3, Liblit et al. would conduct an experiment in which only one out of 1,000 return values of a function was sampled. The impact on performance is less than 4%. Of course, sampling only 1 out of 1,000 function returns requires a large number of runs.

Figure 11.2 shows how the function counters discussed in Section 11.3 are eliminated as the number of runs increases. The process starts with 141 out of 1,710 counters that are ever nonzero. One then adds data from one random run after another. After having considered 1,750 runs, the set of remaining predicates has gone down to 20, and after 2,600 runs just five are left. Again, these five predicates are strongly correlated with failure.

Overall, the results so far demonstrate that statistical sampling can be a powerful, low-overhead tool for detecting anomalies in the field. Now all one needs is users that are willing to have their runs sampled. Liblit et al. (2005) state that "relatively few runs (we used 32,000) are sufficient to isolate all of the bugs described in this paper."

There are situations, though, where several thousand runs are easy to sample. In particular, a centralized *web service* may be called thousands of times a day — and since there is just one program instance doing the actual work behind the scenes, instrumenting a sample of runs is pretty straightforward, as is collecting data of actual failures. In practice, this means that you get anomalies almost for free — and the higher the number of runs, the more significant the correlation of features and failures will be.

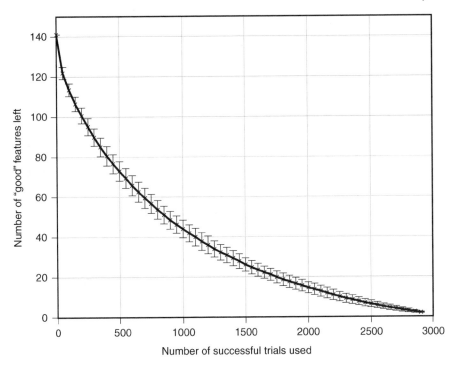

FIGURE II.2 Narrowing down predicates. Crosses mark means; error bars mark one standard deviation.

11.5 DYNAMIC INVARIANTS

So far, we have seen how specific aspects of multiple runs can be collected to detect anomalies. Another approach for leveraging multiple runs is to generate *likely specifications* that hold for all runs and to see whether these can be turned into general *assertions* — which can then be used to detect anomalies.

How does one generate specifications from actual runs? A simple yet highly effective approach has been implemented in the DAIKON tool by Ernst et al. (2001). The main idea behind DAIKON is to discover *invariants* that hold for all observed runs. These invariants come in the form of pre- and postconditions. They can be converted into assertions to check for abnormal behavior. To see what DAIKON does, consider the following piece of code.

```
public static int ex1511(int[] b, int n)
{
    int s = 0;
    int i = 0;
```

```
        while (i != n) {
            s = s + b[i];
            i = i + 1;
        }
        return s;
    }
```

What does this code do? We create a set of concrete runs, processing 100 randomly generated arrays with a length from 7 to 13 and elements from $[-100, +100]$. Running DAIKON on these runs yields two invariants. First is the inferred precondition for ex1511():

```
Ex.ex1511(int[], int):::ENTER
n == size(b[])
b != null
n <= 13
n >= 7
...
```

Obviously, n is the size of the array b[]. This could serve as an assertion, assuming we can access the size of b[]. In addition, in the runs observed n is always in the range from 7 to 13 — but this is obviously an artifact of the runs we observed. The second invariant is the postcondition for ex1511():

```
Ex.ex1511(int[], int):::EXIT
b[] == orig(b[])
return == sum(b[])
...
```

In the first invariant, the orig(b[]) clause stands for the "original" value of b[] — that is, as the function was entered — and the invariant properly states that ex1511() did not change b[]'s values. The second invariant states that the return value of ex1511() is always the sum (sum()) of the elements of b[] — and this is precisely what ex1511() does.

How does DAIKON detect these invariants? The general process, as follows, is shown in Figure 11.3.

1. The program to be observed is instrumented at runtime such that all values of all variables at all entries and exits of all functions are logged to a trace file. For C and JAVA programs, DAIKON uses binary instrumentation techniques

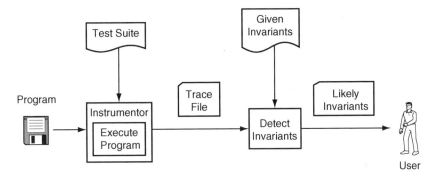

FIGURE 11.3 How DAIKON works. The instrumented program generates a trace file, from which DAIKON extracts the invariants.

built on top of VALGRIND (Section 10.8.3). For PERL programs, DAIKON adds instrumentation to the source code in a preprocessing step.

2. When executing the program under a test suite, the instrumented code generates a trace file.

3. DAIKON processes this trace file. DAIKON maintains a library of invariant *patterns* over variables and constants. Each of these patterns can be instantiated with different variables and constants.

- *Method specifications* come as pre- and postconditions. They can apply to:

    - *Primitive data* such as integers. They compare at most three variables with constants and other variables, as in

```
x = 6;       x ∈ {2, 5, -30}
x < y;       y = 5 * x + 10;
z = 4 * x + 12 * y + 3;
z = fn(x, y).
```

    - *Composite data* such as sequences, arrays, or lists. For instance,
    A subsequence B; x ∈ A; A is sorted.

- *Object invariants* such as the following.

```
string.content[string.length] = '\0';
node.left.value ≤ node.right.value
this.next.last = this
```

Just as method specifications, object invariants can apply to primitive as well as composite data.

For each variable (or tuple of variables), DAIKON maintains a set of potential invariants, initially consisting of all invariants. At each execution point under consideration, for each value recorded in the trace DAIKON checks each invariant in the set whether it still holds. If it does not, DAIKON removes it from the set.

During this process, DAIKON checks individual variables as well as *derived variables*, such as `orig(b[])` or `sum(b[])` in the previous example. Derived variables also include the return values of functions, to be used in postconditions.

4. While detecting invariants, DAIKON makes some optimizations to make the remaining invariants as relevant as possible. In particular, if some invariant A implies an invariant B then B need not be reported.

5. After DAIKON has fully processed the trace file, the invariants that remain are those that held for all execution points.

6. DAIKON ranks the invariants by the number of times they actually occurred. An invariant detected 100 times is less likely to be a random effect than an invariant detected three times.

7. DAIKON reports the relevant and ranked invariants to the user. The invariants can be fed into another tool for further processing.

The benefits of this technique are as clear as its drawbacks. The most obvious drawback of DAIKON is that the invariants it detects are those built into its library. DAIKON cannot generate new abstractions on its own. For instance, DAIKON can discover that "at the end of `shell_sort()`, the value is sorted" (`sample.c` in Example 1.1) but not that "the value returned is the middle number" (`middle.c` in Example 11.1). This is because DAIKON knows about "sorted" things but not about "middle" numbers. It just lacks the appropriate vocabulary.

It is not too difficult to extend DAIKON 's vocabulary by concepts such as middle elements. In general, as long as some property can be observed it can be added to DAIKON's invariant library. However, the more properties there are to be checked (as well as possible combinations thereof) the longer DAIKON has to run. In regard to the current library, invariant detection time for each program point is cubic in the number of variables that are in scope at this point (as patterns involve three variables at most). Hence, a large number of invariants on a large number of variables will quickly bring DAIKON to its knees. Thus, users need to apply DAIKON to the portion of the code that interests them most.

For the user, the central problem is to *assess* the reported invariants. Are these true facts that hold for every possible execution (which is what users are typically interested in), or do the invariants just hold for the examined runs? On the other hand, if the examined runs are typical for the general behavior all reported invariants will be helpful for understanding this general behavior.

Keeping these issues in mind, DAIKON is a great tool for program understanding and for summarizing the properties of several runs in a few conditions. DAIKON can output its assertions in JML format, which JML tools (Section 10.6) can thus check for other runs — for failing runs, for instance, as well as for new runs of a changed version. Whenever a specification is required but a test suite is available, the invariants inferred by DAIKON come in handy as a first take.

11.6 INVARIANTS ON THE FLY

A question not yet answered is whether dynamic invariants can be directly used for anomaly detection — without first selecting those that are useful as general specifications. In the CCRYPT example from Section 11.3, we showed how function return values can be correlated with actual failures. Such return values can also be detected and summarized, making dynamic invariants a potential tool for automatic anomaly detection.

This idea has been explored in the DIDUCE prototype of Hangal and Lam (2002). DIDUCE is built for efficiency, and primarily geared toward anomaly detection. It works for a very specific set of invariants only, but has been demonstrated to be effective in detecting anomalies.

Just like DAIKON, DIDUCE instruments the code of the program in question. In contrast to DAIKON, though, DIDUCE works on the fly — that is, invariants are computed while the program is executed. For each instrumented place in the program, DIDUCE stores three items.

- *Coverage:* DIDUCE counts the number of times the place was executed.

- *Values:* For each accessed variable, DIDUCE stores the found *value* of the variable read or written. This value is converted to an integer, if necessary, and then stored as a pair (V, M), where

  - V is the *initial value* first written to the variable and

  - M is a *mask* representing the *range of values* (the ith bit is 0 if a difference was found in the ith bit, and 1 if the same value has always been observed for that bit)

Formally, if the first value of a variable is W, then $M := \neg 0$ and $V := W$ hold. With each new assignment W', the mask M becomes $M := M \wedge \neg(W' \otimes V)$, where $\otimes$ is the exclusive-or operation.

The following is an example. If some variable i is first assigned a value of 16, then $V = 16 = 1000$ (in binary representation) holds (M is initially $\neg 0 = 11111$). If i is later assigned a value of 18, V is still unchanged, but in M the second bit is cleared because the difference between V and 18 is the second bit. Thus, M becomes 11101.

- *Difference:* For each variable, DIDUCE additionally stores the *difference* between the previous value and the new value. These are again stored as a pair (V, M), as described previously.

  If i's value changes from 16 to 18, as described previously, the initial difference V is 2. In the mask M, all bits are set ($M = \neg 0$). If i's value now increases to 21, the new difference between old and new value is $21 - 18 = 3$. The first bit in M is cleared because the increases 2 and 3 differ in the first bit.

The masks, as collected during a program run, imply *ranges* of values and differences that can easily be translated into invariants over values and differences. Table 11.1 outlines how the mask bits become more and more cleared as value variation progresses. Due to the representation, the ranges are not as exact as could be. The representation. though, is very cost effective. The runtime overhead is limited to a few memory operations and simple logical operations for each instrumentation point, and the slowdown factor reported by Hangal and Lam (2002) lies between 6 and 20.

Once one has collected the invariants and finalized the M masks, this representation is just as effective for reporting invariant violations. Whenever DIDUCE observes further variation of M, it reports a violation. Thus, each value or difference out of the range observed previously becomes an anomaly.

Although far more limited than DAIKON, the invariant violations reported by DIDUCE have successfully uncovered defects in a number of programs. The

TABLE 11.1   Collecting invariants in DIDUCE.

Code	i	Value		Difference		Invariant
		V	M	V	M	
i = 10;	1010	1010	…11111	–/–	–/–	$i = 10$
i += 1;	1011	1010	…11110	1	…11111	$10 \leq i \leq 11 \wedge \lvert i' - i \rvert = 1$
i += 1;	1100	1010	…11000	1	…11111	$8 \leq i \leq 15 \wedge \lvert i' - i \rvert = 1$
i += 1;	1101	1010	…11000	1	…11111	$8 \leq i \leq 15 \wedge \lvert i' - i \rvert = 1$
i += 2;	1111	1010	…11000	1	…11101	$8 \leq i \leq 15 \wedge \lvert i' - i \rvert \leq 2$

following is an example reported by Hangal and Lam (2002). A multiprocessor simulator exhibited rare and presumably random cache errors. Running DIDUCE in a time interval where no failures occurred resulted in a set of invariants. These invariants were then checked in an overnight run of DIDUCE. It turned out that one violation was produced: a status line, which was usually 0 or 1, suddenly turned out to be 2, and a failure occurred. It turned out that the programmer had not checked this condition properly, and the anomaly reported by DIDUCE quickly pointed him to the defect.

As DIDUCE accumulates invariants during a run, and can be switched from "learning" to "detection" mode without interrupting the application, it is particularly easy to use. In particular, users can start using DIDUCE at the start of the debugging process and can switch between inferring and checking during a run.

11.7   FROM ANOMALIES TO DEFECTS

An anomaly is not a defect, and it is not a failure cause. Yet, an anomaly can be a good starting point for reasoning.

- *Does the anomaly indicate an infection?* If so, we can trace the dependences back to the origins.

- *Could the anomaly cause a failure?* If so, we must understand the effects of the anomaly — for instance, by following the forward dependences through the program.

- *Could the anomaly be a side effect of a defect?* If so, we must trace back the anomaly to the common origin of failure and anomaly.

Overall, the case studies in this chapter have shown that abnormal properties of a program run are more likely to indicate defects than normal properties of the run. Therefore, whenever we have the choice of multiple events we should first focus on the abnormal ones — and using scientific method set up an experiment that checks whether the anomaly causes the failure.

11.8 CONCEPTS

✎ As defects are likely to cause abnormal behavior, anomalies frequently point to defects.

✎ Anomalies are neither defects nor failure causes but can strongly correlate with either.

HOW TO   ✎ *To determine abnormal behavior*, determine the normal behavior of passing runs and see how the failing run(s) differ. This can be done

- by *comparing* the summarized properties directly or

- by turning the properties into *assertions*, which can then be used to detect anomalies in failing runs.

HOW TO   ✎ *To summarize behavior*, use inductive techniques that summarize the properties of several program runs into an *abstraction* that holds for all of these runs.

HOW TO   ✎ *To detect anomalies*, researchers so far have focused on *coverage, function return values*, and *data invariants*.

HOW TO   ✎ *To compare coverage*, instrument a program and summarize the coverage for the passing and for the failing runs. Concentrate on statements executed in failing runs only.

HOW TO   ✎ *To sample return values*, at each call site count the numbers within each category of return values. Focus on those categories that occur only in the failing runs.

HOW TO   ✎ *To collect data from the field*, use a sampling strategy such that the impact on performance is minimized.

HOW TO   ✎ *To determine invariants*, use DAIKON or similar tool to check whether given invariants hold at the instrumentation points.

✎ Whenever we have the choice of multiple events, we should first focus on the abnormal ones.

✎ The techniques discussed in this chapter are fairly recent and not yet fully evaluated.

11.9 TOOLS

DAIKON

The DAIKON tool by Ernst et al. (2001) has had a tremendous impact on the field of dynamic program analysis — not only because of its features but because it is available for download. The DAIKON project page offers software, instructions, and papers on the subject. It is found at:

```
http://pag.csail.mit.edu/daikon/
```

DIDUCE

The DIDUCE tool by Hangal and Lam (2002) is also available for download at:

```
http://diduce.sourceforge.net/
```

11.10 FURTHER READING

Dynamic program analysis has taken off as a discipline only in the last decade — an explosion largely due to the wealth of computing power we have today ("why not simply run the program 2,000 times?") and to the presence of cheap communication ("let's collect all data from all users"). As becomes clear in this chapter, the individual approaches are yet isolated, and it is unclear which approach is best suited for which situation. Yet, the tools and techniques merit to be experimented with — to see how they can help with user's programs.

The TARANTULA tool, developed by Jones et al., was the first tool to visualize and leverage code coverage for detecting faults. Jones et al. (2002) offer several details on the tool and a conducted case study.

Renieris and Reiss (2003) introduced the "nearest neighbor" concept. I also recommend their paper because of the careful and credible evaluation method. Sequences of method calls were investigated by Dallmeier et al. (2005).

Liblit et al. were the first to introduce sampling for detecting failures. Liblit et al. (2003) describe details of the approach as well as additional case studies. At the time of writing, you could download instrumented versions of common programs that would report sampled coverage data — thus helping researchers to isolate defects in these applications. See the following address.

```
http://sample.cs.berkeley.edu/
```

Remote sampling is also addressed in the GAMMA project under the name of *software tomography* (Orso et al., 2003). GAMMA primarily focuses on sampling coverage information such that the coverage comparison (as described in Section 11.2) can be deployed on a large number of runs.

Podgurski et al. (2003) apply statistical feature selection, clustering, and multivariate visualization techniques to the task of classifying software failure reports. The idea is to bucket each report into an equivalence group believed to share the same underlying cause. As in GAMMA, features are derived from execution traces.

In addition to DAIKON and DIDUCE, other approaches for extracting behavior models from actual runs have been researched — although not necessarily with the purpose of finding defects. Ammons et al. (2002), for instance, describe how to construct state machines from observed runs that can be used as specifications for verification purposes. Such state machines may also be helpful in uncovering anomalies.

Finally, it is also possible to create abstractions both for passing and failing runs — and then to check a new run as to whether it is closer to one category than the other, effectively *predicting* whether the run will pass or fail. This can be useful for discovering latent defects or otherwise undesirable behavior. Dickinson et al. (2001) describe how to use cluster analysis to predict failures. Brun and Ernst (2004) show how to classify the features of program properties to "learn from fixes." If a program shows properties similar to those that have been fixed in the past, these properties are also likely to be fixed.

11.11 EXERCISES

EXERCISE 11.1. Using your own words, compare

- anomaly detection by comparing coverage and

- anomaly detection by dynamically determined invariants.

in terms of

1. efficiency,

2. applicability to a wide range of programs, and

3. effectiveness in locating defects.

EXERCISE 11.2. Sometimes, bugs reappear that have been fixed before. How can regression testing be used to prevent this? How can regression testing help to detect anomalies?

EXERCISE 11.3. Discuss:

- How assertions could be used to detect anomalies

- Why and why not to use them throughout the program run

EXERCISE 11.4. We have seen that detected anomalies do not necessarily indicate defects (false positives). Explain this phenomenon. What would be false negatives, and how can we explain those?

EXERCISE 11.5. What is the basic idea of invariant analysis? What are the advantages and disadvantages of dynamic compared to static techniques?

EXERCISE 11.6. Use DAIKON to detect invariants in the bigbang program (Example 8.3). Note that you may need to resolve memory issues first.

EXERCISE 11.7. DAIKON generates a huge number of invariants. What techniques does it use to reduce that number to *relevant* invariants? Explain the effectiveness of the techniques.

EXERCISE 11.8. Consider the sample code from Example 1.1 in explaining the effectiveness of:

- DAIKON

- DIDUCE

Discuss strengths and limitations of both tools.

EXERCISE 11.9. Compare DAIKON and DIDUCE regarding efficiency, usability, scalability, performance, and reliability of the results. Discuss when to use which approach.

If you never know failure, how can you know success?

— *The Matrix* (1999)

## CHAPTER 12

CAUSES AND EFFECTS

Dᴇᴅᴜᴄᴛɪᴏɴ, ᴏʙsᴇʀᴠᴀᴛɪᴏɴ, ᴀɴᴅ ɪɴᴅᴜᴄᴛɪᴏɴ are all good in finding *potential* defects. However, none of these techniques alone is sufficient to determine a *failure cause*. How does one identify a cause? How does one isolate not only *a* cause but *the* actual cause of a failure? This chapter lays the groundwork on how to find failure causes systematically — and automatically.

12.1 CAUSES AND ALTERNATE WORLDS

Anomalies and defects, as discussed in the previous chapters, are all good starting points in a debugging session. However, we do not know yet whether these actually *cause* the failure in question.

If we say "a defect causes a failure," what does "cause" mean? Generally speaking, a *cause* is an event preceding another event without which the event in question (the *effect*) would not have occurred. Hence, a defect causes the failure if the failure would not have occurred without the defect.

Because most of debugging is the search for a defect that causes the failure, we must understand how to search for cause-effect relationships. That is, to search for *causality* — with the idea that once we found a cause the defect is not far away.

In natural and social sciences, causality is often difficult to establish. Just think about common disputes such as "Did usage of the butterfly ballot in West Palm Beach cause George W. Bush to be president of the United States?," "Did drugs cause the death of Elvis Presley?," or "Does human production of carbon dioxide cause global warming?"

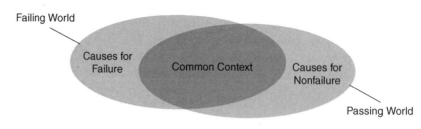

FIGURE 12.1 Causes as differences between alternate worlds.

To determine whether these are actually causes, formally we would have to repeat history *without the cause in question*—in an alternate world that is as close as possible to ours except for the cause. Using this *counterfactual* model of causality, a cause becomes a *difference* between the two worlds (Figure 12.1).

- A world where the effect occurs.

- An *alternate* world where the effect does not occur.

We know already what our actual world looks like. However, if in alternate worlds Albert Gore had been president, Elvis were alive, and global warming were less (and not changing anything else), we would know that butterfly ballots, drugs, and carbon dioxide had been actual causes for the given effects.

Unfortunately, we cannot repeat history like an experiment in a lab. We have to speculate about what *would* have happened. We can have all experts in the world agree with our speculation, but in the real, nondeterministic, and above all nonrepeatable world one can never absolutely know whether a probable cause is a cause. This is why one can always come up with a new theory about the true cause, and this is why some empirical researchers have suggested dropping the concept of causality altogether.

In our domain of computer science, though, things are different. We can easily repeat program runs over and over, change the circumstances of the execution as desired, and observe the effects. Given the right means (Chapter 4 "Reproducing Problems"), the program execution is under (almost) total control and is (almost) totally deterministic. (The "almost" is there because the execution may still be determined by physical effects, as described in Section 4.3.8.)

Scientists frequently use computers to determine causes and effects in models of the real world. However, such causes and effects run the danger of being inappropriate in the concrete, because the model may have abstracted away important aspects. If we are determining causes and effects in the program itself, though, we keep abstraction to a minimum. Typically, we only abstract away the irreproducible physical effects. Minimal abstraction implies minimal risk.

Hence, among all scientific disciplines *debugging is the one that can best claim to deal with actual causality*. In the remainder of this chapter, we shall thus address the key question:

HOW DO I KNOW SOMETHING CAUSES THE FAILURE IN QUESTION?

12.2 VERIFYING CAUSES

How do we check whether some anomaly — or, more generally, any property of a program run — causes the failure in question? The actual world in which the effect occurs is our real world — with the effect, the failing run, occurring before our eyes. The *alternate world,* though, is what we need to show that some property causes the failure. To show causality, we must *set up an experiment with an alternate world* in which the property does not occur. If in this alternate world the failure does not occur either, we have shown that the property caused the failure.

As an example, consider a program that emits a warning message (say, "Configuration file not found") and then fails. How do we show that the missing configuration file causes the failure? We set up an alternate world in which a configuration file is present. In other words, we set up an *experiment* to support or refute our hypothesis about causality. If (and only if) in our experiment the failure no longer occurs have we shown causality (i.e., that the missing file caused the failure).

This reasoning may sound trivial at first ("Of course, we need such an experiment!"), but having such an explicit verification step is crucial for avoiding *fallacies.* In our example, it would only be natural to assume that the warning message is somehow connected to the failure — especially if the warning is all we can observe — and thus attempt to resolve the warning in the hope of resolving the failure.

This type of reasoning is called *post hoc ergo propter hoc* ("after this, therefore because of this"). This means that an anomaly has occurred *before* the failure, and therefore the anomaly must have caused the failure. However, it may well be that the warning is totally unrelated to the failure. In that case, resolving the warning will cost us precious time. Therefore, any systematic procedure will first determine causality by an experiment, as described previously.

12.3 CAUSALITY IN PRACTICE

The following is a somewhat more elaborate example. Consider the following piece of C code.

```
a = compute_value();
printf("a = %d\n", a);
```

This piece of code invokes the compute_value() function, assigns the result to the variable a, and prints the value of a on the console. When executed, it prints a = 0 on the console, although a is not supposed to be zero. What is the cause for a = 0 being printed?

Deducing from the program code (Chapter 7 "Deducing Errors"), we may reason that if variable a is zero we must examine the origin of this value. Following back the dependences from a, we find that the last assignment was from compute_value(), and thus we might investigate how compute_value() can return a zero value. Unfortunately, it turns out that compute_value() is not supposed to return zero. Thus, we may proceed digging into the compute_value() code to find out how the zero came to be.

Unfortunately, reasoning alone does not suffice for proving causality. We must show by experiment that if a cause is not present an effect is not present. Therefore, we must show that a being zero is the cause for a = 0 being printed. Later on, we would show that compute_value() returning zero is the cause for a being zero — and each of these causalities must be shown by an experiment (or, at least, additional observation).

At this point, this may seem like nit-picking. Is not it *obvious* that a is zero? After all, we print its value on the console. Unfortunately, "obvious" is not enough. "Obviously," the program should work, but it does not. Hence, we can trust nothing, and especially not the obvious.

Let's then attempt to show causality using scientific method. We set up a hypothesis:

a *being zero is the cause for* a = 0 *being printed.*

To show that this hypothesis holds, we must set up an experiment in which a is not zero, and in which a = 0 is not being printed. Let's do so by inserting a little assignment a = 1 into the code. This results in our first *alternate world*:

```
a = compute_value();
a = 1;
printf("a = %d\n", a);
```

If the program now prints a = 1, we know that a being zero was the cause for a = 0 being printed. However, if we execute this piece of code we find that a = 0 is still being printed, regardless of the inserted assignment.

This is weird. How can this happen? We set up a new hypothesis:

a = 0 *is being printed regardless of the value of* a.

To prove this hypothesis, we could set a to various values other than 1 — and we would find that the hypothesis always holds. This means that there must be something wrong with the printf invocation. And there is. a is declared a *floating-point* variable:

```
double a;
⋮

a = compute_value();
a = 1;
printf("a = %d\n", a);
```

However, the argument "%d" makes printf expect an *integer* value as a next argument. If we pass a floating-point value instead, this means that only the first four bytes of the floating-point representation are being read — and interpreted as an integer. (In fact, this type of mistake is so common that many compilers issue a warning when the printf format string does not match the later arguments.) What happens on this specific machine is that the first four bytes of the internal representation of 1.0 (and any other small integer) are all zero — and hence a = 0 is printed regardless of the value of a.

But all this, again, is yet only reasoning. Our working hypothesis becomes:

The format %d *is the cause for* a = 0 *being printed.*

To prove the hypothesis, we must again set up an experiment in which the cause does not occur. In other words, we must alter the program to make the failure go away. A proper format for floating-point values in printf is "%f". Let's alter the format to this value:

```
a = compute_value();
printf("a = %f\n", a);
```

Now that the cause "%d" is no longer present, the actual value of a is being printed on the console. That is, the effect of printing a = 0 is gone. This means that "%d" actually was the cause of a = 0 being printed. In other words, "%d" was the defect that caused the failure. Our final hypothesis has become a *theory* about the failure cause. Note how the use of scientific method (Chapter 6 "Scientific Debugging") prevents fallacies from the start, as every hypothesis (about a failure cause) must be verified by an experiment (with an alternate world in which the cause does not occur).

As pointed out in Section 12.1, detecting causes in the real world is difficult, essentially because one cannot turn back history and see what would have happened in the alternate world. This is why the counterfactual definition of causality is often deemed too restrictive. In the context of debugging, though, we can repeat runs over and over. In fact, conducting experiments with alternate worlds is a necessary effect of applying scientific method. Hence, in debugging, experiments are the only way to show causality. Deduction and speculation do not suffice.

12.4   FINDING ACTUAL CAUSES

Now that we have discussed how to *verify* a cause, let's turn to the central problem: how do we find a failure cause? It turns out that finding *a* cause is trivial. The problem is to find *the* cause among a number of alternatives.

In debugging, as in experimental science, the only way to determine whether something is a cause is an experiment. Hence, for example, only by *changing* the program in Section 6.3 could we prove that the defect was actually the *cause* of the failure.

This conjunction of causes and changes raises an important problem. Just as there are infinitely many ways of writing a program, there are infinitely many ways of changing a program such that a failure no longer occurs. Because each of these changes implies a failure cause, there are *infinitely many failure causes.* For example, how can we say that something is *the* defect or *the* cause of a failure, as "%d" in Section 12.3?

- We could also say that the `printf` statement as a whole is a cause for printing a = 0, because if we remove it nothing is printed.

- Anomalies, as discussed in Chapter 11 "Detecting Anomalies," are a cause of a failure because without anomalies (i.e., in a "normal" run) the failure does not occur.

- We can treat the entire program code as a cause, because we can rewrite it from scratch such that it works.

- Electricity, mathematics, and the existence of computers are all failure causes because without them there would be no program run and hence no failure.

This multitude of causes is unfortunate and confusing. In debugging, and especially in automated debugging, we would like to point out a single failure cause, not a multitude of *trivial* alternatives.

To discriminate among these alternatives, the concept of the *closest possible world* comes in handy. A world is said to be "closer" to the actual world than another if it resembles the actual world more than the other does. The idea is that now *the* cause should be a *minimal difference* between the actual world where the effect occurs and the alternate world where it would not (Figure 12.1). In other words, the alternate world should be *as close as possible*. Therefore, we define an *actual cause* as a difference between the actual world where the effect occurs and the closest possible world where it would not.

Another way of thinking about an actual cause is that *whenever we have the choice between two causes we can pick the one whose alternate world is closer.* Consequently, "%d" is *the* defect, but the printf statement is not — because altering just the format string is a smaller difference than removing the printf statement. Likewise, the absence of electricity would result in a world that is quite different from ours. Hence, electricity would not qualify as an actual failure cause. This principle of picking the closer alternate world is also known as *Ockham's Razor,* which states that whenever you have competing theories for how some effect comes to be, pick the simplest.

12.5 NARROWING DOWN CAUSES

Let's now put these general concepts of causality into practice. Given some failure (i.e., the effect), how do we find an actual cause? A simple strategy works as follows.

1. Find an alternate world in which the effect does not occur.

2. Narrow down the initial difference to an actual cause, using scientific method (Chapter 6 "Scientific Debugging").

If you think that this sounds almost too trivial, you are right. The alternate world where the effect does not occur — is not this just what we aim at? Think about a defect causing the failure, for instance. If we have an alternate world in which the defect does not occur, we are already set. Why bother dealing with the differences to the real world if we already know what the alternate world is supposed to be?

The trick is that the alternate world need not be a world in which the program has been corrected. It suffices that the failure does not occur—which implies that there is some other *difference* either in the program input or its execution that eventually causes the differing behavior with respect to the failure. The challenge is to *identify* this initial difference, which can then be narrowed down to an actual cause.

12.6 A NARROWING EXAMPLE

The following is a little example that illustrates this approach. When I give a presentation, I use a little shareware program on my laptop such that I can remote-control the presentation with my Bluetooth phone. (Sometimes it's fun to be a nerd.) Having upgraded this program recently, I found that it quit after moving to the next slide. I exchanged a few e-mails with the author of the shareware. He was extremely helpful and committed, but was not able to reproduce my problem. In his setting (and in the setting of the other users), everything worked fine.

To narrow down the cause, I searched for an alternate world in which the failure did not occur. It turned out that if I created a new user account from scratch, using all of the default settings, the program worked fine. Thus, I had a workaround—but I also had a *cause*, as this alternate account (the alternate world) differed from my account in a number of settings and preferences.

Just having a cause, though, did not help me in fixing the problem. I wanted an *actual* cause. Thus, I had to narrow down the difference between the accounts, and so I copied setting after setting from my account to the new account, checking each time whether the failure would occur. In terms of scientific method, the hypothesis in each step was that the respective setting caused the problem, and with each new copied setting not showing the failure I disproved one hypothesis after another.

Finally, though, I was successful: copying the *keyboard settings* from my account to the new account caused the failure to occur. Mostly living in Germany, I occasionally have to write text in German, using words with funny characters such as those in "Schöne Grüße" (best regards). To type these characters quickly, I have crafted my own keyboard layout such that simple key combinations such as Alt+O or Alt+S give me the ö or ß character, respectively. Copying this layout setting to the new user account resulted in the failure of the shareware program.

Thus, I had an actual cause — the difference between the previous setting and the new setting — and this diagnosis was what I e-mailed the shareware author (who had explored some other alternatives in the meantime). He committed to support such handcrafted layouts in the future, and everybody was happy.

12.7 THE COMMON CONTEXT

As the example in Section 12.6 illustrates, we do not necessarily need an alternate world in which the defect is *fixed*. It suffices to have some alternate world in which the failure *does not occur* — as long as we can narrow down the *initial difference* to an actual cause.

This initial difference sets the frame in which to search for the actual cause. Aspects that do not differ will be part of the *common context* and hence never changed nor isolated as causes. This context is much larger than may be expected. Our common context includes, for instance, the fact that the program is executed, and all other facts required to make the execution possible. One can also think about the common context as defining *necessary conditions* that must be satisfied by every alternate world. Anything that is not part of the common context can *differ*, and thus sets the *search space* — such as the settings in my user account.

In many cases, we have the choice between multiple alternate worlds. For instance, I may find out that some earlier version of the shareware program works nicely, such that I could narrow down the difference between old and new version — with the settings unchanged. I could try different devices and leave everything else unchanged. Perhaps the failure occurs only with specific devices? The choice of an alternate world sets the search space in which to find causes. Whatever alternate world is chosen, one should strive to keep it *as similar as possible to the actual world* — simply because Ockham's Razor tells you that this gives you the best chance of finding the failure cause.

12.8 CAUSES IN DEBUGGING

The concepts *actual cause* and *closest possible world* are applicable to all causes — including the causes required for debugging. Thus, if we want to find the actual cause for a program failure we have to search for the *closest possible world in which the failure does not occur*.

- *Input:* The actual failure cause in a *program input* is a minimal difference between the actual input (where the failure occurs) and the closest possible input where the failure does not occur.

- *State:* The actual failure cause in a *program state* is a minimal difference between the actual program state and the closest possible state where the failure does not occur.

- *Code:* The actual failure cause in a *program code* is a minimal difference between the actual code and the closest possible code where the failure does not occur.

All of these failure causes must be *verified* by two experiments: one in which effect and failure occur and one in which they do not. Once one has verified a cause, one has valuable information for debugging.

- *Causes are directly related to the failure.* As a failure is an effect of the cause, it only occurs when the cause occurs. Neither defects (Chapter 7 "Deducing Errors") nor anomalies (Chapter 11 "Detecting Anomalies") are as strongly related to the failure.

- *Failure causes suggest fixes.* By removing the failure cause, we can make the failure disappear. This may not necessarily be a *correction*, but it is at least a good *workaround*.

Both properties make causes excellent starting points during debugging, which is why in the remainder of this book we will explore how to isolate them automatically.

12.9 CONCEPTS

- ✎ Of all circumstances we can observe during debugging, *causes* are the most valuable.

- ✎ A cause is an event preceding another event without which the event in question (the *effect*) would not have occurred.

- ✎ A cause can be seen as *difference* between two worlds—a world in which the effect occurs and an *alternate* world in which the effect does not occur.

HOW TO   ✎ *To show causality*, set up an experiment in which the cause does not occur.

Causality is shown if (and only if) the effect does not occur either.

✎ *To find a cause*, use scientific method to set up hypotheses on possible causes. `HOW TO`
Verify causality using experiments.

✎ An *actual cause* is the difference between the actual world and the *closest possible world* in which the effect does not occur.

✎ The principle of picking the closest possible world is also known as *Ockham's Razor*, which states that whenever you have competing theories for how some effect comes to be, pick the simplest.

✎ *To find an actual cause*, narrow down an initial difference via scientific `HOW TO`
method.

✎ A common context between actual worlds excludes causes from the search space.

12.10 FURTHER READING

The definitions of cause and effect in this book are based on *counterfactuals*, because they rely on assumptions about nonfacts. The first counterfactual definition of causes and effects is attributed to Hume (1748): "If the first object [the cause] had not been, the second [the effect] never had existed." The best-known counterfactual theory of causation was elaborated by Lewis (1973), refined in 1986.

Causality is a vividly discussed philosophical field. In addition to the counterfactual definitions, the most important alternatives are definitions based on *regularity* and *probabilism*. I recommend Zalta (2002) for a survey and Pearl (2000) for an in-depth treatment.

Ockham's Razor is the principle proposed by William of Ockham in the fourteenth century: "Pluralitas non est ponenda sine neccesitate," which translates as "plurality shouldn't be posited without necessity." A modern interpretation is "If two theories explain the facts equally well, the simpler theory is to be preferred" or just "Keep it simple." The principle was stated much earlier by Aristotle: "For if the consequences are the same it is always better to assume the more limited antecedent."

According to Bloch (1980), *Hanlon's Razor* "Never attribute to malice that which is adequately explained by stupidity" was coined by the late Robert J. Hanlon of Scranton, Pensylvania. (This phrase or very similar statements have been attributed to William James, Napoleon Bonaparte, Richard Feynman, Johann Wolfgang von Goethe, Robert Heinlein, and others.) Reportedly, Hanlon was a winner in a contest to come up with further statements similar to *Murphy's Law* "If it can go wrong, it will."

12.11 EXERCISES

EXERCISE 12.1. Suppose you wish to find out whether:

1. Elvis died on an overdose of drugs

2. The butterfly ballot cost Al Gore the White House

3. Global warming is caused by carbon dioxide

Which experiments would you need to support your views?

EXERCISE 12.2. Consider the experiment in Section 6.3. In each step:

1. What is the hypothesis about the failure cause?

2. How does the hypothesis verify causality?

EXERCISE 12.3. Consider the failure of the `bigbang` program in Example 8.3.

1. List three *actual* failure causes.

2. List three failure causes that are not actual causes.

3. Where would you correct the program? Why?

EXERCISE 12.4. Be creative. Write a failing program with:

1. A *failure cause* that looks like an *error* (but is not)

2. An *error* that looks as if it *caused the failure* (but does not)

EXERCISE 12.5. Site A and site B each send a virus-infected e-mail to site C. A's e-mail arrives first, infecting C. Using the counterfactual definition, what is the cause:

1. For site C being infected?

2. For site C being infected right after A's e-mail arrives?

Try to find your own answer first, and then look at the discussion (and further tricky examples) in Zalta (2002).

EXERCISE 12.6. What are the relationships among

*   failing world,

*   passing world,

*   initial difference, and

*   cause?

EXERCISE 12.7. Explain the meaning of *closest possible world in which a failure does not occur*. What type of failure causes do we distinguish, and how do we verify them? Illustrate using examples.

EXERCISE 12.8. Each of the following statements is either true or false.

1. If c is a cause, and e is its effect, then c must precede e.

2. If c is a circumstance that causes a failure, it is possible to alter c such that the failure no longer occurs.

3. If some cause c is an actual cause, altering c induces the smallest possible difference in the effect.

4. Every failure cause implies a possible fix.

5. For every failure there is exactly one actual cause.

6. A failure cause can be determined without executing the program.

7. A failure is the difference to the closest possible world in which the cause does not occur.

8. If I observe two runs (one passing, one failing) with a minimal difference in input, I have found an actual failure cause.

9. A minimal and successful correction proves that the altered code was the actual failure cause.

10. Increasing the common context between the possible worlds results in smaller causes.

EXERCISE 12.9. "Given enough evidence, an anomaly can qualify as a cause." Discuss.

When you have eliminated the impossible,
whatever remains, however improbable,
must be the truth.
(Sherlock Holmes)

—A. CONAN DOYLE
The Sign of Four (1890)

## CHAPTER 13

ISOLATING FAILURE CAUSES

THIS IS THE CHAPTER THAT AUTOMATES MOST OF DEBUGGING. We show how delta debugging isolates failure causes automatically — in the program input, in the program's thread schedule, and in the program code. In the best case, the reported causes immediately pinpoint the defect.

13.1 ISOLATING CAUSES AUTOMATICALLY

Narrowing down causes as described in Chapter 12 "Causes and Effects" can be tedious and boring — when conducted manually, that is. Therefore, we should aim at narrowing down failure causes *automatically*.

In principle, narrowing down a cause can be easily automated. All it takes is

- an *automated test* that checks whether the failure is still present,

- a means of *narrowing down the difference*, and

- a *strategy* for proceeding.

With these ingredients, we can easily *automate the scientific method* involved. We have some automaton apply one difference at a time; after each difference, the automaton tests whether the failure now occurs. Once it occurs, we have narrowed down the actual cause.

Consider the keyboard layout example from Section 12.6, in which a specific keyboard layout setting caused a presentation shareware to fail. In this example, automation translates to the following points.

- The automated test starts the presentation shareware and checks for the failure.

- The means of narrowing down the difference is copying settings from one account to another.

- The strategy for proceeding could be to copy one setting at a time.

Proceeding one difference at a time can be very time consuming, though. My keyboard layout, for instance, has definitions for 865 key combinations. Do I really want to run 865 tests just to learn that I should not have Alt+O defined? What we need here is a more effective strategy — and this brings us to our key question:

> HOW DO I ISOLATE FAILURE CAUSES AUTOMATICALLY?

13.2   ISOLATING VERSUS SIMPLIFYING

In Chapter 5 "Simplifying Problems," we saw how to leverage automated tests to simplify test cases quickly, using delta debugging. One could think of applying this approach toward simplifying the difference between the real world and the alternate world — that is, to find an alternate world whose difference to the real world is as "simple" or as close as possible. In practice, this means trying to remove all differences that are not relevant for producing the failure — that is, to bring the alternate world as close as possible to the real world. In the remaining difference, each aspect is relevant for producing the failure — that is, we have an actual cause.

When we are thinking about narrowing down differences, though, there is a more efficient approach than simplifying, called *isolating*. In simplifying, we get a test case where each single circumstance is relevant for producing the failure. Isolating, in contrast, produces a *pair* of test cases — one passing the test, one failing the test — with a minimal difference between them that is an actual cause.

Let's highlight isolation using an example. In Example 5.5, we saw how the *ddmin* algorithm eventually simplifies a failure-inducing HTML line from

Simplifying   **Isolating**

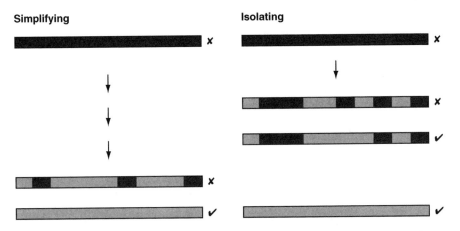

FIGURE 13.1 Simplifying versus isolating. While simplifying, we bring the failing configuration (✗) as close as possible to the (typically empty) passing configuration (✔). When isolating, we determine the smallest difference between the two, moving the passing as well as the failing configuration.

40 characters down to 8 characters in 48 tests. In the result, a <SELECT> tag, every single character is relevant for producing the failure.

Isolating works in a similar fashion: each time a test case fails, the smaller test case is used as the new failing test case. However, we do not just remove circumstances from the failing test case but *add circumstances to the passing test case*, and thus may obtain a new (larger) passing test case. Figure 13.1 highlights the difference between simplification and isolation. Simplifying results in a simplified failing test case, whereas isolation results in a passing and a failing test case with a minimal difference.

Example 13.1 shows how this works on the HTML input of the MOZILLA example. Starting with the empty passing input (bottom) and the 80-character failing input (top), we first remove half the characters — as in *ddmin*. The test passes, and this is where isolation shows the difference. We use the half of the input as a new passing test case and thus have narrowed down the difference (the cause) to the second half of the characters. In the next step, we add half of this half to the passing test case, which again passes the test.

Continuing this pattern, we eventually end up in a minimal difference between the original failing input

```
<SELECT_NAME="priority"_MULTIPLE_SIZE=7>
```

and the new passing input

Input: **<SELECT_NAME="priority"_MULTIPLE_SIZE=7>**⟨40 characters ⟩ ✗
 <SELECT_NAME="priority"_MULTIPLE_SIZE=7>⟨ 0 characters ⟩ ✔

1 <SELECT_NAME="prio**ri ty"_MULTIPLE_SIZE=7>**⟨20 characters ⟩ ✔
2 <SELECT_NA**ME="priority"_MULTIPLE_SIZE=7>**⟨30 characters ⟩ ✔
3 <SELE**CT_NAME="priority"_MULTIPLE_SIZE=7>**⟨35 characters ⟩ ✔
4 <SE**LECT_NAME="priority"_MULTIPLE_SIZE=7>**⟨37 characters ⟩ ✔
5 <S**ELECT_NAME="priority"_MULTIPLE_SIZE=7>**⟨38 characters ⟩ ✔
6 <**SELECT_NAME="priority"_MULTIPLE_SIZE=7>**⟨39 characters ⟩ ✔

Result: **<**

EXAMPLE 13.1 Isolating a failure-inducing difference. After six tests, the < is isolated as failure cause.

SELECT_NAME="priority"_MULTIPLE_SIZE=7>.

The difference is in the first character: adding a < character changes the SELECT text to the full HTML <SELECT> tag, causing the failure when being printed. This example demonstrates the basic difference between simplification and isolation.

- *Simplification* means to make each part of the simplified test case relevant. Removing any part makes the failure go away.

- *Isolation* means to find one relevant part of the test case. Removing this particular part makes the failure go away.

As an allegory, consider the flight test from Section 5.1. Simplifying a flight test returns the set of circumstances required to make the plane fly (and eventually crash). Isolating, in contrast, returns two sets of circumstances that differ by a minimum — one set that makes the plane fly (that is, the "passing" outcome) and a set that makes the plane crash (the "failing" outcome). The difference is a failure cause, and being minimal it is even an actual failure cause.

In general, isolation is much more efficient than simplification. If we have a large failure-inducing input, isolating the difference will pinpoint a failure cause much faster than minimizing the test case. In Example 13.1, isolating requires only five tests, whereas minimizing (Example 5.5) required 48 tests.

The greater efficiency of isolation comes at a price, though. An isolated difference can come in a *large context*, which may require more effort to understand — especially if the isolated cause is not an error. Reconsidering the flight test example, assume we isolate that switching on the cabin light causes the crash. If the light stays off, the plane lands perfectly. Switching on the cabin light is standard procedure, and thus we still have to find out how this event interacts with the context such that it leads to the crash. With minimization, we simplify the context as a whole. We still find that the cabin light is relevant for the crash, but we only keep those other events that are also relevant (e.g., the short-circuit in the cabin light cable).

13.3 AN ISOLATION ALGORITHM

How do we automate isolation? It turns out that the original *ddmin* algorithm, as discussed in Section 5.5, can easily be extended to compute a minimal difference rather than a minimal test case. In addition to reducing the failing test case $c_\mathbf{x}$ whenever a test fails, we now *increase* the passing test case $c_\mathbf{v}$ whenever a test passes. The following is what we have to do to extend *ddmin*.

1. Extend *ddmin* such that it works on two sets at a time:

   - The passing test case $c'_\mathbf{v}$ that is to be maximized (initially, $c'_\mathbf{v} = c_\mathbf{v} = \emptyset$ holds)

   - The failing test case $c'_\mathbf{x}$ that is to be minimized (initially, $c'_\mathbf{x} = c_\mathbf{x}$ holds)

   These two sets are the worlds between which we narrow down the difference.

2. Compute subsets Δ_i as subsets of $\Delta = c'_\mathbf{x} \setminus c'_\mathbf{v}$ (instead of subsets of $c'_\mathbf{x}$).

3. In addition to testing a removal $c'_\mathbf{x} \setminus \Delta_i$, test an *addition* $c'_\mathbf{v} \cup \Delta_i$.

4. Introduce new rules for passing and failing test cases:

   - *Some removal passes:* If $c'_\mathbf{x} \setminus \Delta_i$ passes for any subset Δ_i, then $c'_\mathbf{x} \setminus \Delta_i$ is a larger passing test case. Continue reducing the difference between $c'_\mathbf{x} \setminus \Delta_i$ and $c'_\mathbf{x}$.

   - *Some addition fails:* This is the complement to the previous rule. If $c'_\mathbf{v} \cup \Delta_i$ fails for any subset Δ_i, then $c'_\mathbf{v} \cup \Delta_i$ is a smaller failing test case. Continue reducing the difference between $c'_\mathbf{v}$ and $c'_\mathbf{v} \cup \Delta_i$.

   - *Some removal fails:* This rule is the same as in *ddmin*. If $c'_\mathbf{x} \setminus \Delta_i$ fails for any subset Δ_i, then $c'_\mathbf{x} \setminus \Delta_i$ is a smaller failing test case. Continue reducing the difference between $c'_\mathbf{v}$ and $c'_\mathbf{x} \setminus \Delta_i$.

- *Some addition passes:* Again, this is the complement to the previous rule. If $c'_{\checkmark} \cup \Delta_i$ passes for any subset Δ_i, then $c'_{\checkmark} \cup \Delta_i$ is a larger passing test case. Continue reducing the difference between $c'_{\checkmark} \cup \Delta_i$ and $c'_{\times}$.

- *Increase granularity:* This rule is as in *ddmin*, but applies only if all tests are unresolved. Increase the granularity and split $c_{\times}$ into four (eight, sixteen, and so on) subsets.

The full algorithm, named *dd*, is shown in Example 13.2. It builds on the definitions used for *ddmin* and is called the *general delta debugging algorithm*. The *dd* algorithm returns a pair of configurations $c'_{\times}, c'_{\checkmark}$ which both lie between the original $c_{\checkmark}$ and $c_{\times}$ and whose difference $\Delta = c'_{\times} \setminus c'_{\checkmark}$ is *1-minimal* — that is, each difference in Δ is relevant for producing the failure (Proposition A.17). Although in practice Δ frequently contains only one difference, Δ may contain multiple differences, which must *all* be applied to $c'_{\checkmark}$ in order to produce $c'_{\times}$.

Regarding complexity, *dd* has the same worst-case complexity as *ddmin*. If nearly all test cases result in an unresolved outcome, the number of tests can be quadratic with respect to $|c_{\times} \setminus c_{\checkmark}|$. The more test cases that pass or fail, though, the more efficient *dd* becomes, up to logarithmic complexity when all tests have a resolved outcome (Proposition A.19). When using *dd*, it is thus wise to keep unresolved test outcomes to a minimum, as this keeps down the number of tests required.

The *dd* algorithm can be seen as an *automation of scientific method*. It defines hypotheses (configurations), tests them, and refines or rejects the hypothesis according to the test outcome. One might argue that humans may be far more creative than this simple strategy. However, automating the process makes it less error prone and more systematic than most humans proceed — and it is exactly the type of boring task computers are supposed to relieve us from.

13.4   IMPLEMENTING ISOLATION

Example 13.3 shows a PYTHON implementation of *dd*. Just as with the PYTHON implementation of *ddmin* (Example 5.4), tail recursion and quantifiers have been turned into loops. Again, we rely on a split() function as well as set operations on lists such as listunion() (Example 13.4) and listminus(). [An implementation for listunion() is shown in Example 5.7.] Of course, we also need a test() function that returns either PASS, FAIL, or UNRESOLVED [e.g., a test() function as in Example 5.8 for MOZILLA]. Extending the abstract form

Let a program's execution be determined by a set of circumstances called a *configuration*. By C, we denote the set of all *changes* between configurations.

Let $test : 2^C \rightarrow \{\pmb{\times}, \pmb{\checkmark}, \pmb{?}\}$ be a testing function that determines for a configuration $c \subseteq C$ whether some given failure occurs ($\pmb{\times}$) or not ($\pmb{\checkmark}$) or whether the test is unresolved ($\pmb{?}$).

Now, let $c_{\pmb{\checkmark}}$ and $c_{\pmb{\times}}$ be configurations with $c_{\pmb{\checkmark}} \subseteq c_{\pmb{\times}} \subseteq C$ such that $test\,(c_{\pmb{\checkmark}}) = \pmb{\checkmark}\ \wedge\ test\,(c_{\pmb{\times}}) = \pmb{\times}$. $c_{\pmb{\checkmark}}$ is the "passing" configuration (typically, $c_{\pmb{\checkmark}} = \emptyset$ holds) and $c_{\pmb{\times}}$ is the "failing" configuration.

The *general delta debugging algorithm dd* $(c_{\pmb{\checkmark}}, c_{\pmb{\times}})$ isolates the failure-inducing difference between $c_{\pmb{\checkmark}}$ and $c_{\pmb{\times}}$. It returns a pair $(c'_{\pmb{\checkmark}}, c'_{\pmb{\times}}) = dd(c_{\pmb{\checkmark}}, c_{\pmb{\times}})$ such that $c_{\pmb{\checkmark}} \subseteq c'_{\pmb{\checkmark}} \subseteq c'_{\pmb{\times}} \subseteq c_{\pmb{\times}}$, $test\,(c'_{\pmb{\checkmark}}) = \pmb{\checkmark}$, and $test(c'_{\pmb{\times}}) = \pmb{\times}$ hold and $c'_{\pmb{\times}} \setminus c'_{\pmb{\checkmark}}$ is a *relevant difference* — that is, no single circumstance of $c'_{\pmb{\times}}$ can be removed from $c'_{\pmb{\times}}$ to make the failure disappear or added to $c'_{\pmb{\checkmark}}$ to make the failure occur.

The dd algorithm is defined as $dd\,(c_{\pmb{\checkmark}}, c_{\pmb{\times}}) = dd'(c_{\pmb{\checkmark}}, c_{\pmb{\times}}, 2)$ with

$$
dd'(c'_{\pmb{\checkmark}}, c'_{\pmb{\times}}, n)
$$

$$
= \begin{cases}
(c'_{\pmb{\checkmark}}, c'_{\pmb{\times}}) & \text{if } |\Delta| = 1 \\[4pt]
dd'(c'_{\pmb{\times}} \setminus \Delta_i, c'_{\pmb{\times}}, 2) & \text{if } \exists i \in \{1..n\} \cdot test\,(c'_{\pmb{\times}} \setminus \Delta_i) = \pmb{\checkmark} \\
& \text{("some removal passes")} \\[4pt]
dd'(c'_{\pmb{\checkmark}}, c'_{\pmb{\checkmark}} \cup \Delta_i, 2) & \text{if } \exists i \in \{1..n\} \cdot test(c'_{\pmb{\checkmark}} \cup \Delta_i) = \pmb{\times} \\
& \text{("some addition fails")} \\[4pt]
dd'(c'_{\pmb{\checkmark}} \cup \Delta_i, c'_{\pmb{\times}}, \max(n-1, 2)) & \text{else if } \exists i \in \{1..n\} \cdot test(c'_{\pmb{\checkmark}} \cup \Delta_i) = \pmb{\checkmark} \\
& \text{("some addition passes")} \\[4pt]
dd'(c'_{\pmb{\checkmark}}, c'_{\pmb{\times}} \setminus \Delta_i, \max(n-1, 2)) & \text{else if } \exists i \in \{1..n\} \cdot test\,(c'_{\pmb{\times}} \setminus \Delta_i) = \pmb{\times} \\
& \text{("some removal fails")} \\[4pt]
dd'(c'_{\pmb{\checkmark}}, c'_{\pmb{\times}}, \min(2n, |\Delta|)) & \text{else if } n < |\Delta| \text{ ("increase granularity")} \\[4pt]
(c'_{\pmb{\checkmark}}, c'_{\pmb{\times}}) & \text{otherwise}
\end{cases}
$$

where $\Delta = c'_{\pmb{\times}} \setminus c'_{\pmb{\checkmark}} = \Delta_1 \cup \Delta_2 \cup \cdots \cup \Delta_n$ with all Δ_i pairwise disjoint, and $\forall \Delta_i \cdot |\Delta_i| \approx (|\Delta|/n)$ holds.

The recursion invariant for dd' is $test\,(c'_{\pmb{\checkmark}}) = \pmb{\checkmark}\ \wedge\ test(c'_{\pmb{\times}}) = \pmb{\times}\ \wedge\ n \leq |\Delta|$.

EXAMPLE 13.2 The dd algorithm in a nutshell.

shown in Example 13.2, the concrete implementation has some fine points that reduce the number of tests.

- The order in which the test cases are checked is optimized. In particular, the first two cases require testing of `test(next_c_fail)` but not of `test(next_c_pass)`. This ensures a minimum number of tests, especially in cases where few tests are unresolved.

```
def dd(c_pass, c_fail, test):
    """Return a pair (C_PASS', C_FAIL') such that
       * C_PASS subseteq C_PASS' subset C_FAIL' subseteq C_FAIL holds
       * C_FAIL' - C_PASS' is a minimal difference relevant for TEST."""
    n = 2      # Initial granularity

    while 1:
        assert test(c_pass) == PASS
        assert test(c_fail) == FAIL

        delta = listminus(c_fail, c_pass)
        if n > len(delta):
            return (c_pass, c_fail) # No further minimizing

        deltas = split(delta, n); assert len(deltas) == n

        offset = 0
        j = 0
        while j < n:
            i = (j + offset) % n
            next_c_pass = listunion(c_pass, deltas[i])
            next_c_fail = listminus(c_fail, deltas[i])

            if test(next_c_fail) == FAIL and n == 2:    # (1)
                c_fail = next_c_fail
                n = 2; offset = 0; break
            elif test(next_c_fail) == PASS:             # (2)
                c_pass = next_c_fail
                n = 2; offset = 0; break
            elif test(next_c_pass) == FAIL:             # (3)
                c_fail = next_c_pass
                n = 2; offset = 0; break
            elif test(next_c_fail) == FAIL:             # (4)
                c_fail = next_c_fail
                n = max(n - 1, 2); offset = i; break
            elif test(next_c_pass) == PASS:             # (5)
                c_pass = next_c_pass
                n = max(n - 1, 2); offset = i; break
            else:
                j = j + 1                     # Try next subset

        if j >= n:                            # All tests unresolved
            if n >= len(delta):
                return (c_pass, c_fail)
            else:
                n = min(n * 2, len(delta))    # Increase granularity
```

EXAMPLE 13.3 A PYTHON implementation of the *dd* algorithm.

- We first check those situations that reduce the difference the most, such as cases 1 through 3.

- In principle, case 1 is not necessary, as it is subsumed by case 4. If successful, though, it avoids invoking test(next_c_pass). Together, cases 1 and 2 turn dd() into a binary search if all tests return PASS or FAIL (rather than UNRESOLVED).

```python
def listunion(c1, c2):
    """Return the union of C1 and C2.
       Assumes elements of C1 are hashable."""

    # The hash map S1 has an entry for each element in C1
    s1 = {}
    for delta in c1:
        s1[delta] = 1

    # Add all elements in C2 that are not in C1
    c = c1[:]    # Copy C1
    for delta in c2:
        if not s1.has_key(delta):
            c.append(delta)

    return c
```

EXAMPLE 13.4 A PYTHON implementation of the `listunion()` function.

- The implementation assumes caching of earlier test results (Section 5.8.1). If the `test()` function does not cache, you must rewrite the code shown in Example 13.3 such that it saves and reuses the results of `test(next_c_pass)` and `test(next_c_fail)`.

- The `offset` variable records the subset to check next. When some difference becomes irrelevant (cases 4 and 5), we continue checking the next subset rather than restarting with the first subset. This makes sure each delta has the same chance to be removed.

- Ordering of cases 3 and 4 is tricky. Case 4 simplifies the failing configuration and can rely on the result of a test already performed. Case 3 requires another test, but quickly reduces the difference if successful. Because we want to minimize the difference as quickly as possible, case 3 comes first.

Just like the PYTHON code for *ddmin* (List 5.2), this code should be easy to port to other languages. All you need is an appropriate representation for sets of circumstances such as `c_pass` or `c_fail`.

13.5   ISOLATING FAILURE-INDUCING INPUT

Let's now put *dd* to practice, applying it on a number of failure-inducing circumstances. We have already seen how *dd* pinpoints the < character in the HTML input (Example 13.1) and how this requires much fewer tests than simplifying the entire input (Example 5.5).

Applying *dd* on the fuzz inputs (discussed in Section 5.7) yields even more substantial savings. As reported in Zeller and Hildebrandt (2002), only 12 to 50 tests were required to narrow down the failure-inducing difference to a single character. This confirms the prediction of Proposition A.19, predicting a logarithmic number of tests when all tests have a resolved outcome. In case of the FLEX tests, where *ddmin* requires 11,000 to 17,960 test runs to simplify the input, the *dd* algorithm requires but 23 to 51 runs.

In cases where there were unresolved outcomes, as well as larger failure-inducing differences, the number of tests performed by *dd* was larger. In one of the NROFF test cases, 473 test runs (out of which 390 were unresolved) were needed to isolate a 17-character failure-inducing difference. However, this is still a much lower number than the 5,565 test runs required for simplification of the same input.

13.6   ISOLATING FAILURE-INDUCING SCHEDULES

Again, we can apply isolation on all circumstances that influence the program execution — provided we have a means of controlling and reproducing them. As discussed in Section 4.3.7, *schedules* of process and threads can result in failures that are difficult to debug. With a means of *recording and replaying* schedules, and a means of isolating failure-inducing differences, such defects become far easier to track down. The basic idea uses four building blocks.

- *Deterministic replay:* Use a tool that captures the execution of nondeterministic Java applications and allows the programmer to *replay* these executions deterministically — that is, input and thread schedules are reconstructed from the recorded execution. This effectively solves the problem of reproducing failures deterministically.

- *Test case generation:* A replay tool allows the application to be executed under a given thread schedule. Use the tool to generate *alternate schedules*. For instance, one can alter an original passing (or failing) schedule until an alternate failing (passing) schedule is found.

- *Isolating failure causes:* Use *dd* to automatically isolate the failure cause in a failure-inducing thread schedule. The basic idea is to systematically *narrow the difference* between the passing and the failing thread schedule until only a minimal difference remains — a difference such as "The failure occurs if and only if thread switch #3291 occurs at clock time 47,539." This effectively solves the isolation problem.

- *Relating causes to errors:* Each of the resulting thread differences occurs at a specific location of the program — for instance, thread switch #3291 may occur at line 20 of *foo.java* — giving a good starting point for locating thread interferences.

Choi and Zeller (2002) implemented this idea using IBM's DEJAVU tool to record and replay thread schedules on a single-processor machine. As a proof of concept, they applied the approach on a multithreaded ray-tracing program from the SPEC JVM98 Java test suite, in which they had reintroduced a *data race* that had been commented out by the original authors. This defect, shown in Example 13.5, lead to a failure the first time it was executed.

1. Thread A enters the LoadScene() method and saves the value of ScenesLoaded in OldScenesLoaded (line 84).

2. In line 85, a thread switch occurs, causing the transfer of control from thread A to another thread B.

3. Thread B runs the entire LoadScene() method and properly increments the ScenesLoaded variable.

4. As thread A resumes execution, it assigns the value of OldScenesLoaded plus one to ScenesLoaded (line 130). This effectively undoes the update made by thread B.

Using a fuzz approach (Section 5.7), Choi and Zeller generated random schedules, starting from the failing one. Each schedule consisted of long lists of *yield points* — places in the program code such as function calls or backward branches where a thread switch occurred. After 66 tests, they had generated an alternate schedule where the failure would not occur.

Comparing the original (failing) schedule and the alternate (passing) schedule resulted in 3,842,577,240 differences, each moving a thread switch by one

```
25 public class Scene { ...
44       private static int ScenesLoaded = 0;
45       (more methods...)
81       private
82       int LoadScene(String filename) {
84           int OldScenesLoaded = ScenesLoaded;
85           (more initializations...)
91           infile = new DataInputStream(...);
92           (more code...)
130          ScenesLoaded = OldScenesLoaded + 1;
131          System.out.println("" +
                   ScenesLoaded + " scenes loaded.");
132          ...
134      }
135      ...
733 }
```

EXAMPLE 13.5 Introducing a race condition (Choi and Zeller, 2002). ScenesLoaded may not be properly updated if a thread switch occurs during execution of lines 85 through 130.

yield point. Applying all differences to the passing schedule changed its yield points to those in the failing schedule, thus making the program fail. However, only a few of these 3.8 billion schedule differences were relevant for the failure—which could be uncovered by delta debugging.

The delta debugging run is summarized in Figure 13.2. The upper line is the size of the failing configuration $c'_\times$, and the lower line is the size of the passing configuration $c'_\checkmark$. As the tests only return ✔ or ✘, *dd* requires a logarithmic number of tests such that after 50 tests only one difference remains. The failure occurs if and only if thread switch #33 occurs at yield point 59,772,127 (instead of 59,772,126)—that is, at line 91 of *Scene.java*.

Line 91 of *Scene.java* is the first method invocation (and thus yield point) after the initialization of *OldScenesLoaded*. Likewise, the alternative yield point 59,772,126 (with a successful test outcome) is the invocation of *LoadScene* at line 82 of *Scene.java*—just *before* the variable *OldScenesLoaded* is initialized. Thus, by narrowing down the failure-inducing schedule difference to one single difference the approach had successfully rediscovered the location where Choi and Zeller had originally introduced the error.

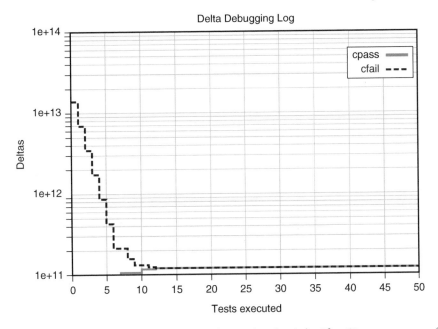

FIGURE 13.2 Narrowing down a failure-inducing thread switch. After 50 tests, one out of 3.8 billion thread switches is isolated as an actual failure cause.

As this example was artificially generated, it does not necessarily generalize to all types of parallel programs. However, it illustrates that once we have a means of automated deterministic testing (as with the DEJAVU tool) adding automated isolation of failure-inducing circumstances is easy. In other words, once one has automated testing automated isolation of failure causes is a minor step.

13.7 ISOLATING FAILURE-INDUCING CHANGES

Failure-inducing inputs and thread schedules do not directly cause a failure. Instead, they cause different executions of the program, which in turn cause the failure. An interesting aspect of thread switches is that they can be *directly associated with code* — the code executed at the moment the thread switch occurs (and is hence a failure cause). Consequently, the programmer can immediately focus on this part of the program code.

This is close to what we'd actually want: some machine where we can simply shove in our program and it will tell us "This line is wrong; please fix it." (or better yet, fix it for us such that we do not have to do any work at all anymore).

As surprising as it seems, such an approach exists, and it is based on delta debugging. It works as follows. Rather than having two different inputs for the same program, we have one input for two versions of the program — one version where the test passes, and one version where it fails. The goal of delta debugging is now to isolate the *failure-inducing difference* between the two versions — the change that turns a failing version into a passing version.

At this point, you may ask "Where should I get the passing version from? Is not this the whole point of debugging?," and you are right. However, there are situations in which some "old" version of a program passed a test that a "new" version fails. This situation is called a *regression*. The new version falls behind the capabilities of the old version.

The following is an example of a regression. From 1997 to 2001, I was maintaining the DDD debugger discussed in Section 8.5. DDD is a front end to the GDB command-line debugger, sending commands to GDB and interpreting its replies. In 1998, I got an e-mail from a user who had upgraded his GDB version and suddenly DDD no longer worked properly.

```
Date: Fri, 31 Jul 1998 15:11:05 -0500
From: ⟨Name withheld⟩
To: DDD Bug Reports <bug-ddd@gnu.org>
Subject: Problem with DDD  and GDB  4.17


When using DDD  with GDB  4.16, the run command correctly
uses any prior command-line arguments, or the value of
"set args".  However, when I switched to GDB  4.17, this
no longer worked:  If I entered a run command in the
console window, the prior command-line options would be
lost. [...]
```

This regression situation is all too common when upgrading your system. You upgrade one part and suddenly other parts that depended on the "old" behavior no longer work. I wondered whether there was a way of isolating the cause automatically — that is, of isolating the change to GDB that caused DDD's failure.

If a regression occurs, a common debugging strategy is to focus on the *changes* one made. In our case, the change was a move from GDB 4.16 to GDB 4.17, and thus this part was clear. However, this change in the GDB release translates into several changes to the GDB source code. Running the `diff` utility to highlight those changes revealed an output of 178,200 lines.

```
$ diff -r gdb-4.16 gdb-4.17
diff -r gdb-4.16/COPYING gdb-4.17/COPYING
5c5
<                           675 Mass Ave, Cambridge, MA 02139, USA
---
>                           59 Temple Place, Suite 330, Boston, MA  02111-1307   USA
282c282
<        Appendix: How to Apply These Terms to Your New Programs
---
>            How to Apply These Terms to Your New Programs
  :
  :
⟨178,192 more lines⟩
```

These 178,200 lines translate into 8,721 individual changes separated by unchanged lines—that is, there were 8,721 locations in the GDB source code that had been changed. At least one of these 8,721 changes caused the regression—but which one?

Again, this is a setting in which delta debugging can isolate the failure cause. The idea is to treat these changes as *input* to a *patch-and-test* program that works in three steps.

1. *Apply changes.* We must apply the changes to the GDB code base. This is done by taking the original GDB 4.16 code base and then running the UNIX PATCH program to apply a subset of the changes. Note that PATCH may fail to apply the changes—for instance, if individual changes depend on each other. In this case, the test outcome is unresolved (**?**).

2. *Reconstruct GDB.* We must reconstruct GDB after all changes have been applied. Normally, this would be a simple matter of invoking the UNIX MAKE program. However, as the MAKE specification itself may have changed we need to recreate the *Makefile* first.

   If we apply a huge set of unrelated changes, we are quite likely to get a compilation error. The *patch-and-test* program must detect this and return an unresolved test outcome.

3. *Run the test.* If we have been successful in recreating GDB, we run it (with DDD) to see whether the failure occurs or not. Because applying arbitrary subsets of changes can result in surprising behavior of the program, it is wise to limit unwanted effects. In the case of GDB, we created a temporary directory for each run, ensuring that personal files would not be touched or overwritten.

Having translated the changes to input, we can now apply delta debugging to minimize the set of changes or to isolate the failure-inducing change (the failure-inducing input). The *patch-and-test* program, instrumented by *ddmin* or *dd*, would apply a subset of the changes, see whether GDB can be reconstructed, and if so return ✔ or ✘ depending on the test outcome. If GDB cannot be reconstructed with the changes applied (which is quite common for random subsets), the *patch-and-test* program would return **?**, and delta debugging would try the next alternative. If we actually do this, and run delta debugging, we end up in a single change that makes DDD fail.

```
diff -r gdb-4.16/gdb/infcmd.c gdb-4.17/gdb/infcmd.c
1239c1278
< "Set arguments to give program being debugged when it is started.\n\
---
> "Set argument list to give program being debugged when it is started.\n\
```

This change in a string constant from arguments to argument list was responsible for GDB 4.17 not interoperating with DDD. Although the string constant is actually part of GDB's online help, it is also the basis for GDB's output. Given the command show args, GDB 4.16 replies

```
Arguments to give program being debugged when it is started is "a b c"
```

but GDB 4.17 issues a slightly different (and grammatically correct) text:

```
Argument list to give program being debugged when it is started is "a b c"
```

Unfortunately, this output could not be parsed by DDD, which expected a reply starting with "Arguments." To solve the problem here and now, one could simply have reversed the GDB change. Eventually, I upgraded DDD to make it work with the new GDB version.

This approach of determining the culprit for a regression has been named the *blame-o-meter* — as a means to know who to blame. However, as the GDB example shows, a *cause* for a problem need not be a defect, it may not even be a mistake. What the GDB programmers did was perfectly sensible. DDD's defect, if any, was to rely on a specific output format. Nonetheless, once one has an automated regression test it may prove useful to add a blame-o-meter on top. This way, whenever a regression test fails one could start the blame-o-meter and tell the developer not only *that* a test fails but also *why* it fails.

Building a blame-o-meter is not very difficult, provided one has automated construction, automated regression tests, and a means of applying changes (such as the UNIX PATCH program). A number of issues call for specific *optimizations*, though.

- *History:* If the changes come from a version archive, they can be grouped according to their creation time. Ensuring that later changes always occur with earlier changes will speed up delta debugging enormously, as this ensures consistent reconstruction and hence resolved test outcomes. In addition, as we know from Proposition A.19, resolved tests outcomes result in a logarithmic number of tests — basically a binary search along the change history.

- *Reconstruction:* As each test requires reconstruction of the program, it is useful to have a means of *incremental* reconstruction. The MAKE program compiles only the code whose sources have changed since the last construction. The CCACHE program speeds up recompilation by caching previous compiles and detecting when the same compile is being done again.

- *Grouping:* Many subsets of changes result in unresolved outcomes because the program cannot be reconstructed. For instance, a change A that references a variable may require a change B that declares that variable. Every subset that contains only A but not B will result in an unresolved outcome, slowing down delta debugging considerably. Therefore, in addition to grouping changes by creation time, it is also useful to group them according to *scope* — that is, to keep those changes together that apply to the same file, class, or function.

- *Failure resolution:* A simple means of dealing with construction errors is to search for changes that may fix these errors. After a failing construction, one could scan the error messages for identifiers, add all changes that reference these identifiers, and try again. This is repeated until construction is possible, or until there are no more changes to add.

In the case of the 8,721 changes to the GDB source code, these optimizations all proved beneficial. CCACHE reduced the average reconstruction time to 20%. Grouping by scope reduced the number of tests by 50%. Overall, as Figure 13.3 shows, using *dd* with scope information required about 97 tests. Assuming that each test takes about two minutes, this boils down to three hours until delta debugging has isolated the cause in the GDB code.

Three hours still sounds like a lot. I am pretty confident that you as a programmer would have found the cause in the GDB code in less than three hours (especially having read this book). However, it is rather uncommon to have 8,721 changes without any temporal ordering and intermediate regression tests, such that typical regressions can be dealt with much faster.

If you want to experiment with delta debugging, Figure 13.4 shows a plug-in named DDCHANGE for the ECLIPSE programming environment. DDCHANGE

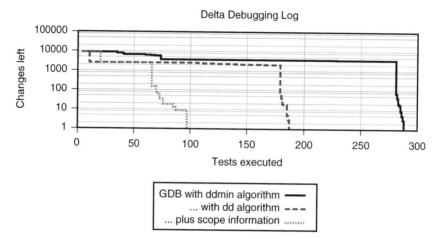

FIGURE 13.3 Isolating failure-inducing code changes. After 97 tests, delta debugging has isolated one of 8,721 code changes as causing the failure.

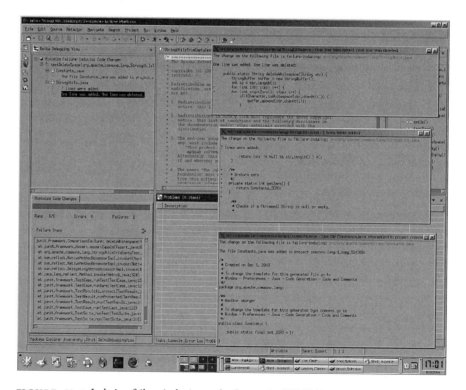

FIGURE 13.4 Isolating failure-inducing code changes in ECLIPSE. As soon as a test fails, the delta debugging plug-in automatically determines the failure-inducing code change—if there were an earlier version where the test did not fail.

keeps track of all tests and all test outcomes. As soon as a test fails that had passed in some previous version, the delta debugging plug-in automatically determines the failure-inducing code change in the background and presents its diagnosis as soon as it is available. This plug-in makes use of the facilities for automated construction, automated testing, and version control, as they are integrated within ECLIPSE (hence, no complex setup is necessary).

DDCHANGE is not that quick, either. As it has to reconstruct the program several times, it can take some time to isolate the failure-inducing change — and again, an experienced programmer might find the cause quicker. However, unless you *need* the cause in the next hour you can easily have delta debugging determine the cause for you. It is slow and dumb, but it will come up with a result — and no programmer I know of has fun running these experiments manually.

13.8 PROBLEMS AND LIMITATIONS

Although delta debugging is generally good at isolating causes, one should be aware of its limits as well as common issues. These include the following.

- *How do we choose the alternate world?* As laid out in Section 12.7, choosing the alternate world (i.e., input or version) determines the *initial difference* in which to search for causes. If we want to search for causes in the input, we should use a passing run with a different input. If we want to search for causes in the configuration, we should search a passing run with an alternate configuration. In general, we should choose an alternate world that is as close as possible to the actual world, in order to keep the initial search space as small as possible.

- *How do we decompose configurations?* Many configurations naturally decompose into smaller parts that can be individually assessed. A text decomposes into lines, an HTML page decomposes into head and body sections, a schedule decomposes into thread switches, and a code difference decomposes into locations. However, there are some configurations for which it is difficult to provide such a decomposition.

  As an example, consider *image processing* — wherein an application fails when processing one specific image but passes on all others. What is the difference between the failure-inducing image and the passing ones? In such cases, it helps to understand how the application works. Does it process the image row by row? In such cases, decomposing the image by rows may make sense. Does it rely on properties such as number of colors, brightness, or contrast? In this case it may make sense to reduce the difference in terms of these properties — for instance, to have each delta adjust the contrast until the difference becomes minimal.

- *When do we know a failure is the failure?* When a program is fed with arbitrary input, it may fail in a number of ways. However, the changed input may cause a *different failure* than the original test case — that is, the program may fail at a different location, produce an alternate error message, or otherwise produce a behavior that is considered "failing" but differs from the original behavior. We call such different failures *artifacts*, which are *artificially generated* during the delta debugging process.

  In the fuzz examples from Section 5.7, for instance, our *test* function would return ✘ whenever a program crashed — regardless of further circumstances. In the fuzz case, ignoring artifacts may be legitimate, as a program must not crash under any input. In general, though, we may want to check further aspects of the failing behavior.

  One of the most important aspects about a failure is to know the location that was active at the moment of the failure — that is, the exact statement that issued the failing message, or the last executed statement in case of a crash. Checking this location is a good protection against artifacts. An even better protection is to take into account the backtrace, the stack of calling functions (Section 8.3.1) at the time of the failure.

  - The *test* function returns ✘ only if the program failed and if the backtrace of the failure was identical to the original backtrace.

  - If the program failed, but with a different backtrace, *test* would return **?**.

  - If the program passed the test, *test* would return ✔.

  In addition to the backtrace, further aspects such as coverage, timing, or exact output can be used to check against artifacts. However, the larger the number of aspects to be considered part of a failure the larger the cause required to create all of these aspects.

- *How do we disambiguate between multiple causes?* For the sake of efficiency, delta debugging always takes the first possibility to narrow down a difference. However, there may be other possibilities, resulting in alternate actual causes. In the MOZILLA example, for instance, *dd* returned < as a failure-inducing difference, but removing any of the <SELECT> characters would have made the failure disappear.

It is fairly easy to extend *dd* such that it considers other alternatives. This is a trade-off between performance and convenience. In my experience, the first cause is typically sufficient to characterize the failure. If it were not, I would run *dd* on the other alternatives. Others may prefer to have *dd* compute multiple alternatives in advance, such that they can consider them all.

- *How do I get to the defect?* Every failure-inducing difference returned by delta debugging is an actual cause. As such, it suggests a *fix*: simply remove the cause and the failure will no longer occur. For instance, we could remove the < from the MOZILLA input, prohibit thread switches during the Raytracer data race, or revert the GDB code to the previous version. This illustrates that such fixes are more *workarounds* than corrections — simply because they do not increase correctness of the program.

  In general, though, the *cause* delta debugging isolates is seldom an *error* — simply because the alternate world need not be correct, either. In fact, if an error is the same in both worlds it will not even be part of the difference in which delta debugging searches for an actual cause.

  To turn the cause into a *correction*, we still have to find out where to correct the program (which is, in fact, *deciding* where and what the defect is). We would have to search the code that handles printing of <SELECT> tags in MOZILLA, set up the Raytracer such that the data race no longer occurs, and adapt DDD such that it handles the outputs from different GDB versions.

  In all three cases, the correction is induced by the cause, and the cause certainly helps in designing and motivating the correction. To get to the actual defect, though, again requires us to examine the innards of the program, as explored in the remainder of this book.

13.9 CONCEPTS

✎ *To isolate failure causes automatically*, you need

HOW TO

- an *automated test* that checks whether the failure is still present

- a means of *narrowing down the difference*, and

- a *strategy* for proceeding.

✎ One possible strategy is the general delta debugging algorithm *dd* (Example 13.2).

✎ *dd* determines the *relevant difference* between two configurations (inputs, schedules, code changes, or other circumstances) with respect to a given test — that is, an actual cause for the failure.

HOW TO ✎ *To isolate a failure cause in the input*, apply *dd* (or another strategy) on two program inputs — one that passes and one that fails the test.

HOW TO ✎ *To isolate a failure cause in the thread schedule*, apply *dd* (or another strategy) on two schedules — one that passes and one that fails the test. You need a means of replaying and manipulating schedules, such as DEJAVU.

HOW TO ✎ *To isolate a failure-inducing code change*, apply *dd* (or another strategy) on two program versions — one that passes and one that fails the test. You need automated reconstruction of the program after a set of changes has been applied.

✎ Any actual cause, as returned by delta debugging, can be altered to make the failure no longer occur. This does not mean, though, that the cause is a defect. It also does not mean that there may be only one actual cause.

✎ Delta debugging on states is a fairly recent technique and not yet fully evaluated.

13.10 TOOLS

Delta Debugging Plug-ins for ECLIPSE

At the time of writing, a number of delta debugging tools were made available for the ECLIPSE programming framework. They can be downloaded at:

http://www.st.cs.uni-sb.de/eclipse/

CCACHE

To apply delta debugging on program changes, you may find the CCACHE tool for incremental compilation useful. It is available at:

http://ccache.samba.org/

13.11 FURTHER READING

Delta debugging on program inputs is described in Zeller and Hildebrandt (2002), a paper discussed in Chapter 5 "Simplifying Problems." The paper cites all data from all experiments. The definitions are general enough to pertain to all types of changes and configurations.

Delta debugging on thread schedules was developed by Choi and Zeller (2002) while the author was visiting IBM research. This paper contains all details on the approach and the experiment. The DEJAVU tool by Choi and Srinivasan (1998) is described in Chapter 4 "Reproducing Problems."

Zeller (1999) describes how to apply delta debugging to code changes. This was the first application of delta debugging. The algorithms used in this paper are now superseded by the more advanced versions in this book, but the case studies are still valid.

Failure-inducing code changes were first handled by Ness and Ngo (1997). In their setting, a compiler consisted of a number of optimization modules. By reverting module after module to an earlier (passing) state, they succeeded in identifying the module whose changes caused the failure and therefore kept it at its earlier revision.

13.12 EXERCISES

EXERCISE 13.1. Repeat the exercises of Chapter 5 "Simplifying Problems" using isolation instead of minimization.

EXERCISE 13.2. Implement simplification of test cases using an unchanged *dd* implementation, but with a wrapper around the *test* function. Which wrapper is needed?

EXERCISE 13.3. Rather than simplifying the failing configuration (as in *ddmin*), one can also think about *maximizing the passing configuration* — that is, having the largest possible configuration that still passes (with a minimal difference to the failing configuration).

- When would such a *ddmax* algorithm be useful?

- Give a mathematical description of *ddmax* (analogously to *ddmin* in List 5.2).

- Implement *ddmax*.

EXERCISE 13.4. Each statement about causes and effects is either true or false. Give a short reason for your answer if appropriate.

1. If C is a cause and E is its effect, C must precede E.

2. If C is a circumstance that causes a failure, it is possible to alter C such that the failure no longer occurs.

3. If some cause C is an actual cause, altering C induces the smallest possible difference in the effect.

4. Every failure cause implies a possible fix.

5. For every failure, there is exactly one actual cause.

6. A failure cause can be determined without executing a program.

7. If I observe two runs (one passing, one failing) with a minimal difference in input, I have found an actual failure cause.

8. A successful fix proves that the altered code was the actual failure cause.

EXERCISE 13.5. In delta debugging, you can either use simplification to simplify failure-inducing input or isolation to isolate a minimal failure-inducing difference.

1. Compare these two approaches with respect to their advantages and disadvantages.

2. Compare the running times of the respective algorithms in their worst-case and best-case behavior.

3. Which are the properties of a 1-minimal result of isolation?

EXERCISE 13.6. Using the logbook format (Section 6.5), describe the first four steps of the delta debugging run in Example 13.1. Which are the hypotheses, predictions, and experiments?

EXERCISE 13.7. Is delta debugging an instance of scientific method? Discuss.

EXERCISE 13.8. Which are the prerequisites in order to apply delta debugging? Discuss situations in which delta debugging is not helpful.

Debugging is still, as it was 30 years ago, a matter of trial and error.

— HENRY LIEBERMAN
The Debugging Scandal (1997)

## CHAPTER 14

ISOLATING CAUSE-EFFECT CHAINS

THIS CHAPTER PRESENTS A WAY of narrowing down failure causes even further. By extracting and comparing program states, delta debugging automatically isolates the *variables and values* that cause the failure, resulting in a cause-effect chain of the failure: "variable x was 42; therefore p became null; and thus the program failed."

14.1 USELESS CAUSES

In Chapter 13 "Isolating Failure Causes," we saw how to isolate inputs, code changes, or schedules that cause a given failure. In many cases, such causes directly lead to the defect in question. There are cases, though, where a difference in the input, for instance, gives few clues, if any, to the nature of the error. This is particularly true if program processes input at several places, such that it is difficult to relate a difference to some specific code.

One typical example of such programs is a *compiler*. A compiler processes the original source code through several stages until it produces an executable.

1. For C, C++, and other languages, the source code is first passed through a *preprocessor*.

2. The compiler proper parses the source code into a *syntax tree*.

3. By traversing the syntax tree, the compiler emits *assembler code*.

```
double mult(double z[], int n) {
  int i, j;

  i = 0;
  for (j = 0; j < n; j++) {
    i = i + j + 1;
    z[i] = z[i] * (z[0] + 1.0);
  }

  return z[n];
}
```

EXAMPLE 14.1 The fail.c program that makes the GNU compiler crash.

4. The *assembler* translates the code into *object code*.

5. The *linker* binds the objects into an *executable*.

In addition, each step can include a number of *optimizations*. The compiler, for instance, optimizes expressions found in the syntax tree, as well as the generated assembler code.

As an example, consider the fail.c program shown in Example 14.1. It is interesting only in one aspect: compiling fail.c with the GNU compiler (GCC) version 2.95.2 on Linux with optimization enabled causes the compiler to crash. In fact, depending on the version of Linux you are using it does not just crash but allocates all memory on the machine, causing other processes to die from starvation. When I tried this example first, every single process on my machine died, until only the Linux kernel and GCC remained — and only then did the kernel finally kill the GCC process. (Actually, this happened while I was remotely logged in on the workstation of our system administrator, effectively terminating his session. I cannot recommend repeating the experience.)

The fail.c program in Example 14.1 is an input (to GCC), and thus we can isolate the actual cause — using delta debugging, for instance. We may thus find that if we change the line

$$z[i] = z[i] * (z[0] + 1.0);$$

to

$$z[i] = z[i] * (z[0]);$$

the program compiles just fine. Thus, we now know that the piece of code + 1.0 in fail.c causes the failure.

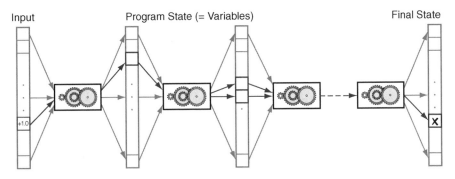

FIGURE 14.1 How differences propagate through a program run. An initial difference in the input, such as + 1.0, causes further differences in the state — up to the final difference in the test outcome.

With this knowledge, we may now be able to *work around* the problem. If the mult() function in fail.c were part of our program, we could rearrange its code such that its semantics remained unchanged but still be capable of being compiled with GCC. To *correct* GCC, though, this knowledge is pretty much useless, even if we were compiler experts. As discussed previously, GCC processes the program code at a large number of places (in particular, optimizations), and thus there is no direct linkage from a piece of input (such as + 1.0) to a piece of code that handles this input. (Contrast this to printing a <SELECT> tag in MOZILLA, for instance. There is one piece of code in MOZILLA which does exactly this.)

To understand what an input such as + 1.0 does, we must take a look into the actual computation and see what is going on. Consider a program execution as a series of states (Figure 14.1). A difference in the input (such as + 1.0) causes a difference in the following states. As the computation progresses, these state differences again cause differences in later states. Thus, the differences propagate through the computation until they become observable by the user — as the difference that makes the program fail.

The difference between the two inputs is a failure cause, as are the later differences between states. Each state difference, however, is also an *effect* of earlier differences. Thus, the chain of differences forms a *cause-effect chain* along the computation — or, in our case, along the GCC run. If we could know what this cause-effect chain looks like, we would obtain a good understanding of how the failure came to be.

The question is: Can we actually leverage such differences by comparing program states? And how do we capture program states up front? We shall work our way through four steps and show:

1. How to capture program states as *memory graphs*

2. How to compare program states to reveal *differences*

3. How to narrow down these differences to reveal *causes*

4. How to combine the causes into *cause-effect chains*

For the sake of simplicity, we shall first study the individual steps on the well-known `sample` program (Example 1.1) — and having mastered that hill, we will face the mountain of complexity that is GCC. Our key question is:

> HOW DO WE ISOLATE CAUSES IN PROGRAM STATE OR CODE?

14.2 CAPTURING PROGRAM STATES

To see how differences propagate along program states, we must find a way of *capturing* program states. At the lowest level, this is simple: as the program stores its state in computer memory, all one needs is a dump of that memory region. When it comes to *comparing* program states, though, we want to use the same abstraction level as when observing a program state — that is, we want to compare (and hence capture) the program state in terms of variables, values, and structures.

Chapter 8 "Observing Facts" discussed how to use a debugger to observe arbitrary parts of the program state during a program run. A debugger also allows us to list all variables of the program — that is, all global variables as well as all local variables of functions that are currently active. We call these variables *base variables*.

As an example, recall the GDB session from Section 8.3.1, where we ran the GNU debugger (GDB) on the `sample` program (Example 1.1). GDB provides three commands for listing variables.

*   `info variables` lists the names of global variables.

*   `info locals` shows all local variables in the current frame.

*   `info args` shows all function arguments in the current frame.

If we stop at the `shell_sort()` function, for instance, we can examine all local variables.

```
(gdb) break shell_sort
Breakpoint 1 at 0x1b00: file sample.c, line 9.
(gdb) run 9 8 7
Breakpoint 1, shell_sort (a=0x8049880, size=4)
    at sample.c:9
9               int h = 1;
(gdb) info args
a = (int *) 0x8049880
size = 4
(gdb) info locals
i = 0
j = 10
h = 0
(gdb) _
```

By moving through the stack frames, we can obtain all variable values for the calling functions.

```
(gdb) frame 1
#1  0x00001d04 in main (argc=3, argv=0xbffff6fc)
    at sample.c:36
36              shell_sort(a, argc);
(gdb) info args
argc = 4
argv = (char **) 0xbffff7a4
(gdb) info locals
a = (int *) 0x8049880
i = 3
(gdb) _
```

sample has no global variables; otherwise, we could have obtained them via GDB's info variables command.

With these names and values, we can easily capture a program state as a mapping of base variables to values, as outlined in Table 14.1. For the sake of avoiding ambiguity, we suffix each (local) variable with its frame number. This way, a_0 — the argument a in frame 0 (shell_sort()) — cannot be confounded with the a_1, the local variable a in frame 1 (main()).

Unfortunately, this naïve approach is not enough. We must record the values of *references*, such as a or argv, and we must take into account the data structures being referenced. In other words, we must also take care of *derived variables* such as argv[0], a[1], and so on. One simple approach toward doing so is to *unfold*

TABLE 14.1 Base variables of the sample program.

Variable	Value	Variable	Value
a_0	0x8049880	$argc_1$	4
$size_0$	4	$argv_1$	0xbffff7a4
i_0	0	a_1	0x8049880
j_0	10	i_1	3
h_0	0	—	—

TABLE 14.2 Derived variables of the sample program.

Variable	Value	Variable	Value	Variable	Value
$a_0[0]$	9	$a_1[0]$	9	$argv_1[0]$	"sample"
$a_0[1]$	8	$a_1[1]$	8	$argv_1[1]$	"9"
$a_0[2]$	7	$a_1[2]$	7	$argv_1[2]$	"8"
—	—	—	—	$argv_1[3]$	"7"
—	—	—	—	$argv_1[4]$	0x0

the program state — that is, follow all references until the state reaches a fix point.

1. Start with a program state consisting of all base variables and their values.

2. For each pointer in the state, include the variables it references.

3. For each array in the state, include its elements.

4. For each composite data in the state (objects, records, and so on), include its attributes.

5. Continue until the state can no longer be expanded.

Such a process can easily be automated (by instrumenting GDB, for instance) as long as we can accurately determine the types and sizes of all objects. (Section A.2.7 sketches how to handle such issues in C.) Doing so for the sample run reveals a number of *derived* variables, outlined in Table 14.2. These are obtained from following the pointers a and argv and including the elements of the arrays being pointed to.

Base and derived variables, as outlined in Tables 14.1 and 14.2, form the entire program state. Every memory location a program can (legally) access is covered. Unfortunately, a simple name/value representation does still not suffice, because *aliasing* is not reflected. Whereas a_0 and a_1 are different variables, $a_0[0]$ and $a_1[0]$ are not. Because the pointers a_0 and a_1 have the same value, $a_0[0]$ and $a_1[0]$ refer to the same location in memory.

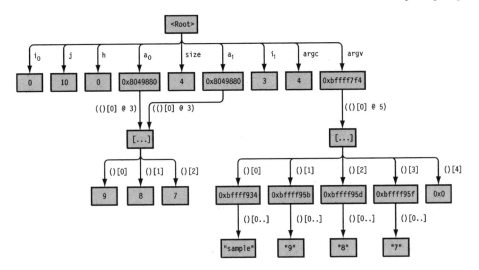

FIGURE 14.2 The state of a passing sample run.

Visual debuggers such as DDD (Section 8.5, on visualizing state) have addressed this problem by showing the program state not as pairs of name and values but as a *graph* in which variable values are represented by *vertices* and references by *edges*. We shall follow the same approach, but (in contrast to a debugger) capture the graph for the entire state, obtaining a so-called *memory graph*. The basic structure of a memory graph is as follows.

- *Vertices* stand for *variable values*. Each memory location that is accessible via some base or derived variable becomes a vertex.

- *Edges* stand for *references*. Each reference points to the location being referenced. Its *expression* shows how to access the location.

As an example, consider the memory graph for sample shown in Figure 14.2. Starting from the root vertex at the top, we can follow the individual edges to the base variables. The size edge, for instance, brings us to the location where the size value (3) is stored. The a variables (one for each frame) both reference the same array [...] referencing the three values 9, 8, and 7. Likewise, argv unfolds into an array of five pointers, referencing the strings "sample", "9", "8", and "7"; the 5th pointer is NULL.

Some of the names attached to the references may appear rather cryptic. What does (()[0] @ 3) mean, for instance? The string () is a placeholder for the expression of the *parent* — in our case, the unambiguous a. The @ operator

is special to GDB, where x @ n means "the array that consists of x and the n −
1 elements following in memory." Thus, (a[0] @ 3) stands for the 3-element
array starting at a[0], and this is exactly what [...] stands for. For a formal
definition see Section A.2.1.

14.3 COMPARING PROGRAM STATES

Once we can extract program states as separate entities, there are many things
we can do with them. We can observe them (as long as we can focus on a
manageable subset), and we can check whether they satisfy specific properties —
although assertions (Chapter 10 "Asserting Expectations") would probably be
better tools for this. The most important thing, though, to do with program
states is *compare* them against program states observed in different runs or from
different program versions.

As an example of comparing program states, consider Figure 14.3. This
memory graph was obtained from a *failing* run of sample; namely, the run with
the arguments 11 and 14. In this visualization, we have highlighted the *differences*
with respect to the passing state shown in Figure 14.2. Out of the 19 values,
only eight have a differing value. This difference in the state is caused by the
difference in the input. However, this difference in the state also causes the
difference in the final outcome. Hence, if we search for failure causes in the
state, we can *focus on the differences* (as highlighted in Figure 14.3).

How does one compute such differences? The basic idea is to compute a
matching between both memory graphs $G_{\checkmark}$ and $G_{\boldsymbol{x}}$.

- A *vertex* in $G_{\checkmark}$ matches a vertex in $G_{\boldsymbol{x}}$ if

  - both vertices are not pointers, and have the same type, value, and size,
    or

  - both vertices are pointers of the same type and are NULL, or

  - both vertices are pointers of the same type and are non-NULL.

  This rule abstracts from memory locations: regardless of where a value is
  stored, it can be matched. In Figure 14.3, for instance, argv[0]'s value differs from the one in Figure 14.2. As both are nonnull pointers, though, they
  match each other.

- An *edge* in $G_{\checkmark}$ matches an edge in $G_{\boldsymbol{x}}$ if

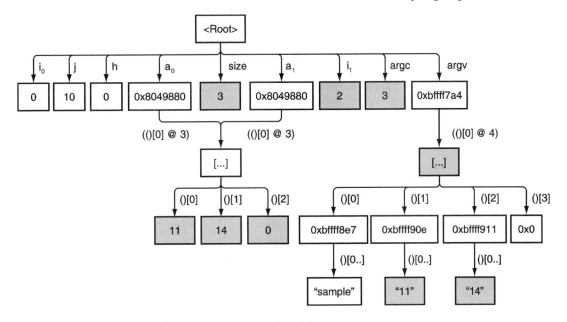

FIGURE 14.3 Differences in the state of the failing sample run.

- the edge expressions are equal and

- the source and target vertices match each other.

Any vertex or edge that is not matched thus becomes a difference.

The question is now: How do we establish the best possible matching? This is an instance of the *largest common subgraph* problem, which is known to be NP-complete. The best-known algorithms have a running time that is exponential in the number of vertices. A pragmatic alternative is to compute a large common subgraph (and thus a large matching) by *parallel traversal*. Starting from the ⟨*Root*⟩ vertex, we determine all matching edges originating from the current vertex and ending in a vertex with matching content. These edges and vertices become part of the common subgraph. The process is then repeated recursively. The resulting common subgraphs are not necessarily the largest but are sufficiently large for practical purposes. The complexity is that of a simple graph traversal. (Details of the algorithm are found in Section A.2.4.)

```
frame 0                         # shell_sort()
set variable size = 3
frame 1                         # main()
set variable a[0] = 11
set variable a[1] = 14
set variable a[2] = 0
set variable i = 2
set variable argc = 3
set variable argv[1] = \
    (char *)strncpy((char *)malloc(3), "11", 3)
set variable argv[2] = \
    (char *)strncpy((char *)malloc(3), "14", 3)
set variable argv[3] = 0x0
```

EXAMPLE 14.2 GDB commands that change the sample state from passing to failing.

14.4 ISOLATING RELEVANT PROGRAM STATES

Focusing on the differences between two states can already be helpful for debugging—simply because the differences in the state cause the failure. As pointed out in Chapter 12 "Causes and Effects," though, we normally do not search for some cause but for actual causes—that is, minimal differences between the world in which the failure occurs and the alternate world in which it does not occur. In Chapter 13 "Isolating Failure Causes" we saw how delta debugging narrows down actual causes in the program input and other circumstances. Can we apply similar techniques to automatically isolate actual causes in the program state?

In principle, we can see each program state as *input* to the remainder of the program run. Thus, we may be able to isolate failure-inducing differences in the state just as we did within the original input. What we need, though, is a difference we can

- *apply* to change the passing state into the failing state and

- *decompose* into smaller differences to narrow down the actual cause.

Applying differences is not too difficult. All we need to do is translate the state differences between $G_\checkmark$ and $G_✗$ into debugger commands that alter the state. In the two sample graphs shown in Figures 14.2 and 14.3 there are 22 vertices and edges that are not matched. Hence, we obtain 22 differences, each adding or removing a vertex or adjusting an edge. These 22 differences translate into 10 GDB commands, shown in Example 14.2.

(Details on how to obtain these commands are listed in Section A.2.5.) We can apply *all* of these GDB commands on the passing run, thus changing the state such that it is identical to the state of the failing run.

```
(gdb) break shell_sort
Breakpoint 1 at 0x1b00: file sample.c, line 9.
(gdb) run 9 8 7
Breakpoint 1, shell_sort (a=0x8049880, size=4)
    at sample.c:9
9           int h = 1;
(gdb) set variable size = 3
(gdb) frame 1
#1  0x00001d04 in main (argc=3, argv=0xbffff6fc)
    at sample.c:36
36          shell_sort(a, argc);
(gdb) set variable a[0] = 11
(gdb) set variable a[1] = 14
     .
     .
     .

(gdb) set variable argv[3] = 0x0
(gdb) _
```

Because the program state determines the remainder of the execution, the remaining behavior is exactly the behavior of the failing run.

```
(gdb) continue
Continuing.
Output: 0 11

Program exited normally.
(gdb) _
```

Let's summarize. If we apply *no* differences, we get the unchanged passing run. If we apply *all* differences, we get the failing run. Consequently, one or more of the differences in the program state must form the actual cause of the failure.

To decompose differences, we could simply take the individual debugger commands and find out which of these are relevant for producing the failure. However, it is wiser to operate at a higher level of abstraction — that is, at the memory graph level. The following is the plan.

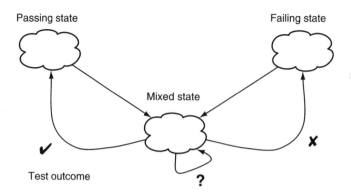

FIGURE 14.4 Narrowing down state differences. Depending on the test outcome, delta debugging uses the mixed state either as passing or as failing state. If the test outcome is unresolved (**?**), delta debugging creates a new mixed state.

1. Take a subset of the memory graph differences.

2. Compute the appropriate debugger commands.

3. Apply them to the passing run.

4. Resume execution.

5. See whether the failure still occurs or not.

This can be easily implemented in a *test* function and then invoked from a delta debugging algorithm such as *dd*. By applying a subset of the differences, we effectively create a *mixed program state* containing parts of the passing state and parts of the failing state. After resuming execution, we assess whether a mixed state results in a passing (**✔**), failing (**✘**), or unresolved (**?**) outcome (Figure 14.4).

Eventually, delta debugging should isolate a relevant difference — at least, this is our hope, as it may well be that such mixed states always result in unresolved outcomes.

Applied to sample, it turns out that delta debugging performs quite well. Figure 14.5 shows what happens if we actually run *dd* on the sample differences.

- *Test 1:* In the first test, *dd* applies half the differences, resulting in all of a[], i_1, size, argc, and argv[] being set to the failing state. It turns out that the failure (0 being output) still persists, and thus the variables j, h, and i_0 are ruled out as causes.

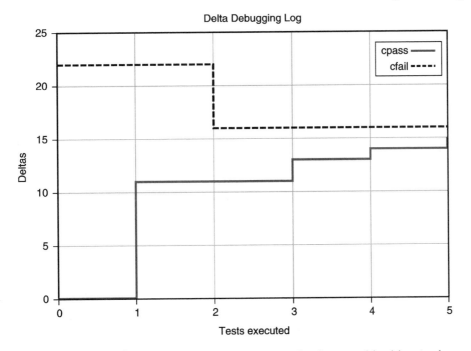

FIGURE 14.5 Isolating failure-inducing state in `sample`. After five tests, delta debugging has narrowed down the failure cause to one single variable.

- *Test 2: dd* only sets a[] and argv[1]. The failure occurs. Now, i_1, size, and argc are ruled out.

- *Test 3: dd* only sets argv[1]. The test passes, ruling out argv[1] as a failure cause. Only a[] remains.

- *Test 4: dd* sets a[0] = 11. The test passes, ruling out a[0].

- *Test 5: dd* sets a[0] = 11 and a[1] = 14. The test also passes, ruling out a[1].

The only difference that remains after five tests is a[2]. Setting a[2] = 0 in the passing run causes the failure in `sample`. Thus, *dd* reports a[2] as an actual failure cause. The failure occurs if and only if a[2] is zero.

Is this a good diagnosis? Yes, because it immediately helps in understanding the failure. If I sort 11 and 14, the value of a[2] should not influence the outcome at all—yet it does. Therefore, this diagnosis points immediately to the defect.

On the other hand, this example raises some of the delta debugging issues discussed in Section 13.8. In particular, it shows that although delta debugging returns causes (such as a[2]) it need not return *infections* (such as size). One might wish to have *dd* isolate an infection such as the value of size. However, although size has a different value in the two runs, and could thus be isolated as cause, changing size from 3 (the value in the failing run) to 4 (the value found in the passing run) only changes the outcome if a[2] is also set to zero.

However, even if delta debugging "only" returns causes, these causes can again be very helpful in understanding how the failure came to be. We have built a prototype called IGOR ("Igor, go fetch bugs!") that runs the previously cited steps automatically. It determines the places to compare states, determines the differences, and runs delta debugging on the differences. IGOR can be downloaded (it is open source) and installed on your system. For a short try, the automated debugging server ASKIGOR provides a public interface. Figure 1.9 shows ASKIGOR with a diagnosis for sample, computed as described in this section.

14.5 ISOLATING CAUSE-EFFECT CHAINS

Let's now go back to the original problem and address the GCC failure. A + 1.0 in the input is the beginning of a long cause-effect chain that eventually leads to the failure.

Because GCC executes for a long time, the first question is: At which locations should IGOR compare executions? For technical reasons, we require *comparable* states. Because we cannot alter the set of local variables, the current program counters and the backtraces of the two locations to be compared must be identical. In addition to this constraint, though, we can choose arbitrary locations during execution. Because the causes propagate through the run, the cause-effect chain can be observed at any location.

However, for crashing programs such as GCC the backtrace of functions that were active at the moment of the crash have turned out to be a good source for locations. Example 14.3 shows the backtrace of the crash. Given a backtrace, IGOR starts with a sample of *three events* from the backtrace.

- After the program start [that is, the location at the bottom of the backtrace, when GCC's subprocess cc1 reaches the function main()]

- In the middle of the program run [that is, in the middle of the backtrace, when cc1 reaches the function combine_instructions()]

```
Frame Address      Location
#0     0x810b19f in  if_then_else_cond() at combine.c:6788
       ⋮
#3189 0x810b19f in  if_then_else_cond() at combine.c:6788
#3190 0x8105449 in  simplify_rtx() at combine.c:3329
#3191 0x8105029 in  subst() at combine.c:3183
       ⋮
#3198 0x8105029 in  subst() at combine.c:3183
#3199 0x8102457 in  try_combine() at combine.c:1758
#3200 0x810110b in  combine_instructions() at combine.c:659
#3201 0x804c7fb in  rest_of_compilation() at toplev.c:4092
#3202 0x8183aa4 in  finish_function() at c-decl.c:7268
#3203 0x81751ea in  yyparse() at c-parse.y:349
#3204 0x804b2f1 in  compile_file() at toplev.c:3265
#3205 0x804e59a in  main() at toplev.c:5440
```

EXAMPLE 14.3 The GCC backtrace.

- Shortly before the failure [that is, the top of the backtrace, when cc1 reaches the function if_then_else_cond() for the 95th time—a call that never returns]

All these events occur in both the passing run $r_✔$ and the failing run $r_✗$. Let's examine these events (and associated locations) in detail.

- *At* main()*:* We start by capturing the two program states of $r_✔$ and $r_✗$ in main(). The graph $G_✔$ and $G_✗$ has 27,139 vertices and 27,159 edges. To squeeze them through the GDB command-line bottleneck requires 15 minutes each.

  It takes a simple graph traversal to determine that exactly one vertex is different in $G_✔$ and $G_✗$ —namely, argv[2], which is "fail.i" in $r_✗$ and "pass.i" in $r_✔$. These are the names of the preprocessed source files as passed to cc1 by the GCC compiler driver. This difference is minimal, and thus IGOR does not need a delta debugging run to narrow it further.

- *At* combine_instructions()*:* As combine_instructions() is reached, GCC has already generated the intermediate code (called RTL for "register transfer list"), which is now optimized. IGOR captures the graphs $G_✔$ with 42,991 vertices and 44,290 edges, as well as $G_✗$ with 43,147 vertices and

44,460 edges. The common subgraph of $G_{\checkmark}$ and $G_{\mathbf{x}}$ has 42,637 vertices. Thus, we have 871 vertices that have been added in $G_{\mathbf{x}}$ or deleted in $G_{\checkmark}$. (The graph $G_{\mathbf{x}}$ is shown in Figure 1.2.)

The deltas for these 871 vertices are now subject to delta debugging, which begins by setting 436 GCC variables in the passing run to the values from the failing run ($G_{\mathbf{x}}$). Is there anything good that can come out of this mixed state? No. GCC immediately aborts with an error message complaining about inconsistent state. Changing the other half of variables does not help either. After these two unresolved outcomes, delta debugging increases granularity and alters only 218 variables. After a few unsuccessful attempts (with various uncommon GCC messages), this number of altered variables is small enough to make GCC pass (Figure 14.6). Eventually after only 44 tests delta debugging has narrowed the failure-inducing difference to one single vertex, created with the GDB commands.

```
set variable $m9 = (struct rtx_def *)malloc(12)
set variable $m9->code = PLUS
set variable $m9->mode = DFmode
```

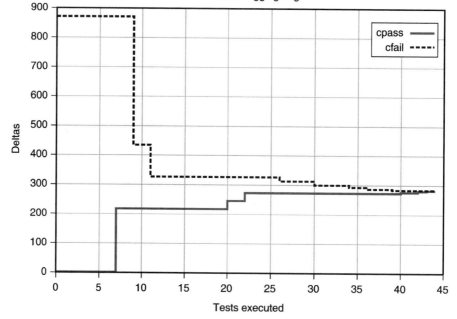

FIGURE 14.6 Narrowing at combine_instructions(). After 44 tests, delta debugging has narrowed down the failure cause to one single state difference—a PLUS operator.

```
set variable $m9->jump = 0
set variable $m9->fld[0].rtx = loop_mems[0].mem
set variable $m9->fld[1].rtx = $m10
set variable first_loop_store_insn->fld[1].rtx->\
    fld[1].rtx->fld[3].rtx->fld[1].rtx = $m9
```

That is, the failure-inducing difference is now the insertion of a node in the RTL tree containing a PLUS operator — the proven effect of the initial change +1.0 from pass.c to fail.c.

- *At* if_then_else_cond(): Shortly before the failure, in if_then_else_cond() IGOR captures the graphs $G_✔$ with 47,071 vertices and 48,473 edges, as well as $G_✘$ with 47,313 vertices and 48,744 edges. The common subgraph of $G_✔$ and $G_✘$ has 46,605 vertices. 1,224 vertices have been either added in $G_✘$ or deleted in $G_✔$.

  Again, delta debugging runs on the 1,224 differing vertices (Figure 14.7). As every second test fails, the difference narrows quickly. After 15 tests, delta debugging has isolated a minimal failure-inducing difference — a single pointer adjustment, created with the GDB command

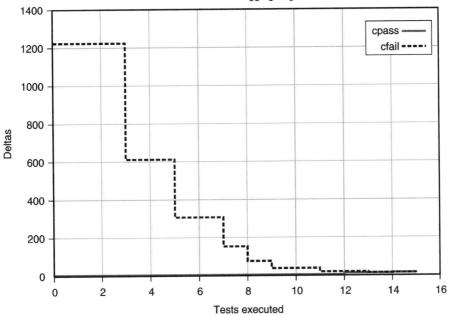

FIGURE 14.7 Narrowing at if_then_else_cond(). After 15 tests, delta debugging has isolated a tree cycle as the cause for the GCC crash.

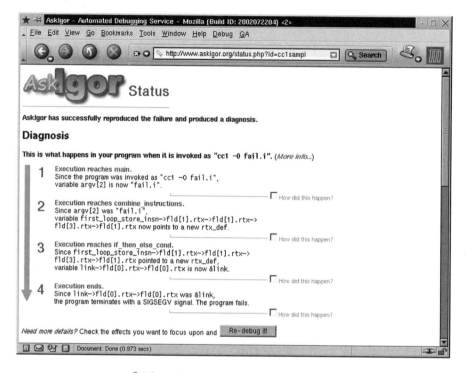

FIGURE 14.8 The GCC cause-effect chain as reported by ASKIGOR.

```
set variable link->fld[0].rtx->fld[0].rtx = link
```

This final difference is the difference that causes GCC to fail. It creates a cycle in the RTL tree. The pointer link→fld[0].rtx→fld[0].rtx points back to link! The RTL tree is no longer a tree, and this causes endless recursion in the function if_then_else_cond(), eventually crashing cc1.

The complete cause-effect chain for cc1, as reported by ASKIGOR, is shown in Figure 14.8.

With this summary, the programmer can easily follow the cause-effect chain from the root cause (the passed arguments) via an intermediate effect (a new node in the RTL tree) to the final effect (a cycle in the RTL tree). The entire diagnosis was generated automatically from the passing and the failing run. No manual interaction was required.

IGOR required six runs to extract GCC state (each taking 15 to 20 minutes) and three delta debugging runs (each taking 8 to 10 minutes) to isolate the failure-inducing differences. (Most of this overhead is due to accessing and manipulating memory via the GDB command line. A nonprototypical implementation, built into GDB or linked with the debuggee, could speed up state access by a factor of 10 to 1,000.)

Again, it should be noted that IGOR produces this diagnosis in a fully automatic fashion. All the programmer has to specify is the program to be examined as well as the passing and failing invocations of the automated test. Given this information, IGOR then automatically produces the cause-effect chain as shown in Figure 14.8.

14.6 ISOLATING FAILURE-INDUCING CODE

So far, we have been able to isolate causes in the program state. Ultimately, though, we are looking for causes in the program code — that is, the *defect that causes the failure*. This implies *searching in time* for the moment the defect executed and originated the infection chain.

In the GCC example, we assume that the states at main() and at combine_instructions() are sane. The RTL cycle at if_then_else_cond() obviously is not. Thus, somewhere between the invocation of combine_instructions() and if_then_else_cond() the state must have changed from sane to infected. An experienced programmer would thus try to identify the moment in time where the transition from sane to infected takes place — for instance, by setting up appropriate invariant assertions such as assert(isAcyclicTree(root)) in all executed functions that modify the RTL tree.

However, there is another way of coming closer to the defect — and this can also be fully automated. The idea is to search for *statements that cause the failure-inducing state*. In other words, when we find a cause in the program state we search the code that created this very cause — in the hope that among these pieces of code we find the actual defect.

To find such causes in the code, one idea is to look at the *variables* associated with the cause in the program state. Assume there is a point where a variable A ceases to be a failure cause, and a variable B begins. (These variables are isolated using delta debugging, as described earlier.) Such a *cause transition* from A to B is an origin of B as a failure cause. A cause transition is thus a good place to *break* the cause-effect chain and to fix the program. Because a cause transition may be a good fix, it may also indicate the actual defect.

How do we locate such transitions? The actual algorithm *cts* is formally defined in Section A.3, but it is easy to see how it works. Figure 14.9 sketches its application to the sample program. Before the call to shell_sort(), delta debugging isolates *argc* as a failure cause. Afterward, $a[2]$ is the failure cause. To find

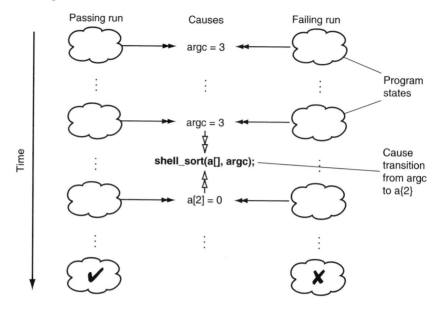

FIGURE 14.9 Locating a cause transition. Delta debugging can detect failure causes in the program state at arbitrary moments in time. When the cause shifts from one variable to another, we can use binary search in time to narrow down the transition — a statement that is likely to cause the failure.

the moment of that cause transition, we apply delta debugging in the middle of the interval. Then we repeat the process for the two subintervals, effectively narrowing down the transitions until we find only *direct* transitions from one moment to the next — that is, at a single statement. Overall, *cts* returns three direct cause transitions.

- From *argc* to $a[2]$ in line 36

- From $a[2]$ to v in line 18

- From v to $a[0]$ in line 22

Each of these cause transitions is where a cause originates — that is, it points to *program code* that causes the transition and hence the failure. $a[2]$ gets its value in lines 32 through 35, v gets its value in line 18, and so on. Each of these cause transitions is thus a candidate for a code correction. Moreover, each is a likely defect. Indeed, the first transition in line 36 of sample is exactly the location of the defect.

TABLE 14.3 Cause transitions in GCC.

#	Location	Cause Transition to Variable
0	⟨Start⟩	`argv[3]`
1	toplev.c:4755	`name`
2	toplev.c:2909	`dump_base_name`
3	c-lex.c:187	`finput→_IO_buf_base`
4	c-lex.c:1213	`nextchar`
5	c-lex.c:1213	`yyssa[41]`
6	c-typeck.c:3615	`yyssa[42]`

7	c-lex.c:1213	`last_insn→fld[1].rtx`
		`→fld[1].rtx→fld[3].rtx`
		`→fld[1].rtx.code`

8	c-decl.c:1213	`sequence_result[2]`
		`→fld[0].rtvec`
		`→elem[0].rtx→fld[1].rtx`
		`→fld[1].rtx→fld[1].rtx`
		`→fld[1].rtx→fld[1].rtx`
		`→fld[1].rtx→fld[1].rtx`
		`→fld[3].rtx→fld[1].rtx.code`

9	combine.c:4271	`x→fld[0].rtx→fld[0].rtx`

Let's apply this concept of cause transitions to the GCC example. Table 14.3 outlines all cause transitions occurring in GCC between the invocation and the failure. We find that the failure cause propagates through the GCC execution in four major blocks.

- Initially, the file name (*fail.c*) is the failure cause. Called with *pass.c*, the alternate input file without + 1.0, the error does not occur. This argument is finally passed to the GCC lexer (transitions 1 through 3).

- In the lexical and syntactical analysis (transitions 4 through 6), it is the actual difference in file content that becomes a failure cause — that is, the characters + 1.0.

- The difference in file content becomes a difference in the abstract syntax tree, where + 1.0 induces `fld[1].rtx` to hold an additional node (`fld[1].rtx.code` is PLUS) in the failing run (transitions 7 through 8). Thus, the + in the input has caused a PLUS node, created at transition 8.

- In transition 9, the failure cause moves from the additional PLUS node to the cycle in the abstract syntax tree. We have

    `x→fld[0].rtx→fld[0].rtx = x,`

```
case MULT:
  /* If we have (mult (plus A B) C), apply the distributive
     law and then the inverse distributive law to see if
     things simplify.  This occurs mostly in addresses,
     often when unrolling loops.  */

  if (GET_CODE (XEXP (x, 0)) == PLUS)
    {
      x = apply_distributive_law
        (gen_binary (PLUS, mode,
                     gen_binary (MULT, mode,
                                 XEXP (XEXP (x, 0), 0),
                                 XEXP (x, 1)),
                     gen_binary (MULT, mode,
                                 XEXP (XEXP (x, 0), 1),
                                 XEXP (x, 1))));

      if (GET_CODE (x) != MULT)
        return x;
    }
  break;
```

EXAMPLE 14.4 The GCC defect.

meaning that the node at *x is its own grandchild. That is, we have again found the cycle in the RTL tree (albeit involving a different base pointer). As discussed in Section 14.5, this cycle ultimately causes an endless recursion and thus the GCC crash. However, transition 9 is where this cycle originates!

At combine.c:4271, the location of the last transition, we find a single statement

```
return x;
```

This line is not likely to be a defect. Let's take a look at the direct origin of x, in combine.c:4013–4019, listed in Example 14.4.

This place is where the infection originates. The call to the function apply_distributive_law() is wrong. This function transforms code using the rule

$$(\text{MULT}\ (\text{PLUS}\ a\ b)\ c) \Rightarrow (\text{PLUS}\ (\text{MULT}\ a\ c_1)(\text{MULT}\ b\ c_2)).$$

(This application of the distributive law allows for potential optimizations, especially for addresses.) Unfortunately, in the `apply_distributive_law()` call (Example 14.4), c_1 and c_2 share a common grandchild (the macro `XEXP(x, 1)` translates into x→`fld[1].rtx`), which leads to the cycle in the abstract syntax tree. To fix the problem, one should call the function with a *copy* of the grandchild — and this is how the error was fixed in GCC 2.95.3.

At this point, one may wonder why cause transitions did not single out the call to `apply_distributive_law()` as a cause transition. The answer is simple: this piece of code is executed only during the failing run. Therefore, we have no state to compare against, and therefore cannot narrow down the cause transition any further. Line 4,271, however, has been executed in both runs, and thus we are able to isolate the failure-inducing state at this location.

Overall, to locate the defect the programmer had to follow just one backward dependency from the last isolated cause transition. In numbers, this translates into just two lines out of 338,000 lines of GCC code. Even if we assume the programmer examines all nine transitions and all direct dependencies, the effort to locate the GCC defect is minimal.

Of course, cause transitions cannot always pinpoint a defect — simply because neither delta debugging nor the isolation of cause transitions has any notion of what is correct, right, or true. However, cause transitions are frequently also defects. In fact, cause transitions predict defect locations significantly better than any of the anomaly-based methods discussed in Chapter 11 "Detecting Anomalies." This was found by Cleve and Zeller (2005).

Applied on the *Siemens* test suite (Section 11.2), cause transitions narrowed down the defect location to 10% or less of the code in 36% of the test runs. In 5% of all runs, they even exactly pinpointed the defect. Again, these figures do not generalize to larger programs but show the potential of the concept.

14.7 ISSUES AND RISKS

Section 13.8 discussed some issues to be aware of when using delta debugging. These issues are also valid for applying delta debugging to program states. In particular,

- the alternate (passing) run should be as close as possible to the actual (failing) run,

- one may be unable to decompose large differences,

- one should take extra care to avoid *artifacts* (for instance, by comparing the backtrace),

- the actual cause reported may be one of multiple actual causes, and

- the actual cause need not be an error.

In addition, applying delta debugging on program states raises its own issues, which one should be aware of.

- *How do we capture an accurate state?* In C and C++, most of memory management is done by convention, and left to the abilities of the programmer. This can lead to ambiguous interpretations of memory content, and hence to inaccurate memory graphs. Section A.2.7 lists some potential pitfalls. This issue is nonexistent for languages with managed memory such as JAVA or C#, because the garbage collector must always know which objects are referenced by which other objects.

- *How do we ensure the cause is valid in the original runs?* Each cause, as reported by delta debugging, consists of two configurations (states) $c'_{\textbf{x}}$ and $c'_{\textbf{v}}$ such that the difference $\Delta = c'_{\textbf{x}} - c'_{\textbf{v}}$ is minimal. This difference Δ between states determines whether the outcome is ✔ or ✘ and thus is an actual failure cause.

  However, Δ is a failure cause only in a specific *context* — the configuration $c'_{\textbf{v}}$ — and this context may or may not be related to the original passing or failing runs. It is conceivable that $c'_{\textbf{v}}$ may not be *feasible* — that is, there is no possible input such that $c'_{\textbf{v}}$ is ever reached. It is yet unknown whether this causes problems in practice. A stronger checking for artifacts may avoid the problem.

- *Where does a state end?* As described here, we assume that the program state is accessible via an interactive debugger. However, differences may also reside *outside* the program memory. For instance, a file descriptor may have the same value in $r_{\textbf{x}}$ and $r_{\textbf{v}}$ but be tied to a different file. To some extent, such "greater" states can be seen as external input, such that the techniques discussed in Chapter 13 "Isolating Failure Causes" may be more appropriate.

- *What is my cost?* Determining cause transitions is very expensive — not because the algorithms are complex but because the states are very huge and because a large number of test runs is required. Furthermore, one needs a significant infrastructure. In contrast, comparing coverage (discussed in Section 11.2) is far more lightweight, can be implemented without much risk, and requires just two test runs (which may even be conducted manually). On the other hand, it is not as precise. Obviously, you get what you pay for.

The most interesting question for the future is how to combine the individual automated debugging techniques. For instance, one could combine coverage and cause transitions and focus on cause transitions occurring in code that executes only in failing runs (Section 11.2). One could have delta debugging focus on state that correlates with failure (Chapter 11 "Detecting Anomalies") — and thus effectively combine correlation, as detected from a large number of runs, with causes, as determined by additional experiments. If one has a specification of what's correct, right, or true (Chapter 10 "Asserting Expectations"), this could effectively guide all searches toward defects. Obviously, we have come quite far, and there is every reason to believe that computer scientists will come up with even better tools and techniques in the future.

How far can we actually go? Unfortunately, there is no chance we will ever be able to automate the entire debugging process — in particular, because there *can be no automated way of determining the defect that causes a failure*. The argument is as follows:

- By definition, the defect is where the program code deviates from what is correct, right, or true. If we know the *correct code*, though, there is no point in debugging. We can simply use the correct code instead.

- Assume that the defect is where the program state becomes infected. To determine whether the state is infected or not requires a *complete specification* of the state — at all moments during execution. Such a specification is called a correct code, and we reenter the argument as previously.

- Furthermore, in the absence of a correct code (or, more precisely, in the absence of a fix) we cannot tell whether a defect *causes* the failure — because we need a fix to verify causality. In fact, determining the defect that causes a failure requires generating a fix (i.e., writing the correct program).

Thus, there is no chance of an automatic device that determines the *defects* — at least not until we find a way of writing programs automatically. As long as we can isolate *causes* automatically, though, we can come very close to the defects — and close to a good explanation of how the failure came to be.

14.8 CONCEPTS

HOW TO

✎ *To understand how a failure cause propagates through the program run*, one can apply delta debugging on *program states*, isolating failure-inducing variables and values.

HOW TO

✎ *To capture program states*, use a representation that abstracts from concrete memory locations, such as *memory graphs*.

HOW TO

✎ *To compare program states*, compute a *large common subgraph*. Any value that is not in the subgraph becomes a difference.

HOW TO

✎ *To isolate failure-inducing program states*, have a *test* function that

1. takes a subset of the memory graph differences,

2. computes the appropriate debugger commands,

3. applies them to the passing run, and

4. sees whether the failure still occurs or not.

Using this *test* function in a delta debugging framework will return a 1-minimal failure-inducing program state.

✎ A failure-inducing variable, as returned by delta debugging, can be altered to make the failure no longer occur. It is thus an actual cause. This does not mean, though, that the variable is infected. It also does not mean that there may be only one failure-inducing variable.

HOW TO

✎ *To find the code that causes the failure*, one can automatically search for *cause transitions* where a variable A ceases to be a failure cause and a variable B begins. Such cause transitions are places where the failure can be fixed, and they are likely defects.

HOW TO

✎ *To narrow down the defect along a cause-effect chain*, search for a cause transition from a sane variable to an infected variable.

✎ Delta debugging on states is a fairly recent technique and not yet fully evaluated.

✎ Whereas finding *failure causes* can be fully automated, finding the *defect* that causes a failure will always remain a manual activity.

14.9 TOOLS

ASKIGOR

The ASKIGOR debugging server is publicly available. At the time of writing, it accepts C (and C++) programs for Linux. This can be found at:

```
http://www.askigor.org/
```

IGOR

At the site, an open-source command-line version of IGOR can be downloaded.

14.10 FURTHER READING

The concept of memory graphs, as described in this book, was first formulated by Zimmermann and Zeller (2002). This paper also contains more details and examples on how to capture and compare memory graphs.

The idea of isolating cause-effect chains by applying delta debugging on program states was developed by Zeller (2002). This paper is also the basis for this chapter. In this paper, the central tool was called HOWCOME, which is now a part of IGOR.

The concept of cause transitions was developed by Cleve and Zeller (2005). The paper describes the details of cause transitions in the sample program, in GCC, and in the *Siemens* test suite. All of these papers, as well as recent work, are available at the delta debugging home page found at:

```
http://www.st.cs.uni-sb.de/dd/
```

Locating a defect becomes much easier if one has a specification handy. Such a specification can be combined with systematic experiments, as discussed in this chapter. A common issue with *model checkers,* for instance, is that they can detect that a program (or, more precisely, its model as a finite automaton) does not satisfy a given specification but fail to give a precise diagnosis why that would be. To this end, Groce and Visser (2003) used multiple passing and failing runs to provide a precise diagnosis, including likely defect locations. In that these runs are generated on demand, the approach is close to delta debugging on program states. In contrast to delta debugging, though, the approach can determine defects from nondefects due to the supplied specification. In Chaki et al. (2004), the technique showed excellent localization capabilities for nontrivial programs.

To actually compute the *largest* common subgraph instead of simply some large subgraph, one can use the approach of Barrow and Burstall (1976), starting from a *correspondence graph* as computed by the algorithm of Bron and Kerbosch (1973). The correspondence graph matches corresponding vertex content and edge labels. This is very suitable in our case, in that we normally have several differing content and labels. However, in the worst case (all content and labels are equal) computing the largest common subgraph has exponential complexity.

Compilers such as GCC have frequently been the subject of automated debugging techniques. Whalley (1994) describes how to isolate failure-inducing RTL optimizations in a compiler, using simple binary search over the optimizations applied.

14.11 EXERCISES

EXERCISE 14.1. Once again, consider the `bigbang` program (Example 8.3). If you change the `mode` variable in line 7, the failure no longer occurs.

1. Sketch how the difference in `mode` propagates through the execution and how it prohibits the failure.

2. Sketch the cause transitions in `bigbang`.

3. Would these cause transitions help in locating the defect? If so, why? If not, why not?

EXERCISE 14.2. Download the IGOR command-line tool from

```
http://www.askigor.org/
```

Use IGOR to obtain a diagnosis for the `sample` program. If you alter the arguments, how does the diagnosis change? Why?

EXERCISE 14.3. Give three examples of cause transitions that are defects, and three examples of cause transitions that are not defects.

So assess them to find out their plans,
both the successful ones and the failures.
Incite them to action in order to find out
the patterns of movement and rest.

—SUN TZU
The Art of War ($\sim$ 400 B.C.)

## CHAPTER 15

FIXING THE DEFECT

ONCE WE HAVE UNDERSTOOD A FAILURE's cause-effect chain, we know how the failure came to be. Still, we must find the place where the infection begins — that is, the actual location of the defect. In this chapter, we discuss how to narrow down a defect systematically — and having found the defect how to fix it.

15.1 LOCATING THE DEFECT

Section 9.5 discussed a general strategy for narrowing down infection sites.

1. We start with the infected value that defines the failure (Figure 15.1a).

2. We determine the possible origins of the infected value, following dependences in the source code (Figure 15.1b).

3. Using observation, we check each single origin to determine whether it is infected or not (Figure 15.1c). Having found the earlier infection, we restart at step 2.

This loop goes on until we find an infection whose origins are all sane. The code producing this infection is the defect.

Although this process is guaranteed to isolate the infection chain, it is pretty tedious — especially if you consider the space and time of a simple program execution. This is where the induction and experimentation techniques discussed in the later chapters come into play. However, although these techniques can determine causes (or at least anomalies that correlate with failure) they cannot

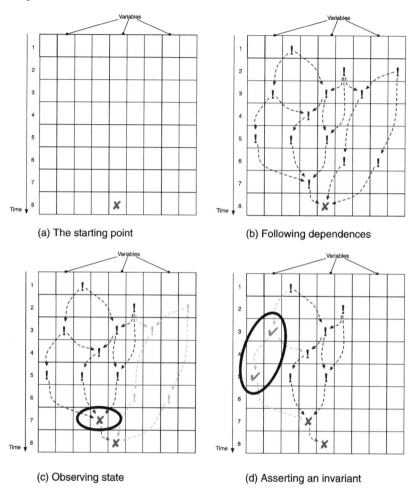

(a) The starting point　　　　(b) Following dependences

(c) Observing state　　　　(d) Asserting an invariant

FIGURE 15.1 Narrowing down a defect.

tell where the defect is — simply because they have no notion of correctness. Therefore, we must combine induction and experimentation with *observation* such that the programmer can tell (or specify) what is correct or not — and eventually fix the program. Our key question is:

How do we actually locate and fix the defect?

15.2 FOCUSING ON THE MOST LIKELY ERRORS

In the previous section, we have resumed the general strategy for locating the defect along the infection chain. It turns out that *induction* and *experimentation* techniques nicely fit into this strategy. The key is to use them to *focus* on specific origins. Whenever we have a choice of multiple origins (or, more generally, hypotheses), we can use automatic induction and experimentation techniques to help us focus on the most likely origin.

As an example, let's reexamine the situation shown in Figure 15.1c and continue to locate the defect.

- *Assertions* (Chapter 10 "Asserting Expectations") ensure data sanity over a long moment in time and a wide range in space. Any *failing* assertion by definition signals an infection. Of course, this is something we must focus on. On the other hand, whatever is covered by a *passing* assertion need no longer be considered. In our example, we can use an assertion to rule out possible infection origins — simply because the assertion guarantees that the state is sane (Figure 15.1d).

- *Anomalies* (Chapter 11 "Detecting Anomalies") are aspects of the execution whose properties are correlated with failure, such as coverage (Section 11.2) or dynamic invariants (Section 11.5). Because of the correlation, it is wise to focus on such anomalies first.

    In Figure 15.1d, we still have the choice between two origins. Observing the one that is abnormal reveals an infection (Figure 15.2a).

- *Causes* (Chapter 13 "Isolating Failure Causes" and Chapter 14 "Isolating Cause-Effect Chains") are aspects of the execution (such as input, state, or code) that are not only correlated with failure but actually cause the failure, as experimentally proven. Therefore, causes are even more likely to indicate the defect than anomalies.

    In Figure 15.2b we have found a cause transition — a statement that causes the failure. As the origin is sane and the target is infected, we have a real defect here — and the complete infection chain.

Although these techniques can help us focusing on specific origins, we still do not know which technique to choose. Starting with those techniques most likely to find the defect, the following is our list.

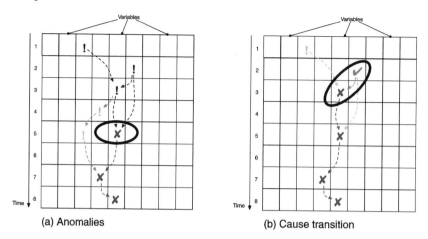

FIGURE 15.2 Narrowing down a defect (continued).

- *Focus on infections.* If you already know that some origin is faulty — from a failing assertion or via observation — focus on this one first and check whether the infection causes the failure. Typically, though, we do not know which of the origins is infected, and thus have nothing to focus on. Therefore, our priority goes to available *automated* techniques (following).

- *Focus on causes.* If delta debugging or any other form of experimentation has highlighted some state or input as a failure cause, focus on these causes and check whether they are infected.

- *Focus on anomalies.* Otherwise, of all possible origins those that are associated with anomalies are more likely to contain errors. Focus on these and check whether they are infected and cause the failure.

- *Focus on code smells.* Otherwise, if you have determined code smells in your program (Section 7.5), *and* if one of these code smells is a possible origin, first focus on the code smell and check whether it causes infection and/or failure.

- *Focus on dependences.* Otherwise, anything that is not in the backward slice of the infected state cannot possibly have caused the infection. Of all possible origins, check the backward slice for infections, starting with the closest statements.

    "Cannot possibly" in fact means "cannot legally." Your program may well find a way to break the rules and use undefined behavior, as discussed in Section 7.6. This can be prevented by system assertions (Section 10.8) or checking for code smells (Section 7.5).

These rules constitute the "Focus on likely origins" step in the TRAFFIC strategy from List 1.1. Each potential origin must then be verified whether it is infected or not, and we repeat the process for the infected origin.

Fortunately, we need not identify every single bit of the infection chain, as we are only interested in its origin. Therefore, we make larger *gaps* — for instance, toward the *boundaries* of functions or packages. These are places where communication is restricted (typically, to function arguments), which makes it easier to assess whether the state is sane or not.

If we find that some state is sane, we need not consider earlier states. Instead, we search forward for the moment in time the infection takes place. Eventually, we will find some piece of code where the state is initially sane but is after execution infected. This is the place where the infection originates — that is, the actual defect.

15.3 VALIDATING THE DEFECT

In the focusing rules in Section 15.2, I have constantly emphasized that whenever we focus on a potentially erroneous origin we must also check whether it actually causes the failure. Why is that so? This is simple: finding an error is not enough, we must also show that the error causes the failure. When tracing back the infection chain, we must show at each step that:

- The origin *is infected* — that is, that the variable value is incorrect or otherwise unexpected

- The origin *causes the infection chain* — that is, that changing the variable value makes the failure (and the remaining infections) no longer occur

Let's briefly examine why both of these steps are necessary.

15.3.1 Does the Error Cause the Failure?

Why do we have to show causality for an infection origin? The first reason is that if we find an origin that is infected but does not cause the failure we are being put on the wrong track. We risk a *post hoc ergo propter hoc* ("after this, therefore because of this") fallacy, as discussed in Section 12.2. As an example of being put on the wrong track, reconsider the example from Section 12.3.

```
a = compute_value();
printf("a = %d\n", a);
```

Because the program outputs a = 0, we assume that `compute_value()` produces an infection. However, we have not shown that a being zero causes the program to output a = 0. Indeed, if we change a to 1 the program still outputs a = 0. Therefore, we know that a does *not* cause the output.

As we found in Section 12.3, the `printf()` format is wrong. The program outputs a = 0 for most values of a. Without verifying the cause, we might have gone for a long search to determine why a could possibly have become zero.

Being put on the wrong track is especially dangerous when dealing with "suspicious" origins — variables where we cannot fully tell whether their values are correct or not. Before following such a scent, you should ensure that the origin actually causes the error — for instance, by replacing its value with a non-suspicious one and checking whether the failure no longer occurs.

15.3.2 Is the Cause Really an Error?

The previous section discussed errors that are not failure causes. Let's now turn to another source of problems: failure causes that are not errors.

Breaking the infection chain for a particular failure is easy. You simply check for the infected value and fix it for the run at hand. The issue, though, is to break the cause-effect chain in such a way that we prevent *as many failures as possible*. In short, we want our fix to actually *correct* the program.

The following is an instance of a fix that makes a failure no longer occur, but nonetheless fails to correct the program. A loop adds up the balance for a specific account.

```
balance[account] = 0.0;
for (int position = 0; position < numPositions; position++)
{
    balance[account] += deposit[position];
}
```

It turns out that the sum for account 123 is wrong, and thus we "fix" it by including:

```
if (account == 123)
    balance[123] += 45.67;
```

Likewise, for some reason, some people do not get their savings bonus:

```
if (account == 890 && balance[account] >= 0)
    balance[account] *= 1.05;
```

These "fixes" are wrong because they do not correct the program. They fix the *symptom rather than the cause*. The origin of the infections may well be in the original claim amounts, which must be investigated.

The following is a less blatant example. Consider once more the `sample` program from Example 1.1. Assume I have no real clue why the program fails. As I always have trouble with loop boundaries, I suspect the number of loop iterations is off by one. Thus, I replace the `for` loop (in line 16)

```
for (i = h; i < size; i++)
```

with

```
for (i = h; i < size - 1; i++) .
```

Does this help? Yes, it does:

```
$ sample 11 14
Output: 11 14
$ _
```

This clearly proves that the loop header caused the failure. I may have no clue why it was wrong, but at least the program now works. Did I really correct the program? I don't know. What we have here is a case of ignorant surgery.

Such a "fix" is even worse than the one described earlier. I have changed the program to make it work, but I actually have no clue how it works. The actual defect that still lurks in the code is likely to produce similar failures in the future. Worse, with my "fix" I have introduced a new defect that will manifest itself as soon as some other part of the program invokes the "fixed" `shell_sort()` function.

The "technique" of twisting and fiddling with the code until the failure miraculously goes away is also known as *debugging into existence*. We change the code although we have not fully understood how the failure came to be. Such a "technique" may eventually help in fixing the failure at hand, but it is so likely to induce new defects (or simply leave defects in the code) that it is best avoided.

The Devil's Guide to Debugging (List 15.1) lists more techniques to be avoided. Have fun.

15.3.3 Think Before You Code

Does one really need to verify causality for every step in the infection chain? Not if you have a clear understanding of how the failure came to be. That is, you

---

The Devil's Guide to Debugging

Find the defect by guessing. This includes:

- Scatter debugging statements throughout the program.

- Try changing code until something works.

- Don't back up old versions of the code.

- Don't bother understanding what the program should do.

Don't waste time understanding the problem. Most problems are trivial, anyway.

Use the most obvious fix. Just fix what you see:

```
x = compute(y);
// compute() doesn't work for y == 17, so fix it
if (y == 17)
    x = 25.15;
```

Why bother going all the way through `compute()`?

LIST 15.1 The Devil's Guide to Debugging (McConnell, 1993).

should have understood the infection chain to a point such that your *hypothesis* about the problem cause becomes a *theory* — a theory that allows you to exactly *predict*

- how your change to the code will break the infection chain and

- how this will make the failure (as well as similar failures) no longer occur.

One way to ensure you have a theory is to have your fix *reviewed* by someone else before applying it. If you can clearly explain how your fix will work, you have a good theory.

Of course, your prediction about how our change will correct the program had better come true. Otherwise, you will know that you have made a huge mistake. If it comes true, though, and the failure is gone, your change *retrospectively validates causality*. Fixing the defect made the failure no longer occur, and therefore the original defect caused the failure.

15.4   CORRECTING THE DEFECT

Assume you have fully understood the infection chain and prepared a correction for the problem. Before you apply the correction, be sure to save the original code — for instance, using the version control system. Then, you actually *correct the code.*

Correcting the code can be a great moment. You have reproduced the failure, observed the execution, carefully tracked back the infection chain, and gained complete understanding of what was going on. All of this has prepared you for this very moment — the actual correcting of the code. (And there was much rejoicing.)

Unfortunately, all great moments are futile. As soon as you have applied your correction, you must take care of four problems.

15.4.1   Does the Failure No Longer Occur?

After correcting the code, you must ensure that the correction makes the failure no longer occur. First, this retrospectively validates causality (Section 15.3.3). Second, it makes sure we actually solved the problem.

Ensuring that the correction was successful is easy to determine: if the original problem (Chapter 4 "Reproducing Problems") no longer occurs with the changed code, the correction was successful. (If you feel like a hero the moment the failure is gone, you have not been systematic enough. As you should be confident about the success of your correction, the problem no longer occurring should give you just the last bit of confirmation you needed.) If the program still fails after your correction has been applied, though, there *is still a defect that must be fixed.*

- It may well be that a failure is caused by multiple defects, and that removing the first defect causes the second defect to become active.

- However, there is also a chance that the code you fixed was not a defect at all, and that your understanding of the infection chain was wrong. To exclude this possibility, work through your earlier observations and experiments, as noted in the debugging logbook (Section 6.5). Check whether your conclusions are valid, and whether other conclusions are possible.

Being wrong about a correction should

- leave you astonished;

- cause self-doubt, personal reevaluation, and deep soul searching; and

- happen rarely.

If you conclude that the defect might be elsewhere, bring back the code to its original state before continuing. This way, your earlier observations will not be invalidated by the code change.

15.4.2 Did the Correction Introduce New Problems?

After correcting the code, you must ensure that the correction did not introduce new problems. This, of course, is a much more difficult issue—especially because many corrections introduce new problems (Table 15.1). Practices that are most useful include the following.

- Having corrections *peer reviewed*, as mandated by the problem life cycle (Chapter 2 "Tracking Problems"). A *software change control board* (SCCB) can organize this.

TABLE 15.1 Facts on fixes.

- In the ECLIPSE and MOZILLA projects, about 30 to 40% of all changes are fixes (Śliwerski et al., 2005).

- Fixes are typically two to three times smaller than other changes (Mockus and Votta, 2000).

- Fixes are more likely to induce failures than other changes (Mockus and Weiss, 2000).

- Only 4% of one-line changes introduce new errors in the code (Purushothaman and Perry, 2004).

- A module that is one year older than another module has 30% fewer errors (Graves et al., 2000).

- Newly written code is 2.5 times as defect prone as old code (Ostrand and Weyuker, 2002).

    (All figures apply to the systems considered in the case studies.)

- Having a *regression test* ready that detects unwanted behavior changes. This is another reason to introduce automated tests (Chapter 3 "Making Programs Fail").

Do not attempt to fix multiple defects at the same time. Multiple fixes can interfere with one another and create failures that look like the original one. Check each correction individually.

15.4.3 Was the Same Mistake Made Elsewhere?

The defect you have just corrected may have been caused by a particular *mistake*, which may have resulted in other similar defects. Check for possible defects that may be caused by the same mistake.

The following is a C example. The programmer copies a character string from a static constant t[] to a memory-allocated area s, using malloc(n) to allocate n characters, strlen(t) to determine the length of a string t, and strcpy(s, t) to copy a string from t to s.

```
char t[] = "Hello, world!";
char *s = malloc(strlen(t));
strcpy(s, t);
```

What's wrong with this code? In C, character strings are NUL-terminated. A five-character string such as Hello actually requires an additional NUL character in memory. The previous code, though, does not take the NUL character into account and allocates one character too few. The corrected code should read:

```
char t[] = "Hello, world!";
char *s = malloc(strlen(t) + 1);
strcpy(s, t);
```

The programmer may have made the same mistake elsewhere, which is why it is useful to check for further occurrences of strlen() and malloc(). This is also an opportunity to *refactor* the code and prevent similar mistakes. For instance, the previous idiom is so common that one might want to use the dedicated function

```
char t[] = "Hello, world!";
char *s = strdup(t);
```

where `strdup(s)` allocates the amount of required memory—using `malloc(strlen(s) + 1)` or similar—and copies the string using `strcpy()`. By the way, `strdup()` can also handle the case that `malloc()` returns `NULL`.

15.4.4 Did I Do My Homework?

Depending on your problem life cycle (Chapter 2 "Tracking Problems"), you may need to assign a *resolution* (such as *FIXED*) as to the problem. You also may need to integrate your fix into the production code, leaving an appropriate log message for version control.

Finally, you may wish to think about how to avoid similar mistakes in the future. We will come to this in Section 15.6.

15.5 WORKAROUNDS

In some cases, locating a defect is not difficult but correcting the defect is. The following are some reasons this might happen.

- *Unable to change:* The program in question cannot be changed—for instance, because it is supplied by a third party and its source code is not available.

- *Risks:* The correction induces huge risks—for instance, because it implies large changes throughout the system.

- *Flaw:* The problem is not in the code, but in the overall design—that is, the system design must undergo a major revision.

In such situations, one may need to use a *workaround* rather than a correction—that is, the defect remains but one takes care that it does not cause a failure. Such a workaround can take care to detect and handle situations that would make the defect cause a failure. It can also take place after the defect has been executed, correcting any undesired behavior.

A workaround is not a permanent solution, and is typically specific to the situation at hand. Workarounds thus tend to reintroduce the failure again after a change has taken place. Therefore, in implementing a workaround it is important to keep the problem open (in the tracking system, for instance) so as to later implement a proper solution.

TABLE 15.2 Some common workarounds.

- *Spam filters* are a workaround for solving a flaw in the e-mail system. Anyone can forge arbitrary messages and conceal his true identity. The proper solution would be to redesign the entire e-mail system, even incurring all associated costs and risks.

- *Virus scanners* are a workaround to what is a flaw of some operating systems. By default, every user has administrator rights, and hence any downloaded program can gain complete control over the machine. The proper solution would be to assign users limited rights and ask them for proper authorization before attempting to change the system. Unfortunately, too many regular programs (and their installation routines) assume administrator rights, and thus the fundamental problem is not easy to change.

- *Date windowing* is a workaround to the inability of many legacy systems to deal with four-digit years. The workaround consists of having the systems still keep two-digit years and resolving ambiguity by defining a 100-year window that contains all years in the data. If the 100-year window begins in 1930, for instance, then 27 refers to the year 2027, whereas 35 means the year 1935. The genuine solution, of course, would be to adapt the legacy system — but again, this incurs costs and risks.

Of course, if there were a better solution available immediately one would use that instead of a workaround. But at least a workaround solves the problem — for now. In practice, customers often find themselves living with workarounds for long periods of time. Table 15.2 outlines a few.

15.6 LEARNING FROM MISTAKES

If a program user experiences a problem, there is not only a problem with the program but also with the way the program came to be. Rather than escape into the field, the problem should have been caught in the local environment — that is, by quality assurance. Hence, the consequence of every problem fixed is to *improve quality assurance* such that the problem will not be missed in the future — and that it can be fixed more quickly should it occur again.

The following are some straightforward suggestions for ensuring that problems will not resurface. The basic idea is to not just fix the mistake but to fix whatever permitted the mistake in the first place.

- *Improve your test suite.* Your test suite has failed to detect the problem. Therefore, you must extend the test suite such that the problem will not occur again. An *automated test* (as discussed in Chapter 3 "Making Programs Fail") that reproduces the original problem is a good starting point.

- *Set up assertions.* If you have inserted assertions to narrow down the infection, *keep them in the code.* If some assertion would have helped catching the infection, go and write one. These assertions will catch similar infections in the future. At the very least, they will help during the debugging process. Consider keeping assertions active in production code (see Section 10.9 for details).

- *Improve training:* Many defects come to be because of simple mistakes. If this is the case, go and make sure your programmers know about *potential pitfalls,* and how to avoid them. Consider organizing your code such that mistakes are caught earlier. This also involves choosing a language or design method for future projects.

- *Improve the software process:* When analyzing how the problem could escape into the field, it may turn out that the software erroneously was not tested before release. It may be that the wrong version was shipped to customers. It may be that some critical part was not reviewed at all. Such blunders indicate an issue not only with the product but with its *production process.* If the history of the problem indicates there is something wrong with the process, go and fix it. To achieve perfection, never stop thinking about how you could improve the process.

- *Improve your analysis tools:* Verify whether common tools could have detected the defect early — in particular tools that detect *code smells* (Section 7.5) or tools that verify *system assertions* (Section 10.8).

Some of these measures can be expensive to realize. Therefore, it is wise to think about

- the effort it took you to detect the defect,

- the damage the defect has done to customers, and

- the risk you take in not implementing these measures.

All of these measures apply to an individual defect only. Over time, though, it may be helpful to explore whether specific defects occur over and over again — that is, over time, we have multiple defects with common properties.

How does one obtain such defect patterns? The obvious sources are the *version archive* (recording all changes to the system) and the *problem database* (recording all problems with the system). Unless both are integrated, we need a means of *linking* problems to changes, and vice versa. This is typically achieved by integrating the PR number into the log message of the version archive, or by storing a change or version identifier in the problem database. By mining these databases, we can explore questions such as the following.

- *Which modules have had the most defects?* If a module had several defects in the past, it is likely to have more waiting to be uncovered. Consider subjecting such a module to thorough quality assurance, or refactor it into smaller, less error-prone, units.

- *When are most defects introduced?* Do they originate in the requirements/design/coding phase? If specific phases are more error prone than others, you may need to increase quality assurance in these phases, or re-work the development process.

- *Which types of errors occur most often?* This can be extracted from *descriptions of the defect* — typically with categories such as "use of noninitialized variable," "bad control flow," "heap misuse," and so on. Consider using (or building) tools that check for these types of errors.

- *Who introduced the defects?* Some people create more defects than others — simply because they write more code, or because they address the most risky issues. If you find that some people or groups create more defects than normal, assign them to less risky tasks, or consider appropriate training.

  Note that this is a sensitive issue. If developers find that information in problem or version archives is used against them, they will no longer use these tools. Rather than blaming people, create an environment that focuses on finding errors.

Of course, this requires that the databases are well kept. The following indicates what the people use that build the space shuttle software (Fishman, 1996).

The database records when the error was discovered; what set of commands revealed the error; who discovered it; what activity was going on when it was discovered — testing, training, or flight. It tracks how the error was introduced into the program; how the error managed to slip past the filters set up at every stage to catch errors — why wasn't it caught during design? during development inspections? during verification? Finally, the database records how the error was corrected, and whether similar errors might have slipped through the same holes in the filters.

All of this is being leveraged to find out how the error came to be — whether by a programmer or as the result of a flaw in the process. That is, the goal is not just to find errors in the code but eventually *errors in the process.* This leads to a very disciplined way of building software.

The most important things the shuttle group does — carefully planning the software in advance, writing no code until the design is complete, making no changes without supporting blueprints, keeping a completely accurate record of the code — are not expensive. The process isn't even rocket science. It's standard practice in almost every engineering discipline except software engineering.

15.7 CONCEPTS

HOW TO
✎ *To isolate the infection chain*, transitively work backward along the infection origins.

HOW TO
✎ *To find the most likely origins*, focus on:

- *Failing assertions* (Chapter 10 "Asserting Expectations")

- *Causes* in state, code, and input (Chapters 14 "Isolating Cause-Effect Chains" and Chapter 13 "Isolating Failure Causes")

- *Anomalies* (Chapter 11 "Detecting Anomalies")

- *Code smells* (Chapter 7 "Deducing Errors")

✎ Function and package boundaries are good places to check for infection origins.

✎ For each origin, ensure that it is an *infection* as well as a *cause.*

✎ If a correction is too costly or too risky, apply a *workaround* (the defect remains in the program but the failure no longer occurs).

HOW TO
✎ *To correct the defect*, wait until you can predict

- how your change to the code will break the infection chain and

- how this will make the failure no longer occur.

HOW TO
✎ *To ensure your correction is successful*, check whether

- the correction makes the failure no longer occur,

- the correction does not introduce new problems, and

- the mistake leading to the defect has caused other similar defects.

✎ *To avoid introducing new problems*, useful techniques include: `HOW TO`

- Having corrections *peer reviewed*

- Having a *regression test* ready

✎ *To learn from mistakes*, use the *problem database* to check for frequently fixed   `HOW TO`
code and frequent types of errors.

15.8 FURTHER READING

Mining version and problem archives to uncover defect patterns is a subject that has recently has seen a lot of attention. Ostrand et al. (2004) describe how to correlate changes with defects to predict which files in a large software system are the most likely to still contain defects. Their model correctly selected files that contained 71 and 92% of the faults.

Researchers are currently applying these techniques to open-source version and problem archives. For up-to-date information, see the workshop on *mining software repositories (MSRs)*.

Humphrey (1996) introduces the *personal software process,* a technique to measure and record what you do during software development — from lines of code produced per unit time to the time spent watching sports games. Of course, you also track any mistakes you make. By correlating this data, you find out how to improve your personal development process.

The article of Fishman (1996) on how the space shuttle software people write their software is a must read for anyone interested in learning from mistakes. It is available online at:

```
http://www.fastcompany.com/online/06/writestuff.html
```

15.9 EXERCISES

EXERCISE 15.1. Sommerville (2001) describes the debugging process in four stages (Figure 15.3). Develop a more detailed model in which "Locate error" is expanded into at least six stages.

EXERCISE 15.2. Consider the `bigbang` code shown in Example 8.3. Where would you locate the defect and how would you correct it?

EXERCISE 15.3. For the `bigbang` code, devise three fixes that make the concrete failure no longer occur, but that do not correct the program — that is, so that minor variations can still reintroduce the failure.

EXERCISE 15.4. In addition to the TRAFFIC model, there can be other systematic processes to locate the defect. Sketch two.

EXERCISE 15.5. Illustrate, using an example, the difference between "good" and "bad" fixes.

EXERCISE 15.6. The following piece of code is supposed to read in a number of elements, and to print their sum.

```
n = read(); // Number of elements
for (int i = 0; i < n; i = i + 1)
    a[i] = read();

// sum up elements in a[0]..a[n - 1]
sum = computeSum(a, n - 1);
print(sum);
```

Unfortunately, this program has a defect. If you read in the numbers

```
2       // n
2       // a[0]
2       // a[1]
```

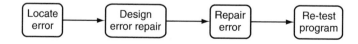

FIGURE 15.3 The debugging process (Sommerville, 2001).

the program prints 2 as the sum, rather than 4. It turns out that rather than summing up the elements from a[0] to a[n] it computes only the sum of a[0] to a[n - 1].

1. The following are suggestions for fixing the bug. Which one of these actually causes the failure to disappear?

   a) Replace the computeSum() call by the following piece of code.

   ```
   sum = 0;
   for (int i = 0; i < n; i = i + 1)
       sum += a[i];
   ```

   b) Add the following piece of code after the computeSum call.

   ```
   if (n == 2 && a[0] == 2 && a[1] == 2)
       sum = 4;
   ```

   c) Fix computeSum() such that it conforms to its specification.

   d) Replace the computeSum(a, n - 1) call with computeSum(a, n) and fix the specification such that it conforms to the actual behavior of computeSum.

2. How do these fixes rate in terms of generality (fixing as many failures as possible) and maintainability (preventing as many future failures as possible)? Rank the alternatives, justifying your choices.

EXERCISE 15.7. Consider the "fix" to the sample program in Section 15.3.2. Is the program actually correct?

Would that I discover truth
as easily as I can uncover falsehood.

— CICERO
(44 B.C.)

FORMAL DEFINITIONS

A.1 DELTA DEBUGGING

A.1.1 Configurations

DEFINITION A.1 (Configurations and Runs). We assume that the execution of a specific program is determined by a number of *circumstances*. Denote the set of possible *configurations* of circumstances by $\mathcal{R}$. □

DEFINITION A.2 (*rtest*). The function *rtest*: $\mathcal{R} \to \{✗, ✔, ?\}$ determines for a program run $r \in \mathcal{R}$ whether some specific failure occurs (✗) or not (✔), or whether the test is unresolved (?). □

DEFINITION A.3 (Change). A *change* δ is a mapping $\delta\colon \mathcal{R} \to \mathcal{R}$. The set of changes $\mathcal{C}$ is the set of all mappings from $\mathcal{R} \to \mathcal{R}$ (i.e., $\mathcal{C} = \mathcal{R}^{\mathcal{R}}$). The *relevant change* between two runs $r_1, r_2 \in \mathcal{R}$ is a change $\delta \in \mathcal{C}$ such that $\delta(r_1) = r_2$. □

DEFINITION A.4 (Composition of changes). The *change composition* $\circ\colon \mathcal{C} \times \mathcal{C} \to \mathcal{C}$ is defined as $(\delta_i \circ \delta_j)(r) = \delta_i(\delta_j(r))$. □

A.1.2 Passing and Failing Run

AXIOM A.5 (Passing and failing run). We assume two runs $r_✔, r_✗ \in \mathcal{R}$ with $rtest(r_✔) = ✔$ and $rtest(r_✗) = ✗$. □

In the following, we identify $r_✔$ and $r_✗$ by the changes applied to $r_✔$.

DEFINITION A.6 ($c_{\checkmark}$). We define $c_{\checkmark} \subseteq \mathcal{C}$ as the empty set $c_{\checkmark} = \emptyset$, which identifies $r_{\checkmark}$ (no changes applied). □

DEFINITION A.7 (Failing configuration). The set of all changes $c_{\textbf{X}} \subseteq \mathcal{C}$ is defined as $c_{\textbf{X}} = \{\delta_1, \delta_2, \ldots, \delta_n\}$, identifying $r_{\textbf{X}} = (\delta_1 \circ \delta_2 \circ \cdots \circ \delta_n)(r_{\checkmark})$. □

A.1.3 Tests

DEFINITION A.8 (*test*). The function $test: 2^{c_{\textbf{X}}} \rightarrow \{\textbf{X}, \checkmark, \textbf{?}\}$ is defined as follows: Let $c \subseteq c_{\textbf{X}}$ be a configuration with $c = \{\delta_1, \delta_2, \ldots, \delta_n\}$. Then, $test(c) = rtest((\delta_1 \circ \delta_2 \circ \cdots \circ \delta_n)(r_{\checkmark}))$ holds. □

COROLLARY A.9 (Passing and failing test case). The following holds:

$$test(c_{\checkmark}) = test(\emptyset) = rtest(r_{\checkmark}) = \checkmark \quad \text{and}$$
$$test(c_{\textbf{X}}) = test(\{\delta_1, \delta_2, \ldots, \delta_n\}) = rtest(r_{\textbf{X}}) = \textbf{X}$$

A.1.4 Minimality

DEFINITION A.10 (n-minimal configuration). A configuration $c \subseteq c_{\textbf{X}}$ is *n-minimal* if $\forall c' \subset c \cdot |c| - |c'| \leq n \Rightarrow (test(c') \neq \textbf{X})$ holds. □

DEFINITION A.11 (Relevant configuration). A configuration is called *relevant* if it is *1-minimal* in the sense of Definition A.10. Consequently, c is relevant if $\forall \delta_i \in c \cdot test(c \setminus \{\delta_i\}) \neq \textbf{X}$ holds. □

A.1.5 Simplifying

PROPOSITION A.12 (*ddmin* minimizes). For any $c \subseteq c_{\textbf{X}}$, *ddmin* (c) returns a relevant configuration in the sense of Definition A.11.

PROOF: According to the *ddmin* definition (Figure 5.6), *ddmin* $(c'_{\textbf{X}})$ returns $c'_{\textbf{X}}$ only if $n \geq |c'_{\textbf{X}}|$ and $test(\nabla_i) \neq \textbf{X}$ for all $\Delta_1, \ldots, \Delta_n$ where $\nabla_i = c'_{\textbf{X}} \setminus \Delta_i$. If $n \geq |c'_{\textbf{X}}|$, then $|\Delta_i| = 1$ and $|\nabla_i| = |c| - 1$. Because all subsets of $c' \subset c'_{\textbf{X}}$ with $|c'_{\textbf{X}}| - |c'| = 1$ are in $\{\nabla_1, \ldots, \nabla_n\}$ and $test(\nabla_i) \neq \textbf{X}$ for all ∇_i, the condition of Definition A.10 applies and c is 1-minimal. □

PROPOSITION A.13 (*ddmin* complexity, worst case). The number of tests carried out by *ddmin* $(c_{\textbf{X}})$ is $(|c_{\textbf{X}}|^2 + 3|c_{\textbf{X}}|)/2$ in the worst case.

PROOF: The worst case can be divided into two phases. First, every test has an unresolved result until we have a maximum granularity of $n = |c_{\mathbf{x}}|$. Then, testing only the last complement results in a failure until $n = 2$ holds.

- In the first phase, every test has an unresolved result. This results in a reinvocation of *ddmin'* with a doubled number of subsets, until $|c_i| = 1$ holds. The number of tests t to be carried out is $t = 2 + 4 + 8 + \cdots + |c_{\mathbf{x}}| = |c_{\mathbf{x}}| + \frac{|c_{\mathbf{x}}|}{2} + \frac{|c_{\mathbf{x}}|}{4} + \cdots = 2|c_{\mathbf{x}}|$.

- In the second phase, the worst case is that testing the *last* set $c_{\mathbf{x}}' \setminus \{c_n\}$ fails. Consequently, *ddmin'* is reinvoked with $ddmin'(c_{\mathbf{x}}' \setminus \{c_n\})$. This results in $|c_{\mathbf{x}}| - 1$ calls of *ddmin*, with one test per call. The total number of tests t' is thus $t' = (|c_{\mathbf{x}}| - 1) + (|c_{\mathbf{x}}| - 2) + \cdots + 1 = 1 + 2 + 3 + \cdots + (|c_{\mathbf{x}}| - 1) = \frac{|c_{\mathbf{x}}|(|c_{\mathbf{x}}| - 1)}{2} = \frac{|c_{\mathbf{x}}|^2 - |c_{\mathbf{x}}|}{2}$.

The overall number of tests is thus $t + t' = 2|c_{\mathbf{x}}| + (|c_{\mathbf{x}}|^2 - |c_{\mathbf{x}}|)/2 = (|c_{\mathbf{x}}|^2 + 3|c_{\mathbf{x}}|)/2$. $\qquad\square$

PROPOSITION A.14 (*ddmin* complexity, best case). *If there is only one failure-inducing change $\delta_i \in c_{\mathbf{x}}$ and all configurations that include δ_i cause a failure as well, the number of tests t is limited by $t \leq \log_2(|c_{\mathbf{x}}|)$.*

PROOF: Under the given conditions, the test of either initial subset c_1 or c_2 will fail. $n = 2$ always holds. Thus, the overall complexity is that of a binary search. $\qquad\square$

A.1.6 Differences

DEFINITION A.15 (*n-minimal difference*). *Let $c_{\checkmark}'$ and $c_{\mathbf{x}}'$ be two configurations with $\emptyset = c_{\checkmark} \subseteq c_{\checkmark}' \subset c_{\mathbf{x}}' \subseteq c_{\mathbf{x}}$. Their difference $\Delta = c_{\mathbf{x}}' \setminus c_{\checkmark}'$ is n-minimal if*

$$\forall \Delta_i \subset \Delta \cdot |\Delta_i| \leq n \Rightarrow (test(c_{\checkmark}' \cup \Delta_i) \neq \checkmark \wedge test(c_{\mathbf{x}}' \setminus \Delta_i) \neq \mathbf{x})$$

holds. $\qquad\square$

DEFINITION A.16 (*Relevant difference*). *A difference is called relevant if it is 1-minimal in the sense of Definition A.15. Consequently, a difference Δ is 1-minimal if*

$$\forall \delta_i \in \Delta \cdot test(c_{\checkmark}' \cup \{\delta_i\}) \neq \checkmark \wedge test(c_{\mathbf{x}}' \setminus \{\delta_i\}) \neq \mathbf{x}$$

holds. $\qquad\square$

A.1.7 Isolating

PROPOSITION A.17 (*dd* minimizes). Given $(c'_{\checkmark}, c'_{\checkmark}) = dd\,(c_{\checkmark}, c_{\checkmark})$, the difference $\Delta = c'_{\checkmark} \setminus c'_{\checkmark}$ is 1-minimal in the sense of Definition A.15.

PROOF: (Compare proof of Proposition A.12) According to the *dd* definition (Figure 13.3), $dd'(c'_{\checkmark}, c'_{\checkmark}, n)$ returns $(c'_{\checkmark}, c'_{\checkmark})$ only if $n \geq |\Delta|$ where $\Delta = c'_{\checkmark} \setminus c'_{\checkmark} = \Delta_1 \cup \ldots \cup \Delta_n$. That is, $|\Delta_i| = 1$ and $\Delta_i = \{\delta_i\}$ hold for all i.

Furthermore, for dd' to return $(c'_{\checkmark}, c'_{\checkmark})$, the conditions $test(c'_{\checkmark} \cup \Delta_i) \neq \mathbf{X}$, $test(c'_{\checkmark} \setminus \Delta_i) \neq \checkmark$, $test(c'_{\checkmark} \cup \Delta_i) \neq \checkmark$, and $test(c'_{\checkmark} \setminus \Delta_i) \neq \mathbf{X}$ must hold.

These are the conditions of Definition A.15. Consequently, Δ is 1-minimal. □

PROPOSITION A.18 (*dd* complexity, worst case). The number of tests carried out by $dd\,(c_{\checkmark}, c_{\checkmark})$ is $|\Delta|^2 + 7|\Delta|$ in the worst case, where $\Delta = c_{\checkmark} \setminus c_{\checkmark}$.

PROOF: The worst case is the same as in Proposition A.13, but with a double number of tests. □

PROPOSITION A.19 (*dd* complexity, best case). If all tests return either $\checkmark$ or $\mathbf{X}$, the number of tests t in *dd* is limited by $t \leq \log_2(|c_{\checkmark} \setminus c_{\checkmark}|)$.

PROOF: We decompose $\Delta = \Delta_1 \cup \Delta_2 = c'_{\checkmark} \setminus c'_{\checkmark}$. Under the given conditions, the test of $c'_{\checkmark} \cup \Delta_1 = c'_{\checkmark} \setminus \Delta_2$ will either pass or fail. $n = 2$ always holds. This is equivalent to a classical binary search algorithm over a sorted array: with each recursion, the difference is reduced by $1/2$; the overall complexity is the same. □

COROLLARY A.20 (Size of failure-inducing difference, best case). Let $(c'_{\checkmark}, c'_{\checkmark}) = dd(c_{\checkmark}, c_{\checkmark})$. If all tests return either $\checkmark$ or $\mathbf{X}$, then $|\Delta| = |c'_{\checkmark} \setminus c'_{\checkmark}| = 1$ holds.

PROOF: Follows directly from the equivalence to binary search, as shown in Proposition A.19. □

A.2 MEMORY GRAPHS

A.2.1 Formal Structure

Let $G = (V, E, root)$ be a memory graph containing a set V of vertices, a set E of edges, and a dedicated vertex *root* (Figure A.1):

Vertices. Each vertex $v \in V$ has the form $v = (val, tp, addr)$, standing for a value *val* of type *tp* at memory address *addr*. As an example, the C declaration

```
int i = 42;
```

results in a vertex $v_i = (42, \text{int}, 0x1234)$, where *0x1234* is the (hypothetical) memory address of i.

Edges. Each edge $e \in E$ has the form $e = (v_1, v_2, op)$, where $v_1, v_2 \in V$ are the related vertices. The operation *op* is used in constructing the expression of a vertex (see Figure A.2). As an example, the C declaration of the record ("struct") f,

```
struct foo { int val; } f = {47};
```

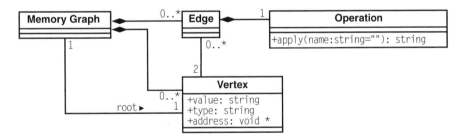

FIGURE A.I. UML object model of memory graphs.

FIGURE A.2. Edge construction.

results in two vertices $v_f = (\{\dots\}, \text{struct foo}, \textit{0x5678})$ and $v_{f.val} = (47, \text{int}, \textit{0x5678})$, as well as an edge $e_{f.val} = (v_f, v_{f.val}, op_{f.val})$ from v_f to $v_{f.val}$.

Root. A memory graph contains a dedicated vertex $root \in V$ that references all base variables of the program. Each vertex in the memory graph is accessible from root. In the previous examples, i and f are base variables. Thus, the graph contains the edges $e_i = (root, v_i, op_i)$ and $e_f = (root, v_f, op_f)$.

Operations. *Edge operations* construct the name of descendants from their parent's name. In an edge $e = (v_1, v_2, op)$, each operation op is a function that takes the expression of v_1 to construct the expression of v_2. We denote functions by $\lambda x.B$ — a function that has a formal parameter x and a body B. In our examples, B is simply a string containing x. Applying the function returns B where x is replaced by the function argument.

Operations on edges leading from *root* to base variables initially set the name. Thus, $op_i = \lambda x."\text{i}"$ and $op_f = \lambda x."\text{f}"$ hold.

Deeper vertices are constructed based on the name of their parents. For instance, $op_{f.val} = \lambda x."x\ .\text{val}"$ holds, meaning that to access the name of the descendant one must append ".val" to the name of its parent.

In our graph visualizations, the operation body is shown as edge label, with the formal parameter replaced by "()". That is, we use $op("()")$ as label. This is reflected in the previous figure.

Names. The following function *name* constructs a name for a vertex v using the operations on the path from v to the root vertex. As there can be several parents (and thus several names), we nondeterministically choose a parent v' of v along with the associated operation op.

$$name(v) = \begin{cases} op(name(v')) & \text{if } \exists (v', v, op) \in E \\ "" & \text{otherwise (root vertex)} \end{cases}$$

As an example, see how a name for $v_{f.val}$ is found: $name(v_{f.val}) = op_{f.val}(name(v_f)) = op_{f.val}(op_f("")) = op_{f.val}("\text{f}") = "\text{f.val}"$.

A.2.2 Unfolding Data Structures

To obtain a memory graph $G = (V, E, root)$, as formalized in Section A.2.1, we use the following scheme.

1. Let *unfold*(*parent*, *op*, *G*) be a procedure (sketched in the following) that takes the name of a parent expression *parent* and an operation *op* and unfolds the element *op*(*parent*), adding new edges and vertices to the memory graph *G*.

2. Initialize $V = \{root\}$ and $E = \emptyset$.

3. For each base variable *name* in the program, invoke *unfold*(*root*, λx."*name*").

The *unfold* procedure works as follows. Let $(V, E, root) = G$ be the members of *G*, let *expr* = *op*(*parent*) be the expression to unfold, let *tp* be the type of *expr*, and let *addr* be its address. The unfolding then depends on the structure of *expr*.

Aliases. If *V* already has a vertex v' at the same address and with the same type [formally, $\exists v' = (val', tp', addr') \in V \cdot tp = tp' \wedge addr = addr'$], do not unfold *expr* again. However, insert an edge (*parent*, v', *op*) in the existing vertex. As an example, consider the C statements:

```
struct foo f; int *p1; int *p2; p1 = p2 = &f;
```

If f has already been unfolded, we do not need to unfold its aliases *p1 and *p2. However, we insert edges from p1 and p2 to f.

Records. Otherwise, if *expr* is a record containing *n* members $m_1, m_2, \ldots, m_n$, add a vertex $v = (\{\ldots\}, tp, addr)$ to *V*, and an edge (*parent*, *v*, *op*) to *E*. For each $m_i \in \{m_1, m_2, \ldots, m_n\}$, invoke *unfold*(*expr*, λx."$x.m_i$", *G*), unfolding the record members.

As an example, consider the "Edges" example shown in Figure A.2. Here, the record f is created as a vertex and its member f.val has been unfolded.

Arrays. Otherwise, if *expr* is an array containing *n* members $m[0], m[1], \ldots, m[n-1]$, add a vertex $v = ([\ldots], tp, addr)$ to *V*, and an edge (*parent*, *v*, *op*) to *E*. For each $i \in \{0, 1, \ldots, n\}$, invoke *unfold*(*expr*, λx."$x[i]$", *G*), unfolding the array elements. Arrays are handled very much like records, and thus no example is given.

Pointers. Otherwise, if *expr* is a pointer with address value *val*, add a vertex $v = (val, tp, addr)$ to *V*, and an edge (*parent*, *v*, *op*) to *E*. Invoke *unfold*(*expr*, λx."*(x)*", *G*), unfolding the element *expr* points to (assum-

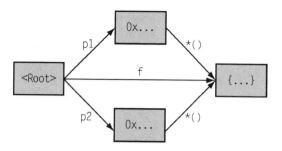

FIGURE A.3. Alias graph.

ing that $*p$ is the dereferenced pointer p). In the previous "Aliases" example, we would end up with the graph shown in Figure A.3.

Atomic values. Otherwise, *expr* contains an atomic value *val*. Add a vertex $v = (val, tp, addr)$ to V, and an edge $(parent, v, op)$ to E. As an example, see f in the previous figure.

A.2.3 Matching Vertices and Edges

Let $G_{\checkmark} = (V_{\checkmark}, E_{\checkmark}, root_{\checkmark})$ and $G_{\mathbf{x}} = (V_{\mathbf{x}}, E_{\mathbf{x}}, root_{\mathbf{x}})$ be two memory graphs.

Matching vertices. Two vertices $v_{\checkmark} \in V_{\checkmark}$ and $v_{\mathbf{x}} \in V_{\mathbf{x}}$ *match* (written $v_{\checkmark} \leftrightarrow v_{\mathbf{x}}$) if

- both are not pointers, and have the same type, value, and size, or

- both are pointers of the same type and are NULL, or

- both are pointers of the same type and are non-NULL.

Note that two pointers of the same type, but pointing to different addresses, match each other. This is exactly the point of memory graphs: to abstract from concrete addresses.

Matching edges. Two edges $e_{\checkmark} = (v_{\checkmark}, v_{\checkmark}') \in E_{\checkmark}$ and $e_{\mathbf{x}} = (v_{\mathbf{x}}, v_{\mathbf{x}}') \in E_{\mathbf{x}}$ *match*, written $e_{\checkmark} \leftrightarrow e_{\mathbf{x}}$ if

- the edge expressions are equal,

- $v_{\checkmark} \leftrightarrow v_{\checkmark}'$, and

- $v_{\mathbf{x}} \leftrightarrow v_{\mathbf{x}}'$ — that is, the vertices match.

A.2.4 Computing the Common Subgraph

To compare two memory graphs $G_{\checkmark} = (V_{\checkmark}, E_{\checkmark}, root_{\checkmark})$ and $G_{\mathbf{x}} = (V_{\mathbf{x}}, E_{\mathbf{x}}, root_{\mathbf{x}})$, we use the following *parallel traversal* scheme.

1. Initialize $M = (root_{\checkmark}, root_{\mathbf{x}})$.

2. For all $(v_{\checkmark}, v_{\mathbf{x}}) \in M$, determine the set of *reachable matching vertices* $(v_{\checkmark}', v_{\mathbf{x}}')$ with $v_{\checkmark}' \in V_{\checkmark}, v_{\mathbf{x}}' \in V_{\mathbf{x}}$ such that

    - $(v_{\checkmark}', v_{\mathbf{x}}') \notin M$,

    - $(v_{\checkmark}, v_{\checkmark}') \in E_{\checkmark}$ (i.e., there is an edge from $v_{\checkmark}$ to $v_{\checkmark}'$),

    - $(v_{\mathbf{x}}, v_{\mathbf{x}}') \in E_{\mathbf{x}}$ (i.e., there is an edge from $v_{\mathbf{x}}$ to $v_{\mathbf{x}}'$), and

    - $(v_{\checkmark}, v_{\checkmark}') \leftrightarrow (v_{\mathbf{x}}, v_{\mathbf{x}}')$ (i.e., the edges match, implying $v_{\checkmark}' \leftrightarrow v_{\mathbf{x}}'$).

    Set $M := M \cup (v_{\checkmark}', v_{\mathbf{x}}')$ for each matching pair $(v_{\checkmark}', v_{\mathbf{x}}')$ so found.

3. Continue with step 2 until no further matching vertices can be found.

The matching vertices in M form a common subgraph of $G_{\checkmark}$ and $G_{\mathbf{x}}$. All vertices $v_{\checkmark} \in V_{\checkmark} \cdot (\neg \exists v \cdot (v_{\checkmark}, v) \in M)$ and $v_{\mathbf{x}} \in V_{\mathbf{x}} \cdot (\neg \exists v \cdot (v, v_{\mathbf{x}}) \in M)$ are *nonmatching* vertices and thus form differences between $G_{\checkmark}$ and $G_{\mathbf{x}}$.

Note that M as obtained by parallel traversal is not necessarily the *largest common subgraph*. To obtain this, use the algorithm of Barrow and Burstall (1976), starting from a *correspondence graph* as computed by the algorithm of Bron and Kerbosch (1973).

A.2.5 Computing Graph Differences

We not only need a means of detecting differences in data structures but a means of *applying* these differences. We shall first concentrate on applying *all* differences between $r_{\checkmark}$ and $r_{\mathbf{x}}$ to $r_{\checkmark}$ — that is, we compute debugger commands that change the state of $r_{\checkmark}$ such that eventually its memory graph is identical to $G_{\mathbf{x}}$.

For this purpose, we require three graph traversals. During these steps, $G_{\checkmark}$ is transformed to become equivalent to G_{x} and each graph operation is translated into debugger commands that perform the equivalent operation on $r_{\checkmark}$.

As an example, we consider the two memory graphs shown in Figure A.4, where the dotted lines indicate the matching M between vertices, obtained from the common subgraph. (Actually, this matching cannot be obtained from parallel traversal, as described in Section A.2.4, but would be obtained from the largest common subgraph.) It is plain to see that element 15 in G_{x} has no match in $G_{\checkmark}$. Likewise, element 20 in $G_{\checkmark}$ has no match in G_{x}.

1. **(Set and create variables)** *For each vertex v_{x} in G_{x} without a matching vertex in $G_{\checkmark}$, create a new vertex $v_{\checkmark}$ as a copy of v_{x}. v_{x} is matched to $v_{\checkmark}$.* After this step, each vertex v_{x} has a matching vertex $v_{\checkmark}$.

Figure A.5 shows our example graphs after this step. To generate debugger commands, for each addition of a vertex $v_{\checkmark}$ we identify the appropriate variable v in r_{x} and generate a command that

- creates v in $r_{\checkmark}$ if it does not exist yet and

- sets v to the value found in r_{x}.

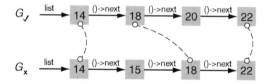

FIGURE A.4. Graph matchings.

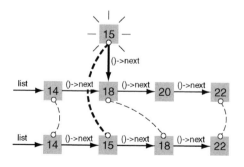

FIGURE A.5. Creating new variables.

In our example, we would obtain the following GDB commands.

```
set variable $m1 = (List *)malloc(sizeof(List))
set variable $m1->value = 15
set variable $m1->next = list->next
```

2. **(Adjust pointers)** *For each pointer vertex* p_x *in* G_x, *determine the matching vertex* $p_✓$ *in* $G_✓$. *Let* $*p_x$ *and* $*p_✓$ *be the vertices that* p_x *and* $p_✓$ *point to, respectively (reached via the outgoing edge). If* $*p_✓$ *does not exist, or if* $*p_✓$ *and* $*p_x$ *do not match, adjust* $p_✓$ *such that it points to the matching vertex of* $*p_x$.

In our example, the *next* pointers from 14 to 18 and from 18 to 20 must be adjusted. The resulting graphs are shown in Figure A.6. Again, any adjustment translates into appropriate debugger commands.

3. **(Delete variables)** *Each remaining vertex* $v_✓$ *in* $G_✓$ *that is not matched in* G_x *must be deleted, including all incoming and outgoing edges. After this last step,* $G_✓$ *is equal to* G_x.

In our example, vertex 20 must be deleted. The resulting graphs are shown in Figure A.7.

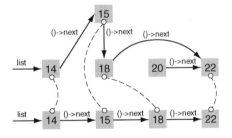

FIGURE A.6. Adjusting pointers.

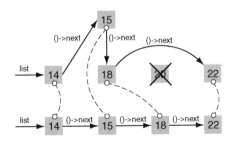

FIGURE A.7. Deleting variables.

Such a deletion of a vertex v translates into debugger commands that set all pointers that point to v to null, such that v becomes unreachable. Additionally, one might want to free the associated dynamic memory.

After these three steps, we have successfully transferred the changes in a data structure from a run $r_{\mathbf{x}}$ to a run $r_{\mathbf{v}}$.

A.2.6 Applying Partial State Changes

For the purpose of delta debugging, transferring *all changes* is not sufficient. We need to apply *partial* state changes as well. For this purpose, we associate a delta δ_v with each vertex v in $G_{\mathbf{v}}$ or $G_{\mathbf{x}}$ that is not contained in the matching. If v is in $G_{\mathbf{v}}$ only, applying δ_v is supposed to delete it from $G_{\mathbf{v}}$. If v is in $G_{\mathbf{x}}$ only, applying δ_v must add it to $G_{\mathbf{v}}$.

Let $c_{\mathbf{x}}$ be the set of all deltas so obtained. As always, $c_{\mathbf{v}} = \emptyset$ holds. In Figure A.4, for instance, we would obtain two deltas $c_{\mathbf{x}} = \{\delta_{15}, \delta_{20}\}$. The idea is that δ_{15} is supposed to add vertex 15 to $G_{\mathbf{v}}$. δ_{20} should delete vertex 20 from $G_{\mathbf{v}}$. Applying both δ_{15} and δ_{20} should change $G_{\mathbf{v}}$ to $G_{\mathbf{x}}$.

To apply a *subset* $\Delta \subseteq c'_{\mathbf{x}} \setminus c'_{\mathbf{v}}$ only, we run the state transfer method of Section A.2.5, but with the following differences.

- In steps 1 and 3 we generate or delete a vertex v only if δ_v is in Δ.

- In step 2 we adjust a pointer $p_{\mathbf{v}}$ with a matching $p_{\mathbf{x}}$ only if $\delta_{*_{p_{\mathbf{x}}}}$ is in Δ or $\delta_{*_{p_{\mathbf{v}}}}$ is in Δ.

As an example, apply $\Delta = \{\delta_{15}\}$ only. Step 1 generates the new vertex. Step 2 adjusts the pointer from 14 such that it points to 15. However, the pointer from 18 to 20 is not changed, because δ_{20} is not in c. We obtain a graph (and appropriate GDB commands) where only element 15 has been inserted (Figure A.8).

Likewise, if we apply $\Delta = \{\delta_{20}\}$ only step 1 does not generate a new vertex. However, step 2 adjusts the pointer from 18 such that it points to 22, and step 3 properly deletes element 20 from the graph.

A.2.7 Capturing C State

In the programming language C (and its sibling C++), pointer accesses and type conversions are virtually unlimited, which makes extraction of data structures difficult. The following are challenges and how one can deal with them.

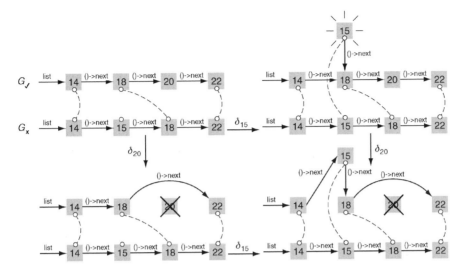

FIGURE A.8. Applying partial state changes.

Invalid pointers. In C, uninitialized pointers can contain arbitrary addresses. A pointer referencing invalid or uninitialized memory can quickly introduce a lot of garbage into the memory graph.

To distinguish valid from invalid pointers, we use a *memory map.* Using debugger information, we detect individual memory areas such as stack frames, heap areas requested via the *malloc* function, or static memory. A pointer is valid only if it points within a known area.

Dynamic arrays. In C, one can allocate arrays of arbitrary size on the heap via the *malloc* function. Although the base address of the array is typically stored in a pointer, C offers no means of finding out how many elements were actually allocated. Keeping track of the size is left to the discretion of the programmer (and can thus not be inferred by us).

A similar case occurs when a C struct contains arrays that grow beyond its boundaries, as in

```
struct foo {
    int num_elements;
    int array[1];
}.
```

Although array is declared to have only one element, it is actually used as a dynamic array, expanding beyond the struct boundaries. Such structs are allocated such that there is sufficient space for both the struct and the desired number of array elements.

To determine the size of a dynamic array, we again use the memory map as described earlier. An array cannot cross the boundaries of its memory area. For instance, if we know the array lies within a memory area of 1,000 bytes the array cannot be longer than 1,000 bytes.

Unions. The biggest obstacle in extracting data structures are C *unions*. Unions (also known as variant records) allow multiple types to be stored at the same memory address. Again, keeping track of the actual type is left to the discretion of the programmer. When extracting data structures, this information is not generally available.

To disambiguate unions, we employ a couple of heuristics, such as expanding the individual union members and checking which alternative contains the smallest number of invalid pointers. Another alternative is to search for a *type tag* — an enumeration type within the enclosing struct whose value corresponds to the name of a union member. Although such heuristics mostly make good guesses, it is safer to provide explicit disambiguation rules — either handcrafted or inferred from the program.

Strings. A char array in C has several uses. It can be used for strings, but is also frequently used as placeholder for other objects. For instance, the *malloc()* function returns a char array of the desired size. It may be used for strings, but also for other objects.

Generally, we interpret char arrays as strings only if no other type claims the space. Thus, if we have both a char array pointer and pointer of another type both pointing to the same area, we use the second pointer for unfolding.

In languages with managed memory such as JAVA or C#, none of these problems exist, as the garbage collector must be able to resolve them at any time. Most languages are far less ambiguous when it comes to interpreting memory contents. In object-oriented languages, for instance, dynamic binding makes the concept of unions obsolete.

A.3 CAUSE-EFFECT CHAINS

A program run r is a sequence of states $r = [s_1, s_2, \ldots, s_n]$. Each state s_i consists of at least a memory graph G_i as well as a backtrace b_i; that is, $s_i = (G_i, b_i)$.

Let $s_{\textbf{x}}$ be a program state from a failing run $r_{\textbf{x}}$. Let $r_{\checkmark}$ be a passing run. Then, $s_{\checkmark} = match(s_{\textbf{x}})$ is a *matching state*.

Matching states. Two states $s_{\checkmark} = (G_{\checkmark}, b_{\checkmark})$ and $s_{\times} = (G_{\times}, b_{\times})$ match if their backtraces are identical ($b_{\checkmark} = b_{\times}$). This implies that the set of local variables is equal. The function $match : (r_{\times} \rightarrow r_{\checkmark} \cup \{\bot\})$ assigns each state $s_{\times t} \in r_{\times}$ a *matching state* $s_{\checkmark t} \in r_{\checkmark}$, or $\bot$, if no such match can be found.

Individual state differences, as determined by delta debugging, can be composed into a cause-effect chain.

Relevant deltas. For each $s_{\times t} \in r_{\times}$ let a *relevant delta* Δ_t be a failure-inducing difference, as determined by delta debugging:
Let $s_{\checkmark t} = match(s_{\times t})$. If $match(s_{\times t}) = \bot$ holds, then $\Delta_t = \bot$. Otherwise, let $c_{\times t}$ be the difference between $s_{\checkmark t}$ and $s_{\times t}$, and let $c_{\checkmark t} = \emptyset$. Let $(c'_{\checkmark t}, c'_{\times t}) = dd(c_{\checkmark t}, c_{\times t})$. Then, $\Delta_t = c'_{\checkmark t} \setminus c'_{\times t}$ is a relevant delta.

Cause-effect chains. A sequence of relevant deltas $C = [\Delta_{t_1}, \Delta_{t_2}, \ldots]$ with $t_i < t_{i+1}$ is called a *cause-effect chain* if each Δ_{t_i} causes the subsequent $\Delta_{t_{i+1}}, \Delta_{t_{i+2}}, \ldots$ as well as the failure.

Within a cause-effect chain, *cause transitions* occur as follows.

Cause transitions. Let $var(\Delta_t)$ be the set of variables affected by a state difference Δ_t. $var(\bot) = \emptyset$ holds. Then, two moments in time (t_1, t_2) are called a *cause transition* if

- $t_1 < t_2$,

- a cause-effect chain C with $[\Delta_{t_1}, \Delta_{t_2}] \subseteq C$ exists, and

- $var(\Delta_{t_1}) \neq var(\Delta_{t_2})$.

A cause transition is called *direct* if $\neg \exists t : t_1 < t < t_2$.

To isolate direct cause transitions, we use a *divide-and-conquer* algorithm. The basic idea is to start with the interval $(1, |r_{\times}|)$, reflecting the first and last state of $r_{\times}$. If a cause transition has occurred, we examine the state at the middle of the interval and check whether the cause transition has occurred in the first half and/or in the second half. This is continued until all cause transitions are narrowed down.

Isolating cause transitions. For a given cause-effect chain C, the algorithm $cts(t_1, t_2)$ narrows down the cause transitions between the moments in time t_1 and t_2:

$$cts(t_1, t_2) = \begin{cases} \emptyset & \text{if } var(\Delta_{t_1}) = var(\Delta_{t_2}) \\ cts(t_1, t) \cup cts(t, t_2) & \text{if } \exists t : t_1 < t < t_2 \\ \{(t_1, t_2)\} & \text{otherwise} \end{cases}$$

where $[\Delta_{t_1}, \Delta_{t_2}] \subseteq C$ holds.

Our actual implementation computes C (and in particular, Δ_t) on demand. If we isolate a Δ_t between Δ_{t_1} and Δ_{t_2}, but find that Δ_t was not caused by Δ_{t_1}, we recompute Δ_{t_1} such that the cause-effect chain property is preserved.

We think in generalities, but we live in detail.

— Alfred North Whitehead (1861–1947)

GLOSSARY

This glossary gives definitions for important terms as used in this book. If multiple definitions are given, definition 1 is the one as used in this book (definition 2 and later are found in other places). References within the glossary always refer to definition 1.

Accident An unplanned event or series of events resulting in death, injury, occupational illness, damage to or loss of data and equipment or property, or damage to the environment. Synonym of *mishap*.

Adaptive testing Executing a sequence of tests in which later tests depend on the outcome of earlier tests.

Algorithmic debugging An automated technique that narrows down an error by querying the correctness of intermediate results.

Anomaly A program behavior that deviates from expectations based on other runs or other programs. Also known as *incident*.

Backward slice The *slice* that may influence a specific statement.

Bug 1. Synonym of *defect*. 2. Synonym of *failure*. 3. Synonym of *problem*. 4. Synonym of *infection*.

Bug report Synonym of *problem report*.

Cause An event preceding the *effect* without which the effect would not have occurred.

Cause-effect chain A sequence of events in which each event is a *cause* of the following event.

Change request Synonym of *problem report*.

Circumstance An event or aspect that may affect the function of a system.

Code smell A program property likely to be a *defect*. See also *Defect pattern*.

Configuration An arrangement of *circumstances* that affect the function of a system.

Correction A *fix* to the code that removes a *defect* from the program. See also *Debugging*. Compare *Workaround*.

Correctness The degree to which software is free from *errors* in its specification, design, and coding.

Crash The sudden and complete *failure* of a computer system or component.

Debuggee The program that is subject to *debugging*.

Debugger Tool to facilitate *debugging*.

Debugging 1. Relating a *failure* or an *infection* to a *defect* (via an *infection chain*) and subsequent *fixing* of the defect. 2. Removing defects from software. See also *Validation* and *Verification*.

Deduction Reasoning from the abstract to the concrete. See also *Static analysis*. Compare *Induction*.

Defect An *error* in the program — especially one that can cause an *infection* and thus a *failure*. Also known as *bug* or *fault*. Compare *Flaw*.

Defect pattern A pattern matching a *code smell*.

Delta Difference between (or change to) *configurations* — especially code, states, or circumstances.

Delta debugging An automatic technique that narrows down a cause by running automated *experiments*.

Diagnosis A *theory* that explains a *failure*.

Dynamic analysis Runtime techniques for *observing* or *inducing* abstractions to the set of values or behaviors seen so far when executing a program. Compare *Static analysis*.

Effect An event following the *cause* that would not have occurred without the cause.

Error 1. An unwanted and unintended deviation from what is correct, right, or true. 2. Synonym of *infection*. 3. Synonym of *mistake*.

Exception An event that causes suspension of normal program operation.

Experiment A set of actions and *observations*, performed to verify or falsify a *hypothesis*.

Experimental analysis A *dynamic analysis* in which program executions are initiated and/or conducted by the technique, typically within *experiments*.

Failure An externally visible *error* in the program behavior. Also known as *malfunction*. See also *Problem*.

Fallacy An *error* in logical argument that is independent of the truth of the premises.

Fault Synonym of *defect*.

Feature An intended property or behavior of a program. Compare *Problem*.

Fix A *delta* such that the failure in question no longer occurs. See also *Correction* and *Workaround*.

Fixing The act of applying a *fix*.

Flaw A *defect* that cannot be attributed to some specific location within the program, but rather its overall design or architecture.

Forward slice The *slice* that may be influenced by a specific statement.

Hanging Waiting for an event that will never occur.

Heisenbug A *failure* that is altered or disappears when one attempts to probe or isolate it.

Hypothesis A proposed explanation for a phenomenon. See also *Theory* and *Diagnosis*.

Incident Synonym of *anomaly*.

Induction Reasoning from the concrete to the abstract. Compare *Deduction*.

Inductive analysis A *dynamic analysis* technique that uses *induction* over multiple program executions to find common abstractions.

Infection An *error* in the program state — especially one that can cause a *failure*.

Infection chain A *cause-effect chain* from *defect* to *failure* along *infections*.

Invariant A property that does not change under a set of transformations, such as loop iterations (for loop invariants) or method calls (for class invariants).

Issue Synonym of *problem*.

Malfunction Synonym of *failure*.

Mishap Synonym of *accident*.

Mistake A human act or decision resulting in an *error*.

Observation Watching something and taking note of anything it does — for instance, observing a program run using a *debugger*.

Observational analysis A *dynamic analysis* technique that *observes* a single program execution to gather findings.

Oracle A device that is able to decide any problem of a certain type — in particular, correctness.

Patch 1. Synonym of *fix*. 2. A change made directly to an object program without reassembling or recompiling from the source program.

Problem A questionable property or behavior of a program. Also known as *issue*. See also *Failure*. Compare *Feature*.

Problem report The information required to reproduce a *problem*.

Regression testing *Testing* that functionality present in the past is still working in the present.

Scientific method A collection of processes that are considered characteristic for the acquisition of new scientific knowledge based on physical evidence.

Slice A subset of a program; either a *forward slice* or a *backward slice*.

Specification A document that specifies in a complete, precise, and verifiable manner the behavior and other characteristics of a program.

Static analysis Compile-time techniques for *deducing* safe and computable approximations to the set of values or behaviors arising dynamically at runtime when executing a program. Compare *Dynamic analysis*.

Surprise A property or behavior of a program that cannot be classified as *feature* or *problem*, due to the lack of *specification*.

Test case A documentation specifying inputs, predicted results, and a set of execution circumstances for a program.

Testing The execution of a program with the intent to produce some *problem*—especially a *failure*. In the context of *debugging*, testing is typically intended to produce a given problem.

Theory A *hypothesis* offering valid predictions that can be *observed*.

Validation Producing evidence that the program meets its *specification* for a specific intended use. In other words, "you built the right thing." Compare *Verification*.

Verification Proving the absence of *defects* with regard to a *specification*. In other words, "you built it right." Compare *Validation*.

Workaround A *fix* to the code where the *defect* remains in the program. Compare *Correction*.

"And hast thou slain the Jabberwock?
Come to my arms, my beamish boy!
O frabjous day! Callooh! Callay!"
He chortled in his joy.

— LEWIS CARROLL
Through the Looking-Glass (1872)

BIBLIOGRAPHY

Agrawal, H. and Horgan, J.R. (1990). "Dynamic Program Slicing," in *Proceedings of the ACM SIGPLAN 1990 Conference on Programming Language Design and Implementation (PLDI)*, volume 25(6) of *ACM SIGPLAN Notices*, pp. 246–256, White Plains, New York.

Aho, A.V., Sethi, R., and Ullman, J.D. (1986). *Compilers — Principles, Techniques and Tools*. Reading, Massachusetts: Addison-Wesley.

Ammons, G., Bodik, R., and Larus, J. R. (2002). "Mining Specifications," in *Proceedings of the ACM SIGPLAN/SIGACT Symposium on Principles of Programming Languages (POPL)*, Portland, Oregon.

Barnett, M., DeLine, R., Fähndrich, M., Leino, K.R.M., and Schulte, W. (2004). "Verification of Object-Oriented Programs with Invariants," *Journal of Object Technology*, 3(6):27–56. Special issue: ECOOP 2003 workshop on Formal Techniques for Java-like Programs.

Barron, C.A. (2000). "High Tech's Missionaries of Sloppiness," *Salon Magazine*, December 2000.

Barrow, H.G., and Burstall, R.M. (1976). "Subgraph Isomorphism, Matching Relational Structures and Maximal Cliques," *Information Processing Letters*, 4(4):83–84.

Beizer, B. (1990). *Software Testing Techniques*. Boston, Massachusetts: International Thomson Computer Press.

Beizer, B. (1999). "Unbanning the 'Bug'." Posting *79q48lncc1@fir.prod.itd. earthlink.net to comp.software.testing*.

Beizer, B. (2000). "Definition of the word *bug*." Posting *8kcV4.4008$S31. 103769@newsread2.prod.itd.earthlink.net to comp.software.testing*.

Beveridge, W.I.B. (1957). *The Art of Scientific Investigation* (3d ed.). New York: Vintage Books.

Binkley, D., and Harman, M. (2003). "A Large-scale Empirical Study of Forward and Backward Static Slice Size and Context Sensitivity," in *ICSM '03: Proceedings of the International Conference on Software Maintenance*. IEEE Computer Society.

Bloch, A., editor (1980). *Murphy's Law Book Two: More Reasons Why Things Go Wrong!* Price/Stern/Sloan Publishers.

Booch, G. (1994). *Object-oriented Analysis and Design* (2d ed.). Reading, Massachusetts: Addison-Wesley.

Bron, C., and Kerbosch, J. (1973). "Algorithm 457—Finding All Cliques of an Undirected Graph," *Communications of the ACM*, 16(9):575–577.

Brun, Y., and Ernst, M. (2004). "Finding Latent Code Errors via Machine Learning over Program Executions," in *Proceedings of the International Conference on Software Engineering (ICSE)*, pp. 480–490, Edinburgh, Scotland.

Burdy, L., Cheon, Y., Cok, D., Ernst, M., Kiniry, J., Leavens, G.T., Leino, K.R.M., and Poll, E. (2003). "An Overview of JML Tools and Applications," in *Proceedings of the Eighth International Workshop on Formal Methods for Industrial Critical Systems (FMICS 03)*, Trondheim, Norway.

Buschmann, F., Meunier, R., Rohnert, H., Sommerlad, P., and Stal, M. (1996). *Pattern-Oriented Software Architecture: A System of Patterns*, volume 1 of *Pattern-Oriented Software Architecture*. New York: John Wiley & Sons.

Chaki, S., Groce, A., and Strichman, O. (2004). "Explaining Abstract Counterexamples," in *SIGSOFT '04/FSE-12: Proceedings of the 12th ACM SIGSOFT International Symposium on Foundations of Software Engineering*, pp. 73–82. Newport Beach, California: ACM Press.

Chelf, B. (2004). "Squashing Bugs at the Source," *Linux Magazine* 55; 16–20.

Choi, J.-D., and Srinivasan, H. (1998). "Deterministic Replay of Java Multithreaded Applications," in *Proceedings of the ACM SIGMETRICS Symposium on Parallel and Distributed Tools (SPDT)*, pp. 48–59.

Choi, J.-D., and Zeller, A. (2002). "Isolating Failure-inducing Thread Schedules," in *Proceedings of the International Symposium on Software Testing and Analysis (ISSTA)*, pp. 201–220, Rome, Italy.

Cleve, H., and Zeller, A. (2005). "Locating Causes of Program Failures," in *Proceedings of the International Conference on Software Engineering (ICSE)*, St. Louis, Missouri.

Cohn, R., and Muth, R. (2004). *Pin 2.0 User Guide. http://rogue.colorado.edu/Pin/documentation.php.*

Condit, J., Harren, M., McPeak, S., Necula, G.C., and Weimer, W. (2003). "Ccured in the Real World," in *PLDI '03: Proceedings of the ACM SIGPLAN 2003 Conference on Programming Language Design and Implementation*, pp. 232–244. San Diego, California: ACM Press.

Dallmeier, V., Lindig, C., and Zeller, A. (2005). "Lightweight Defect Local-ization for Java," in *Proceedings of the 19th European Conference on Object-Oriented Programming*, Glasgow, Scotland.

DeMillo, R.A., Pan, H., and Spafford, E.H. (1996). "Critical Slicing for Soft-ware Fault Localization," in *Proceedings of the of the 1996 International Symposium on Software Testing and Analysis (ISSTA)*, pp. 121–134. ACM SIG-SOFT.

Demsky, B., and Rinard, M. (2003). "Automatic Detection and Repair of Er-rors in Data Structures," in *Proceedings of the 18th Annual ACM SIGPLAN Conference on Object-Oriented Programming, Systems, Languages, and Appli-cations (OOPSLA)*, pp. 78–95, Anaheim, California.

Dickinson, W., Leon, D., and Podgurski, A. (2001). "Finding Failures by Clus-ter Analysis of Execution Profiles," in *Proceedings of the International Con-ference on Software Engineering (ICSE)*, pp. 339–348, Toronto, Ontario, Canada.

Dijkstra, E.W. (1972). "Notes on Structured Programming," in Dahl, O.-J., Dijkstra, E.W., and Hoare, C.A.R., editors, *Structured Programming*, Chap-ter 1, pp. 1–82. London: Academic Press.

Dijkstra, E.W. (1982). "On Webster, Users, Bugs, and Aristotle," in *Selected Writings on Computing: A Personal Perspective*, pp. 288–291. New York: Springer-Verlag. Originally published as EWD 618 in 1977.

Dijkstra, E.W. (1989). "On the Cruelty of Really Teaching Computer Science," *Communications of the ACM*, 32(12):1398–1404.

Ducassé, M. (1999). "Coca: An Automated Debugger for C," in *Proceedings of the International Conference on Software Engineering (ICSE)*, pp. 504–513, Los Angeles, California.

Dunlap, G.W., King, S.T., Cinar, S., Basrai, M.A., and Chen, P.M. (2002). "Re-virt: Enabling Intrusion Analysis Through Virtual-machine Logging and Replay," in *Proceedings of the Symposium on Operating Systems Design and Implementation (OSDI)*, Boston, Massachusetts.

Dustin, E., Rashka, J., and Paul, J. (2001). *Automated Software Testing: Intro-duction, Management, and Performance*. Reading, Massachusetts: Addison-Wesley.

Eisenstadt, M. (1997). "My Hairiest Bug War Stories," *Communications of the ACM*, 40(4):30–37.

Ernst, M.D., Cockrell, J., Griswold, W.G., and Notkin, D. (2001). "Dynam-ically Discovering Likely Program Invariants to Support Program Evolu-tion," *IEEE Transactions on Software Engineering*, 27(2):1–25.

ESEC/FSE 99 (1999). *Proceedings of ESEC/FSE'99 – 7th European Software En-gineering Conference/7th ACM SIGSOFT Symposium on the Foundations of*

Software Engineering, volume 1687 of *Lecture Notes in Computer Science*, Toulouse, France: Springer-Verlag.

Fewster, M., and Graham, D. (1998). *Software Test Automation*. Reading, Massachusetts: Addison-Wesley.

Fishman, C. (1996). "They Write the Right Stuff," *Fast Company Magazine*, 06.

Fritzson, P., Shahmehri, N., Kamkar, M., and Gyimothy, T. (1992). "Generalized Algorithmic Debugging and Testing," *ACM Letters on Programming Languages and Systems*, 1(4):303–322.

Gamma, E., Helm, R., Johnson, R., and Vlissides, J. (1994). *Design Patterns: Elements of Reusable Object-Oriented Software*. Reading, Massachusetts: Addison-Wesley.

Geiger, L., and Zündorf, A. (2002). "Graph-based Debugging with Fujaba," in *Workshop on Graph Based Tools, International Conference on Graph Transformations*, Barcelona, Spain.

Gould, J.D. (1975). "Some Psychological Evidence on How People Debug Computer Programs," *International Journal of Man-Machine Studies*, 7:151–182.

Graves, T.L., Karr, A.F., Marron, J.S., and Siy, H. (2000). "Predicting Fault Incidence Using Software Change History," *IEEE Transactions on Software Engineering*, 26(7):653–661.

Groce, A., and Visser, W. (2003). "What Went Wrong: Explaining Counterexamples," in *Proceedings of the SPIN Workshop on Model Checking of Software*, pp. 121–135, Portland, Oregon.

Gyimóthy, T., Beszédes, Á., and Forgács, I. (1999). "An Efficient Relevant Slicing Method for Debugging," in ESEC/FSE 99 (1999), pp. 303–321.

Hailpern, B., and Santhanam, P. (2002). "Software Debugging, Testing, and Verification," *IBM Systems Journal*, 41(1):4–12.

Hangal, S., and Lam, M.S. (2002). "Tracking Down Software Bugs Using Automatic Anomaly Detection," in ICSE-2002 (2002), pp. 291–302.

Hopper, G.M. (1981). "The First Bug," *Annals of the History of Computing*, 3(3):285–286.

Hovemeyer, D., and Pugh, W. (2004). "Finding Bugs Is Easy," *Proceedings of the Conference on Object-Oriented Programming Systems Languages and Applications (OOPSLA)*, pp. 132–136, Vancouver, Canada.

Hume, D. (1748). *An Enquiry Concerning Human Understanding*. London: A. Millar.

Humphrey, W.S. (1996). *Introduction to the Personal Software Process*. Reading, Massachusetts: Addison-Wesley.

Humphrey, W.S. (1999). "Bugs or Defects?," Technical Report Vol. 2, Issue 1, Carnegie Mellon Software Engineering Institute.

ICSE 2002 (2002). *Proceedings of the International Conference on Software Engineering (ICSE)*, Orlando, Florida.

Jacky, J. (1996). *The Way of Z: Practical Programming with Formal Methods*. Cambridge, England: Cambridge University Press.

Jim, T., Morrisett, J.G., Grossman, D., Hicks, M.W., Cheney, J., and Wang, Y. (2002). "Cyclone: A Safe Dialect of C," in *Proceedings of the General Track: 2002 USENIX Annual Technical Conference*, pp. 275–288. USENIX Association.

Jones, J.A., Harrold, M.J., and Stasko, J. (2002). "Visualization of Test Information to Assist Fault Localization," in ICSE 2002 (2002), pp. 467–477.

Kaner, C., Falk, J., and Nguyen, H.Q. (1999). *Testing Computer Software*. New York: John Wiley & Sons.

Kernighan, B.W., and Pike, R. (1999). *The Practice of Programming*. Reading, Massachusetts: Addison-Wesley.

Kiczales, G., Hilsdale, E., Hugunin, J., Kersten, M., Palm, J., and Griswold, W.G. (2001). "An Overview of AspectJ," in *Proceedings of the 15th European Conference on Object-Oriented Programming*, Budapest, Hungary. pp. 327–353. Springer-Verlag.

Kidder, T. (1981). *The Soul of a New Machine*. New York: Atlantic Monthly Press.

Knight, J.C., and Leveson, N.G. (1986). "An Experimental Evaluation of the Assumption of Independence in Multiversion Programming," *IEEE Transactions on Software Engineering*, 12(1):96–109.

Ko, A.J., and Myers, B.A. (2004). "Designing the Whyline: A Debugging Interface for Asking Questions About Program Behavior," in *CHI '04: Proceedings of the 2004 Conference on Human Factors in Computing Systems*, Vienna, Austria. pp. 151–158. New York: ACM Press.

Ko, A.J., and Myers, B.A. (2005). "A Framework and Methodology for Studying the Causes of Software Errors in Programming Systems," *Journal of Visual Languages and Computing*. In press.

Kolawa, A. (2002). "Using Bug-Tracking Systems as Idea Repositories," *stickyminds.com*.

Konuru, R., Srinivasan, H., and Choi, J.-D. (2000). "Deterministic Replay of Distributed Java Applications," in *Proceedings of the International Parallel and Distributed Processing Symposium (IPDPS)*, Cancun, Mexico.

Korel, B., and Laski, J. (1990). "Dynamic Slicing of Computer Programs," *The Journal of Systems and Software*, 13(3):187–195.

Larman, C. (2002). *Applying UML and Patterns*. Englewood Cliffs, New Jersey: Prentice-Hall.

Leavens, G.T., Baker, A.L., and Ruby, C. (1999). "JML: A Notation for Detailed Design," in *Behaviora; Specifications of Businesses and Systems*, pp. 175–188. Boston, Massachusetts: Kluwer Academic Publishers.

Leavens, G.T., and Cheon, Y. (2004). "Design by Contract with JML," Technical report, Iowa State University. Available at http://www.jmlspecs.org/.

Lencevicius, R. (2000). *Advanced Debugging Methods*. Boston, Massachusetts: Kluwer Academic Publishers.

Leveson, N.G., Cha, S.S., Knight, J.C., and Shimeall, T.J. (1990). "The Use of Self-Checks and Voting in Software Error Detection: An Empirical Study," *IEEE Transactions on Software Engineering*, 16(4):432–443.

Lewis, B. (2003). "Debugging Backward in Time," in Ronsse, M., editor, *Proceedings of the Fifth International Workshop on Automated and Algorithmic Debugging (AADEBUG)*, Ghent, Belgium.

Lewis, D. (1973). "Causation," *Journal of Philosophy*, 70:556–567. Reprinted in Lewis (1986).

Lewis, D. (1986). *Philosophical Papers: Volume II*. Oxford, England: Oxford University Press.

Liblit, B., Aiken, A., Zheng, A.X., and Jordan, M.I. (2003). "Bug Isolation via Remote Program Sampling," in *Proceedings of the SIGPLAN 2003 Conference on Programming Language Design and Implementation (PLDI)*, San Diego, California.

Liblit, B., Naik, M., Zheng, A.X., Aiken, A., and Jordan, M.I. (2005). "Scalable Statistical Bug Isolation," in *Proceedings of the SIGPLAN 2005 Conference on Programming Language Design and Implementation (PLDI)*, Chicago, Illinois.

Martin, R.C. (1996). "The Dependency Inversion Principle," *C++ Report* May 8, 1996.

McConnell, S.C. (1993). *Code Complete: A Practical Handbook of Software Construction*. Redmond, Washington: Microsoft Press.

Meyer, B. (1997). *Object-Oriented Software Construction*. (2d ed.). Englewood Cliffs, New Jersey: Prentice-Hall.

Miller, B.P., Fredrikson, L., and So, B. (1990). "An Empirical Study of the Reliability of UNIX Utilities," *Communications of the ACM*, 33(12):32–44.

Mirrer, B. (2000). "Organize Your Problem Tracking System," *Software Testing & Quality Engineering (STQE) Magazine*, 2(5).

Mockus, A., and Votta, L. G. (2000). "Identifying Reasons for Software Changes Using Historic Databases," in *Proceedings of the International Conference on Software Maintenance (ICSM 2000)*, pp. 120–130. San Jose, California: IEEE Computer Society.

Mockus, A., and Weiss, D.M. (2000). "Predicting Risk of Software Changes," *Bell Labs Technical Journal*, 5(2):169–180.

Morgenstern, C. (1964). "The Impossible Fact," in Knight, M., editor, *The Gallows Songs*. Berkeley, California: University of California Press. Original poem published in 1905.

Muchnik, S.S. (1997). *Advanced Compiler Design and Implementation*. San Francisco, California: Morgan Kaufmann.

Müller, M.M., Typke, R., and Hagner, O. (2002). "Two Controlled Experiments Concerning the Usefulness of Assertions as a Means for Programming," in *Proceedings of the 18th International Conference on Software Maintenance (ICSM 2002)*, pp. 84–92. San Jose, California: IEEE Computer Society.

Myers, G.J. (1979). *The Art of Software Testing*. New York: John Wiley & Sons.

Naish, L. (1997). "A Declarative Debugging Scheme," *The Journal of Functional and Logic Programming*, 1997(3).

Necula, G.C., McPeak, S., and Weimer, W. (2002). "Ccured: Type-Safe Retrofitting of Legacy Code," in *POPL '02: Proceedings of the 29th ACM SIGPLAN-SIGACT Symposium on Principles of Programming Languages*, Portland, Oregon. pp. 128–139. New York: ACM Press.

Ness, B., and Ngo, V. (1997). "Regression Containment Through Source Code Isolation," in *Proceedings of the 21st Annual International Computer Software & Applications Conference (COMPSAC '97)*, pp. 616–621. Washington, DC: IEEE Computer Society Press.

Nethercote, N. (2004). "Dynamic Binary Analysis and Instrumentation," Ph.D. thesis, University of Cambridge, UK.

Nethercote, N., and Seward, J. (2003). "Valgrind: A Program Supervision Framework," *Electronic Notes in Theoretical Computer Science*, 89(2).

Neuburg, M. (2003). *AppleScript: The Definitive Guide*. Sebastopol, California: O'Reilly.

Orso, A., Apiwattanapong, T., and Harrold, M.J. (2003). "Leveraging Field Data for Impact Analysis and Regression Testing," in *ESEC/FSE-11: Proceedings of the 9th European Software Engineering Conference Held Jointly with 11th ACM SIGSOFT International Symposium on Foundations of Software Engineering*, pp. 128–137. New York: ACM Press.

Ostrand, T., and Weyuker, E. (2002). "The Distribution of Faults in a Large Industrial Software System," in Frankl, P.G., editor, *Proceedings of the ACM SIGSOFT 2002 International Symposium on Software Testing and Analysis (ISSTA-02)*, volume 27, 4 of *Software Engineering Notes*, pp. 55–64. New York: ACM Press.

Ostrand, T.J., Weyuker, E.J., and Bell, R.M. (2004). "Where the Bugs Are," in *ISSTA '04: Proceedings of the 2004 ACM SIGSOFT International Symposium on Software Testing and Analysis*, pp. 86–96. New York: ACM Press.

Ottenstein, K.J., and Ottenstein, L.M. (1984). "The Program Dependence Graph in a Software Development Environment," in *Proceedings of the ACM SIGSOFT/SIGPLAN Software Engineering Symposium on Practical Software Development Environments*, volume 19 of *ACM SIGPLAN Notices*, pp. 177–184.

Pearl, J. (2000). *Causality: Models, Reasoning, and Inference*. New York: Cambridge University Press.

Pezzè, M., and Young, M. (2005). *Software Testing and Analysis: Process, Principles, and Techniques*. New York: John Wiley & Sons. In press.

Pirsig, R.M. (1974). *Zen and the Art of Motorcycle Maintenance*. New York: William Morrow Publishers.

Podgurski, A., Leon, D., Francis, P., Masri, W., Minch, M., Sun, J., and Wang, B. (2003). "Automated Support for Classifying Software Failure Reports," In *ICSE '03: Proceedings of the 25th International Conference on Software Engineering*, pp. 465–475. Portland, Oregon: IEEE Computer Society.

Popper, K. (1959). *The Logic of Scientific Discovery*. London: Hutchinson. Translation of *Logik der Forschung*, Vienna, Austria, 1935.

Purushothaman, R., and Perry, D.E. (2004). "Towards Understanding the Rhetoric of Small Changes," in *Proceedings of the International Workshop on Mining Software Repositories (MSR 2004)*, pp. 90–94, Edinburgh, Scotland.

Raymond, E.S., editor (1996). *New Hacker's Dictionary* (3d ed.) Cambridge, Massachusetts: MIT Press. See also http://www.jargon.org/.

Renieris, M., and Reiss, S.P. (2003). "Fault Localization with Nearest Neighbor Queries," in *Proceedings of the 18th International Conference on Automated Software Engineering*, Montreal, Canada.

Ronsse, M., Bosschere, K.D., Christiaens, M., de Kergommeaux, J.C., and Kranzlmüller, D. (2003). "Record/Replay for Nondeterministic Program Executions," *Communications of the ACM*, 46(9):62–67.

Rosenberg, J.B. (1996). *How Debuggers Work—Algorithms, Data Structures, and Architecture*. New York: John Wiley & Sons.

RTI (2002). "The Economic Impacts of Inadequate Infrastructure for Software Testing," Technical Report, Planning Report 02-3, National Institute of Standards & Technology.

Saff, D., and Ernst, M. (2004a). "Automatic Mock Object Creation for Test Factoring," in Flanagan, C. and Zeller, A., editors, *Proceedings of the ACM SIGPLAN/SIGSOFT Workshop on Program Analysis for Software Tools and Engineering (PASTE)*, Washington, DC.

Saff, D., and Ernst, M. (2004b). "An Experimental Evaluation of Continuous Testing During Development," in *ISSTA 2004, Proceedings of the 2004 International Symposium on Software Testing and Analysis*, pp. 76–85, Boston, Massachusetts.

Schmidt, D.C., Stal, M., Rohnert, H., and Buschmann, F. (2000). *Pattern-Oriented Software Architecture: Patterns for Concurrent and Networked Objects*, volume 2 of *Pattern-Oriented Software Architecture*. New York: John Wiley & Sons.

Shapiro, E.Y. (1982). "Algorithmic Program Debugging," Ph.D. thesis, MIT Press. ACM Distinguished Dissertation.

Shapiro, F.R. (1994). "Exposing the Myth Behind the First Bug Reveals a Few Tales," *BYTE*.

Shore, J. (2004). "Fail Fast," *IEEE Software*, 21(5):21–25.

Śliwerski, J., Zimmermann, T., and Zeller, A. (2005). "When Do Changes Induce Fixes?," *Proceedings of the Workshop on Mining Software Repositories (MSR)*, St. Louis, Missouri.

Sommerville, I. (2001). *Software Engineering* (6th ed.). Reading, Massachusetts: Addison-Wesley.

Sosič, R., and Abramson, D. (1997). "Guard: A Relative Debugger," *Software—Practice and Experience*, 27(2):185–106.

Stallman, R.M., and Pesch, R.H. (1994). *Debugging with GDB* (4th ed.). Free Software Foundation. Distributed with GDB 4.13.

Tip, F. (1995). "A Survey of Program Slicing Techniques," *Journal of Programming Languages*, 3(3):121–189.

Viega, J., and McGraw, G. (2001). *Building Secure Software*. Reading, Massachusetts: Addison-Wesley.

Voas, J.M. (1992). "PIE: A Dynamic Failure-based Technique," *IEEE Transactions on Software Engineering*, 18(8):717–727.

Wahbe, R. (1992). "Efficient Data Breakpoints," in *ASPLOS-V: Proceedings of the Fifth International Conference on Architectural Support for Programming Languages and Operating Systems*, pp. 200–212. New York: ACM Press.

Weinberg, G.M. (1971). *The Psychology of Computer Programming*. New York: Van Nostrand Reinhold.

Weiser, M. (1982). "Programmers Use Slices When Debugging," *Communications of the ACM*, 25(7):446–452.

Weiser, M. (1984). "Program Slicing," *IEEE Transactions on Software Engineering*, 10(4):352–357.

Whalley, D.B. (1994). "Automatic Isolation of Compiler Errors," *ACM Transactions on Programming Languages and Systems*, 16(5):1648–1659.

Wilson, E.B. (1952). *An Introduction to Scientific Research*. New York: McGraw-Hill.

Xie, Y., and Engler, D. (2002). "Using Redundancies to Find Errors," In *SIGSOFT '02/FSE-10: Proceedings of the 10th ACM SIGSOFT Symposium on Foundations of Software Engineering*, pp. 51–60. New York: ACM Press.

Zachary, G.P. (1994). *Showstopper!: The Breakneck Race to Create Windows NT and the Next Generation at Microsoft*. New York: The Free Press.

Zalta, E.N., editor (2002). *Stanford Encyclopedia of Philosophy*. Stanford University. *http://plato.stanford.edu/*.

Zeller, A. (1999). "Yesterday, My Program Worked. Today, It Does Not. Why?" in ESEC/FSE 99 (1999), pp. 253–267.

Zeller, A. (2000). *Debugging with DDD*, version 3.2 edition, Universität Passau and Free Software Foundation. Distributed with GNU DDD.

Zeller, A. (2002). "Isolating Cause-Effect Chains from Computer Programs," in Griswold, W. G., editor, *Proceedings of the Tenth ACM SIGSOFT Symposium on the Foundations of Software Engineering (FSE-10)*, pp. 1–10, Charleston, South Carolina. New York: ACM Press.

Zeller, A., and Hildebrandt, R. (2002). "Simplifying and Isolating Failure-inducing Input," *IEEE Transactions on Software Engineering*, 28(2):183–200.

Zeller, A., and Lütkehaus, D. (1996). "DDD — A Free Graphical Front-end for UNIX Debuggers," *SIGPLAN Notices*, 31(1):22–27.

Zhang, X., and Gupta, R. (2004). "Cost-effective Dynamic Program Slicing," in *Proceedings of the 2004 ACM SIGPLAN Conference on Programming Language Design and Implementation (PLDI 2004)*, pp. 94–106, Washington, DC.

Zimmermann, T., and Zeller, A. (2002). "Visualizing Memory Graphs," In Diehl, S., editor, *Proceedings of the International Dagstuhl Seminar on Software Visualization*, volume 2269 of *Lecture Notes in Computer Science*, pp. 191–204, Dagstuhl, Germany. Heidelberg: Springer-Verlag.

INDEX